John Aberth

CRIMINAL CHURCHMEN
—————— in the ——————
AGE OF EDWARD III
The Case of Bishop Thomas de Lisle

The Pennsylvania State University Press
University Park, Pennsylvania

Library of Congress Cataloging-in-Publication Data

Aberth, John, 1963–
   Criminal churchmen in the age of Edward III : the case of Bishop
Thomas de Lisle / John Aberth.

      p.   cm.
   Includes bibliographical references and index.
   ISBN 0-271-01518-7 (cloth : alk. paper)
   1. Law—England—History. 2. De Lisle, Thomas. 3. Crime—
England—East Anglia—History. 4. Clergy—Legal status, laws, etc.—England—
History. 5. Criminal justice, Administration of—England—History. 6. Church
and state—England—History. 7. Great Britain—Politics and government—1327–
1377. 8. England—Social conditions—1066–1485. I. Title.
KD610.A24   1996
349.42'09'023—dc20
[344.2009023]
                                                                    95-49869
                                                                        CIP

It is the policy of The Pennsylvania State University Press to use acid-free paper
for the first printing of all clothbound books. Publications on uncoated stock
satisfy the minimum requirements of American National Standard for Information Sciences—Permanence of Paper for Printed Library Materials, ANSI
Z39.48-1992.

Frontispiece. Seal of Thomas de Lisle (British Library, Seal LV 36)

In Memoriam
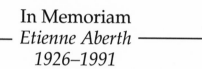
Etienne Aberth
1926–1991

Contents

List of Tables

List of Illustrations

List of Abbreviations

AS	*Anglia Sacra*, 2 vols., ed. H. Wharton (London, 1691).
ASV	Archivio Segreto Vaticano
BL	British Library
CCR	*Calendar of the Close Rolls Preserved in the Public Record Office: Edward III, 1327–1377*, 14 vols. (London, 1896–1913).
CFR	*Calendar of the Fine Rolls Preserved in the Public Record Office*, 22 vols. (London, 1911–62).
CPL	*Calendar of Entries in the Papal Registers Relating to Great Britain and Ireland: Papal Letters*, 14 vols. (London, 1893–1960).
CPP	*Calendar of Entries in the Papal Registers Relating to Great Britain and Ireland: Petitions to the Pope, 1342–1419*, 1 vol. (London, 1896).
CPR	*Calendar of the Patent Rolls Preserved in the Public Record Office: Edward III, 1327–1377*, 16 vols. (London, 1891–1916).
CUL	Cambridge University Library
CYS	Canterbury and York Society
DNB	*Dictionary of National Biography*, 63 vols., eds. S. Lee and L. Stephen (London, 1885–1900).
EDR	Ely Diocesan Records
EHR	*English Historical Review*
Foedera	*Foedera, Conventiones, Litterae et Cujuscunque Generis Acta Publica*, 3 vols. in 6 parts, ed. T. Rymer et al. (London, 1816–30).
LAO	Lincolnshire Archives Office
LPL	Lambeth Palace Library
NRO	Norfolk Record Office
PRO	Public Record Office
RDP	*Reports from the Lords' Committees for All Matters Touching the Dignity of a Peer of the Realm*, 4 vols. (London, 1826).
RP	*Rotuli Parliamentorum*, 6 vols. (London, 1783).
RS	Rolls Series
SR	*Statutes of the Realm*, 9 vols. (London, 1810–22).
SS	Selden Society
TRHS	*Transactions of the Royal Historical Society*

VCH Cambs.   *The Victoria History of the Counties of England: Cambridgeshire*
                  and the Isle of Ely, 9 vols. (London, 1938–89).
VCH Hamps.   *The Victoria History of the Counties of England: Hampshire and*
                  the Isle of Wight, 5 vols. (London, 1900–12).
VCH Hunts.   *The Victoria History of the Counties of England: Huntingdonshire,*
                  3 vols. (London, 1926–36).
Yearbooks   *Les Reports des Cases en Ley,* ed. R. Brooke and A. Fitzherbert,
                  black letter edition, 11 vols. (London, 1678–80).

Acknowledgments

This book is the product of many minds beside my own. First and foremost, I must thank my dissertation supervisor at Cambridge, Barrie Dobson, who provided insightful comments on every chapter and constantly reminded me to look at De Lisle within the general context of his times. I also owe a debt of thanks to Paul Hyams at Cornell University for his many useful comments, particularly with regard to De Lisle's dispute with Richard Spynk, and to Peter J. Potter at the Penn State Press for his patient faith in the manuscript. Others have contributed their special knowledge relating to different aspects of De Lisle's life. Christopher Brooke contributed much needed feedback on De Lisle's relations with monasteries; Patrick Zutshi helped me greatly with my investigations of De Lisle's supposed education at Cambridge; Sandy Heslop at the University of East Anglia put at my disposal his vast knowledge of heraldry; and Jeus Röhrkasten at the University of Birmingham graciously informed me about his latest research on approvers.

Profuse thanks must also be offered to librarians and archivists for their enduring patience and assistance. I wish especially to thank Godfrey Waller, superintendent of the manuscripts reading room in the Cambridge University library, and his assistants. In addition, I have been ably assisted by staff at the Public Record Office, the British Library, and the Lambeth Palace Library in London and at the Norfolk Record Office in Norwich. Also worthy of mention are the archivists and librarians at various colleges in Cambridge, including Catherine Hall at Corpus Christi, Anne Neary at Gonville and Caius, Jayne Ringrose at Pembroke, and Roger Lovatt at Peterhouse.

On a more personal note, I have been blessed with the friendship of many who have helped me on the way to my goal. My fellow Cantabrigians, Clive Powell, William Kelly, John Murphy, and Surreya Yigit, were steadfast drinking companions and intellectual sounding boards during my time at the University. In London, I was able to rely on old friends such as Adam Boxall and Michael Kerr, and Alex Cameron, to whom I will always be grateful for providing me with a room of my own in that vast city.

Last, but most important, I have received the eternal love and support of my family, without which this book never would have been possible. Thanks are long overdue to my mother, Sally, who is my best and sternest critic; my brother, Roger; and my sister-in-law, Aileen. But most of all, this book is dedicated to my father, Etienne, who, while he was alive, inspired me in all things, and still does.

——————Introduction——————

On 24 July 1345, Thomas de Lisle was consecrated bishop of Ely at Avignon by Gaucelin, cardinal-bishop of Albano.[1] The service did not pass without incident. Just as the host was about to be blessed, a glass vessel containing the sacramental wine suddenly and violently broke, without a hand having been laid on it, spilling its contents over the altar. Those present who saw the accident judged it an evil omen.[2]

Future events were amply to justify this dire premonition. By 1356, just eleven years later, the bishop's temporalities had been seized and De Lisle himself was banished from the kingdom, having become the personal enemy of King Edward III, and nearly lynched by a vengeful mob. The immediate cause of this disastrous change in the bishop's fortunes was his ill-advised attack on the king's cousin, Blanche (Lady Wake), widow of Thomas (Lord Wake of Liddell), and sister of Henry of Grosmont, duke of Lancaster. Lady Wake's prosecution of De Lisle seems to have encouraged other alleged victims to come forward with their tales of oppression at the hands of the bishop. What these and numerous other indictments suggest is that De Lisle's assault on Lady Wake may have been merely the culmination of a career in crime that lasted throughout his eleven-year tenure at Ely. According to the accusations, the bishop supported a number of criminals, including his own brother, his cousins, manorial officials, and even beneficed priests, who on their master's orders terrorized the inhabitants of East Anglia. De Lisle's followers were indicted for but rarely, it seems, convicted of a host of crimes ranging from petty theft and extortion to kidnapping, arson, assault, and murder. Both men and women complained of being arbitrarily seized by the bishop's officers and dragged away to his prisons, where they were kept until they ransomed themselves. Some of De Lisle's men were said to have looted and burned people's houses, breaking and entering at night while the occupants were asleep. They were accused of extorting fines from tenants, stealing men's goods, and driving away their livestock. Supposedly they assaulted, threatened, and even killed anyone who dared try to bring them to justice.

1. *CPL*, 3:188.
2. *AS*, 1:655; see also Appendix B, page 228.

Was De Lisle guilty of such violent behavior? Although conclusive ver-
dicts are hard to come by in any age, this book will argue that De Lisle in
fact did maintain a criminal "gang," mainly composed of his manorial
officials, whose primary motive for their crimes was to accrue profit to
the bishop. The case against De Lisle will evolve out of the abundant
legal records of medieval England, as well as the testimony of the bishop's
medieval biographer and evidence of De Lisle's persistent maintenance
of habitual criminals. But how did a bishop come to be involved in such
bloodthirsty activity so at odds with his pastoral and religious function?
To answer that question, this book takes a different approach from that of
most biographies of medieval English bishops. Such studies usually focus on the bishop's political role as the king's administrator, diplomat, or
councilor, in addition to the standard chapter on diocesan duties. However, Bishop De Lisle seems to have taken no active role or interest in
politics, precluding a study of a bishop-cum-curialist that forms the staple
of other episcopal biographies for the later medieval period.[3] Rather, the
criminal nature of De Lisle's career necessitates a look at the social and
economic side of his rule, an aspect of episcopal history that has been
relatively ignored by historians.[4] The bishop of Ely was one of the great
landowners of medieval England. The dynamics between De Lisle, his
tenants, and manorial officials—who formed the bulwark of his criminal
band—and his management of household and estate may provide clues
that can help unravel the mystery of De Lisle's involvement in crime.

De Lisle was a complex and enigmatic personality, and the organization of this book reflects that. Part One explores his role as bishop, both
in terms of his pastoral duties and as lord of a vast network of manors,
and how this role relates to his alleged sponsorship of criminals. De Lisle's
background prior to becoming bishop, that of a Dominican friar preacher
and papal protégé, was fairly unique among his fellow prelates. His relative inexperience in episcopal affairs and royal court politics undoubt-

---

3. See, for example, A. Judd, *The Life of Thomas Bekynton, Secretary to King Henry
VI and Bishop of Bath and Wells, 1443–1465* (Chichester, 1961); R. L. Storey, *Thomas
Langley and the Bishopric of Durham, 1406–1437* (London, 1961); J. H. Dahmus, *William
Courtenay: Archbishop of Canterbury, 1381–1396* (University Park, Pa., 1966); M.
Aston, *Thomas Arundel: A Study of Church Life in the Reign of Richard II* (Oxford,
1967); M. Buck, *Politics, Finance and the Church in the Reign of Edward II: Walter
Stapeldon, Treasurer of England* (Cambridge, 1983); R. M. Haines, *The Church and
Politics in Fourteenth-Century England: The Career of Adam Orleton, 1275–1345*
(Cambridge, 1978); idem, *Archbishop John Stratford: Political Revolutionary and
Champion of the Liberties of the English Church* (Toronto, 1986).

4. An exception is L. H. Butler, "Robert Braybrooke, Bishop of London (1381–
1404), and His Kinsmen" (D.Phil. diss., Oxford, 1952); idem, "Archbishop Melton,
His Neighbours, and His Kinsmen, 1317–1340," *Journal of Ecclesiastical History* 2
(1951), 54–67.

edly affected his later, more violent career. It also made him a rather quix-otic bishop. While his diocesan affairs were unexceptional, his encoun-ters with several monasteries were stormy and litigious, and his house-hold and manorial administration was marked by ruinous extravagance and the presence of officials with a penchant for extralegal activities. The fact that the bishop consistently supported his officials' abuse of power on his estate is one of the strongest arguments for his guilt, and at the same time is a feature that sets him apart from his contemporaries.

De Lisle's putative role as criminal is the subject of Part Two. First, the general context of crime in medieval English society must be established. How violent was medieval England? Until recently, historians have re-lied on anecdotal evidence to answer that question. But beginning in the 1970s, researchers have increasingly applied statistical, sociological, and even psychological techniques to the problem. How effective are these techniques and can they be sustained by the primary sources, the well-preserved records of the medieval English law courts?

The debate concerning the medieval practitioners of crime will also be reviewed: Who were the criminal elements of society or those most re-sponsible for violent behavior? Traditionally, scholars have blamed the so-called fur-collar criminals: members of the nobility or gentry who, for one reason or another, formed Robin Hood–style outlaw bands or oper-ated as individual "robber barons" and supported, or maintained, vio-lent men and who themselves were so maintained. According to this ar-gument, it was the upper classes of society—the ones who, ironically, were charged with keeping the peace, advising the king in council, and pro-posing legislation in parliament—who were most disruptive of law and order. "Maintenance" is the term generally used to express this idea that the elite of medieval English society were employing and defending crimi-nals in defiance of the common law.

Yet, maintenance was merely symptomatic of a wider phenomenon called "bastard feudalism," in which the traditional ties of land between vassal and lord were gradually replaced by a money fee, or retainer. This buying, or retaining, of men's loyalty was thought to be a late medieval corruption, or bastard form, of the earlier, purer feudal bonds. Crime thus was allowed to flourish as vassals were much less accountable to their lords, and patrons were less discriminating in the distribution of their largess. However, the recent work of a number of historians of gen-try and magnate affinities has challenged these traditional interpretations.[5] The medieval English nobility's reaction to De Lisle's prosecution by the crown in 1356 reveals something of how they themselves viewed the is-sues of maintenance and crime.

5. See pages 77–82.

De Lisle's feuds will next be studied, including one with a merchant of Norwich, Richard Spynk, whom De Lisle allegedly harassed shortly after he had become bishop. The dispute with Spynk has added interest because it was decided by the king's council in parliament, where it became entangled with issues of villeinage of great concern to De Lisle's peers. Then, of course, there is the bishop's notorious attack on Lady Wake and his subsequent feud with the king himself, which has received the attention of contemporary chroniclers and, more recently, of a few modern historians.[6] Nevertheless, the full implications of the Lady Wake affair, in which Edward III attempted to flout the law in order to punish De Lisle, have yet to be explored. Crimes allegedly perpetrated by individual members of De Lisle's retinue will be the subject of a separate chapter. Despite the hefty fines and poor reputation such unruly elements created, De Lisle continued to support these men throughout their respective careers.

Part Three, De Lisle as "victim," presents the bishop's case against his conviction at the hands of Lady Wake and examines the king's role in that conviction. In the aftermath of the feud, De Lisle appealed his case to the papal see at Avignon, where he was to remain until his death in 1361. His challenge to the king's judgment interfered with the pope's efforts to negotiate a peaceful settlement to the Hundred Years' War. The appeal also deeply affected politics back home in England, as De Lisle's messengers and loyalists in his diocese attempted to publish papal summons in violation of the Statute of *Praemunire*. Edward proved to be the master, not only of his subject bishops to whom De Lisle looked for support, but likewise of international diplomacy with a supposedly pro-French papacy.

Finally, there are issues of justice and law and order to consider. Edward's effectiveness in combating crime within the context of contemporary expectations and of the shortcomings of the medieval English legal system has yet to be fully explored. The way in which Edward inter-

6. For medieval accounts of De Lisle's dispute with Lady Wake and its aftermath, see *AS*, 1:44–45 and 655–62 (Appendix B, pages 229–38); Henry Knighton, *Chronicon*, ed. J. R. Lumby, 2 vols. (RS, xcii, 1889–95), 2:103–4; Thomas Walsingham, *Historia Anglicana*, ed. H. T. Riley, 2 vols. (RS, xxviii, 1863–64), 1:285–86; John de Reading, *Chronica Johannis de Reading et Anonymi Cantuariensis*, ed. J. Tait (Manchester, 1914), 129–30. Modern analyses include F. Godwin, *A Catalogue of the Bishops of England* (London, 1601), 214–16; J. Bentham, *The History and Antiquities of the Conventual and Cathedral Church of Ely* (Cambridge, 1771), 161–62; *DNB*, 33:344; B. H. Putnam, *The Place in Legal History of Sir William Shareshull, Chief Justice of the King's Bench, 1350–1361: A Study of Judicial and Administrative Methods in the Reign of Edward III* (Cambridge, 1950), 140–42; J.R.L. Highfield, "The Relations Between the Church and the English Crown from the Death of Archbishop Stratford to the Opening of the Great Schism, 1349–78" (D.Phil. diss., Oxford, 1951), 141–46; and see also Tait's commentary in John de Reading, *Chronica*, 272–73.

vened in the Lady Wake dispute says much about his judicial policy in general. By extension, the king's judicial policy reflects his domestic government as a whole, since, according to most contemporary theories of kingship, one of the main responsibilities of the medieval king was to maintain good order in his realm.[7] Opinion among modern historians has long been divided as to Edward's abilities as a ruler: Most recently, assessments of the domestic government of the reign have been largely favorable.[8] Edward, the hero of the Hundred Years' War and the embodiment of chivalry, was also the architect of a long and happy consensus among his political community of barons and bishops. The fact that De Lisle miserably failed to obtain the support of his colleagues in the course of his feud with the king seems to support such a conclusion. But there remains the king's behavior as a theoretically impartial arbitrator of the bishop's suit with his rival, Lady Wake. It is disturbing that, at a time when Edward was supposedly at his most mature and powerful, he attempted to dispense justice in an arbitrary way, without recourse to the law, in accordance with his very personal conception of honor. It was a performance typical of his approach to judicial reform in general, and it bodes ill for any representation of Edward III as one of the great kings of medieval England.

A word must be said about the primary sources used in this study. The most important, of course, with regard to crime are the legal records contained in the Public Record Office (PRO) in London. Ever since the Assize of Clarendon was instituted by Henry II in 1166, indictments of criminal conduct were brought by a jury of twelve from each hundred and four men from each town. Eventually, the jury was called on to decide the guilt or innocence of the accused as well, thus replacing the outdated trial by ordeal. By the thirteenth century, two main courts were established in England: the court of king's bench and the court of common pleas. King's bench decided criminal cases, which included accusations of felony (the more heinous crimes such as homicide, rape, theft, and arson, for which the penalty was death) and trespass (crimes that usually carried a monetary penalty or fine, such as assault, conspiracy, and extortion). The court of common pleas decided civil cases, mostly dealing with recovery of debt and disputes over property.[9]

---

7. See pages 189–91.

8. W. M. Ormrod, *The Reign of Edward III: Crown and Political Society in England, 1327–1377* (New Haven, 1990), 197–203; S. L. Waugh, *England in the Reign of Edward III* (Cambridge, 1991), 230–36.

9. For more information, see F. Pollock and F. W. Maitland, *The History of English Law*, 2 vols. (Cambridge, 1899–1923); T.F.T. Plucknett, *A Concise History of the Common Law* (London, 1922); M. Blatcher, "The Workings of the Court of King's Bench in the Fifteenth Century" (D.Phil. diss., London, 1936); M. Hastings, *The Court of Common Pleas in Fifteenth-Century England* (New York,

Each of these courts had its own records, called plea rolls, which were written down by law clerks on long strips of parchment or vellum made out of animal skins, a far more durable material than paper. However, because the vellum is covered in cursive, heavily abbreviated medieval script in the Latin language (but also occasionally in Anglo-Norman French), some quite technical paleographical and linguistic skills are required to decipher them. These documents equally are demanding in a very physical sense; they are at least a yard long, and, since the membranes are stitched together at one end, they become twice as long when opened. They also can be extremely heavy, particularly in the case of the common plea rolls, which often run in excess of five hundred membranes. Entries are enrolled by the county of England in which the suit originated and are, for the most part, written in formulaic language employing stock phrases (such as *vi et armis*, "by force and arms"). It is rare, in fact, that a case came to trial in the plea rolls.[10] By one estimate, more than 94 percent of pleas of trespass from East Anglia between 1422 and 1442 failed to reach a verdict in the king's bench.[11] Time and again the sheriff delayed the proceedings because he could not find the accused (*non est inventus*) or because he could not impanel a quorum of jurors (*pro defectu juratorum*) or because he could not produce the original writ of *venire facias* (*non misit brevem*). Consequently, most entries produce only the indictments against the accused and thus have a built-in bias, or one-sided view, toward the case, namely from the perspective of the prosecutor, the crown. It is rare that defendants were allowed to make a defense in the plea rolls.

Other legal records worthy of the researcher's attention include gaol delivery rolls, compiled when an itinerant justice "delivered" or visited the king's gaol in a city or town. These records have much the same format as the plea rolls and present similar problems in interpretation. Also of great interest from a legal perspective are the *Yearbooks*, or *Reports of Cases in Law*, printed in a "black letter" edition during the seventeenth century in the original, heavily abbreviated Anglo-Norman French. These

---

1947); G. O. Sayles, *The Court of King's Bench in Law and History* (London, 1959); A. Harding, *The Law Courts of Medieval England* (London, 1973); R. C. Van Caenegem, *The Birth of the English Common Law*, 2d edition (Cambridge, 1988); J. H. Baker, *An Introduction to English Legal History*, 3d edition, 2 vols. (London, 1990); P. Brand, *The Making of the Common Law* (Hambledon, 1992).

10. *Select Cases in the Court of King's Bench*, ed. G. O. Sayles, 7 vols. (SS, LV, LVII, LVIII, LXXIV, LXXVI, LXXXII, LXXXVIII, 1936–71), 2:cvi.

11. P. C. Maddern, *Violence and Social Order: East Anglia, 1422–1442* (Oxford, 1992), 33. Other estimates cite a 30 percent rate of trial verdict: J. B. Given, *Society and Homicide in Thirteenth-Century England* (Stanford, 1977), 93–94; J. B. Post, "Criminals and the Law in the Reign of Richard II" (D.Phil. diss., Oxford, 1976), 15.

records are especially valuable as they record the deliberations of the judges on the case, in addition to the arguments made by the counsel, as transcribed by the clerks of the court. The *Yearbooks* thus provide a more intimate, and even-handed, view of the workings of a medieval English court. Much important administrative material issuing out of chancery and accessible in print include the letters patent, which record special commissions of "oyer and terminer" (literally, to "hear and determine") issued by the crown to investigate individual offenses in the shires, and letters close. In addition, there are the great series of printed editions of the *Rolls of Parliament, Statutes of the Realm,* and Rymer's *Foedera,* which includes various royal documents of interest.

De Lisle's diocesan and administrative acts can be studied through his episcopal register, which is complete up to the time of his departure for exile in Avignon in 1356. None of the bishop's household accounts and few of his manorial account rolls survived the depredations of the Peasants' Revolt of 1381.[12] Nevertheless, this meager material is supplemented by two exhaustive surveys of the bishop's estates made by the king's sheriffs and his clerk, Roger de Clown, in 1356 and 1357 following De Lisle's conviction of complicity in the murder of Lady Wake's valet, William Holm. Since the confiscation of episcopal temporalities was a relatively rare event, these surveys are unique and provide complete records of all the bishop's material holdings, including his manor-houses, lands, tenants and their customary rents and duties, profits of manorial courts, and so on.

Finally, there is a medieval biography of De Lisle that forms part of a series of histories of the bishops of Ely from the death of Bishop Nigel in 1169 to the death of Bishop Philip Morgan in 1434. Written by two anonymous monks of the Ely Cathedral Chapter, the *Monachi Eliensis Anonymi Continuatio Historiae Eliensis* survives in four fifteenth-century manuscripts.[13] Based on the evidence of one of these manuscripts, Cotton MS Nero A.xvi, now located in the British Library (BL), the seventeenth-century editor of the biographies, Henry Wharton, postulated that they were written in a single, fourteenth-century hand up until 1388, after which a new hand continued on until 1434.[14] It is therefore possible that Nero A.xvi was written by a contemporary, or near contemporary, of De Lisle, a possibility made even greater by the fact that the biographer reveals an intimate knowledge of the bishop's famous feud with Lady Wake,

12. D. M. Owen, *Ely Records: A Handlist of the Records of the Bishop and Archdeacon of Ely* (Cambridge, 1971), 7.

13. The four manuscripts are: Corpus Christi College Library, Cambridge, MS 287, 118–36; BL, Cotton MS Titus A.i, fols. 128v–142r; BL, Cotton MS Nero A.xvi, fols. 36v–72r; and LPL, MS 448, fols. 63r–76r.

14. BL, Cotton MS Nero A.xvi, fol. 79v; *AS,* 1:xlvi.

knowledge that he most likely received firsthand. The De Lisle biography is also by far the longest of the series, comprising nineteen pages compared to an average of between two and three pages for the other bishops.[15]

Several Ely monks are known to have served in De Lisle's retinue.[16] Although the biographer betrays a strong bias in favor of the bishop, there are places where he seems to criticize De Lisle's behavior or at least show his hero in a bad light.[17] Contrasted with the otherwise positive tone of the work, these criticisms probably can be taken at face value and, for that reason, are most revealing. Compared to the rather dry, formulaic records of royal and diocesan administration, De Lisle's biography bequeaths to us a more human and tangible subject through the dark glass of the intervening centuries.

15. Corpus Christi College Library, Cambridge, MS 287, 143.
16. See pages 38–40.
17. See pages 41, 129–30, 134–35.

PART ONE

De Lisle as Bishop

1

Early Years

Thomas De Lisle's origins are perhaps the most obscure of those of any of his contemporary bishops. He did not belong to any great noble family, nor does his surname, derived from the Old French for "island," designate any particular town or region of the country.[1] The genealogist's task is complicated by the fact that "Lisle" occurs quite often in medieval English records, turning up in rolls from various counties.

One clue to the identity of De Lisle's family lies in his episcopal coat of arms. A 1691 edition of De Lisle's medieval biography describes these arms as "in three roundels three kings of Cologne in a field red."[2] This rather odd coat (De Lisle's connection with a city in Germany is never explained) is derived from Robert Steward's depiction of the arms of the various bishops of Ely compiled in the previous century.[3] The coat is quite false. As early as 1747, the antiquarian William Cole pointed out that Bishop De Lisle's true coat of arms is "a chevron between three trefoils slipped."[4] Cole deduced these arms from a wax impression of the bishop's great seal, which still survives in the archives of Corpus Christi College, Cambridge.[5] Nevertheless, the three kings coat is attributed to De Lisle

1. *A Dictionary of British Surnames*, ed. P. H. Reaney and rev. R. M. Wilson, 2d edition (Sheffield, 1976), 217; *A Dictionary of Surnames*, ed. P. Hanks and F. Hodges (Oxford, 1988), 328. De Lisle's name also is sometimes rendered in Latin as *Insula*.
2. *AS*, 1:652.
3. LPL, MS 448, fol. 63v.
4. BL: Add. MS 33491, 55; Add. MS 5822, fol. 140v.
5. Corpus Christi College Archives, Cambridge, XXVII-9. Other impressions of the same seal, in various conditions of repair, survive in ibid., XXVII-17, XXVII-20, XXVII-21; Pembroke College Archives, Cambridge, Box A.2; Gonville and Caius College Archives, Cambridge, RM I.11, RM I.25 (see Fig. 4); BL, Seal LV 35. An impression of a different seal of the bishop's, also showing his coat of arms, survives in BL, Seal LV 36 (see Frontispiece).

in the windows made in the 1950s by the glazier Charles Blakeman for St. Etheldreda's church in Ely Place, Holborn, London.[6]

Next, Cole identified De Lisle's coat with that of a Hampshire Lisle family listed in an alphabetical roll of arms dated 1604.[7] Thus, "gules, a chevron between three leaves or slipt vert," became the bishop's standard entry in modern works of heraldry.[8] This coat does not correspond with those of the great Hampshire baronial families of Lisle of Rougemont or Kingston Lisle,[9] nor does it match the arms of Sir John de Lisle of Wootton in the Isle of Wight, whom J.R.L. Highfield believed was related to the bishop.[10] However, another Sir John de Lisle from Hampshire was enrolled with the arms, "or, a chevron between three leaves gules," in a list of knights banneret from the early fourteenth century.[11] Around the same time, Sir Walter de Lisle was enrolled as a knight with the arms, "or, a chevron of gules [between] three trefoils of gules," while the Lisle family, which held the manor of Mainsbridge-alias-Swaythling, Hampshire, bore on their shield, "gules, a chevron between three burdock leaves or."[12]

All of these Hampshire coats are sufficiently close to Bishop De Lisle's own to indicate that the families might have been related in some way, but without additional information, the exact nature of the relationship will never be known. In actual fact, the most powerful evidence we have as to where in England De Lisle and his immediate family came from

6. *St. Etheldreda's and Ely Place: A Brief Account of the Church and its Surroundings* (Leicester, n.d.), 19.

7. King's College, Cambridge, MS 15, "A Common-Place Book," 223, 395.

8. *Papworth's Ordinary of British Armorials,* ed. A. W. Morant (London, 1874), 425; W.K.R. Bedford, *The Blazon of Episcopacy* (Oxford, 1897), 44.

9. The arms of these two families were, respectively, "or, a fess between two chevronels" and "gules, a lion passant argent crowned or." See *Papworth's Ordinary,* 77, 739; B. Burke, *The General Armory of England, Scotland, Ireland and Wales* (London, 1884), 611.

10. Highfield, "Relations Between the Church and the English Crown," 667. The Wootton arms are "or, on a chief azure three lions rampant of the first." See Burke, *Armory of England,* 611; *Papworth's Ordinary,* 566; *VCH Hamps.,* 5:204–5. The basis for Highfield's connection between the two men is that Sir John de Lisle employed a Dominican as his confessor and the young Thomas de Lisle was ordained in the Winchester Dominican convent. The identification of the employer with Sir John de Lisle of Wootton, however, itself is tenuous. See *The Registers of John de Sandale and Rigaud de Asserio, Bishops of Winchester, 1316–1323,* ed. F. J. Baigent (London, 1897), 509–10, 551, and 510, n. 1.

11. Burke, *Armory of England, 611;* C. R. Humphery-Smith, *General Armory Two: Alfred Morant's Additions and Corrections to Burke's General Armory* (London, 1973), 102 and bibliography under "N."

12. "The 'Nativity' Roll of Arms, Temp. Edward I," ed. J. Greenstreet, *The Reliquary* 15 (1874–75), 230; G. J. Brault, *Early Blazon, Heraldic Terminology in the Twelfth and Thirteenth Centuries with Special Reference to Arthurian Literature* (Oxford, 1972), 284; *VCH Hamps.,* 3:484.

points not to Hampshire but to the county of Kent. Several of De Lisle's known relatives, including his brother John, who were to join their successful kinsman at Ely, seem to have had their roots there. In 1349, De Lisle petitioned the pope on behalf of himself, John de Lisle (probably the bishop's brother), and John's wife, Joan, for plenary remission at the hour of death. When the pope granted the remission, John de Lisle was called "of the diocese of Canterbury."[13] A "John de Lisle of Kent" was one of the bishop's *domicelli* (a page or squire) commissioned in 1345 to take seisin of the Ely temporalities in De Lisle's stead and receive from the prior and chapter of Ely Cathedral the bishop's pontifical ornaments and muniments.[14] John de Lisle of Kent also was associated with the bishop's men in several criminal and civil suits.[15] Sir John de Colville, a knight from Kent, was among those who bailed John de Lisle and his friends before the king's bench in Easter term 1355, when they were indicted for the arson of Lady Wake's houses.[16]

In addition to his brother, Bishop De Lisle petitioned the pope on behalf of three of his "nephews," Thomas, Richard, and Robert Michaelis (or Michel), who, like John de Lisle, were described as men "of the diocese of Canterbury."[17] A "Robert Michel of Kent" is recorded in Bishop De Lisle's register.[18] De Lisle probably had a sister who married into a Michel family that came from Kent. She may have been Ancilla de Lisle (or Michel), the bishop's sister who stayed at Downham manor in Cambridgeshire during her brother's episcopate.[19] Important men in De Lisle's curia likewise had a Kentish connection. William de Pecham, one of the bishop's vicars-general appointed in his absence, is described as a "clerk of the diocese of Canterbury" and was rector of the church of Kingswood, Kent.[20] Magister John Thursteyn, the bishop's official, was rector of the church of Bishopsbourne, Kent.[21] Thomas de Baa, the bishop's constable of Wisbech Castle, Cambridgeshire, seems to have been a native of the diocese of Canterbury.[22]

There remains, however, the enigma of De Lisle's arms. They cannot be attributed to any known Kentish Lisle family. This suggests that the bishop's immediate family was not of the knightly class, which had been allowed to bear arms since at least 1300. Nevertheless, the family very

---

13. *CPP*, 174; *CPL*, 3:326.
14. CUL, EDR, G/I/1, Reg. De Lisle, fol. 54r.
15. See page 154.
16. PRO, KB 27/379, rex m. 9.
17. *CPP*, 100, 173, 283; *CPL*, 3:213, 306, 352.
18. CUL, EDR, G/I/1, Reg. De Lisle, fol. 25r.
19. CUL, EDR, D 10/2/19, *opera yemalia et estivallia*.
20. CUL, EDR, G/I/1, Reg. De Lisle, fols. 17r, 18v, 20r.
21. Ibid., fol. 41v; *CPP*, 127.
22. LPL, Reg. Simon Islip, fol. 150r.

well could have belonged to the lower half of the gentry, known as the esquires or armigerous class, who did not assume coats of arms until 1350.[23] Membership in the gentry would help explain the family's apparent connection with the Hampshire Lisles, who occupied the slightly higher status of knights. On his elevation to the see of Ely, therefore, De Lisle seems to have appropriated for himself the arms of his nearest kin who were of arm-bearing status, namely one of the Hampshire Lisle families mentioned above. Apparently it was not uncommon for bishops who had no inheritable arms of their own to borrow them from someone else or indeed make them up altogether.[24]

As best we can tell, then, De Lisle was a Kentish man born and bred, whose family probably belonged to the lower gentry of esquires who could not yet bear arms. Fortunately for the future bishop, however, he seems to have had richer relations in Hampshire, some of whom were knights and who may have had influence with the Winchester Dominicans and the powerful local nobility. It was the latter consideration that conceivably determined the young Thomas De Lisle to begin his ecclesiastical career as a Dominican preaching friar at the Winchester convent.

Dominican Friar and Papal Protégé

The priory at Winchester perhaps was not the most prestigious of the English Dominican convents that De Lisle could have joined. It was half as large as that at London and did not have the university credentials of those at Oxford and Cambridge. Nevertheless, the Winchester convent was one of the older and larger Dominican foundations in England, founded in c. 1234. The buildings of the convent were said to be able to house between forty and fifty friars, and in all the site, including buildings, occupied approximately two and one-half acres. In 1325 the house was recorded as containing forty-six friars and in 1331 to have numbered thirty-six. Throughout its early history it was the recipient of generous royal patronage, a tradition that continued into De Lisle's day. In 1331, Edward III gave the convent 12s., and in 1339, he assigned to it a total of £35.[25] Thus, the presence of De Lisle's Hampshire relatives notwithstand-

23. C. Given-Wilson, *The English Nobility in the Late Middle Ages: The Fourteenth-Century Political Community* (London, 1987), 70.

24. J. Woodward, *A Treatise on Ecclesiastical Heraldry* (Edinburgh and London, 1894), 22, 81.

25. C.F.R. Palmer, "The Friar-Preachers, or Blackfriars, of Winchester," *The Reliquary*, new series, 3 (1889), 207–10; *VCH Hamps.*, 2:189; J.R.H. Moorman, *Church Life in England in the Thirteenth Century* (Cambridge, 1945), 408; W. A. Hinnebusch,

ing, the Winchester convent was probably an attractive place for an ambitious young man seeking to enter the Dominican Order to make his profession.

The first we hear of De Lisle as a Dominican was when he was ordained a priest by Peter de Bologna, bishop of Corbava in Croatia, acting for Bishop Assier of Winchester, in the chapel of St. Elizabeth near Winchester on 18 December 1322.[26] If De Lisle adhered to the canonical age of twenty-five at the time of his ordination, then we have a *terminus post quem* for his date of birth of 1297.[27] According to the sixteenth-century antiquarian John Bale, De Lisle studied at Cambridge and received a doctorate there, an assertion repeated by succeeding generations of historians.[28] However, as is often the case with Bale, there is tantalizingly little surviving evidence to support his statements. We cannot be certain, therefore, that in his youth De Lisle attended the Cambridge Dominican convent or, indeed, that he received an academic degree of any kind.

Nonetheless, at Winchester at least, De Lisle was a rising star in the Dominican hierarchy. When next we hear of him, in 1341, he is recorded as prior of the Winchester Dominicans as he was about to go on a royal diplomatic mission in the company of John Walwayn to the papal court at Avignon. Once there, he and Walwayn were to liaison with William Bateman, dean of Lincoln and later bishop of Norwich, the king's proctor at the papal curia. The messengers were to communicate to Bateman Edward III's latest proposals for a resumption of the peace conference with France at Tournai and his objections to the election of William de la Zouche in the previous year to the archbishopric of York.[29] On the same day, 14 March, De Lisle and Walwayn also were entrusted with instructions from the king to his proctor, Bateman, concerning Edward's bitter

The Early English Friars Preachers (Rome, 1951), 107–8, 493–95; M. D. Knowles and R. N. Hadcock, *Medieval Religious Houses: England and Wales,* 2d edition (London, 1971), 219.

26. *Registers of Sandale and Asserio,* 545, 551.

27. *Dictionnaire de Droit Canonique,* ed. R. Naz et al., 6 vols. (Paris, 1935–57), 1:340–41.

28. J. Bale, *Scriptorum Illustrium Maioris Brytanniae Catalogus* (Basle, 1557–59), 469–70. Most recently, Bale's information has been repeated by A. B. Emden, *A Biographical Register of the University of Cambridge to 1500* (Cambridge, 1963), 370–71.

29. *Foedera,* 2, no. 2:1118. The year of 1340 assigned to this document in *Foedera* is incorrect, and in this instance the editors apparently failed to account for the medieval system of dating from 25 March. Zouche was elected to York on 2 May 1340, and on 18 January 1341, Edward appointed Bateman his proctor at the papal court in order to object to Zouche's election. See J. Le Neve, *Fasti Ecclesiae Anglicanae, 1300–1541,* rev. J. M. Horn, B. Jones, and H.P.F. King, 12 vols. (London, 1962–67), 6:3; *CPR, 1340–43,* 109–19. I also have updated from 1340 to 1341 Edward's letters of 16 March on behalf of the earl of Salisbury.

dispute with the archbishop of Canterbury, John Stratford. Edward had fallen out with his former chancellor as a result of the failure of his latest military campaign in France. Stratford was held to blame for the fact that the tax that was to finance the war yielded disappointing returns. In his letter to the pope against the archbishop, Edward repeated the charges of treason that he had leveled against Stratford in the *libellus famosus*.[30]

In spite of the importance of the missions that he was undertaking in the king's name, De Lisle played a secondary role to that of the resident proctor at Avignon, Bateman. His chief patron on this occasion seems to have been not the king but the earl of Salisbury, William de Montagu. On 16 March 1341, just two days after his appointments on royal business, De Lisle was commissioned to petition Pope Benedict XII for confirmation of the earl's foundation of Bisham Priory, Berkshire, and for a dispensation to allow the marriage between Hugh le Despenser and the earl's daughter, Elizabeth.[31] Significantly, De Lisle was to act alone on Montagu's behalf. It is quite possible that De Lisle was introduced into Montagu's service by one of his Hampshire Lisle relatives. Alternatively, De Lisle may have been pressed into royal diplomacy by one of the king's confessors, who tended to be Dominicans.[32]

An event now was to happen that would change the entire course of De Lisle's life, without which he probably never would have become bishop. Still haunting the halls of the papal palace long after he had fulfilled his diplomatic mission, De Lisle very likely was present at Avignon when Pope Benedict XII died on 25 April 1342 and the new pope, Clement VI, was elected and consecrated in May of the same year. The successor to the throne of Saint Peter was altogether different from his predecessor. The contrast must have been striking: Jacques Fournier, who had become Benedict XII, had come from humble origins, had been brought up in the Cistercian order, and had been known as ascetic in his personal habits, stingy toward his friends, and a zealous reformer of the religious orders.[33] But the election of Pierre Roger, the scion of a noble house who

---

30. *Foedera*, 2, no. 2:1152–53; Haines, *Archbishop John Stratford*, 306. For standard histories of the Stratford crisis, see W. Stubbs, *The Constitutional History of England*, 3 vols. (Oxford, 1874–78), 2:384–92; D. Hughes, *A Study of Social and Constitutional Tendencies in the Early Years of Edward III* (London, 1915), 100–152; G. T. Lapsley, "Archbishop Stratford and the Parliamentary Crisis of 1341," *EHR* 30 (1915), 6–18, 193–215, and reprinted in *Crown, Community and Parliament*, ed. H. M. Cam and G. Barraclough (Oxford, 1951), 231–72.

31. *Foedera*, 2, no. 2:1119. The petition for the marriage dispensation between Despenser and Salisbury's daughter was granted almost immediately by Pope Benedict, on 27 April 1341. See *CPL*, 2:553.

32. For example, Richard de Wynkeley, a friar preacher and master of theology, was mentioned as royal confessor in 1340 and 1342. See *CPP*, 2; *CPL*, 3:580.

33. G. Mollat, *The Popes at Avignon, 1305–1378*, trans. J. Love (London, 1963), 35–36.

chose the apt name Clement VI, heralded a lax and luxurious regime. Declaring that "my predecessors did not know how to be popes," Clement inaugurated his papacy with banquets featuring fountains of flowing wine, endless courses of food, and trick bridges that betrayed their travelers into the river. The pope's reputation for generosity soon spread far and wide as he became a magnet for artists from all over Europe, thus making Clement an early prototype of the princely patrons of the Renaissance.[34]

"His court was the most civilized in Europe, the haunt of the highest nobility, enlivened with feasts, balls and tournaments," writes Guillaume Mollat, a historian of the Avignon popes. "The finest figures of the time were to be found there, painters from Italy and Germany, French sculptors and architects, poets and men of letters, physicians, doctors and astronomers."[35] Seekers of plum jobs in the Church flocked to the papal curia as Clement announced in 1344 that the power of disposing of all such offices, wherever they might be, was vested in himself alone. A new building program to enlarge the papal palace on a grand scale was begun, and in 1348, Clement made Avignon a more permanent place of exile from Rome by purchasing the city from the beautiful Queen Joanna of Naples. It was rumored that the purchase price of 80,000 gold florins was accompanied by sexual favors.[36]

Surrounded by such a dazzling, and almost secular, court, it is no wonder that the ambitious and perhaps impressionable De Lisle decided to marry his future fortunes to Avignon and stayed on to become the pope's protégé. On 14 March 1343, two years to the day when he had been dispatched on king's business, De Lisle returned to his native land, and to Edward III's court, in his new capacity as pope's messenger. Clement entrusted his protégé with a letter asking Edward to appoint ambassadors who were to represent him in the peace conference between England and France to be mediated by his holiness at Avignon the following year.[37] De Lisle probably returned there shortly after discharging this mission. Although he is not mentioned as part of the English delegation, he may have taken part in the lengthy negotiations leading up to and during the Avignon conference.[38] He was definitely at the papal court on 20 January

34. Ibid., 38; D. Wood, *Clement VI: The Pontificate and Ideas of an Avignon Pope* (Cambridge, 1989), 51–52.

35. Mollat, *Popes*, 39.

36. Ibid., 38; Wood, *Clement VI*, 48–50, 52–61.

37. *Foedera*, 1, no. 2:981–82. The letter is mistakenly dated 1306 and attributed to Pope Clement V. See P.N.R. Zutshi, *Original Papal Letters in England, 1305–1415* (Vatican City, 1990), 91–92.

38. E. Déprez, "La Conférence d'Avignon, 1344: L'Arbitrage Pontifical Entre la France et l'Angleterre," in A. G. Little and F. M. Powicke, eds., *Essays in Medieval History Presented to Thomas Frederick Tout* (Manchester, 1925), 301–20.

1345, when he, along with William Bateman, now bishop of Norwich, and John Offord, dean of Lincoln, were instructed by Edward III to persuade the pope to excuse the bishop of Worcester, Wulstan de Bransford, from personally appearing before the papal auditors.[39]

What happened next was a stroke of luck for De Lisle. The incumbent of the see of Ely, Simon Montacute, died on 20 June 1345,[40] and De Lisle probably was opportunistic enough to sense that he was "in the right place at the right time." He was by now the pope's penitentiary, or "familiar," and Clement VI was quick to fill the vacancy with a trusted and native follower. The formal bull of provision, addressed to Archbishop Stratford, was issued on 15 July, and De Lisle's career move to the papal curia finally was vindicated.[41]

There were obstacles to be overcome, however. The pope had overridden the election by the monastic chapter of the Ely Cathedral prior, Alan Walsingham, as bishop on 7 July.[42] Early in the fourteenth century, the Ely chapter had succeeded in installing two of its members in the episcopal chair, but Clement VI was to make papal provisions a normal procedure with regard to English bishoprics.[43] After De Lisle's superstitious consecration at the papal palace on 24 July, he was given safe conduct by the pope to return to England seven days later.[44] That same day, 31 July 1345, Clement wrote to Edward III, explaining that he had provided De Lisle, an Englishman, to the see of Ely "chiefly because he ought to be agreeable to you, most beloved son, because we have continually found in him a faithful promoter and fervid zealot of your honor and well-being."[45] If the king did not have grounds for believing the pope's hyperbole, he nevertheless did not protest and reject De Lisle's provision. By

39. *Foedera*, 3, no. 1:27.

40. Le Neve, *Fasti, 1300–1541*, 4:13. *AS*, 1:652 (see Appendix B, page 225) dates Montacute's death a year earlier, in 1344.

41. ASV, Registra Vaticana 139, Clement VI, no. 120 (from a microfilm in the Seeley Historical Library, Cambridge); *CPL*, 3:19; *Clement VI (1342–1352): Lettres Closes, Patentes et Curiales Intéressant les Pays Autres que la France*, ed. E. Déprez and G. Mollat (Paris, 1960), 92. *AS*, 1:655 (see Appendix B, page 228) again gives the wrong date, 1344.

42. *AS*, 1:652–53, and see Appendix B, page 225. The *congé d'élire* was requested from the crown on 22 June 1345 and granted on 28 June. See PRO, C 84/24/42; *CPR*, 1343–45, 486.

43. Highfield, "Relations Between the Church and the English Crown," 133–34; W. A. Pantin, *The English Church in the Fourteenth Century* (Cambridge, 1955), 55.

44. *CPL*, 3:26, 188.

45. ". . . ex eo presertim tibi fili carissime debebat esse grata, quia ipsum reperimus continue tui honoris et com[m]odi promotorem fidelem, et fervideum zelatorem" (ASV, Registra Vaticana 139, Clement VI, no. 178). A similar letter announcing the provision was sent to John Thoresby, at that time canon of Lincoln and keeper of the privy seal. See *Foedera*, 3, no. 1:55.

10 September of the same year, Edward signified his assent by releasing to De Lisle the Ely temporalities, with the exception of Haddenham church in Cambridgeshire, which the king retained until 11 February 1346.[46] It was not until 9 September 1348 that De Lisle professed his obedience to Archbishop Stratford.[47] However, it seems that neither of the two most important participants, the bishop or the archbishop, was present: De Lisle is recorded in his episcopal register as being at his manor of Somersham, Huntingdonshire, on the same day, and Stratford was dead by 23 August 1348, with his successor, John Offord, not chosen until the following 24 September.[48]

Edward III's successes in the Hundred Years' War are largely attributed to the fact that he could rely on a political community of magnates to support his policies both at home and abroad.[49] Since Church prelates figured large in this community, it was obviously in Edward's interest to pack the episcopal bench as much as possible with his long-time clerical servants. This action had the added advantage of rewarding these servants at the Church's expense rather than the crown's. It has been calculated that at least thirty percent of the bishops during Edward III's reign served the crown at some stage in their careers prior to their promotion.[50] Among this group numbered some of the wealthiest and most influential prelates in the country. The keepership of the privy seal was almost a prerequisite office for many powerful churchmen. It had been held by Thomas Hatfield, bishop of Durham; John Thoresby, archbishop of York; Simon Islip, archbishop of Canterbury; and Michael Northburgh, bishop of London. Thoresby continued to serve the crown as chancellor after his provision to York. His colleague, William Edington, bishop of Winchester, likewise had a long career at the royal court, serving as keeper of the wardrobe before becoming bishop and then throughout almost his entire episcopal career as either treasurer or chancellor.[51]

De Lisle, by contrast, belonged to a small minority of Edward's bishops, 14 percent, who had obtained their bishoprics through the pope's patronage.[52] Thomas Ringstead, De Lisle's penitentiary and a fellow friar preacher, followed in the footsteps of his patron by residing at Avignon

46. *CPR, 1343–45*, 548–49; *CPR, 1345–48*, 44; CUL, EDR, G/I/1, Reg. De Lisle, fol. 67r.

47. *Canterbury Professions*, ed. M. Richter (CYS, LXVII, 1972–73), 103.

48. CUL, EDR, G/I/1, Reg. De Lisle, fol. 16r; Le Neve, *Fasti, 1300–1541*, 4:3.

49. Ormrod, *Reign of Edward III*, 95–120; Waugh, *England in the Reign of Edward III*, 117–35.

50. Highfield, "Relations Between the Church and the English Crown," 686.

51. For précis of the careers of these men, see ibid., 499–505, 531–35, 543–52, 564–68, 574–78.

52. Ibid., 686.

and becoming papal penitentiary prior to his elevation to the Welsh see of Bangor.[53] Another of De Lisle's contemporaries, Thomas Fastolf, became bishop of St. David's after having served the pope as one of his auditors.[54] John Grandisson, bishop of Exeter, had been a chaplain and close friend of Pope John XXII.[55]

The bishop of Ely was even more alone if we consider the number of his fellow prelates who were Dominicans like himself. Aside from Ringstead, there was, in fact, no British bishop of the order whose episcopacy coincided with De Lisle's own, although before his time John de Eaglescliff had been bishop of Llandaff and afterward, Gervase de Castro succeeded Ringstead to Bangor. In any event, these men were heads of marginal Welsh sees not of much consequence in English politics. Even if we extend our scope to the whole fifty years of Edward's reign, the only other Dominican to head an English see was John Gilbert, who at the very end of the reign was translated from Bangor to Hereford in 1375.[56] Aside from royal confessors, therefore, Dominicans generally did not attain high office in England during the fourteenth century.

De Lisle thus was isolated from his episcopal colleagues by dint of his very background, an isolation that seems to have continued after he became bishop. The isolation was not only political but geographical: The fens of medieval Cambridgeshire made travel within the diocese hazardous and difficult (Fig. 1). In only a few instances can it be shown that De Lisle attended general convocation or provincial council in the company of his fellow prelates.[57] Many of these prelates shared a certain esprit d' corps fostered by a patronage system whereby clerks in the fourteenth century climbed a ladder of promotion to their bishoprics through administrative service and collection of benefices. The fact that De Lisle had managed to circumvent this system through his closeness to the pope made him something of an outsider. Bishops Bateman, Hatfield, Edington, John Gynwell of Lincoln, and Robert Wyville of Salisbury all, for example, had been at one time or another members of the chapter of Lincoln Ca-

53. Ibid., 673–74. Ringstead acknowledged De Lisle's patronage in his will of 3 December 1365, in which he left a total of £11 for masses to be said for the souls of his family and for "Thomas, bishop of Ely." See P.N.R. Zutshi and R. Ombres, "The Dominicans in Cambridge, 1238–1538," *Archivum Fratrum Praedicatorum* 60 (1990), 353.

54. Pantin, *English Church*, 21; J.R.L. Highfield, "The English Hierarchy in the Reign of Edward III," *TRHS*, 5th series, 6 (1956), 121.

55. Highfield, "English Hierarchy," 122; *The Register of John de Grandisson, Bishop of Exeter, A.D. 1327–1369*, ed. F. C. Hingeston-Randolph, 3 vols. (London, 1894–99), 3:v.

56. Highfield, "English Hierarchy," 125–26; M. D. Knowles, *The Religious Orders in England*, 3 vols. (Cambridge, 1948–59), 1:321, 2:370–71.

57. See page 25, and Appendix A, pages 212, 223.

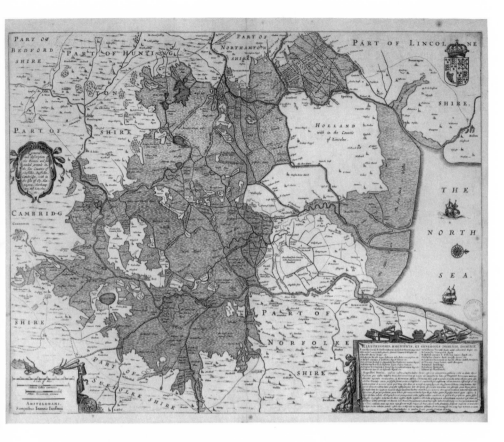

Fig. 1. Ely before the draining of the fens, 1646.

thedral. Bateman had been the chapter's dean before his promotion to
Norwich. Archbishop Islip had been vicar-general to the bishop of Lincoln, Henry Burghersh, during the first part of the fourteenth century.[58]
All this was to have political repercussions when De Lisle sought support
for his efforts to win back his confiscated temporalities from the king.[59]

De Lisle's unique background not only hurt him politically, but also
contributed to the ruinous financial situation in which the bishop found
himself early in his episcopate and which seems to have provided a ratio-
nale for his subsequent crimes. Despite their reputation for extravagance,
most medieval nobles and high churchmen were pretty hard-headed when
it came to their business affairs. They might have to support a large retinue and supply a lavish household in keeping with their status, but to

58. Highfield, "Relations Between the Church and the English Crown," 547–48.
59. See pages 167–74.

keep pace with this expenditure they often maximized the profit from their estates. Nevertheless, the margin for error was becoming smaller as the Black Death took its toll in the middle of the fourteenth century. Most aristocratic families, therefore, if they were to survive, had to spend within their means.[60]

Unfortunately, De Lisle, unlike many other prelates, came to his see with little or no practical experience in diocesan and manorial administration. He had been prior of the Dominican convent in Winchester, but the physical size, and therefore the administrative machinery required, was not very great and would not have prepared him for the sheer enormity of the Ely patrimony. In all, the bishop of Ely's estate included in the mid-fourteenth century forty-one manors in seven counties (Fig. 2) and was worth anywhere from £2000 to £2500 a year.[61] This probably translates into millions of pounds in modern-day money. It made De Lisle the third richest bishop in England and put him among the upper echelons of the entire medieval English aristocracy.[62] He indeed had risen far from his relatively humble origins in Kent and his position as a poor friar of St. Dominic.

The success seems to have gone to his head. In contrast to his colleagues' prudent management of their estates,[63] De Lisle, perhaps drunk with his recent conquest of one of the richest bishoprics in the land, squandered his considerable financial resources in celebration of his new-found status as one of the great men of the kingdom. Even before he reached England, the new bishop of Ely was already in debt: On 16 July 1345 the pope gave him leave to contract a loan of 12,000 florins, or between £1800 and £2400, representing a year's worth of his episcopal income.[64] On 29

60. K. B. McFarlane, *The Nobility of Later Medieval England* (Oxford, 1973), 4, 98–103; M. C. Carpenter, "The Fifteenth–Century English Gentry and their Estates," in M. Jones, ed., *Gentry and Lesser Nobility in Late Medieval Europe* (Gloucester, 1986), 45–56; Given-Wilson, *The English Nobility in the Late Middle Ages*, 87–89; K. Mertes, *The English Noble Household, 1250–1600: Good Governance and Politic Rule* (Oxford, 1988), 102–3; A. Goodman, *John of Gaunt: The Exercise of Princely Power in Fourteenth-Century Europe* (Harlow, Essex, 1992), 345–49.

61. For valuations of the bishop of Ely's estate, see *CCR, 1333–37*, 642–43; *CCR, 1354–60*, 392; *CFR*, 7:172; E. Miller, *The Abbey and Bishopric of Ely* (Cambridge, 1951), 81.

62. Ely was ranked third richest behind Winchester and Durham in 1291, but fourth richest behind Winchester, Durham, and Canterbury in 1535. See *Taxatio Ecclesiastica Angliae et Walliae Auctoritate P. Nicholai IV circa A.D. 1291* (London, 1802), 215, 270, 318; *Valor Ecclesiasticus Temp. Henr. VIII Auctoritate Regia Institutus*, 6 vols. (London, 1810–34), 1:7, 2:2, 3:499. For the value of De Lisle's income relative to that of the fourteenth-century nobility as a whole, see Ormrod, *Reign of Edward III*, 96.

63. See, for example, Butler, "Archbishop Melton," 54–67.

64. ASV, Registra Vaticana 139, Clement VI, no. 1283 (from a microfilm in the Seeley Historical Library, Cambridge); *CPL*, 3:26.

July of the same year, Clement VI granted him license to receive a "charitable subsidy," in reality a tax, from his diocese.[65]

But although the loan may seem excessive, it was, in fact, a standard initiation to a medieval bishopric. In the words of the pope's faculty for the loan, it was contracted so that De Lisle could meet his "necessary expenses . . . at the apostolic see."[66] What this means is that at least half the money probably went toward the enormous *servitia*, 7500 florins, or between £1125 and £1500, which the new bishop of Ely had to pay into the papal camera as the price of his promotion.[67] This bribe, which the *servitia* in essence was, was a normal and expected part of the provision procedure. All bishops had to pay it, and many needed a loan in order to do so. Between 1344 and 1351, at least six prelates besides De Lisle were dispensed by the pope to contract loans: John Offord, archbishop of Canterbury, borrowed 16,000 florins; the bishop of Dunkeld in Ireland needed 3000 florins; the abbot of St. Augustine's Priory in Canterbury, 1000 florins; the abbot of St. Albans, 1000 florins; and the prior of Westminster Abbey, 800 florins.[68] The levying of a charitable aid also was quite common. During the same time period, seven ecclesiastics, not including De Lisle, received such subsides: William Edington, bishop of Winchester; Thomas Hatfield, bishop of Durham; John Offord, archbishop of Canterbury; Offord's successor, Simon Islip (twice); John Thoresby (also twice), as bishop of St. David's and of Worcester; John de St. Paul, archbishop of Dublin; and the bishop of Sodor in Ireland.[69]

It was not the Italian loan, therefore, that broke De Lisle's bank, but apparently his reckless spending once in office. Perhaps in imitation of his liberal patron, Pope Clement, the bishop is said to have gathered about him a large and sumptuous following. His anonymous medieval biographer, most likely a monk in the Ely Cathedral chapter, notes that early in his episcopate, De Lisle "used to keep the strongest knights and squires of the land and men skilled in law in great abundance for his livery and for his counsel, so that in parliament and in other public places, surrounded by a multitude of knights and squires and other servants, he appeared glorious among the other nobles of the realm."[70] That a magnate such as De Lisle, especially one newly created, should want to advertise his status before his peers is not unusual. But the bishop's inexpe-

65. *CPL,* 3:189; *CPP,* 100.

66. ". . . tam pro tuis expensis necessarijs quam ecclesie tue Elien' [Ely] negocijs apud sedem apostolicam expendendis." ASV, Registra Vaticana 139, Clement VI, no. 1283.

67. W. E. Lunt, *Papal Revenues in the Middle Ages,* 2 vols. (New York, 1934), 2:285–86.

68. *CPL,* 3:4, 9, 39, 350, 396.

69. *CPP,* 91, 100, 124, 143, 169, 180, 190, 194, 222.

70. *AS,* 1:655, and see Appendix B, pages 228–29.

rience in such a high position seems to have caught up with him. The biographer adds that later, when De Lisle finally realized that "so great a household was exceedingly burdensome to him," he used a "hoe of discretion" to weed out all but his most essential servants.[71] Although the biographer is our only witness to the bishop's excessive expenditure on retinue, since household accounts do not survive, there are nonetheless good reasons to trust his testimony.[72]

Lastly, one may ask why, given De Lisle's rather meager credentials in royal service, Edward III should have tolerated him in such a valuable and much sought after bishopric as Ely. The king was not one to treat such matters lightly. Just two years prior to De Lisle's appointment, in 1343, Edward had withheld his consent to William Bateman's provision to Norwich, even though Bateman's diplomatic service to the king had been far more extensive than De Lisle's. As it turned out, Edward's protest was short-lived, as he seems to have had no personal objection to Bateman but acted under pressure from a parliament complaining of Clementine provisions.[73] Yet in the next year, Edward again opposed the installment of bishops chosen by the pope.

At this crucial juncture, a tacit agreement seems to have been reached between the two leaders.[74] Clement wrote to the king suggesting that, should Edward cooperate, papal provisions would prove to be a more amenable instrument for the royal wishes with regard to bishoprics than independent capitular elections. As the pope pointed out, democratic principles were often hostile to monarchical aspirations, "because rarely or never would elections occur except by martial influence and also contrary to the king, whose councilors could be promoted by the Roman Church rather than anywhere else."[75] Edward no doubt agreed, since by mere economy of numbers, a single pope was more easily influenced than a whole body of men. Clement, for his part, seems to have gone out of his way to uphold his side of the bargain. When his cardinals objected to his provision in 1345 of the king's servant, Thomas Hatfield, as bishop of Durham because the candidate was considered to be of "little consequence and a layman," the pope was said to have replied, "Truly, if the king had asked for an ass [as bishop], he would have obtained his wish, on this occasion."[76]

71. Ibid.

72. See pages xxiii–xxiv.

73. *CPL*, 3:9; *RP*, 2:141, 143–45. For modern accounts of the dispute, see A. H. Thompson, "William Bateman, Bishop of Norwich, 1344–1355," *Norfolk Archaeology* 25 (1935), 106–8; Highfield, "Relations Between the Church and the English Crown," 520.

74. Highfield, "Relations Between the Church and the English Crown," 76; Pantin, *English Church*, 56.

75. BL, Cotton MS Cleopatra E.II, fol. 47r/49r.

76. *Chronicon Angliae, 1328–1388*, ed. E. M. Thompson (RS, LXIV, 1874), 20.

By the time of De Lisle's provision to Ely, therefore, Edward may have been unwilling to provoke the pope's anger and upset the delicate balance so recently reached between the two sides, a situation Clement may have exploited in order to intrude his choice. But other factors may help explain the king's mute assent to the pope's coup. Edward already may have been satiated by the fact that in 1345, two of his most trusted servants, Thomas Hatfield, keeper of the privy seal, and William Edington, treasurer, were in line for the two richest bishoprics in the land. On 8 May 1345 Hatfield was elected to Durham, valued at over £2666 per year, while Edington, at the king's request, was provided by Clement to Winchester, valued at nearly £3000 per year, on 9 December 1345—although the bishopric had been known to be vacant since the previous 18 April.[77] In addition, De Lisle seems to have done his best to placate the king. The fourteenth-century chronicler Adam Murimuth wrote that the temporalities of Ely were handed over to De Lisle through the procurement of the king's secretaries, but "not without the intercession of promises and gifts."[78]

On 27 November 1345, Advent Sunday, De Lisle formally was enthroned in his episcopal chair at Ely. The ceremony in the Cathedral church apparently was carried off in magnificent style.[79] After his enthronement, the new bishop gave a celebratory feast, to which the local lords and high monks from the abbey no doubt were invited and that most likely was held at the bishop's palace nearby. We know that the celebrants ate stewed rabbit and enjoyed the warmth of a roaring fire, the ingredients of both having been gathered at the bishop's manor of Downham, Cambridgeshire, "for the expenses of the enthronement."[80] It marked the end of the process of De Lisle's provision, and he now could take pleasure in officially calling himself the bishop of Ely. It was a satisfaction he was not to enjoy untroubled for long.

77. Le Neve, *Fasti, 1300–1541*, 4:46, 6:108. Valuations of Winchester and Durham are from *Taxatio Ecclesiastica*, 215, 318.

78. ". . . et cito postea fuerunt sibi temporalia liberata per regem, procurantibus secretariis regis, non absque promissionum et munerum interventu." Adam Murimuth, *Continuatio Chronicarum Robertus de Avesbury, de Gestis Mirabilibus Regis Edwardi Tertii*, ed. E. M. Thompson (RS, xciii, 1889), 172.

79. *AS*, 1:655. The adverb used to describe the enthronement ceremony, *solempniter*, literally means "solemnly" but was interpreted by the *DNB* and Highfield in the sense of "grand" or "magnificent." See *DNB*, 33:343; Highfield, "Relations Between the Church and the English Crown," 667–68.

80. "In auxilium pro cuniculis captis tam pro expensis Intronizacionis. . . . In bosco [boscum] focalem prostrandum tam pro expensis domini ibidem quam pro expensis intronizacionis domini apud Ely." CUL, EDR, D 10/2/17, *expense forinsece*.

2

Diocesan Business, Monastic Disputes, and Manorial Administration

When modern readers see the word "bishop," they usually think of a spiritual pastor benevolently guarding the souls of his flock, not a maintainer of criminals rapaciously fleecing the earthly possessions of his neighbors. That De Lisle may have been both seems to have required an almost schizophrenic personality, rather like the Dr. Jekyll and Mr. Hyde of Robert Louis Stevenson's story. However, the gulf between the two worlds, religious and secular, was not as wide then as it is today. People of the twentieth century in Western Europe and North America, particularly in the United States, have become accustomed to a separation of Church and state, the idea that churchmen should not concern themselves with politics or wealth. We expect, even demand in the form of laws, that religion not interfere with the more mundane issues affecting our lives.

It was not so in the Middle Ages. The sheer number of biographies of medieval prelates who doubled as diplomats, royal councilors, and career politicians testifies to the seamless marriage of heaven and earth that defined the times.[1] Indeed, the medieval king more often than not encouraged the participation of the Church in his government; bishoprics had long been the preferred method for a monarch, with limited resources, to reward his trusted officials.[2] Not even military service was off-limits to adventurous churchmen, despite the prohibitions of canon law against bloodshed. Thomas Hatfield, bishop of Durham, led one of the English armies against the Scots in the Battle of Neville's Cross of 1346, while Hugh Despenser, bishop of Norwich, put down the Peasants' Revolt in

---

1. See works cited in the Introduction, note 3.
2. A. H. Thompson, *The English Clergy and Their Organization in the Later Middle Ages* (Oxford, 1947), 41–45; Pantin, *The English Church*, 11–14; R. N. Swanson, *Church and Society in Late Medieval England* (Oxford, 1989), 103–8.

East Anglia in 1381. Both these bishops at times acted more like soldiers than priests. Equally ensnaring of the medieval Church in the real world were the vast lands and estates that it had to administer. Even monasteries and nunneries could not insulate themselves entirely from outside responsibilities, the more so as their bequests and benefactions grew.

With the dual life led by so many Church leaders, De Lisle's contemporaries may have been shocked far less than we to learn of his extracurricular activities. It is unlikely that they would have declared him unfit for his pastoral duties. We hold our priests to a different, and far stricter, moral standard than did our medieval forebears. As early as the fifth century, the greatest of the Church fathers, Saint Augustine, warned against applying a test of moral purity to any occupant of ecclesiastical office. To do so would be to subscribe to the Donatist heresy, which implied that the grace of the sacraments came from the minister performing them rather than, more properly, from God. As late as the fourteenth and fifteenth centuries, John Wycliffe and Jan Huss were persecuted for demanding ethical behavior as a precondition for spiritual authority.

The rudiments of diocesan and manorial administration have been outlined elsewhere in sufficient detail as to obviate the need to explain them here.[3] Rather, this chapter discusses these issues within the context of the bishop's criminal and litigious history. There is little to indicate that De Lisle's effectiveness as diocesan was diminished in any way by his nonreligious activities. However, his litigation with numerous monastic houses reveals an evident concern to preserve his episcopalian rights and privileges, an aspect that also features in his criminal suits. Moreover, an examination of the official duties performed by members of his curia, many of whom were suspect criminals, illustrates the extent of their support from the bishop, their power over the local community, and their abundant opportunities for extortion.

Diocesan Business

De Lisle was a competent, if perhaps uninspiring, diocesan, judging by the evidence of the register of his episcopal *acta*, which is complete up until his departure for Avignon in 1356. Assessments of bishops based on their registers are limited by the dry, formulaic nature of their entries.

3. For the classic study of late medieval diocesan administration, see R. M. Haines, *The Administration of the Diocese of Worcester in the First Half of the Fourteenth Century* (London, 1965). An authority on manorial administration is to be found in P.D.A. Harvey, *Cuxham Manorial Records* (Oxford Record Society, 1976), and idem, *Manorial Records* (Gloucester, 1984).

Nevertheless, some aspects of De Lisle's register are not without interest. One discernible policy of the bishop's was his expectation that clerics reside in their churches, or at least that they obtain a license if they are to be nonresident. Early in his episcopate, De Lisle confiscated the possessions of six royal clerks beneficed in Cambridgeshire who, by the nature of their business, had to reside in Westminster. The king naturally supported their cause and ordered De Lisle to restore their goods on 25 September 1345; yet it was not until 6 May 1346 that the king's writ reached the bishop.[4] On 8 July 1348, De Lisle ordered the archdeacon of Ely's official to warn Edmund de Benhale, rector of Wimpole, to reside in his church "within the time established by [canon] law."[5] Two months later, however, on 14 September, Benhale was given a license for absence until the bishop revoked it.[6] Similarly, process was begun against Roger de Breynton, rector of Doddington, for nonresidence without license, but the process was revoked when the license was granted for one year on 17 August 1348.[7]

De Lisle likewise moved against corrupt confessors, or penitentiaries. On 15 September 1348, he revoked his license granted to all confessors in the diocese because he heard that they "bore our duties in this office and conferred our medicine with languid spirits."[8] Subsequently, the bishop embarked on an extended absence abroad: His last recorded act before his departure was done at Cambridge on 6 December 1348.[9] Yet with the advent of the Black Death in East Anglia by March 1349,[10] the vastly increased mortality brought on by the plague necessitated a corresponding increase in the number of confessors. On 26 March 1349, Pope Clement VI granted an indulgence to the diocese to allow parishioners to choose a confessor in their hour of death "in all the places in which the epidemic

4. CUL, EDR, G/1/1, Reg. De Lisle, fol. 69v.
5. ". . . mandamus quatenus infra decem dies a recepcione presentes moneatis canonice Dominum Edmundum de Benhale qui se dicit rectorem ecclesie de Wympul' nostre diocesis quod in dicta ecclesia infra tempus a iure statut[u]um sub pena iuris moram trahat continuam et residenciam faciat personalez [personales]." Ibid., fol. 15r.
6. Ibid., fol. 16r.
7. Ibid., fol. 15v.
8. "Licet olim diversis temporibus certas personas religiosas et seculares, tam vive vocis oraculo quam litteratorie, in penitenciarios nostros ordinaverimus, qui vices nostras in officio huiusmodi gererent et medelam conferrent languidis animabus." Ibid., fol. 88r.
9. Ibid., fol. 16v.
10. A breakdown by month of the year ending March 1350, when a total of eighty-seven vacancies of parish churches was recorded in the bishop's register, reveals that six people died in April 1349, one more than in all of 1348 (see Table 2). One must take into account, however, the one-month delay that is thought to have passed between the actual death of the incumbent and the institution of his successor. See A. H. Thompson, "Registers of John Gynwell, Bishop of Lincoln, for the Years 1347–50," *Archaeological Journal* 68 (1911), 317; A. Jessopp, *The Coming*

or mortality of people, which at present, by the Lord's will, flourishes in many parts of the world, now is or will be."[11] By 20 November 1350, De Lisle was back in his diocese at Downham, Cambridgeshire.[12] Shortly thereafter, on 11 March 1351, he revoked all penitentiaries who had been appointed in his absence.[13]

De Lisle's register is one of ten in England that survived the Black Death of 1348–49.[14] Despite the bishop's absence abroad at this time, the register is an invaluable record of mortality among the beneficed priests of East Anglia, one of the areas hardest hit by the plague in England.[15] During the height of the disease between March 1349 and March 1350, 87 out of 176 beneficed priests in the diocese died—a mortality rate approaching 50 percent—compared to a normal year in which no more than four or five incumbents had to be replaced (Tables 1 and 2). The high rate of death had far-reaching social and economic effects that also are recorded by the register.[16]

De Lisle made elaborate preparations for his departure abroad: On 1 October 1348, he appointed no less than five vicars-general, an unusually high number. They were Alan Walsingham, prior of Ely Cathedral; John de Brunne, prior of Barnwell in Cambridgeshire; John de Oo, the bishop's chancellor; William de Pecham, friar preacher; and Edmund de Gonville, rector of Terrington, Norfolk and founder of Gonville Hall. The vicar-general had authority to act in the bishop's name and carry out all duties normally expected of him. Nevertheless, De Lisle made the stipulation that if "any monasteries, priories or any other benefices requiring election or any benefices or ecclesiastical offices pertaining to our collation" fell vacant in the meantime, at least two vicars-general, one of whom must be the prior of Barnwell, were to supervise the granting of such benefices.[17] If five vicars-general were appointed for fear of the impending mortality

---

of the Friars and Other Historic Essays, 5th edition (London, n.d.), 200.

11. CUL, EDR, G/1/1, Reg. De Lisle, fol. 19v.

12. Ibid., fol. 37r.

13. Ibid., fol. 87v.

14. The others are Lincoln, York, Exeter, Winchester, Norwich, Bath and Wells, Worcester, Hereford, and Lichfield.

15. Estimates of plague mortality in England range from a quarter to a half. See P. Ziegler, *The Black Death* (Harmondsworth, Middlesex, 1969), 232–39; Z. Razi, *Life, Marriage and Death in a Medieval Parish: Economy, Society and Demography in Halesowen, 1270–1400* (Cambridge, 1980), 99–100; Waugh, *England in the Reign of Edward III*, 87–89. Shrewsbury's estimate of only 5 percent plague mortality has attracted controversy. See J.F.D. Shrewsbury, *A History of Bubonic Plague in the British Isles* (Cambridge, 1970), 36, and the review by C. Morris, "The Plague in Britain," *Historical Journal* 14 (1971), 205–15.

16. See J. Aberth, "The Black Death in the Diocese of Ely: The Evidence of the Bishop's Register," *Journal of Medieval History* 21, no. 3 (1995): 275–87.

17. ". . . quod si medio tempore aliqua monasteria, prioratus, aut quecumque alia

Table 1. Institutions to Benefices by Year

1345	2
1346	2
1347	5
1348	5
1349	83
1350	13
1351	11
1352	4
1353	3
1354	0
1355	0
Total	176[a]

SOURCE: CUL, EDR, G/ı/1, Reg. De Lisle, fols. 2r–46r.
[a]Total number of benefices in diocese is from *Taxatio Ecclesiastica Angliae et Walliae Auctoritate P. Nicholai IV circa A.D. 1291* (London, 1802), 265–67.

Table 2. Institutions to Benefices by Month, 1349–50.

March	0
April	6
May	6
June	17
July	22
August	10
September	7
October	6
November	4
December	4
January	3
February	1
March	1
Total	87

SOURCE: CUL, EDR, G/ı/1, Reg. De Lisle, fols. 18v–36r.

of the Black Death, De Lisle nevertheless felt compelled to add still more. Writing from Rome on 9 April 1349, the bishop named three other men empowered to act as vicar-general: Richard Norreys, canon of Exeter and

beneficia eleccionem requirencia, vel eciam aliqua beneficia, vel officia ecclesiastica, ad nostram collacionem, presentacionem, seu quamvis aliam disposicionem spectancia vacaverint, quod tam confirmacionem electorum huiusmodi quam eciam collacionem, presentacionem, aut aliam disposicionem beneficorum seu officiorum predictorum, quatuor, tres, vel ad minus duo, vestrum, quorum duorum vos Johannem priorem de Bernewell' predictum alterum esse volumus, excerceatis, examinetis, confirmetis, vel infirmetis, conferatis, et presentetis, et fine debito terminetis." CUL, EDR, G/ı/1, Reg. De Lisle, fol. 17r.

the bishop's chancellor; John Thursteyn, the bishop's official; and Nicholas de Cambridge, rector of Cottenham, Cambridgeshire. He also established a precise order of succession should each succumb to the pestilence: Brunne, Pecham, Oo, Walsingham, Norreys, Thursteyn, Gonville, and Cambridge.[18] On De Lisle's second, and more permanent, departure in 1356, he left behind John Thursteyn as the sole vicar-general to act on his behalf.[19]

The bishop's presence in Rome was no doubt in order to attend the 1350 jubilee. Perhaps he awaited the new half-century with his future enemy, Lady Wake, who also made the pilgrimage.[20] Despite the religious character of the journey, it is not entirely clear why De Lisle went abroad. His missive of 1 October 1348 had informed his vicars-general that he was going abroad "as much on behalf of certain business of our lord king as also on behalf of our own."[21] What this pressing business was is not known, but it probably was conducted at the papal court of Avignon, to which the bishop had sent two friar preachers, John Gatenhale and William Keylmerch, with letters of safe conduct dated the previous 5 September.[22] Early in 1349 De Lisle himself may have been seeking an audience with the pontiff. The same year he submitted a petition to the pope for appropriation to his episcopal income of three churches—Leverington and Haddenham in Cambridgeshire and Somersham, Huntingdonshire—whose combined value, £200, would have added considerably to his yearly revenue. Prophetically, De Lisle justified his request on the grounds that "it often happens in England that the temporalities of prelates of the said realm . . . are at length taken into the royal hands and detained for not a short time by royal ministers."[23] On 9 September 1349 Pope Clement VI granted De Lisle permission to appropriate only one of the churches; the bishop, predictably, chose the most valuable benefice, Leverington, worth £85.[24]

The medieval diocese of Ely cannot have been the easiest to administer. In terms of land mass, it comprised one of the smallest dioceses of medieval England. Nevertheless, it was covered by impenetrable swamp and thick undergrowth that made travel possible only by treacherous

---

18. Ibid., fol. 21r.

19. *The Register of William Edington, Bishop of Winchester, 1346–1366*, ed. S. F. Hockey, 2 vols. (Hampshire Record Series nos. 7–8, 1986–87), 1:168.

20. *Foedera*, 3, no. 1:203.

21. "Cum nos tam pro quibusdam domini nostri Regis negociis quam eciam nostris propriis, habeamus ad partes ultra marinas et remotas, ductore domino, proficisci." CUL, EDR, G/1/1, Reg. De Lisle, fol. 17r.

22. Ibid., fol. 15v.

23. "Contingit eciam sepius in Anglia temporalitates prelatorum dicti regni, mandatis regijs iuri canonico quandoque dissonis non perencium consistari, vel alias ad manus regias applicari, et per non modica tempora per ministros regios detineri." Gonville and Caius College Library, Cambridge, MS 253/497.

24. *CPP*, 175; *CPL*, 3:306 (wrongly dated 1348).

roads, or, more comfortably, by boat along the fenland's rivers (see Fig. 1). The large number of licenses granted by the bishop for a private oratory—137 in all—testify to the difficulty of just getting to the local parish church on Sunday. Bad weather could play havoc with medieval travel in the fens. Thomas de la More of Balsham obtained permission from De Lisle to celebrate Mass in his oratory "in time of rain and at other times when he cannot conveniently go to his mother church."[25] Roger, vicar of Wisbech, received a license for a private oratory in "Piggesdrave" where priests could celebrate Mass in wet weather.[26]

The difficulty of travel in the fens may have determined De Lisle's political as well as geographical isolation. A quick glance at his itinerary (see Appendix A) shows that, except for his absence abroad from December 1348 until November 1350, De Lisle resided mostly at his large, opulent manors at Downham, Cambridgeshire, or at Somersham in the next county of Huntingdonshire. He is known to have personally attended provincial council convened by the archbishop of Canterbury only twice, at the beginning and toward the end of his episcopate. On 17 January 1346, De Lisle was at Leicester where his colleagues decided on procurations due from the beneficed clergy to pay for the expenses of the papal nuncio, Nicholas, archbishop of Ravenna.[27] In May of 1356 the bishop was present at St. Paul's Cathedral in London to hear the crown's exorbitant demand for a sexennial tenth payable in three years.[28] On another occasion, De Lisle appointed John de Carleton, canon of Wells, and Richard Norreys as his proctors to attend convocation in his place.[29]

On the whole, De Lisle appears to have been an unexceptional diocesan. His long periods of residence in his diocese do not seem to have made him any more conscientious in the performance of his episcopal duties than his colleagues who managed to combine service to the state with service to the Church. De Lisle was by no means the only bishop to take action against nonresident priests and corrupt confessors, as the registers of John Thoresby, archbishop of York, William Edington, bishop of Winchester, and Thomas Hatfield, bishop of Durham—all career royal servants—show.[30] Particularly after the Black Death, concern about clerical standards seems to have been shared by many of England's prelates.

25. ". . . dominus concessit Thome de la More de Balsham quod posset facere celebrari in oratorio suo apud Balsham tempore pluviali et alterius vicibus quando non poterit commodo ad suam ecclesiam accedere matricem." CUL, EDR, G/1/1, Reg. De Lisle, fol. 2r.

26. Ibid., fol. 10r.

27. Ibid., fols. 55r–56v; CPL, 3:20.

28. LPL, Reg. Simon Islip, fols. 117r–v.

29. CUL, EDR, G/1/1, Reg. De Lisle, fol. 59v.

30. Register of William Edington, 1:xi; J. Hughes, Pastors and Visionaries: Religion and Secular Life in Late Medieval Yorkshire (Woodbridge, Suffolk, 1988), 140; R. M.

Fig. 2. Manors of the Bishop of Ely, 1356–57.

Admittedly, the bishop's register is full of tedious repetition as it describes the bishop's daily routine: the granting of special licenses, admission to benefices, confirmation of chantry and college foundations, and so on. Yet mediocrity may help reconcile De Lisle's criminal activities with his religious ones: By looking on the latter as simply a job to be done, the bishop may not have been too concerned with morality.

Haines, *Ecclesia Anglicana: Studies in the English Church of the Later Middle Ages* (Toronto, 1989), 49.

Monastic Disputes

Unlike his other pastoral duties, De Lisle's relations with various religious houses in the area were anything but ordinary. In the diocese of Ely, the bishop had jurisdiction over two foundations of Benedictine monks: Thorney Abbey and Ely Cathedral Priory; four houses of Benedictine nuns, St. Radegund's in Cambridge, Chatteris, Ickleton, and Swaffham Bulbek; and three houses of Augustinian canons, Anglesey, Barnwell, and Spinney (see Fig. 2). In the second year of his episcopate, 1346, De Lisle conducted his primary visitation, examining the Ely Cathedral chapter from 3 to 5 April 1346; Ickleton on 15 May; Swaffham Bulbeck on 16 May; Barnwell on 18 May; St. Radegund's on 19 May; Thorney on 2 October; Anglesey on 12 October; and Chatteris on 24 May 1347.[31] Although on this occasion no injunctions were copied into the register, De Lisle's second visitation of Thorney on 18 June is more fully recorded. It was necessitated by a pornography scandal involving the prior, the senior cellarer, and the manorial steward, perhaps the only one of its kind in visitation records. Naturally the deviant monks resisted De Lisle's corrections, and he had to press his visitation rights in the court of arches in Bow Church, London.

A second general visitation of the diocese was conducted in 1352 after De Lisle's return from abroad. The register records that in that year he dedicated or consecrated seven high altars and ten parish churches, representing a total of sixteen new churches at or near completion: two at Cambridge and one each at Teversham, Great Childerley, Chatteris, Papworth Everard, Hungry Hill, Toft, Clopton, East Hatley, Arrington, Little Gransden, Caxton, Kingston, Whittlesford, and Haslingfield. In addition, De Lisle dedicated the conventual church and cemetery of Ickleton Priory on 3 June 1352, the church belonging to Chatteris on 27 September and that of Swaffham on 4 November.[32] De Lisle also conducted at least one visitation at this time, that of Ickleton Priory, whose recalcitrance likewise earned it immortality. On this occasion, De Lisle attempted to remove a corrupt prioress who threatened violent resistance and tried to halt his efforts through a lawsuit brought in the court of common pleas.

But the litigation did not stop there. In addition to his visitation disputes with Thorney and Ickleton, De Lisle quarreled with Ramsey Abbey in Huntingdonshire and even with his Cathedral chapter, Ely Priory, whose relations with the bishop were otherwise friendly. Clearly, De Lisle

31. CUL, EDR, G/1/1, Reg. De Lisle, fols. 5r–v.
32. Ibid., fol. 65v. The year of De Lisle's visits to Great Childerley and Ickleton was given as 1351, but this would be out of sequence with the rest of the visitation. Most likely, the scribe forgot to update the year after 25 March.

was anxious to preserve the traditional episcopalian rights of his predecessors, and such efforts are understandable, even laudatory. However,
an overzealous litigator could create a backlash of ill-feeling that he might
have cause to regret, as the example of other contentious prelates proves.
In 1347 William Bateman, bishop of Norwich, was fined £10,000 and thirty
talents of gold and had his temporalities seized by the crown for attempting to force himself as visitor on the exempt monks of Bury St. Edmunds.
Fortunately for the bishop, these penalties were revoked by 1349.[33] The
poisonous relations between Alexander Neville, archbishop of York, and
the inhabitants of Durham Priory and Beverly Minster may have contributed to the archbishop's political exile to France in 1388.[34]

The fact that De Lisle was not afraid to engage in so much litigation with
his spiritual brethren throws an interesting light on his legal defense of more
secular activities. The bishop may even have had a legal turn of mind and
been on the lookout for any loophole to turn to his advantage. His suit
with Ramsey Abbey, in particular, contains aspects reminiscent of other cases.
Like his feud with Richard Spynk, De Lisle distrained abbey property on a
technical point of law, based on a perambulation of county boundaries made
more than half a century earlier. And as in the dispute with Lady Wake, his
clash with the Ramsey monks centered around rival claims to land in
Huntingdonshire. Combined with his criminal suits in king's bench and
elsewhere, the bishop's disputes with monasteries must have provided almost continual litigation throughout his eleven-year tenure at Ely.

Thorney

The first indication that all was not well at Thorney came in 1345 when
Hugh de Seton, canon of Exeter, visited several monasteries in the diocese on behalf of the archbishop of Canterbury, John Stratford, who was
exercising his visitation rights during the vacancy in the see. At his visitation, Seton found that a certain book, "containing things improper and
shameful, not at all commending of scripture," had been stolen from the
keeping of the prior of the convent, John de Chatteris, and was still missing, "giving rise to evil speech and scandals."[35] The popularity of the

33. *CPR*, 1345–48, 251, 535; *CPR*, 1348–50, 297; *CCR*, 1346–49, 338; and see
Thompson, "William Bateman," 118–21.

34. A. F. Leach, "A Clerical Strike at Beverly Minster in the Fourteenth Century,"
Archaeologia 55 (1896), 1–20; Aston, *Thomas Arundel*, 289–91; R. G. Davies,
"Alexander Neville, Archbishop of York, 1374–1388," *Yorkshire Archaeological Journal*
47 (1975), 95–96.

35. "Ad hec quia comperimus quod ex invencione et occupacione cuisdam libri
in custodia Fratris Johannis de Chateriz, tunc prioris ipsius monasterii, existentis
inordinata et pudenda, scripture nequaquam commendanda continentis,
oblocuciones, et scandala pulularunt." CUL, EDR, G/I/1, Reg. De Lisle, fol. 47r.

book and the jocularity that seemed to follow in its wake strongly suggests that Seton objected to it on decorous rather than doctrinal grounds.[36] Perhaps it contained some kind of collection of ribald Latin verses as are found in *The Cambridge Songs* or *Carmina Burana*. Seton enjoined the monks to obey the prior's order to burn the book and that this be done by whoever was in possession of the offending volume within six days of his admonition. In the meantime, no monk was to inspect the book or make copies of it, and if any copies were made then these were to be burned also. In addition, no monk henceforth was to speak of the matter to Prior Chatteris, not even in the form of a "provoking objection or rebuke."[37]

Two years later, De Lisle considered Thorney's situation serious enough to warrant a second visitation on 18 June 1347, which the bishop's scribes recorded in detail. Previously, at his first visitation of the monastery, De Lisle had adjourned the meeting three-quarters of the way through "on account of business of the lord king as well as on account of the arduous points of the *comperta* and *detecta*."[38] Clearly, the bishop had found little improvement since Seton's visit and much that still needed correction. In the meantime, De Lisle had issued an "inhibition" against the convent forbidding it from attempting anything that would prejudice his next visitation. Nevertheless, the abbot, Reginald de Water Newton, and his monks had decided to challenge the new bishop and test his resolve. They had obtained a counterinhibition against De Lisle's next visitation from the court of arches, dated 9 November 1346. Water Newton had claimed that the correction and punishment of his monks pertained to him alone and not to the diocesan. He also had complained about the "excessive expense" to his monastery that De Lisle's visitation had caused, perhaps an allusion to the bishop's overlarge household.[39]

From the outset, however, the odds had been against Thorney winning its case, simply because the archbishop as well as the bishop had recently and successfully exercised their rights of visitation and both would have been threatened by the monks' suit. On 2 March 1347 the dean of the

36. D.M.B. Ellis and L. F. Salzman concluded, in their account of the incident, that "there is no hint as to whether the book was heretical or obscene, but the latter seems more probable." *VCH Cambs.*, 2:215.

37. ". . . ne de contento seu aliquo contentorum in dicto libro predicto Johanni de Chateriz obiectio fiat decetero irritativa seu increpacio aliqualis." CUL, EDR, G/1/1, Reg. De Lisle, fol. 47r.

38. "Et quia ipsam suam visitacionem tum propter negocia domini regis tum propter puncta ardua compertorum et detectorum ibidem in ipsa visitacione tunc complere nec excessus iuxta naturam et qualitatem detectorum absque magna deliberacione tunc corrigere nequivit." Ibid., fol. 48r.

39. ". . . prefatus reverendus pater per triduum ad sumptus dicit monasterii excessivos visitacionem suam ibidem excertens." Ibid.

court of arches had dismissed the abbot's inhibition and given De Lisle free faculty to carry out his visitation. Shortly thereafter, on 27 April, certain clerks commissioned by De Lisle had visited the monastery, and those monks excommunicated for disobedience toward the bishop had sought absolution and declared their willingness to submit to his visitation and corrections.[40] The same day also had witnessed an election in the convent for a new abbot to replace the deceased Water Newton. It had been a contest between William de Haddon, formerly Water Newton's penitentiary, and Robert de Corby, the senior cellarer, who had been implicated in the abbey's pornography scandal. Haddon's election, after a close vote, suggests that the reforming party of the monastery finally had won sway and would inaugurate a new spirit of cooperation with the bishop.[41]

Appeasement was, in fact, in evidence when, on 18 June 1347, at the hour of prime, De Lisle sat in the Thorney chapter-house to deliver his final set of injunctions. Corby and his accomplice, William de Sutton, custodian of the abbey's manors, were confronted with their crime: that they had stolen the by now notorious "defamatory book" from the head of the prior's bed and secretly were passing it around to the other monks. Sutton and Corby confessed their error before the bishop, who absolved them provided that the monks would burn the book and all copies of it without delay. The prior, John de Chatteris, was cleared of any blame in the affair, and De Lisle ordered the convent to be reconciled with the kiss of peace, forbidding anyone from harassing another in the future "by reason of the said book or the process held therein."[42]

Ickleton

The nearly four-month hiatus between De Lisle's dedication of Ickleton Priory church on 3 June 1352 and an ordination he held in Over parish church on the following 22 September[43] probably was due to a heated dispute between the nuns and the bishop that threatened to escalate into violence. As in the case of Thorney, the rebellious nuns of Ickleton resisted De Lisle's attempts to improve the moral condition of their house. Although the bishop's visitation is not recorded in his register, the bitter struggle for authority over the nunnery between its prioress, Alice Lacy, and De Lisle resulted in a lawsuit that was enrolled two years later in the rolls of the court of common pleas. According to De Lisle's version of

40. Ibid.
41. Ibid., fols. 49r–51r; *VCH Cambs.*, 2:215. Reginald de Water Newton died on 16 April 1347.
42. ". . . ne quis eorum inposterum racione dicti libri seu processus inde habiti aut alicuius dicti vel facti alteri inproperet verbo vel facto vel alium infestet quovis quesito colore." CUL, EDR, G/1/1, Reg. De Lisle, fol. 48r.
43. Ibid., fols. 84v, 98v.

events, he had found, in the course of his visitation in 1352, that Prioress Lacy had been prone to "various enormous defects" that are not specified in the court record.[44] As a result, the bishop had deposed Lacy and sequestered the priory's goods, entrusting them to the care of her second-in-command, the subprioress. In addition, De Lisle had found that many secular women were staying in the convent without license, and he had enjoined the subprioress that she was to warn the laywomen to remove themselves from the priory.

Besieged by the bishop's forces, Lacy had not relinquished her privileged position without a struggle. With the help of her supporters, she had broken the doors of the granges and other buildings of the priory and seized its goods. In a further reckless act of defiance, she had had it proclaimed from her place of forced occupation that if any of the bishop's clerks were to dare return to the priory in order to carry out his reforms, "they would be beheaded."[45] Heedless of the danger of decapitation, De Lisle had returned once more to the house and found, as he no doubt suspected, Prioress Lacy still in control of the nuns' affairs. The bishop had excommunicated her, but the subprioress as yet had been unable to eject the outcast's secular friends. De Lisle had resolved to take harsher measures and ordered the dean of Camps and others to instruct all secular women still staying in the priory to leave within a certain period of time or themselves face excommunication.

Dislodging laywomen from the comfortable surroundings of a religious house proved difficult, however, especially as some of them claimed to have property interests in the priory. In Trinity term 1354, two secular women residing with the nuns, Elizabeth Sanzanoir and Elizabeth Spigurnel, sued a writ of prohibition *de laico feodo* against De Lisle in the court of common pleas. Such writs go back to the reign of Henry II in the twelfth century and originally were designed to prevent encroachments of ecclesiastical courts on cases belonging within royal jurisdiction. Toward the later Middle Ages, writs of prohibition became increasingly popular and apparently were being used to escape the strictures of Church courts altogether.[46] The plaintiffs claimed a message within the monas-

---

44. ". . . pro enormibus defectibus in quadam Alicia Lacy, tunc priorissa eiusdem prioratus, in visitacione sua compertis ipsam priorissam ab officio suo deposuit." PRO, CP 40/378, m. 46.

45. ". . . publice dictum erat ibidem quod si clerici predicti episcopi redirent ad impediendam predictam Aliciam de admin[i]stracione sua vel ad ammovendas predictas mulieres seculares a prioratu predicto ipsi decollarentur." Ibid.

46. N. Adams, "The Writ of Prohibition to Court Christian," *Minnesota Law Review* 20 (1935–36), 272–93; G. B. Flahiff, "The Writ of Prohibition to Court Christian in the Thirteenth Century: Part I," *Mediaeval Studies* 6 (1944), 261–313; R. H. Helmholz, "The Writ of Prohibition to Court Christian before 1500," *Mediaeval Studies* 43 (1981), 297–314, reprinted in idem, *Canon Law and the Law of England* (London, 1987), 59–76.

tery that they said had been surrendered to them by its previous owner, Philip le Gras, on 29 July 1352. De Lisle, they alleged, was challenging their lay fee in a court Christian, which was expressly forbidden by the "king's prohibition."[47]

On 29 July 1352, Alan, the vicar of the church of St. John the Baptist in Duxford, had come to Ickleton and, in the bishop's name, warned all secular women residing within the priory to depart on pain of excommunication by the following Wednesday, 1 August. When the day of ultimatum had arrived, the plaintiffs had sent their own envoy, Robert Hert, to the bishop's manor at Somersham where he had served a writ of prohibition to De Lisle. Nonetheless De Lisle had continued his legal actions against the plaintiffs until finally, on 10 August 1352, the vicar of Duxford had excommunicated them on the bishop's behalf. The plaintiffs now claimed £1000 in damages.[48] De Lisle countered that the plaintiffs "have not shown in court that they were endamaged excessively concerning their freehold."[49] The plaintiffs replied that "they would lose their houses and thus were endamaged."[50] The final verdict handed down by the common bench is not recorded.

However, De Lisle's admonitions against laywomen living in the nunnery are supported by an earlier visit to the house made by Seton on 10 August 1345. He had found it necessary to enjoin the nuns that "henceforth married secular women be not admitted in order to sojourn or loiter within the enclosure of your aforesaid priory."[51] Seton's command that these women leave the priory by the following 29 September obviously had not been obeyed.

Ramsey

De Lisle's stormy feuds with monasteries were not confined to those within his own diocese. He came to loggerheads with Ramsey Abbey in Huntingdonshire[52] over rights to land straddling the two medieval counties of Cambridge and Huntingdon. Perhaps it should come as no surprise,

47. ". . . predictus episcopus prosecutus fuit aliquod placitum de laico feodo vel aliquid fecit contra prohibicionem regis." PRO, CP 40/378, m. 46.

48. Ibid.

49. "Et l'evesque dit qu'ils n'avoient monstré en countant qu'ils fueront en damagés auxi come oustes de lour franktenement." *Yearbooks* 2–3, Trinity term, 28 Edward III, 19.

50. "Et les autrez disoient qu'ilz weyveront lour measons, et issint en damagés." Ibid.

51. ". . . vobis in virtute sancte obediencie inhibemus ne mulieres seculares coniugate ad perhendinandum vel morandum infra septa vostri prioratus predicti deceptero admittantur." CUL, EDR, G/1/1, Reg. De Lisle, fol. 47v.

52. According to medieval shire boundaries. Under present county divisions, Ramsey is part of Cambridgeshire.

however, that antagonisms flared up between them. Disputes between the abbey, one of the oldest monastic foundations in England, and the bishopric date back to at least the twelfth century.[53] In the time of Geoffrey Ridel, who had occupied the see of Ely from 1173 to 1189, the abbey's tenants at Chatteris, Cambridgeshire, had refused to do their customary work on Aldreth causeway for the bishop. Ridel had agreed to release the tenants from their work in exchange for a payment of 2s. per year.[54] John de Hothum, bishop from 1316 to 1337, had quarreled bitterly with Abbot Simon de Eye over rights to a market fair at St. Ives, Huntingdonshire.[55]

The first sign of trouble between Bishop De Lisle and Ramsey is recorded in a Downham manorial account roll of 1345–46 in which, under forinsec (foreign) expenses, there is entered the amount of 3d. paid for six works to "help drive distrained [animals] taken from the abbot of Ramsey unto Ely."[56] In 1347–48, the reeve of Downham took possession of a mare and a two-year-old chicken from the abbey.[57] The animals were perhaps strays that had wandered onto the bishop's land and therefore could be legitimately confiscated as trespassing livestock.

Hostilities finally came out into the open when the abbot of Ramsey, Richard de Sheningdon, sued De Lisle in the court of common pleas in Michaelmas term 1355. Sheningdon, represented by his attorney, Roger de Elynton, claimed five hundred acres[58] of moorland that he said lay in the village of Ramsey and on which he sought to deny entry to the bishop. In a writ of entry *sine assensu capituli*, the abbot claimed that during the 1250s his predecessor, Hugh de Sullegrave, had leased the land to the bishop of Ely, William de Kilkenny, "without the assent and will of his chapter" and that the land belonged to the abbey "by right."[59]

De Lisle, represented by his own lawyer, John de Northwold, responded by producing a document under the privy seal that purported to be a

53. *VCH Hunts.*, 1:380.

54. *Chronicon Abbatiae Rameseiensis*, ed. W. D. Macray (RS, LXXXIII, 1886), 294; *Cartularium Monasterii de Rameseia*, ed. W. H. Hart and P. A. Lyons, 3 vols. (RS, LXXIX, 1884–93), 2:187–88.

55. *Chronicon Abbatiae*, 350–51.

56. "In auxilium fugandi districciones captas de Abbate de Ramseia usque Ely: iij.d. in vj. operibus." CUL, EDR, D 10/2/17, *expense forinsece*.

57. CUL, EDR, D 10/2/18, 21–22 Edward III, dorse, *jumenta* and *pulle biennales*.

58. The records of the case differ as to the acerage contested. The common plea rolls say five hundred acres but the *Yearbooks* mention only one hundred acres. See PRO, CP 40/383, m. 49, and *Yearbooks* 2–3, Michaelmas term, 29 Edward III, 45.

59. "Abbas de Rammeseye per Rogerum de Elynton' attornatum suum petivit versus Thomam episcopum Eliensis quingintas acras marisci cum pertinenciis in Rammeseye ut ius ecclesie sue Sancti Benedicti de Rammeseye et in quas idem episcopus non habet ingressum nisi post dimissionem quam Hugo de Sullegrave quondam abbas de Rammeseye predecessor predicti abbatis sine assensu et voluntate capituli sui inde fecit Willelmo de Kilkenny quondam episcopo Eliensis

perambulation of the boundaries between Cambridgeshire and Huntingdonshire undertaken in accordance with a commission from Edward I to his justices on 20 March 1284 and confirmed in a subsequent commission on 13 June 1285.[60] The perambulation, which was transcribed into the court record, was based on the testimony of twenty-four jurors drawn from Cambridgeshire and Huntingdonshire and from the adjacent counties of Lincoln and Northampton. De Lisle claimed that his evidence proved that the disputed moorland lay not in Ramsey but approximately eight miles away across the county border in the village of Doddington, Cambridgeshire. The plaintiff refused to recognize the perambulation or its boundaries and continued to maintain that the moor lay in Ramsey in Huntingdonshire as he originally had alleged.[61]

The bench presiding over the case included the chief justice of the king's bench, Sir William Shareshull, and three justices of the court of common pleas: Sir Henry Green, Sir Thomas Seton, and Sir Richard Willoughby. Four king's serjeants were also present: William de Witchingham and William de Finchdean for the defense, and Edmund de Childrey and William de Fyfield for the plaintiff. John Kirton, a clerk of the king's bench, also argued on behalf of the abbot of Ramsey.

Witchingham opened the disputation by presenting the evidence of the perambulation issued to Sir Thomas de Weyland, at that time chief justice of the court of common pleas, and to others that proved, he argued, that the disputed moorland lay in the village of Doddington. Kirton countered that the perambulation had been made under different circumstances, by parties who were "estranged," or far removed, from the present litigants.[62] Furthermore, the perambulation did not specify where the tenants of the moorland lived, and in fact, Kirton contended, they were residents of Ramsey. Witchingham then demanded judgment in accordance with the original perambulation, which, he argued, "would bind all people of both the two counties."[63] Justice Seton, however, preferred to settle the matter through "another writ of perambulation to be executed with the

---

et cetera." PRO, CP 40/383, m. 49. The chronicler Matthew Paris briefly mentions that in the year 1256 a peace was made between the abbot of Ramsey and the bishop of Ely "concerning a quarrel moved about resolving the boundaries of a moor." ("Tempore quoque sub eodem, facta ex pax inter episcopum Elyensem W[illelmum] et H[ugonem] abbatem Rameseiensem, super lite mota de terminis in marisco statuendis.") See Matthew Paris, *Chronica Majora*, ed. H. R. Luard, 7 vols. (RS, LVII, 1872–83), 5:570.

60. *CPR*, 1281–92, 140, 209.

61. PRO, CP 40/383, m. 49.

62. "A cest record sumes estrangé de ambideus parties." *Yearbooks* 2–3, Michaelmas term, 29 Edward III, 45.

63. ". . . car c'est un record qui liera touts gens de les ii. contes ambedeus." Ibid.

assent of both parties, which . . . will be to the prejudice of no one."[64] Yet Justice Willoughby complained that it would be extremely hard on sheriffs, coroners, and other royal ministers if the county boundaries were always in debate, for they would not know where the limits of their jurisdiction lay. He seems to have been in favor of keeping the boundaries as they were in accordance with the existing perambulation.

Pleading on behalf of the defense, Finchdean declared that a "writ to survey land is worthless if all the common people be not named."[65] Since a new writ of perambulation would be brought at the suit of only one party, namely the plaintiff, "it would not bind those who were not party to it."[66] Justice Seton then addressed Witchingham and instructed him that there was a difference in law between arguing that at one time tenants had lived in Huntingdonshire but after a perambulation lived in Cambridgeshire, and claiming that they had lived in one county, Cambridgeshire, the whole time, "as your writ assumes."[67] The court ruled that "if the tenants were in Ramsey in the county of Huntingdonshire but by the perambulation they are people of the county of Cambridge, that from now on they are in the same village as they were in before."[68] Witchingham then opted to ask for a new perambulation based on the testimony of people from both counties.

The bench was divided, however, as to whether to solicit evidence from only one county, Huntingdonshire, or from Cambridgeshire as well. Childrey argued on behalf of the plaintiff that the people of the county where the original writ of entry had been brought, that is, from Huntingdonshire, would best know where the disputed tenants belonged. He also noted that this was the standard procedure in the assize courts. Both Justices Willoughby and Green, on the other hand, were of the opinion that the new inquest into the matter should be decided by a jury drawn

---

64. ". . . et autre brief de perambulacion facienda d'assent des parties, qui servit in semble cas, et sera entre eux de record: Mes cest chose qui fuit a nully suit forsque d'office, sera prejudiciale a nully." Ibid.

65. "Brief d'amesurement de pasture ne vaut rien si touts les comones ne soient només." Ibid.

66. ". . . et coment que ce soit amesuré a la suit d'ascuns, ceo ne liera pz ceux que ne fuerent partys." Ibid.

67. "Si vous voilez conustre que a un temps les tenants fuerent deins le conte de H[untingdon] et que puis par l'ambulacion ils furent gettes a le conte de C[ambridge], ascun chose seroit de pleder issint in ley. . . . Et puis dit, come avant est dit que les tenants fuerent gettes a le conte de C[ambridge] in le ville de D[oddington] et nemy in le conte de H[untingdon] come vostre brief suppose." Ibid.

68. "Et nota, que le court dit que si les tenants fuerent in Ra[msey] in le conte de H[untingdon] mesque par le perambulacion ils sont gettes a le conte de C[ambridge], que uncore ils sont in meme le ville come ils fuerent adevant." Ibid.

from both counties. Yet Fyfield pleaded with the bench that it "not judge except by mandate of the evidence," presumably referring to the abbot's writ of entry.[69] Finally, Chief Justice Shareshull ruefully observed "that henceforth he would not issue a writ to two sheriffs, except where the whole matter is in one county" and there could not be any confusion about the proper locality of the case.[70] In the end, the bench was unable to decide whether a verification of the earlier perambulation should be tried by a jury from both counties of Cambridge and Huntingdon or by a jury from Huntingdonshire alone. Their deliberation therefore was adjourned until the following Hilary term. At their next sitting, on 27 January 1356, the bench ruled that the issue should be decided by a jury from Huntingdonshire and ordered the sheriff to draw twelve jurors from the neighborhood of Ramsey, but the end result is not recorded.[71]

In the same term, Abbot Sheningdon also brought a writ of trespass against De Lisle, alleging that the bishop unlawfully had taken his beasts at Ramsey. De Lisle justified the seizure on the grounds that the animals actually had been taken at Doddington in Cambridgeshire in order to compensate for damages done in a trespass on his private property. The court noted that the issue here concerned the same matter of disputed boundaries as in the earlier suit of entry *sine assensu capituli*. The plaintiff asked to be awarded damages because "he should not be held accountable at all for the seizure" and because, he said, the monastery could not sustain such a loss.[72] Justice Seton advised the defense that if it could prove that the beasts had not been taken at Ramsey, it would be "quit of this action."[73] Whereupon Witchingham tried to convince the bench that this was indeed the case, that the disputed animals had been seized at Doddington on the bishop's property, as De Lisle claimed. However, the plaintiff obstinately insisted that the livestock had been taken at Ramsey, and once again the court seems to have been unable to make up its mind.[74]

The dispute over moorland and beasts still was unresolved by the time De Lisle left England for exile in Avignon in November 1356. Once at the papal court, the bishop pressed his suit against Ramsey at the same time

---

69. "Sir, non adjuggez mes come par mandement d'evidence: Car il le weyva." Ibid.

70. Sch[areshull] dit pur ley, que jammes n'issera brief a ij. vicontes, forsque l'ou le gros est in un conte, et l'appelle in autre conte come de comen appelle, et auxi in gard de corps ou priorite est pledé de tenants in autre conte." Ibid.

71. PRO, CP 40/383, m. 49.

72. "Le pleintif demand jugement, depuis que il ne respoigne point a le pris dont cest accion est puis, et sera nul autre pris poit estre maintenu: Et pria ses damages." *Yearbooks* 2–3, Hilary term, 30 Edward III, 2.

73. "Il vous surmet que vous pristes les bests in R[amsey], et si vous poies escaper de le pris in R[amsey], vous estes quité a cest action." Ibid.

74. Ibid.

that he was appealing his conviction and punishment as accessory to the murder of William Holm. This, combined with the fact that some of the very justices whom De Lisle was having summoned to Avignon were about to rule in his favor against the abbey, prompted Sheningdon to write a letter to the king laying forth his grievances against the bishop. The letter, which is undated, almost certainly was written in 1357–58, the years that record the processes held in Avignon before the pope's auditor, Aymeric Hugonis, concerning De Lisle's suit with Lady Wake.[75] Sheningdon opened his letter to Edward III by piously presenting his abbey as the victim of "the great evils, grievances, and wrongs that Thomas, bishop of Ely, before his departure out of your kingdom, committed and plotted to commit in various ways against your humble chaplains and servants, the abbot and convent of Ramsey," who "were very poor and in such hardship and state that they could not defend themselves."[76] The abbot complained that De Lisle recently had taken his case to the pope's "court of Rome," and he tried to link his own "distress" with that of the king concerning the bishop's actions against his justices. Sheningdon seemed to imply that De Lisle's appeal against Ramsey violated the Statute of *Praemunire* of 1353, which forbade appeals outside the king's courts, just as much as did his appeal of the king's judgment in favor of Lady Wake.[77] Yet the royal justices, Sheningdon claimed, were about to hand down a verdict attainting the abbey and imposing "great and grievous fines and ransoms," which the abbot urged the king to reverse.[78] To press home his point, Sheningdon at the end of his letter raised the specter that his abbey would be "completely destroyed" and made "desolate" and "the monks driven away and the service of God entirely abandoned" should their case go against them.[79]

No doubt Sheningdon exaggerated his plight to the king in order to take advantage of the new political climate of antagonism between De Lisle and Edward III. The abbot's protestations of poverty and financial ruin of the house, for example, are suspicious in light of the fact that the abbey was able to initiate a long and costly legal suit against the bishop. The unfavorable attitude of the bench toward the abbey's suit also is surprising given its previous indecision and Ramsey's long tradition of bribing justices with fat retainers. Sir Henry Green, one of those who presided in Michaelmas term 1355, received a £2 fee from the abbey every year. The Ordinance of Justices of 1346 and Sir William Thorp's disgrace as chief justice of the court of common pleas in 1350 seem to have made

75. See pages 166–71.
76. BL, Add. charter 33657, and see Appendix B, page 238.
77. See page 177.
78. BL, Add. charter 33657, and see Appendix B, page 239.
79. Ibid.

no difference in the abbey's retainers. But the arrival of the Black Death in 1349 and again in 1361 eventually may have taken its toll on the abbey's finances; by 1362 Ramsey was cutting back its largess, including the fees to Green.[80] In addition, the unpleasant experience of the suit with De Lisle may have convinced the abbey to place less reliance on judicial favors. Sheningdon's letter thus provides some new and interesting details that are unavailable from the court records.

As in England, De Lisle's dispute with the abbey of Ramsey in the papal court at Avignon ended in his favor, although he did not live long enough to enjoy the profits of justice. In December 1361, six months after De Lisle's death, there was recorded in the expenditure accounts of the apostolic camera a payment of 300 florins, or between £45 to £60, to Thomas de Paxton, a papal auditor who had acted as surety for the abbot of Ramsey in his suit with De Lisle. The payment to Paxton was deducted from the 500 marks sterling, or approximately £333, which had been awarded to De Lisle against Ramsey but that now, on the bishop's death, reverted to the papal camera.[81]

Ely Cathedral Priory

Despite the fact that De Lisle had been imposed as bishop on the monks of Ely over one of their own, relations between the two seem to have been friendly. Like Bishop William Bateman at Norwich, De Lisle cultivated good relations with the chapter by involving its members in his diocesan administration.[82] Prior Alan Walsingham, for example, acted as one of De Lisle's vicars-general during the bishop's absence abroad from 1348 until 1350.[83] The sacrist of the convent was commissioned jointly with the prior of Barnwell to hold a synod at Barnwell on 24 October 1345 and regularly was called on to induct new members into the Hospital of Sts. Mary Magdalene and John the Baptist in Ely.[84] Two monks from the priory, Robert de Rykeling and Robert d'Aylesham, sacrist, were appointed bishop's penitentiaries on 1 December 1345, and a third monk, John de Repynghale, was appointed penitentiary on 12 July 1346. Rykeling and D'Aylesham were among the six confessors reappointed by De Lisle on 15 September 1348. Ely monks were likewise among an even more select

80. J. R. Maddicott, *Law and Lordship: Royal Justices as Retainers in Thirteenth-and Fourteenth-Century England* (Past and Present Supplement no. 4, Oxford, 1978), 56–59.

81. C. Burns, "Sources of British and Irish History in the Instrumenta Miscellanea of the Vatican Archives," *Archivum Historiae Pontificiae* 9 (1971), 60.

82. Thompson, "William Bateman," 125–26.

83. CUL, EDR, G/1/1, Reg. De Lisle, fol. 17r.

84. Ibid., fols. 1v, 2r, 15v, 23v, 25v, 36r, 40v, 42r, 44v.

Fig. 3. Ely Cathedral, west front.

group of only three penitentiaries spared De Lisle's second purge on 11 March 1351, when Walter de Walsoken, subprior, and Adam de Linstead, sacrist, were reappointed.[85]

Another Ely sacrist, Robert de Sutton, who held the office from 1354 until at least 1360,[86] seems to have had particularly close relations with De Lisle. According to the bishop's biographer, he accompanied his diocesan on the journey from Somersham to London on 29 August 1355, during which De Lisle was attacked by an angry mob; the day before, his servants allegedly had murdered Lady Wake's valet, William Holm.[87] Sutton also accompanied the bishop at his canonical trial for complicity in Holm's murder at Mayfield, Sussex, on 14 November 1356.[88] In 1354–55, Sutton was paid 6s. 5d. from the monastery's coffers in order to travel down to Hatfield, Hertfordshire, so that he could attend De Lisle at his manor there.[89] Just before his departure into exile in 1356, the bishop reputedly entrusted some richly adorned episcopal vestments and precious silver vessels for the Mass to Sutton for safekeeping. On 30 January 1359, the crown ordered that all episcopal goods in Sutton's possession be seized, but, according to De Lisle's biographer, "the king out of his mercy" later had them returned to the monastery.[90]

In addition, De Lisle bequeathed to the priory shortly before his exile 19s. 6d. that was to go toward the fabric of the Lady Chapel, built during the first half of the fourteenth century and consecrated by 1353. The money for the bequest came from the proceeds of the sale of fruit on the bishop's manor of Littleport, Cambridgeshire, on 15 October 1356.[91] These riches were joined by two relics the cathedral chapter also was fortunate to add to its treasury during De Lisle's episcopate: a lance that a soldier, Hugh de Hinton, fighting against the Moors in Spain, had managed to pull out of the bone of his groin, and a gold ring that a Benedictine monk, John Lavenham, from the abbey of Bury St. Edmunds in Suffolk, gave in gratitude for being cured of quinsy, or tonsillitis. Both these miracles allegedly had occurred at the intercession of Blessed Etheldreda, the seventh-century foundress of the original abbey.[92]

---

85. Ibid., fols. 87v–88r.
86. *Sacrist Rolls of Ely*, ed. F. R. Chapman, 2 vols. (Cambridge, 1907), 2:111.
87. *AS*, 1:657–58, and see Appendix B, page 232.
88. Ibid., 659, and see Appendix B, page 234; LPL, Reg. Islip, fols., 125r, 128r.
89. *Sacrist Rolls*, 2:169.
90. PRO, KB 27/394, rex m. 13; *AS*, 1:662, and see Appendix B, page 238.
91. PRO, E 143/9/2, m. 47. For the dating of the Lady Chapel, see N. Coldstream, "Ely Cathedral: The Fourteenth-Century Work," in N. Coldstream and P. Draper, eds., *Medieval Art and Architecture at Ely Cathedral* (British Archaeological Association Conference Transactions, 2, 1979), 28.
92. *AS*, 1:653–54, and see Appendix B, pages 226–28.

On several occasions the Ely chapter presented gifts to its bishop. While the exact purpose behind these gifts is not known, the monastery's continued generosity toward De Lisle indicates that a spirit of goodwill persisted between the two. In 1349–50, the convent sent two deer calves, valued at 4s.; six bitterns, valued at 6s.; and wine costing 18s. 6d., which De Lisle shared with several other recipients. In 1352–53, the monks sent to the bishop two deer calves, two muttons, five bitterns, two pigs, six capons, and three pike from its storeroom, the value of the gifts totaling £1 1s. 7d. In the same year, the priory also sent wine and gave the bishop's messengers and his other ministers 2s. 10d. in the autumn and the bishop's vintner 4d. as a gratuity. In 1354–55, the monastery sent to De Lisle's manor at Hatfield, Hertfordshire, bitterns worth 11s. 9 1/2d. and also that year gave him a cow's carcass, two deer carcasses, and two sheepskins totaling 19s. 4d.[93] It is quite possible, however, that some of this food was enjoyed by the monks themselves. On 29 July 1345, Pope Clement VI had granted De Lisle his petition for license to dispense religious persons so that they could eat meat at his table.[94]

Yet in spite of these abundant signs of amicability, De Lisle still managed to quarrel at least once with his cathedral chapter. His biographer, himself an Ely monk and an admirer of the bishop, writes that De Lisle "caused the prior and convent much difficulty, in that he denied them [license] to dig up clay and sand for the [building] work of the church, as they had been accustomed [to do] in the time of all [other] bishops." De Lisle was incited to take this uncompromising stand, the biographer believes, by "certain wicked men, not by the impulse of his own spirit." The bishop, he says, "was good in and of himself, nevertheless he lent extremely credulous and open ears to certain flatterers and narrators of perverse things, which were [told] to him in secret." The monks tried repeatedly, through hand-delivered letters and messages, to persuade the bishop to let them have clay, sand, and gravel for their cathedral fabric, but all to no avail. De Lisle would not let them have the material unless the convent formally requested a "license of his special grace." Eventually, the prior and chapter sent the required "deprecatory letter," which De Lisle returned unopened, and the bishop gave the monks free access to dig on his land.[95] The biographer's indignation notwithstanding, it was quite natural that De Lisle should seek to prevent the monks from establishing a precedent that could prove detrimental to his episcopal privilege. The incident caused only a temporary rupture in what seemed otherwise friendly relations between the bishop and the priory.

93. *Sacrist Rolls*, 2:141, 152–53, 157, 163.
94. *CPP*, 101.
95. *AS*, 1:655, and see Appendix B, page 229.

Manorial Administration

A study of the bishop's criminal career needs to look at his manorial and estate management for two reasons. One, the economic fate of the manors, particularly in the years immediately following the Black Death of 1348–49, may help gauge the strength (or weakness) of the bishop's income. A poor harvest and lower rents, combined with an expensive household, undoubtedly would have put pressure on the bishop to find additional sources of revenue, such as that provided by crime. Second, it may be possible to trace the major instigators of De Lisle's criminal raids to the various officials named in the manorial records. Such information would be valuable because it would help establish the opportunity and means by which these crimes were carried out: A manorial official, such as a reeve or steward, had unparalleled knowledge of the local terrain and the tenants who inhabited it. In addition, if it can be demonstrated that the alleged perpetrators of these crimes acted together as a close-knit group in the course of their official duties and saw long service with the bishop, the case that De Lisle supported a criminal band would be strengthened greatly.

The estate for which De Lisle's manorial officials were responsible was vast: It comprised forty-one manors in seven counties, including the bishop's townhouse of Holborn in London (see Fig. 2). Yet the number of manorial records surviving from De Lisle's episcopate are few: Scattered documents are available for Downham, Wisbech Barton, and Wisbech Castle. The rest probably fell victim to the destruction of the Peasants' Revolt that swept East Anglia in 1381.[96] The Downham account rolls are particularly important as they yield much information about the administration of one of the bishop's largest and most frequently visited manors. These sources are supplemented by two surveys conducted of De Lisle's temporalities in 1356 and 1357, ordered by the crown in the wake of the bishop's conviction of complicity in the murder of William Holm.[97] It is unfortunate that the picture is not completed by any surviving household accounts. The only such records relating to Ely date from the episcopate of Thomas Arundel, bishop from 1373 until 1388.[98]

The end of the accounting year, 29 September, saw the manorial reeve submit his roll of account, listing all his income and expenses, or credits and debits, to the auditors for inspection. He was expected to maintain a certain level of profitability and efficiency on the manor from year to year,

---

96. Owen, *Ely Records*, 7.
97. See pages 138–41.
98. Aston, *Thomas Arundel*, 166–68.

but his job became much more difficult with the advent of the plague in East Anglia in 1349. The account rolls of all three manors—Downham, Wisbech Barton, and Wisbech Castle—provide information on income and agricultural output in the years immediately following the Black Death.

At Downham, the recorded increases in total gross and net income during the years 1350–52 are illusory. In 1350–51, a large chunk of the profit came from sales at the audit, totaling more than £49, and in 1351–52, rent arrears reached an unprecedented high of more than £57, a bad sign in any manorial economy. If these artificial revenues are taken away, then profits at Downham in reality declined after the plague. Rents of land remained stable at just over £15 throughout De Lisle's episcopate, and sale of corn stayed high, but other sources of income suffered. The years 1350–52 saw no income whatsoever from rents of mills or forinsec receipts, and the sale of stock fell sharply from just over £10 to little more than £2 (Table 3).

At Wisbech Barton and Wisbech Castle, the economic devastation wreaked by the plague is more readily apparent. Total gross income at Wisbech Barton plummeted more than 50 percent in 1349–50 from the previous year's total. Rents were nearly half what they had been in 1348–49 and corn sales dropped by more than two-thirds. By the following year, 1350–51, figures for these two income sources were even lower (Table 5). Wisbech Castle saw its rents fall by more than 50 percent in 1349–50 and its arrears more than triple (Table 7).

Agricultural production at Downham and Wisbech Barton also suffered. Total output of all kinds of grain at Downham was halved in 1350–51, while grain production at Wisbech Barton fell sharply in 1349–50 and by the following year was well under half its former output in 1348–49 (Tables 4 and 6).[99]

Despite these glum statistics, other figures show that, after an initial sharp drop in revenue immediately following the Black Death, income on the manors was beginning to recover to its former, pre-plague levels. Total gross income at Wisbech Barton in 1352–53 nearly equaled that for 1346–47, and rents were slightly more than two-thirds their pre-1349 level while corn sales surpassed all previous records. Grain issues at Downham sharply improved in 1351–52 and at Wisbech Barton were roughly equal in 1352–54 to what they had been six years previously. At Wisbech Castle, a strong and steady flow in court profits from 1349 to 1355 helped offset weak returns in other, formerly reliable revenue sources such as rents and forinsec receipts. Evidence from other parts of the country confirms that

99. Agricultural production already had been in decline at Wisbech Barton for a decade prior to the plague. See Miller, *Abbey and Bishopric*, 105.

Table 3. Downham Account Rolls: Manorial Income[a]

	1341–42	1342–43	1345–46	1346–47	1347–48	1348–49	1350–51	1351–52
Arrears	£7.6s.1¼d.	£2.6s.11d.	£4.19s.7¾d.	£3.11s.6¾d.	£3.11s.8½d.	£3.11s.9½d.	£6.12s.5d.	£57.15s.2¼d.
Assessed rents	3.11.5	3.11.5½	3.11.6½	0	0	0	3.11.9½	3.11.9½
Rents of land	10.5.6½	10.5.6½	10.9.8½	15.14.7¼	15.14.7¼	15.14.7¼	15.14.7¼	15.14.7¼
Rents of fisheries	0.12.10	0.12.10	0.11.2	0.11.2	0.11.2	0.11.2	0.11.2	0.11.2
Rents of mills	3.0.0	3.0.0	2.13.4	3.0.0	3.0.0	4.2.0	0	0
Rents of cows	4.15.0	5.0.0	0	0	0	0	5.0.0	5.10.0
Sale of corn[b]	1.9.1½	4.1.6	0	4.18.9	35.8.1¼	21.9.1¾	33.6.10	28.1.9
Sale of stock & labor[c]	10.6.10	10.14.0	10.6.8½	9.9.10¾	10.13.6¼	10.9.3	2.4.3½	2.7.5
Issues of the manor	0.8.0	1.1.0	0.2.0	3.18.1	0	0.3.2	0.3.1	3.15.2½
Profits of the court	7.5.0	3.11.0	6.13.8½	8.14.11½	2.7.7	14.17.5	2.5.7	7.10.11
Forinsec (foreign) receipts	0	0	23. 8.5¾	1.15.5	26.10.2	9.0.0	0	0
Sales at the audit	10.8.2	0.2.6	0.6.3	6.10.8	1.4.4¾	12.10.5¾	49.19.0	4.0.3½
Other	0	0	0	0	0	0.1.4	0	0
Total (gross)[d]	59.8.0¼	44.6.9	63.2.6½	63.5.1¼	104.19.4½	94.10.4¼	118.17.1¾	128.18.4½
Total (net)[d]	12.8.2	—[e]	2.2.11½	13.1.3½		20.4.9	65.19.8¼	89.8.3½

a data are missing for the years 1343–44 and 1344–45.
b including malt
c including plow service
d totals are taken from those given in the documents
e indicates missing data
SOURCE: CUL, EDR, D 10/2/11, D 10/2/13, D 10/2/17–20.

Table 4. Downham Account Rolls: Issues of the Grange (quarters/bushels)[a]

	1341–42	1342–43	1345–46	1346–47	1347–48	1348–49	1350–51	1351–52
Fruit	33/5	44/2	0	27/0	48/5	42/7	32/4	22/7
Rye	11/2	0/7	0	3/1	5/2	8/3	1/3	6/2
Beans	1/1	1/1	0	0	0	0	0	0
Peas	28/1	43/0	0	51/4	49/5	62/1	25/4	31/2
Barley	69/7	94/3	0	110/4	115/4	108/4	59/1	75/1
Oats	8/2	10/0	0	0/6	7/5	0	0	0
"Dredge"(*dragetum*)	0	0	0	0	0	0	0	13/2
Total	152/2	193/5	0	192/7	226/5	221/7	118/4	148/6

[a]data are missing for the years 1343–44 and 1344–45.
Source: CUL, EDR, D 10/2/11, dorse; D 10/2/13, dorse; D 10/2/17–20, dorse.

Table 5. Wisbech Barton Account Rolls: Manorial Income[a]

	1337–38	1338–39	1340–41	1341–42	1342–43	1343–44	1345–46	1346–47
Arrears	£10.8s.11$\frac{1}{4}$d.	£13.10s.2$\frac{3}{4}$d.	£12.12s.5$\frac{3}{4}$d.	£16.1s.4d.	£27.5s.6$\frac{1}{4}$d.	£6.5s.7d.	£5.0s.0d.	£1.2s.2$\frac{1}{2}$d.
Rents of land	38.17.11$\frac{1}{2}$	39.18.4	40.13.11$\frac{1}{2}$	40.13.11$\frac{1}{2}$	40.13.11$\frac{1}{2}$	40.13.11$\frac{1}{2}$	48.9.2$\frac{1}{2}$	48.9.2$\frac{1}{2}$
Sale of corn[b]	19.0.11$\frac{1}{2}$	36.18.4$\frac{1}{2}$	28.9.9$\frac{3}{4}$	38.18.5$\frac{3}{4}$	39.11.11$\frac{1}{2}$	40.9.7$\frac{1}{2}$	0	36.3.0$\frac{1}{2}$
Sale of stock	0	6.16.11	2.9.9	8.8.4	4.18.0$\frac{1}{2}$	8.10.7	6.4.0	4.4.0
Dairy	0	2.0.0	3.10.0	3.19.11	4.19.9	5.5.0	0	0
Sale of labor	6.13.9	6.19.9	7.5.11$\frac{1}{2}$	7.5.4$\frac{1}{2}$	7.5.6$\frac{1}{2}$	7.7.0	8.12.5	7.14.11
Issues of the manor	3.15.9	3.12.0	3.7.7	2.10.3	1.17.0	0.6.0	10.3.2	8.0.0
"Foldage" (*faldagium*)	0	0.7.9	0.5.0	0.16.8	0	0.16.8	0	0.13.4
Forinsec (foreign) receipts	0	0	0	0	0	0	4.0.0	0
Sales at the audit	10.11.11	4.1.4	0.6.6	1.3.10$\frac{1}{2}$	1.6.3$\frac{1}{2}$	2.9.5$\frac{3}{4}$	3.5.10	9.12.11$\frac{1}{2}$
Other	0	0	0	0	0	0	0	0
Penalties	0	0	0	0	0	0	0	50.0.0
Total (gross)[c]	89.9.3$\frac{1}{4}$	114.4.8$\frac{1}{4}$	99.1.0$\frac{1}{2}$	120.8.2$\frac{1}{4}$	127.18.0$\frac{3}{4}$	111.7.2$\frac{3}{4}$	85.15.3$\frac{1}{2}$	165.19.8
Total (net)[c]	19.5.4$\frac{1}{4}$	33.5.2$\frac{1}{4}$	19.13.1	27.16.11$\frac{1}{4}$	25.11.7	18.0.0$\frac{3}{4}$	1.2.2$\frac{1}{2}$	63.12.0

Table 5 *cont'd*

	1347–48	1348–49	1349–50	1350–51	1351–52	1352–53	1353–54
Arrears	£10.0s.0d.	0	£3.6s.8¼d.	0	0	£8.12s.8¼d.	£9.1s.5d.
Rents of land	48.9.2½	48.9.2½	26.12.8	19.5.8½	23.7.5½	32.15.5	29.2.11½
Sale of corn[b]	54.18.8½	68.17.9	20.12.2½	16.18.10	56.3.1½	91.2.9½	32.8.1
Sale of stock	4.13.7	6.1.4½	3.8.10½	11.11.6	7.7.4	13.10.7	12.6.3
Dairy	0.1.8	2.0.0	0	2.7.3	3.0.0	3.10.0	3.0.0
Sale of labor	7.15.9	7.11.2½	6.5.5½	6.10.3	6.11.10	6.9.9¼	7.11.10¾
Issues of the manor	6.5.6	0.6.4	1.15.11	1.13.8	0.8.4	1.12.4	2.2.4
"Foldage" (*faldagium*)	0	0	0.6.5	0	0	0.1.8	0.16.2
Forinsec (foreign) receipts	14.12.6	0	0	0	0	0	0
Sales at the audit	4.19.11¼	2.3.1½	2.19.11¾	3.15.9¼	24.4.10½	6.15.4¼	—[d]
Other	0	0	0	0	8.1.4	0	—
Total (gross)[c]	151.16.10¼	135.9.0	65.8.2½	62.2.11¾	129.4.3½	164.10.7¼	—
Total (net)[c]	29.6.1	—	—	—	—	38.6.6½	—

[a] data are missing for the years 1339–40 and 1344–45
[b] including malt
[c] totals are taken from those given in the documents
[d] indicates missing data

SOURCE: CUL, EDR, D 8/1/12–17, D 8/1/19, D 8/2/1–2, D 8/2/4, D 8/2/6, D 8/2/8, D 8/2/10–12.

Table 6. Wisbech Barton Account Rolls: Issues of the Grange (quarters/bushels)[a]

	1337–38	1338–39	1340–41	1341–42	1342–43	1343–44	1345–46	1346–47
Fruit	55/6½[b]	45/1	82/3	51/7	64/1	52/2	0	48/5
Fruit and rye	2/2	16/4	20/2	12/6	6/0	5/4	0	4/0
Mixed corn	168/6	213/6	184/7	182/6	161/2	165/5	0	127/0
"Rackmalt"(*rackbrasium*)	0	0	46/0	17/3	41/2	77/2	0	89/0
Early corn	52/0	80/0	80/3	45/1	40/0	23/2	0	0
Beans	4/0	33/0	13/2	14/1	0	0	0	61/6
"Dredge"(*dragetum*)	0	0	26/2	12/2	0	0	0	0
Oats	290/2	430/1	428/6	296/3	522/6	482/5	0	309/3
Other	0	0	0	0	0	0	0	0
Total	573/0½	818/4	882/1	632/5	835/3	806/4	0	639/6

	1347–48	1348–49	1349–50	1350–51	1351–52	1352–53	1353–54
Fruit	43/0	98/4	55/6	35/0	60/2	103/1	47/4¾
Fruit and rye	0/5½	12/2	6/1	4/7	0	0	0
Mixed corn	203/6	214/1	122/0	115/3	161/3	276/2	281/4
"Rackmalt"(*rackbrasium*)	0	62/7	74/1	13/6	74/0	0	30/5
Early corn	0	0	0	0	0	15/1	0
Beans	41/5	22/1	10/4	3/6	0	11/1	0
"Dredge"(*dragetum*)	0	0	0	0	0	0	8/0
Oats	311/5	396/7	252/2	214/2	201/4	201/2	241/1½
Other	0	0	0	0	12/1	7/0	25/1
Total	600/5½	806/6	520/6	387/0	509/2	613/7	634/0¼

[a]data are missing for the years 1339–40 and 1344–45
[b]fractions used in this table indicate parts of packs or bales

SOURCE: CUL, EDR, D 8/1/12–17, dorse; D 8/1/19, dorse; D 8/2/1–2, dorse; D 8/2/4, dorse; D 8/2/6, dorse; D 8/2/8, dorse; D 8/2/10–12, dorse.

Table 7. Wisbech Castle Account Rolls: Manorial Income[a]

	1343–44	1346–47	1347–48	1349–50	1350–51	1354–55
Arrears	£15.3s.3$_{1/2}$d.	£8.7s.6$_{1/2}$d.	£7.17s.4d.	£30.3s.1d.	£12.10s.4d.	£24.12s.8d.
Assessed rents	111.17.11$_{3/4}$	111.18.11$_{3/4}$	111.19.1$_{1/4}$	111.19.1$_{1/4}$	111.19.1$_{1/4}$	112.1.1$_{1/4}$
Rents	39.10.3	48.13.1	54.4.5	24.15.9	27.15.5	25.18.11
Sale of stock	0.4.2$_{1/2}$	1.5.8$_{1/4}$	0.9.1$_{3/4}$	0.5.7$_{3/4}$	0.0.2$_{3/4}$	0.5.6$_{1/2}$
Rushes	0.19.7$_{3/4}$	0.19.7$_{3/4}$	0.19.7$_{3/4}$	0.19.7$_{3/4}$	0.19.7$_{3/4}$	0.19.7$_{3/4}$
Profits of the court	42.19.10$_{3/4}$	38.3.1$_{1/2}$	47.6.6$_{3/4}$	66.7.6$_{3/4}$	50.6.8$_{1/4}$	46.6.4$_{1/2}$
Sale of labor	0	0.5.5$_{1/2}$	0	0	0.4.2	0
Issues of the manor	0.19.2	1.11.8	2.0.7	0.4.0	0.6.4	1.1.1
Forinsec (foreign) receipts	30.13.8	48.9.2$_{1/4}$	48.9.2$_{1/2}$	26.12.8	19.5.8$_{1/2}$	23.15.4$_{1/2}$
Sales at the audit	2.1.6	0.5.3	0.3.9$_{1/2}$	2.8.11$_{1/2}$	6.1.4$_{1/2}$	0.12.0
Other	9.5.0	5.0.0	0	0	0.10.6	8.6.10
Total (gross)[b]	253.14.7$_{1/4}$	264.19.7$_{1/2}$	273.9.9$_{1/2}$	263.16.5	229.19.6	243.19.6$_{1/2}$
Total (net)[b]	23.13.0$_{1/2}$	28.8.1$_{1/4}$	69.13.7$_{3/4}$	85.9.6$_{3/4}$	63.5.0$_{3/4}$	——[c]

[a]data are missing for the years 1344–46, 1348–49, and 1351–54
[b]totals are taken from those in the documents
[c]indicates missing data
Source: CUL, EDR, D 7/1/5–10.

seigniorial incomes in general, including those from ecclesiastical estates, recovered from plague setbacks during the second half of the fourteenth century.[100] There is nothing to suggest, therefore, that the Black Death permanently affected De Lisle's manorial income and precipitated his career in crime. At most, the short-lived economic shortfall caused by the plague aggravated an already worsening situation allegedly created by the bishop's reckless household spending.[101] It was the need to balance the household side of the books, for which manorial profits apparently were insufficient, that, among possibly other factors, set De Lisle on the path that would eventually lead him before the king's courts and then into exile.

Perhaps it should come as no surprise that a large proportion of the men alleged to have committed crimes associated with the bishop were employed as officials in his administrative bureaucracy. Their legitimate duties entailed a practical ability to organize men, a familiarity with local terrain, and close contact with tenants and other potential victims. John de Lisle, in particular, was in an ideal position to organize raids and coordinate extralegal activities since, as chief steward, he controlled the entire machinery of estate management and personnel. He led the raids on Richard and William Spynk in 1346, an arson raid on the Duke of Lancaster's lands in 1350, and the arson raid on Lady Wake in 1354. He was helped in the raid on the Spynks by Osbern le Hawker, keeper of the bishop's parks at Downham, and by William Michel, the bishop's nephew and John de Lisle's assistant; in the raid on the Duke of Lancaster by John de Brownsley and John de Essex, both described as the bishop's bailiffs of the liberty of Ely, and by Thomas Canville, porter of Wisbech Castle, and by Thomas Bacon and Martin Lowen, both sometime reeves of Wisbech Castle; and in the raid on Lady Wake by Thomas Durant, steward of Downham, and by Robert de Godington and Henry de Shankton, De Lisle's auditors.

In 1355, Ralph Carles, the bishop's chamberlain, allegedly murdered Lady Wake's valet, William Holm; both men occupied roughly equivalent positions in their respective master's household. William de Stansted, steward of the liberty of Ely, and Robert de Godington, acting as De Lisle's bailiff, allegedly extorted fines for the bishop from men falsely accused by approvers. Robert Hale and Richard Mody, respectively the bailiff and

100. G. A. Holmes, *The Estates of the Higher Nobility in Fourteenth–Century England* (Cambridge, 1957), 114–15; J. Hatcher, *Plague, Population and the English Economy, 1348–1530* (London, 1977), 32; J. L. Bolton, *The Medieval English Economy, 1150–1500* (London, 1980), 209–13; C. Dyer, "The Social and Economic Background to the Rural Revolt of 1381," in R. H. Hilton and T. H. Aston, eds., *The English Rising of 1381* (Cambridge, 1984), 29–30 and n. 62.

101. *AS*, 1:655, and see Appendix B, pages 228–29.

reeve of Somersham manor, were said to have committed several abductions and extortions against the tenants and free men of Somersham. Thomas de Baa, constable of Wisbech Castle, John de Brownsley, Thomas Bacon, and Thomas Canville supposedly carried out arson and pillage raids in 1351–52 on John Daniel and others in Norfolk following the escape of Reginald de Wilton, a prisoner in the custody of Brownsley, Godington, and Canville at Wisbech. In 1356, William de Stretford, the bishop's bailiff of Hadstock, Essex, and Thomas de Chilton, keeper of the bishop's parks at Downham, were accused of assaulting John de Grey at Balsham, Cambridgeshire, and killing one of his servants.

The alleged misdeeds of all these men are examined in subsequent chapters.[102] It is the aim of the following section to illustrate the more legitimate side of their activities.

As on almost every other estate, the most important official in the bishop of Ely's manorial administration was the estates steward, an office that was invested with various judicial and financial duties. At Ely, the steward traditionally assumed custody of the bishop's temporalities whenever he went abroad.[103] He controlled virtually the entire source of the bishop's income, and therefore he had to be someone on whom the bishop could rely absolutely. The high priority of the office can be gauged by the fact that De Lisle entrusted it to none other than his brother, John. He first appears in the records as one of the bishop's *domicelli* who were commissioned on 13 and 14 September 1345 to take possession of the bishop's temporalities as well as his books, muniments, and pontifical ornaments in the keeping of the prior and chapter of Ely Cathedral.[104]

One of the steward's main duties was to hold the manorial courts and generally supervise the estate. In 1351–52, for example, the steward and his clerk were ferried several times by the bishop's tenants from Downham to Doddington "in order to hold court there."[105] This same year also saw John de Lisle holding court at Somersham, in preparation for which the Downham tenants carried his letters to the Somersham reeve.[106] The steward's prodigious duties required almost constant travel among the various manors of the estate. At Downham alone, at least 7s. was paid over three years to men who helped transport the steward and his attendants, mostly by boat through the waterways of the fens, from the manor to Doddington and Chatteris in Cambridgeshire.[107] In 1348–49, fifteen

102. See pages 99–107, 119–31, 143–58.
103. Miller, *Abbey and Bishopric,* 260.
104. CUL, EDR, G/1/1, Reg. De Lisle, fol. 54r.
105. "In batellagandum senescalli et clerici usque Dodyngton' per diversas vices pro curiam ibidem tenendo: xxx. opera." CUL, EDR, D 10/2/20, dorse, *opera yemalia et estivallia.*
106. Ibid.
107. CUL, EDR, D 10/2/17, *expense forinsece;* D 10/2/18, 20–21 Edward III, *expense forinsece;* D 10/2/18, 22–23 Edward III, *expense forinsece.*

men were employed to ferry "in many boats . . . John de Lisle, steward, and several others" from Downham to Somersham, Huntingdonshire.[108] In the winter of this same year, ice was broken near Manea, Cambridgeshire, so that John de Lisle and others could pass by river from Doddington to Downham around Christmas.[109] In 1350–51, John de Lisle and his sister, Ancilla, were ferried several times to Doddington and Chatteris.[110]

As steward, the bishop's brother also authorized the reeves to pay wages, hand out charitable gifts, and make purchases. In 1345–46, John de Lisle ordered the payment of 13s. 4d. to a carpenter hired to enlarge the "chamber above the pantry" in the Downham *aula*,[111] and he ordered that 7d. be paid for seven autumn works performed by men sent to pitch rushes and peat on the bishop's cart destined for the manor. In this same year, the steward ordered that four shovels be purchased at 5d. to replace those broken by the bishop's ministers in his new garden, and his letters authorized the payment of £1 8s. 5d. to strong diggers who had filled ponds in the bishop's park.[112] In 1346–47, he instructed the reeve to buy ale and give it to men coming from Lyndonbury in Haddenham, Cambridgeshire, with the bishop's carts loaded with hay and to give three and a half quarters of barley as a gift to Agnes, the widow of Geoffrey Skut.[113] In 1348–49, at a time when the Black Death so afflicted the Downham manor that no peat could be cut that year "by reason of the great mortality of men from the pestilence,"[114] John de Lisle ordered that 1d. be given every Tuesday to eighteen poor men among the bishop's customary tenants at Downham from 30 September 1348 until 29 September 1349, the alms totaling £3 18s. In the same year, he ordered that five members of the bishop's *familia* at Downham be granted five bushels of fruit in the autumn as a gratuity.[115]

Assisting the chief steward was a number of subordinates, also called stewards, each of whom was assigned to a portion of the estate, a practice

---

108. "In stipendium xv. hominum quasi j. vice licet per plures batellos usque Somersham cum Johanne de Insula senescallo et cum alijs diversis: ij.s. vj.d. cuilibet ij.d." CUL, EDR, D 10/2/18, 22–23 Edward III, *expense forinsece.*

109. Ibid.

110. CUL, EDR, D 10/2/19, dorse, *opera yemalia et estivallia.*

111. "In stipendium unius carpentarii elargienti cameram ultra panetriam secundum ordinacionem Johannis de Insula fratris domini: xiij.s. iiij.d." CUL, EDR, D 10/2/17, *custume domorum.*

112. Ibid., *expense forinsece* and *expense necessarie.*

113. CUL, EDR, D 10/2/18, 20–21 Edward III, *expense forinsece* and dorse, *ordium.*

114. "De facto nihil hoc anno pro defectu hominum et causa pestilencia magne mortalitatis hominum." CUL, EDR, D 10/2/18, 22–23 Edward III, dorse, *turba.*

115. CUL, EDR, D 10/2/18, 22–23 Edward III, *elemosina* and dorse, *liberationes familie.*

at Ely dating from at least the thirteenth century.[116] William de Stansted, for example, was mentioned in one record as "the steward of the bishop of Ely's liberty of Ely."[117] Thomas Durant, or Darent, rector of Snailwell, Norfolk, and subsequently of Stretham, Cambridgeshire, was given the title of steward in the Downham manorial account roll of 1351–52, when he ordered that seventy-five pigs be sent out to pasture.[118] In the previous year, he had set out in a boat for Doddington and Chatteris with the bishop's sister, Ancilla, and a "slater."[119] John de Lisle may also have been assisted by his nephew, William Michel. In 1345–46, Michel and "Jonger, Ponger, and others with him" were transported to Doddington "on behalf of the lord's business concerning [the village of] March [in Norfolk]."[120] This may have been for violent purposes: Michel was accused by a Norwich merchant, Richard Spynk, of leading a raid on his house and livestock at March.[121] The names "Jonger" and "Ponger" may have been pseudonyms designed to keep the identities of the perpetrators secret, similar to the "Brothers Muf, Cuf, and Puf" whom John de Bannebury of Hackney, Middlesex, accused of robbing and terrorizing him in 1327.[122] In the next year, 1346–47, Michel ordered the payment of 14s. to William de Elm for timber carried from Brandon, Suffolk, to Littleport, Cambridgeshire, to be used for construction of the bishop's new chamber.[123]

Below the steward, the next most important tier of officers in the bishop's manorial administration were the auditor and receiver. The former acted as a medieval accountant who made a yearly review of the balance sheet compiled by the reeve of each manor and tried to ensure that the manor remained profitable. It was the auditor's job to keep the reeve honest: The opportunities for corruption presented to the reeve were many and tested the auditor's vigilance. In the accounting year ending on 29 September 1347, for example, the auditors penalized the reeve of Wisbech Barton, John Fairy, £40 "for various falsehoods and concealments

---

116. Miller, *Abbey and Bishopric,* 263.

117. "De Willelmo de Stanstede senescallo libertatis episcopi Eliensis de Ely." PRO, JUST 3/8/4, m. 1 (undated). See also *AS,* 1:658, and Appendix B, page 233.

118. CUL, EDR, D 10/2/20, dorse, *pise.* His title was crossed out by a later hand.

119. "In batellagandum Domini Thome Darrent cum Ancilla sorore domini et j. sclatore usque Dodington' et Chateriz per vices: viij. opera." CUL, EDR, D 10/2/19, dorse, *opera yemalia et estivallia.*

120. "In batellagandum Willelmi Michel et clericorum usque Dodyngton et eiusdem Willelmi, Jonger, Ponger, et aliorum secum existenciorum usque Dodyngton' pro negociis domini de March': xiiij.d. per xiiij. opera autumpnalia." CUL, EDR, D 10/2/17, *expense forinsece.*

121. See page 99.

122. R. W. Kaeuper, "Law and Order in Fourteenth-Century England: The Evidence of Special Commissions of Oyer and Terminer," *Speculum* 54 (1979), 734–35.

123. CUL, EDR, D 10/2/18, 20–21 Edward III, *expense et liberationes.*

concerning his account discovered by his own cognizance."[124] In addition, Fairy was fined a further £10 "because he did not serve the days assigned to him."[125]

As the records indicate, more than one auditor visited the manors. The office typically seems to have been filled by long-standing servants of the bishop who doubled as his clerks. A case in point is Robert de Godington, who was identified by Clown's inquest at Kelshall, Hertfordshire, on 2 March 1357, as "one of the bishop's auditors."[126] Godington began his career in De Lisle's service as bailiff, an office that he held from 1347 until as late as 20 July 1349.[127] The turmoil caused by the Black Death among the clergy in the latter year gave Godington the opportunity to occupy a succession of benefices by exchange. In one year, 1349, he was made rector of Whittington, Norfolk, then Conington, Cambridgeshire, and finally Newton, Cambridgeshire.[128] By 8 June 1350, he was being called the bishop's clerk.[129]

Henry de Shankton, another clerk who briefly took Godington's place at Whittington on 25 June 1349 before being presented on the following 4 August to the church of Hadstock, Essex,[130] acted as auditor from the beginning of De Lisle's episcopate. In 1347, six and a half quarters of malt "counted by Henry de Shankton" were delivered from Downham to Ely for the auditors' victuals in the months of November and December.[131] In 1348–49, Shankton accounted for one quarter of fruit, one oxen, one cow, and six pigs for the provision of his fellow auditors of accounts.[132]

If any profits did accrue to the manor, they were collected in quarterly cash payments by the receiver, of whom the bishop employed several. Obviously, the receiver had to be someone whom the bishop could trust to handle large sums of money on a regular basis. One of De Lisle's most reliable receivers was Richard de Middleton, rector of Littlebury, Essex,

124. "De eodem preposito pro diversis falcitatibus et concellamentis super compoto compertis per cognicionem suam propriam." This fine was pardoned. CUL, EDR, D 8/2/1, *misericordia.*

125. "De preposito quia non servavit dies sibi fixos de diversis denariorum summis per eos faciendis sub diversis penis." Also pardoned. Ibid., *pena.*

126. "Stephanus Wyne messor in eodem manerio liberavit Roberto de Godyngton' uni [uno] auditorum dicti episcopi post dictas octabas: xx.s. per j. talliam." PRO, E 143/9/2, m. 72.

127. PRO, KB 27/381, rex m. 24.

128. CUL, EDR, G/I/1, Reg. De Lisle, fols. 18v, 19r, 21r, 26r.

129. *CPR,* 1348–50, 585.

130. CUL, EDR, G/I/1, Reg. De Lisle, fols. 21r, 25v.

131. "Et liberavit usque Ely pro expensis auditorum compoti mensibus Novembris et Decembris vj. quartas dimidietatem per talliam contra Henricum de Schanketon." CUL, EDR, D 10/2/18, 21–22 Edward III, dorse, *braseum.*

132. CUL, EDR, D 10/2/18, 22–23 Edward III, dorse, *fructum, boves, vacce, porcelli.*

and custodian of the bishop's palace at Ely.[133] Middleton discharged the office almost from the very beginning of De Lisle's episcopate: He received £3 from Geoffrey Cardinal, reeve of Downham, in Michaelmas term 1346.[134] When the bishop determined to liquidate his estate preparatory to fleeing England in 1356, the one person entrusted with receiving the profits of the surreptitious sale was Middleton. He was assisted in his collection by Godington, Shankton, and another of the bishop's clerks, John de Dunsterre.[135] Even after the temporalities of Ely had been seized into the king's hand on 21 October 1356, Middleton allegedly continued to receive the bishop's moneys and deliver them to his former employer. Although he was indicted by the crown for his loyalty to De Lisle, Middleton was eventually granted a king's pardon on 1 June 1362.[136]

In common with other manorial estates, the lands belonging to the bishop of Ely were divided into hundreds or bailiwicks, each supervised by a salaried official called a bailiff.[137] These officers rarely appear in the Ely manorial records and thus not much can be said about them. On the other hand, the account rolls are quite informative about their authors, the reeves and *messors* who were held accountable for their contents. Unlike the bailiff, the reeve typically received no salary but instead was rewarded for his labors with an acquittance of customary services owed to his lord. At Downham, the reeve's exemption meant more work for his fellow tenants: Each customary tenant holding a virgate, or twelve acres, of land performed more than two hundred works during the year on Cardinal's behalf. The reeve and *messor* also were acquitted of four chickens and forty sheep owed to the bishop each year. The only money paid to them was when they served the bishop's table for so many weeks in every autumn: In 1351–52, for example, they were paid a total of 8s. for four weeks and four days of attendance, taken at 1 1/2d. per man per day.[138]

The bishop's departure to Avignon in 1356 signaled a breakdown in discipline among the manorial reeves. In the course of his inquest into the temporalities of Ely in 1357, Roger de Clown found that many reeves throughout Norfolk and Suffolk still owed money in arrears from their accounts of the previous year. A total of nearly £50 was withheld by De Lisle's former servants. Normally, this would indicate that the reeves were attempting to keep the profits of the manor for themselves, which was the principal reason they were required to render yearly accounts. However, in this case, the reeves (or some of them at any rate) may have been

133. CUL, EDR, G/1/1, Reg. De Lisle, fols. 75v, 77r.
134. CUL, EDR, D 10/2/17, *liberationes donorum*.
135. See pages 139–40.
136. *CPR*, 1361–64, 204.
137. Miller, *Abbey and Bishopric*, 255, 264–65.
138. CUL, EDR, D 10/2/20, *custume autumpnales*.

withholding their revenues from the king's agents out of loyalty to De Lisle.[139]

The manors of the bishop were supposed to supply food and, if profitable, money to support the household. It is therefore only natural that the reeve, in addition to his other duties, such as reckoning the issues of the grange, collecting rents, and paying the salaries and food liveries of the manor's officials and *familia*, should be responsible for delivering grain, livestock, and fuel to the household larder. Each delivery had to be confirmed by a sealed bill of the wardrobe. In 1350–51, almost all of the reeve's charges, totaling £47 15s. 1d., to the household at Downham were disallowed by the auditors because they had been made without the warrant or indenture of the wardrobe or "because the indenture is not sealed."[140] The bishop's peripatetic movements meant that a large amount of grain and livestock had to be transferred each year among the reeves of neighboring manors. Downham's reeve, for example, received a variety of grain and livestock from his counterparts at other manors including Stretham, Littleport, Wilburton, Ely, Doddington, and Haddenham in Cambridgeshire, Barking in Suffolk, Shipdham in Norfolk, and Somersham in Huntingdonshire. In return, the Downham reeve sent produce to Somersham in Huntingdonshire, Haddenham, Willingham, and Balsham in Cambridgeshire, and even fourteen partridges down to the bishop's townhouse in Holborn, London. The labor required to drive livestock, ranging from pigs and chickens to oxen and deer, from Downham to neighboring manors was drafted in part from hired hands and partly from the bishop's customary tenants.[141]

Another manorial officer, the parker, frequently doubled as an important member of the household. Ralph Carles, who was keeper of the bishop's park, warren, and free chase at Somersham, where he enjoyed a salary of 3d. per day, was also employed as De Lisle's chamberlain, who traditionally looked after the lord's living quarters.[142] Other parker-cum-chamberlains include Peter Blanchard, chamberlain at Downham who was granted keepership of the parks and warrens there on a wage of 2d. per day, and John Pecham, chamberlain at Doddington and parker, also at 2d. per day.[143] Blanchard's predecessor as Downham parker was Osbern

---

139. PRO: E 143/9/2, mm. 53, 55–57, 59, 61, 64–66, 72; E 143/13/1, m. 11.

140. ". . . quia indentura non sigillatur." CUL, EDR, D 10/2/19, dorse, *opera autumpnalia.*

141. CUL, EDR, D 10/2/17, dorse; D 10/2/18, 20–21 Edward III, dorse, and 21–22 Edward III, dorse; D 10/2/19, dorse.

142. BL, Add. MS 41612, fol. 113v; PRO, KB 27/382, rex m. 17. Blanchard probably died of the plague: His last payment as keeper was on 4 June 1349, after which his place was taken by Cok de Stratford. CUL, EDR, D 10/2/18, 22–23 Edward III, *custume parci cum vadijs parcarij.*

143. BL, Add. MS 41612, fols. 107v–108r.

le Hawker, who held the office from 20 November 1345 until 20 September 1348.[144] On occasion the bishop took recreation in his parks, as at Downham in 1345–46, when men were paid to help "drive deer from one part of the park to the other so that the bishop may see them."[145]

A discussion of De Lisle's manorial administration would not be complete without mention of the constable of Wisbech Castle, who by the fourteenth century had lost any military role and served a purely administrative function. Under the terms current during De Lisle's day, the constable received a generous remuneration for his services. It consisted of living quarters within the castle, including a hall near the castle gates, chambers on either side of the hall and above the gates an easement, kitchen, and a stable for three horses; twenty marks, or £13 6s. 8d., per year in wages taken in four equal installments; a robe like that worn by the bishop's shield-bearers, or £1 per year for such a robe; a robe for the constable's clerk like that worn by the bishop's clerks, or £1 per year for such a robe; 40,000 turves per year for fuel; necessary litter each year for himself and his familiars; twelve cartloads of hay per year; and sufficient litter and a bushel of oats each day for his three horses. In addition, the constable was to take for himself all profits pertaining to his office.[146]

In return, the constable was expected to act as custodian of the castle; to supervise the stock yields and all profits issuing within the castle and on the bishop's manors and lands within the Marshland bailiwick; to hold, when necessary, the bishop's hundred, halimote, and leet courts; and to imprison securely all prisoners taken within his jurisdiction. The constable was held liable for all prisoners who escaped on account of his negligence or that of his deputies, and he swore an oath on taking office that he would "perform a faithful and diligent administration."[147] The first person in De Lisle's curia to take that oath was Thomas Lovet, who is recorded as receiving a full year's wages in the Downham manorial account roll ending on 29 September 1347.[148] Lovet was still in possession of the office on 8 June 1350, but by Easter term 1355, a new constable,

---

144. Ibid.; CUL, EDR, D 10/2/17, *custume parci cum vadijs parcarij*. In spite of Blanchard's grant, the manorial account roll for the year ending on 29 September 1349 records that Hawker was paid up until 3 November 1348. CUL, EDR, D 10/2/18, 22–23 Edward III, *custume parci cum vadijs parcarij*.

145. "In auxilium pro damis fugandis de una parte parci usque ad aliam ut eos videre dominus." CUL, EDR, D 10/2/17, *expense forinsece*.

146. BL, Add. MS 41612, fols. 107r–v; *CPR*, 1358–61, 43.

147. "Idem vero Thomas corporale prostabit juramentum futuris successoribus nostris, priori eciam et conventui sive domino regi, quociens et quandocumque tempus vacacionis adesse contigerit, de fideli et diligenti administracione sua eisdem facienda in custodia predicta." BL, Add. MS 41612, fol. 107r.

148. CUL, EDR, D 7/1/6, *expense et liberationes*.

149. *CPR*, 1348–50, 584–85; PRO, KB 27/379, rex m. 9.

Thomas de Baa, was registered in the king's bench plea rolls.[149] Baa held the constableship until 3 May 1358, when he surrendered it to the crown, and the king granted it to his yeoman, John Herlyng.[150]

The diocesan business recorded in De Lisle's register may tell us nothing more than that he was a competent bishop who, in true medieval style, kept a foot in both worlds, spiritual and secular. Yet, the bishop's stormy dealings with various monasteries confirm his appetite for litigation in defense of potentially lucrative rights, while the declining revenues evidenced by his manorial account rolls strengthen his motives for doing so. Most significant, the high proportion of De Lisle's manorial administrators who committed crimes, the fact that they tended to act together, and their continued employment by him, all suggest that their "unofficial" actions were by no means unplanned or unsanctioned by the bishop. As an examination of their legitimate activities shows, De Lisle's officials were well prepared for such double duty.

150. *CPR*, 1358–61, 43.

PART TWO

De Lisle as "Criminal"

3

The State of Disorder
in Medieval England

Nearly every modern scholar agrees that medieval England was a violent place. R. H. Hilton characterizes England at the end of the thirteenth century as "a society where violence, bribery and corruption were normal means of settling the issues which arose between men."[1] J. G. Bellamy, who wrote the first general history of crime in medieval England since the nineteenth century, asserts that "late medieval England was known throughout Europe for its high rate of crime," an opinion echoed by B. A. Hanawalt.[2] J. B. Given states baldly: "Thirteenth-century England was a violent society. The threat of violence and the effects of violence were, if not a common part of the average Englishman's day, something that he could expect to experience, if only as a spectator, at some time in his life."[3]

It is reasonable to assume that any society lacking a standing, professional police force to maintain local order was bound to be violent. This probably was no less true of the "wild west" of nineteenth-century America as of medieval England. In the isolated towns and villages of the medieval English countryside, or the "shires" as they were called, there simply was no one to turn to for defense against violent criminals. One was forced to rely on personal resources and the support of friendly neighbors. Most houses were made of wattle and daub, a fancy term for mud, and were exceptionally easy to break into. An intruder simply could punch his fist through the walls, or more conveniently, set fire to the house, which would "smoke out" the inhabitants, after which the burglars would rush

1. R. H. Hilton, *A Medieval Society: The West Midlands at the End of the Thirteenth Century* (London, 1966), 55.

2. J. G. Bellamy, *Crime and Public Order in England in the Later Middle Ages* (London, 1973), 3; B. A. Hanawalt, *Crime and Conflict in English Communities, 1300–1348* (Cambridge, Mass., 1979), 45.

3. Given, *Society and Homicide*, 188.

in to grab as much as they could before immolating themselves. The latter tactic was thought to have been used at Boston, Lincolnshire, in 1288 in order to steal some merchant goods; unfortunately, the fires that had been set burned down the greater part of the village, including the Dominican priory there.[4] According to his accusers, arson was likewise a favorite tactic of Thomas de Lisle and his cohorts.[5]

Since medieval people generally had to rely on themselves for their own defense, they probably carried with them knives, swords, sticks, or other potential weapons that they did not seem reluctant to use when provoked. Indeed, a cursory glance through the rex membranes of the *coram rege* rolls of the king's bench (which record criminal indictments) leaves one with the impression that violence was not uncommon in medieval English society. In Michaelmas term 1360, William Dumberdale of Essex was indicted for killing Hugh Pytman in a brawl in his house, after which William fled to the church for sanctuary.[6] William de Moreby of Yorkshire was accused in Trinity term 1362 of killing a man and then burning the corpse in a cemetery.[7] At this same session, a particularly vicious crime was recorded against Thomas Porter, chaplain. On 17 February 1362, Porter allegedly came to the house of William Webster of Pocklington, Yorkshire, carried off five pounds' worth of Webster's goods and cattle, abducted his wife, Agnes, and "against William's will carnally knew" her. On 14 April of the same year, Porter returned to Webster's house, entered it by force and, when Agnes would not consent to sex with him a second time, attacked and wounded her and set fire to the Websters' two-year-old son, burning off one of his feet so that the child was permanently maimed.[8] In the Middle Ages, however, "rape" was defined as abduction and did not imply sexual abuse; nor was it committed always by force, for sometimes wives used it to escape their husbands. In Easter term 1361, John Froile was indicted of nocturnally abducting Elizabeth, the wife of John son of Richard de Wodeford, "against the king's peace but not against the will" of Elizabeth.[9]

Like all periods of history, medieval England, too, had its serial killers. In Michaelmas term 1360, Adam de Sale, son of John de Croft, was accused of killing and mutilating at least twenty-nine men in Liverpool.[10]

4. *Annales Monastici*, ed. H. R. Luard, 5 vols. (RS, xxxvi, 1864–69), 315; William Rishanger, *Chronica et Annales, 1259–1307*, ed. H. T. Riley (RS, xxviii, 1865), 117; Walter de Guisborough, *Chronicle*, ed. H. Rothwell (Camden Society, 3d series, lxxxix, 1957), 224.

5. See pages 119–24, 149–53.

6. PRO, KB 27/401, rex m. 28.

7. PRO, KB 27/407, rex m. 15.

8. PRO, KB 27/407, rex m. 6.

9. ". . . noctanter rapuit Elizabetham uxorem Johannis filii Ricardi de Wodeford contra pacem domini regis set non contra voluntatem." PRO, KB 27/ 403, rex m. 11d.

10. PRO, KB 27/401, rex mm. 28, 31d.

One of the ways in which criminal networks could be uncovered was if one of the members of the gang, a notorious villain who was certain to be convicted and hung, turned approver, whereby he was spared his life if he named his accomplices in crime.[11] In Hilary and Easter terms of 1361, one such approver, William Knyght, a well-known thief, revealed an astonishing geographical range of crime, extending from Buckinghamshire in the south through the midland counties of Nottingham and Lincoln up to Yorkshire in the north.[12] Not even the dignity of the dead in their graves was safe from the depredations of determined thieves. Adam Kyng, for example, was indicted in Trinity term 1360 of despoiling the tomb of a chaplain in order to obtain the precious vestments of the corpse.[13] Innocent games could turn deadly. The king's bench in Michaelmas term 1358 heard how John Templere of Stanwell in Somerset accidentally struck a pillar with a stick with which he was playing, whereupon the pillar fell and struck Nicholas Shepherd on the head below the ear, killing him.[14]

Ironically, the very reason historians can tell such entertaining anecdotes about crime in medieval England is because English administrative records were so well kept and preserved relative to those on the Continent. The blackness of the picture that emerges from the medieval English legal system is in part a tribute to its success: Quite obviously, crimes were being reported and investigated, if not punished altogether. Therefore, medieval England may have been perceived, even by contemporaries, as being more violent than the rest of Europe simply because its system for detecting such crimes was so much better. As K. B. McFarlane pointed out in his Ford Lectures in 1959, there is no simple correlation between complaint and crime. The greater evidence we have for disorder in later medieval England may only reflect increased opportunities to obtain legal redress.[15] The dilemma for the historian is how much his role as an observer impinges on the result he seems to find. A good example is the interpretation of the itinerary of the king's bench. On occasion during the fourteenth century it acted like a "superior eyre," traveling to certain counties rather than staying in Westminster.[16] Was the king's bench's visit to a shire an indication that crime was rampant there? Or rather, does the predominance of crime from that county simply reflect the fact

11. F. C. Hamil, "The King's Approvers: A Chapter in the History of English Criminal Law," *Speculum* 11 (1936), 238–58; J. Röhrkasten, "Some Problems of the Evidence of Fourteenth-Century Approvers," *Journal of Legal History* 5, no. 3 (1984), 14–22.

12. PRO, KB 27/402, rex mm. 1–2, 9d., 15d., and KB 27/403, rex mm. 3, 6, 20, 26d.

13. PRO, KB 27/400, rex m. 9d.

14. PRO, KB 27/393, rex m. 34d.

15. K. B. McFarlane, *England in the Fifteenth Century* (London, 1981), xx, 42; Kaeuper, "Law and Order in Fourteenth-Century England," 736.

16. For the itinerary of the king's bench during the fourteenth century, see *Select Cases in the Court of King's Bench*, 6:xlvi.

that people took advantage of the presence of the court in their vicinity to report their crimes instead of having to make the trip to London? Unless we can know the intention of the judges who performed the circuit, we will never be able to answer this question.

Complaints in Parliament

Perhaps a more reliable marker of the general state of disorder in medieval England, or at least the popular conception of it, can be found in the pronouncements of the king and the petitions of the commons in parliament. At least three times during the reign of Edward III, for example, widespread dissatisfaction with the state of the king's peace expressed itself in the rolls of parliament.[17] At the assembly held in March 1332, Sir Geoffrey le Scrope, chief justice of the king's bench, explained to the assembled prelates, earls, barons, and other great men how it had come to the king's attention:

> that various people, disregarding the law, have raised great companies to destroy the faithful people of our lord king, as well as the members of Holy Church, the king's justices, and others; they take some and detain them in prison until they receive grievous fines and ransoms of their lives at the will of the said malefactors, and they put others to death; they rob some men of their goods and chattels, and commit many other evils and felonies, in contempt of the king and in disturbance of his peace and to the destruction of his people.[18]

Even the members of parliament themselves feared the "disputes, riots, and brawls" around London committed by people "armed with padded

17. Bellamy, *Crime and Public Order*, 5–6.
18. ". . . si pronuncia Monsieur Geffrei le Scrope, par le comandement nostre seignur le roi, et en sa presence et des touz les autres prelatz, countes, barons, et autres grantz, coment le roi avoit entendu, et si feust ce chose conue as touz, que divers gentz, diffuantz la lei, feurent levéz en grant compaignies en destruantz les liges gentz nostre seignur le roi, auxi bien les gentz de Seinte Esglise, les justices le roi, come autres; prenantz acuns de eux et detenauntz en prisone, tant q'ils avoient receu pur lur vies sauver greves fyns et raunceouns a la volunte des ditz mesfesours, et acuns mettantz a la mort, acuns desrobeaunz de lur biens et chatelx, et fesant plusours autres malx et felonies, en despit du roi et en affrai de sa pees, et destructioun de son poeple." *RP*, 2:64.

jerkins, plate armour, lances, long coats, and other manner of arms."[19] To remedy the situation, the king, on the advice of his commons, was to appoint keepers of the peace in each county, who would arrange for suspects to be pursued, arrested, and kept for trial.[20]

At the parliament held in April 1343, the commons petitioned the king to appoint general commissions of oyer and terminer that would investigate "felonies, trespasses, conspiracies, confederations, and false maintenance" in the shires in order to "maintain the peace" and "in chastisement of evildoers and for the salvation and aid of good people."[21] At the assembly held in January 1348, the members pleaded with the king "to have pity and regard to the great mischief of your said commons, and to the great duress and charges which it suffers and has suffered annually."[22] According to the petition, "the peace is very troubled and disturbed and the law hindered and almost ignored" on account of the fact that the great men of the land maintain and endorse "traitors, felons, robbers, trespassers against the peace" as well as those who distort the law for their own ends.[23] An ordinance was called for to be enacted to punish the offenders.[24]

At the parliament in January 1352, Edward admitted that:

> the peace of his realm is not as well kept as before and that the disturbers of the peace and maintainers of quarrels and of riots committed in the countryside are extremely grievous to his people, without the fact that a due punishment is made of them; and also, that the statutes made previously for the amendment of the laws

19. "Por ce que avant ces hours, as parlementz et as conselx nostre seignur le roi, debatz, riotz, et conteks ont esté sourtz et meuz, par tant que gentz se sont aléz es lieuz ou les parlementz et conselx ont esté somons et assembléz, arméz d'aketouns, des plates, des espeyes, des longes cotelx, et des autres maneres des armes." Ibid.
   20. Ibid., 64–65.
   21. "Tresexcellent et treshonurable seignur, les gentz de vostre commune soi recomandent a vous . . . de ce que tant tendrement prenez a quer a meyntenir la pees a la quiete de vostre poeple. Et semble a eux, que bien-seante chose serroit, que en chastiement des malveys, et salvation et eide des bones gentz, que certeyns justices . . . soient juréz ore a ce parlement . . . d'oier et terminer felonies, trespasses, conspiracies, confederacies, et malveys meyntenance." Ibid., 136.
   22. "Treshonure et tresredoute seignur, les gentz de vostre commune esmercient . . . vous plest pitee et regarde avoir al grant mescheif de vostre dite commune, et as grandes duresses et charges q'ele soeffre et ad suffert annuelement." Ibid., 165.
   23. ". . . ils priount . . . que nul grant de la terre, ne autre, ne meigntiegne ne endosse traitours, felouns, robbeours, trespassours contre la pees, barettours, meyntenours des quereles et barettz, embraceours des busoignes, conspiratours, confederatours, chaumpartours, ne autres tieux, par queux fauxine et fauxes engines la pees est tout trublée et destourbée, et les leyes arreriés et a poy anientéez." Ibid.
   24. Ibid.

of the land and of the people are not kept nor used to their full effect, nor that the judgements rendered by the king's courts . . . duly executed.[25]

Nevertheless, complaint about the king's peace did not surface again until the end of the reign, when it became entangled in the political issues raised by the Good Parliament of 1376.[26]

Yet again, there is a question as to how to interpret the evidence. Was complaint by the commons a reliable indicator of a situation in the country at large? The complaint of 1332, for instance, was probably inspired by a notorious kidnapping and ransom earlier in that year of a puisne justice of the king's bench, Sir Richard Willoughby, by the Folville and Coterel gangs.[27] Such an assault on the dignity of the bench was enough to provoke the government into action, but whether kidnapping was widespread in England at this time we probably will never know. On the other hand, the fact that complaint about lawlessness was sparse between 1352 and 1376 is not a sure indication that "good order prevailed" during those years.[28] For it was during this period when, according to his accusers, De Lisle and his gang were active. Likewise, there was little outcry about excessive violence during the reign of Edward II, although scholars suspect that it was a common phenomenon hidden by the larger political issues in the realm.[29] The absence of complaint is therefore no guarantee that crime did not occur, nor, for that matter, is its presence any proof that such crime was commonplace.

Quantitative Measures of Crime

Where does the historian turn to prove that England in the Middle Ages was violent? One answer favored in recent years is to count the actual number of criminals who appeared before the bench in medieval England and correlate this figure with a general index of population or some other variable. This is an extremely daunting and, as we will see, treacherous task.

25. Ibid., 237; J. G. Bellamy, *The Law of Treason in England in the Later Middle Ages* (Cambridge, 1970), 78.

26. See, in particular, G. A. Holmes, *The Good Parliament* (Oxford, 1975).

27. E.L.G. Stones, "The Folvilles of Ashby-Folville, Leicestershire, and their Associates in Crime, 1326–1347," *TRHS*, 5th series, 7 (1957), 122–28; J. G. Bellamy, "The Coterel Gang: An Anatomy of a Band of Fourteenth-Century Criminals," *EHR* 79 (1964), 707–11.

28. Bellamy, *Crime and Public Order*, 6.

29. Ibid., 5.

Nevertheless, two historians in the late 1970s attempted to provide a statistical and scientific basis for the common perception that medieval England was a dangerous place. Their efforts are testimony to the rich survival of medieval legal records in the Public Record Office (PRO) in London, as well as to the toil and pertinacity of the researchers themselves. It remains to be seen, however, whether the records can support such an endeavor.

The first attempt to make a statistical analysis of medieval crime came from J. B. Given in *Society and Homicide in Thirteenth-Century England*, published in 1977. Given counted the indictments for homicide in twenty eyre rolls from five counties and two cities over the course of the thirteenth century. The eyre was an itinerant court that periodically visited each shire dispensing justice in the king's name but relying on juries composed of local men.[30] Although the eyre was empowered to investigate all crimes, Given limits himself to murder. Given estimates that on average, 15.1 homicides occurred per 100,000 population in thirteenth-century England, as opposed to 9.7 per 100,000 in the United States in 1974.[31]

Despite the "impressive and persuasive tables" and the complex battery of statistical tests he uses, Given's calculations both of number of slayings and of population have been shown to be fundamentally flawed.[32] While Given assumes that "all those accused of having committed a murder probably did so," only a third of those indicted actually appeared before the eyre, according to his own statistics.[33] Another study finds that 10 to 20 percent of those tried for homicide in England in the Middle Ages were actually convicted.[34] Given's estimates of thirteenth-century population are not reliable, since his sources are at least a century out of date.[35]

Similar pitfalls awaited another statistical study of medieval crime that appeared in 1979, Barbara Hanawalt's *Crime and Conflict in English Communities, 1300–1348*. Hanawalt bases her study on over two hundred gaol delivery rolls from eight counties dating from the first half of the fourteenth century.[36] Gaol deliveries were cases heard locally in the county when the king's justices came to "deliver" a town's gaol. With the demise of the eyre by the beginning of the fourteenth century, the sessions of gaol delivery emerged as the new, although not exclusive, itinerant courts of justice, bringing the king's law into the shires.

---

30. Given, *Society and Homicide*, 4–6.
31. Ibid., 36, 39, and errata slip for Warwick.
32. E. Powell, "Social Research and the Use of Medieval Criminal Records," *Michigan Law Review* 79 (1980–81), 967–78.
33. Given, *Society and Homicide*, 93–94.
34. T. A. Green, "The Jury and the English Law of Homicide, 1200–1600," *Michigan Law Review* 74 (1975–76), 431.
35. Given, *Society and Homicide*, 29–31.
36. Hanawalt, *Crime and Conflict*, 5, 7–8, 12–13.

Although Hanawalt attempts a more broad-based study of crime than Given, she repeats his mistake of basing her conclusions on indictments rather than convictions.[37] Hanawalt assumes that "indictments had to be plausible in order to be recorded," yet she finds that, on average, 80 percent of those who appeared before gaol deliveries between 1300 and 1348 were in fact acquitted.[38] Yet another study of gaol delivery cases, drawn from East Anglia between 1422 and 1442, points to an 84 percent acquittal rate.[39]

The social and psychological speculations of these authors also have come in for criticism.[40] Given subscribes to the sociologist Albert Bandura and his modern theory of "aversive experiences." According to Given, people were violent in the Middle Ages because life was violent. Their violent surroundings conditioned their violent behavior. Thus, the medieval criminal was a victim of lifelong flogging: husbands beating wives, fathers beating children, priests beating husbands. One gets the impression from Given that everyone in the Middle Ages was beating someone else. In addition, the violence of medieval Englishmen was conditioned by such bloodthirsty sports as jousting and wrestling.[41] Needless to say, such speculations are hard to prove.

Given's other explanation for medieval crime is that it was a form of "conflict resolution."[42] Given finds that the vast majority of suspects in the eyre rolls, 77.9 percent, either had no possessions or whose chattels were valued at less than 5s.[43] He concludes from this that poor people were more likely to commit crime since they had less to lose if caught and had few opportunities for legal resolutions of their disputes.[44] Yet Given himself admits that the foundation for his assumptions is unreliable: "Chattels were often deliberately undervalued by jurors" in the records of the eyre, and "it can be suspected that the rolls may not give a complete picture of violent activity among the aristocracy."[45] These qualifications fundamentally undermine the validity of his thesis.

Hanawalt explains medieval crime in terms of "conflict theory," a term she borrows from A. T. Turk and that "views law as a powerful instrument of social control."[46] In other words, various social groups, accord-

37. Ibid., 14; Powell, "Social Research," 969.
38. Hanawalt, *Crime and Conflict*, 14, 58.
39. Maddern, *Violence and Social Order*, 53.
40. Powell, "Social Research," 970–72, 977–78.
41. Given, *Society and Homicide*, 193–99.
42. Ibid., 200.
43. Ibid., 69.
44. Ibid., 70–71, 90.
45. Ibid., 67, 72.
46. Hanawalt, *Crime and Conflict*, 3, 62–63. Hanawalt's ideas on conflict theory were first developed in idem, "Community Conflict and Social Control: Crime and Justice in the Ramsey Abbey Villages," *Mediaeval Studies* 39 (1977), 402–23.

ing to Hanawalt, compete with each other for power by attempting to manipulate the legal system in their favor. Hanawalt matches her suspects in Huntingdonshire with the J. A. Raftis Regional Data Bank at the University of Toronto, which reconstructs the social makeup of several villages in the county using the records of Ramsey Abbey.[47] On this basis, the vast majority of her suspects, 79.8 percent, came from the wealthiest members of society, the so-called primary and secondary villagers.[48] Thus, in contrast to Given, Hanawalt claims that it was the nobility of medieval England who were most responsible for crime; in fact, they comprised a "fur-collar" criminal community equivalent to the modern-day Mafia.[49]

However, this 79.8 percent represents only a minority of those who actually appeared before the bench. By one estimate, just 30 percent of offenders indicted before local peace sessions in the fourteenth century appeared for their trial.[50] And, as Given argues, it is likely that poor men indicted to appear before the courts fled and risked outlawry, since they had little to lose. The wealthy members of society, on the other hand, risked confiscation of their land and possessions and were more likely to be acquitted by their peers.[51]

Well before statistical studies of medieval crime became fashionable, K. B. McFarlane and J. G. Bellamy warned against such endeavors. Medieval records, they argue, survive in too quixotic a pattern to support the rigors of accuracy and completeness that the tools of statistical analysis demand.[52] The recent research of other investigators of medieval crime confirms that the qualitative approach is preferable to the quantitative. Studies of individual court cases seem to yield far more important and fruitful results than general statistical surveys.[53]

Bellamy also was reluctant to find an all-encompassing cause of crime in the medieval psychosis. Medieval people themselves, Bellamy points out, would have little understood such explanations: "Medieval man had little curiosity about causation of crime, although he was aware of the importance of opportunity. Revenge was understood, but not much else."[54]

---

47. Hanawalt, *Crime and Conflict*, 6–7; idem, "Community Conflict," 404–5.

48. Hanawalt, *Crime and Conflict*, 129; idem, "Community Conflict," 407.

49. B. A. Hanawalt, "Fur-Collar Crime: The Pattern of Crime Among the Fourteenth-Century English Nobility," *Journal of Social History* 8, no. 4 (1975), 1–17; idem, *Crime and Conflict*, 138–44, 214–16.

50. Post, "Criminals and the Law in the Reign of Richard II," 15.

51. Given, *Society and Homicide*, 70–71; Powell, "Social Research," 971–72.

52. McFarlane, *England in the Fifteenth Century*, xx; Bellamy, *Crime and Public Order*, 3.

53. S. J. Payling, *Political Society in Lancastrian England: The Greater Gentry of Nottinghamshire* (Oxford, 1991), 189–90; Maddern, *Violence and Social Order*, 7–9.

54. Bellamy, *Crime and Public Order*, 31.

Instead, medieval men sought explanations for crime "in terms of obligations shirked, wrongs done, and rules broken or badly administered."[55]
Case studies of the better documented criminals in the pleas rolls will
give a better understanding of medieval motives for crime, Bellamy contends, than trying to find it in the vast and inhuman terrain of statistics.[56]

Even if the incidence of medieval crime could be known absolutely, it
is hard to see how this would advance our understanding of the period.
Rather than attempting modern statistical comparisons, should we not
ask: How did medieval people themselves view the problem of crime?
Based on the evidence of complaints in the rolls of parliament referred to
at the beginning of the chapter, it seems that medieval Englishmen wanted
to know basically two things with regard to disorderly conduct: Who,
specifically, was responsible for it, and how were they to be punished?

Maintenance and Bastard Feudalism

The identity of the criminal class in medieval England always has been rather
elusive. It has been speculated that a criminal "underworld" existed in the
England of the Middle Ages consisting of vagabonds and vagrant paupers
who made a life of crime. This was a self-perpetuating underclass of desperate men and women whose chief means of survival was a combination
of petty theft and confidence trickery.[57] Although such subsistence criminals may have been common, they are difficult to trace in the medieval legal records. Consequently, aside from the studies of Hanawalt and Given,
not much scholarly attention has been devoted to this subject.

Instead it has been the gentry and aristocracy that traditionally have
attracted the most blame for the high level of violence and crime in medieval England. An understanding of this question is essential if we are to
place Thomas De Lisle within the context of his times. If the bishop indeed was guilty of masterminding a criminal gang, as accusations against
him claim, was this in any way typical of fourteenth-century magnate
behavior? If De Lisle was a maintainer of criminals, was he an aberration
to be condemned by his contemporaries, or simply one among many such
figures? The outcome of the debate on medieval English noble crime will
therefore greatly influence how we interpret De Lisle's supposed criminal behavior.

55. Ibid., 32.
56. Ibid., 37–38.
57. I owe this information to a lecture given by Jeus Röhrkasten at the Institute
of Historical Research in London in 1990. See also Bellamy, *Crime and Public Order*,
38–41.

First, we must establish who the gentry and aristocracy were. Below the king was a group of men, numbering no more than seventy-eight during Edward III's reign, who were distinguished by receiving a personal summons to parliament in the house of lords.[58] Collectively, they were known as the lords, magnates, barons, or peers of the realm. Their titles ranged from duke or earl at the upper end of the scale, to the majority of barons who styled themselves as "lord" before their name and, at the very bottom of the heap, the knights banneret (literally, "little barons").[59] The wealth of members of this group likewise varied considerably. Aside from the king, by far the richest member was the duke of Lancaster, who in the late fourteenth century boasted an annual income of £11,750.[60] For the earls, £1000 seems to have been considered a minimum income, but peers below this status could earn as little as £250. Most of the magnates seem to have enjoyed incomes between £500 and £4000 per year. All together, the magnates and their families probably numbered between two hundred and five hundred persons.[61]

The other, poorer half of the nobility of medieval England commonly is known as the gentry. Whereas the magnates sat in the house of lords, the gentry occupied the house of commons. It was a group whose membership was in a state of flux during the fourteenth century. At the beginning of the century, there were only two classes among the gentry: knights and esquires, each numbering about fifteen hundred persons, or three thousand all together.[62] Knights enjoyed an annual income of on average £40, although their incomes could reach as high as £200. Esquires generally earned half that of knights, or £20 per year on average, but their incomes ranged between £5 and £40.[63] In the retinue of John of Gaunt in the late fourteenth century, the average fee paid to knights in time of peace was a little over £32, and in time of war, £43. Squires were paid on average just over £9 in time of peace and about £11 in time of war.[64] Membership in the gentry was distinguished by the right to bear a family coat of arms. Originally this extended only to knights, but by the middle of the

---

58. Given-Wilson, *The English Nobility in the Late Middle Ages*, 1, 56; Ormrod, *Reign of Edward III*, 95–96.

59. Given-Wilson, *English Nobility in the Late Middle Ages*, 61; Ormrod, *Reign of Edward III*, 95.

60. Goodman, *John of Gaunt*, 329, 341.

61. Given-Wilson, *The English Nobility in the Late Middle Ages*, 13–14, 18, 37, 66; Ormrod, *Reign of Edward III*, 96.

62. Given-Wilson, *The English Nobility in the Late Middle Ages*, 14, 18, 69–70.

63. Ibid., 18, 71; N. Saul, *Knights and Esquires: The Gloucestershire Gentry in the Fourteenth Century* (Oxford, 1981), 12, 18.

64. J.M.W. Bean, *From Lord to Patron: Lordship in Late Medieval England* (Manchester, 1989), 251–64; S. Walker, *The Lancastrian Affinity, 1361–1399* (Oxford, 1990), 91–92.

fourteenth century, this right also was possessed by esquires.[65] By the end of the century, a third rank was added to the gentry, that of gentleman or yeoman, who occupied the lowest rung of gentry society and boasted an annual income of between £5 and £20.[66]

Two terms are critical to the debate over noble crime in medieval England. One is maintenance. According to the *Oxford English Dictionary*, maintenance is defined as "the action of wrongfully aiding and abetting litigation," particularly when a party who has no personal interest in the case sustains a suitor at law.[67] A related term, champerty, denotes a variation of maintenance in which the maintainer of the suit conspires to divide the profits of litigation with the plaintiff or defendant. Maintenance, it is argued, was practiced in the late Middle Ages by almost every lord on behalf of his retainers, who advertised the value they attached to their lord's patronage by wearing his livery, an article of clothing or badge that signified that one was the lord's "man." This would not present a problem if the lord's retainers were law-abiding pillars of their community, but very often, so the argument goes, they were quite the opposite. The act of maintaining is thus synonymous in some historians' minds with subverting the English common law to rule in favor of men who otherwise would have been punished. This was done by such means as embracery, whereby the jury is bribed to acquit, or by payments to court officials such as the sheriff and judges of the bench. If the members of the court could not be corrupted, then more persuasive tactics, such as violence and intimidation, could be used.[68] Ecclesiastical patrons could maintain criminals just as readily as lay ones, as the employment of the Folville and Coterel outlaw gangs by Crowland Abbey, St. Mary's Abbey, and Lichfield Cathedral demonstrate.[69]

The other term associated with maintenance and noble crime is bastard feudalism. The phrase was first coined by the Victorian Charles Plummer in 1885 to describe a phenomenon that he perceived to have made its appearance in England during the reign of Edward III. For Plummer, bastard feudalism has a negative connotation: It represents a

---

65. Saul, *Knights and Esquires*, 20–23; Given-Wilson, *The English Nobility in the Late Middle Ages*, 70.

66. Saul, *Knights and Esquires*, 16–18; Given-Wilson, *The English Nobility in the Late Middle Ages*, 71.

67. *Oxford English Dictionary*, 2d edition (Oxford, 1989). See also the definition in N. F. Cantor, *The English: A History of Politics and Society to 1760* (New York, 1969), 270.

68. Cantor, *The English*, 269; Bellamy, *Crime and Public Order*, 22–23.

69. Stones, "The Folvilles," 124; Bellamy, "The Coterel Gang," 713–14; E. D. Jones, "The Church and 'Bastard Feudalism': The Case of Crowland Abbey from the 1320s to the 1350s," *Journal of Religious History* 10 (1978–79), 148–49.

corruption of simple feudalism whereby the old ties of homage between lord and vassal were replaced by money contracts, or indentures. Plummer traces this practice to the French campaigns of Edward III during the middle of the fourteenth century, which, although they resulted in English victories, weakened the power of the crown relative to that of the barons. Indentures enabled the great lords to make enormous profits at the expense of the government and at the same time to gather around themselves "a horde of retainers, who wore his livery and fought his battles," while the lord "in turn maintained their quarrels and shielded their crimes from punishment." As long as the lords and their criminal following were out of the country on campaign, there was peace; once the war was over, however, they returned back home to resume their warlike ways and wreak havoc on the land.[70]

Thus, in Plummer's view, the nobility of medieval England was the enemy of good order and sound government. Although they outwardly followed a code of chivalry and honor, the lords of medieval England, Plummer argues, were in fact characterized by an "ingrained lust and cruelty" and a "reckless contempt for the rights and feelings of all who were not admitted within the charmed circle."[71] Their power and independence of the crown increased to the point that by the fifteenth century, during the reign of the weak King Henry VI, they engaged in numerous private wars that divided the kingdom and led to the chaos and misery of the War of the Roses.[72] Plummer bases his negative assessment of the nobility on the writings of Sir John Fortescue, a chief justice of the king's bench who lived through the struggles between the Lancastrian and Yorkist factions in fifteenth-century England. Based on his experience, Fortescue saw any lord who was richer and more powerful than the king (what he called the "over-myghtye subgette") as a potential threat to the crown and the peaceful government of the kingdom.[73]

Plummer's interpretation of maintenance and bastard feudalism has remained influential and still is followed in its essentials by some scholars.[74] According to this school, the overmighty subject undermined law and order in two ways. One was to bribe or intimidate juries, sheriffs, justices of the peace, and even royal judges in order to render favorable judgments in court. Second, the fact that the lord was successful in the former activity meant that men were eager to gain his patronage in order

70. Sir John Fortescue, *The Governance of England*, ed. C. Plummer (Oxford, 1885), 15–16.
71. Ibid., 15.
72. Ibid., 17–19.
73. Ibid., 127–30.
74. R. L. Storey, *The End of the House of Lancaster* (London, 1966), 15–17; Bellamy, *Crime and Public Order*, 21–25; Hanawalt, "Fur-Collar Crime," 7–14; P. R. Coss, "Bastard Feudalism Revised," *Past and Present*, no. 125 (1989), 54–59.

that they might benefit from his "good lordship." Bastard feudalism and maintenance, in this view, created a vicious circle in which each fed off the other. By keeping a large retinue that was no longer bound by traditional oaths of homage but by the more precarious ties of indentures, the overmighty subject manipulated the law in order to protect his followers and maintain his reputation as a good lord. By the same token, the corruption of local and royal officers of the law was made possible by the new money contracts lords regularly issued to their followers, and their intimidation by the large private armies lords now were able to command.

Much of the support for the maintenance and bastard feudalism thesis comes from complaints reflected in the fifteenth-century statute rolls and rolls of parliament, and from the private correspondence of the Pastons, a Norfolk gentry family who engaged in much litigation over land.[75] Naturally, this evidence falls within the period that saw the most violence among the nobility. Nevertheless, it is worth examining the statute rolls and rolls of parliament for the reign of Edward III in order to determine if the commons complained about livery and maintenance as much in the fourteenth century as they did in the fifteenth.

In the very first year of Edward's reign, 1327, the commons petitioned the king that none of his councilors, "nor any of the other great men of the realm, nor any of the king's court, great or small, nor any minister who be under the king, maintain by himself or by another, nor by command of his letters, neither suitors nor quarrels, by which the common law be disturbed."[76] The king replied by transcribing the commons' request into a royal command contained in the second statute issued that year. If anyone was to be found guilty of maintenance at the next parliament, he was to be brought before the king's council and make good the damages done to the injured party.[77]

The statute of 1330 complained that:

> in times past several people of the realm, great men as well as others, have made alliances, confederacies, and conspiracies to maintain parties, pleas, and quarrels, whereby several people have been wrongfully disinherited, and some ransomed and destroyed, and some, for fear of being maimed and beaten, dare not sue of their right, nor complain, nor the jurors of inquests give their verdicts, to the great damage of the people and to the scandal of the law.

---

75. See note 88 below, and *The Paston Letters*, ed. J. G. Gairdner, 3 vols. (London, 1896).
76. "La commune prie . . . que nul de ceux, ne nul autre graunt de la terre, ne nul de l'oustel le roy, ne grant ne petit, ne nul ministre qe soit desouz le roi, ne meinteigne par lui ne par autre, ne par maundement de lettres, parties, ne quereles, par quei que comun droit soit desturbé." *RP*, 2:10.
77. *SR*, 1:256.

As a remedy, the justices of the courts of king's bench and common pleas, as well as the justices of assize and of the eyre, were to investigate "such maintainers, bearers, and conspirators, and also of them that commit champerty." Accusations were to be brought both at the king's suit and by private parties. If the case could not be heard before the king's courts on the writ of *nisi prius*, it was to be adjourned until such time as was convenient.[78]

In 1331, each of the magnates was examined before full parliament and required to swear publicly that "henceforth he not retain in giving or receiving [of livery] nor maintain nor avow, privately or openly, by himself or by another, any robber, malefactor, fugitive indicted of felony, anyone sued by writ of exigent, common trespasser, nor any other who is of evil fame or of bad reputation."[79] The magnates further promised to aid the king's justices, sheriffs, and other officers in the execution of the king's judgment against such criminals, "of whatever estate or condition they may be."[80] At the parliament held at York in 1334, the royal justices as well as the keepers of the peace in the shires were instructed to inquire "of false jurors and maintainers," who also were to be excommunicated by the prelates of the Church.[81] In the second statute of 1336, the king promised to issue writs to his sheriffs to arrest and imprison "notorious malefactors, or maintainers of malefactors" who were said to be responsible for "the great mischiefs that have happened in the realm." The king also promised to appoint in each county "good men and true" who would hold inquests "upon the doings of the said malefactors and maintainers."[82]

By far the most concerted effort made in Edward's reign to address the problem of maintenance came in the Ordinance for Justices of 1346, which attacked not only corruption on the bench but also bad behavior among the peers of the realm. Every great man, from the king on down to the queen, his son, the Prince of Wales, the members of the king's court, prel-

---

78. Ibid., 264.

79. "Acordé est par nostre seignur le roi, prelatz, countes, barouns, et autres grantz du roialme, en pleyn parlement, chescun des ditz grantz ent especiaument examiné, et a ce assentant, que nul grant de la terre desore ne reteigne en menage n'en recevaunce, ne meyntiegne ne avowe en prive n'en apert, par lui ne par autre, nul robeour, mesfesour, n'endite de felonie qui est futyf, ne celui qui est mis en exigende, ne comune trespassour, ne autre qui soit de male fame ou de male rette." *RP*, 2:62, 446.

80. "Et ont les ditz grantz promis q'ils deyvent ayder od tut lur poer les justices, viscountes, et touz les autres ministres le roi, queux q'ils soient, a faire execution des jugementz, et de totes autres choses qe attiegnent a lur office, auxi bien devers grantz come devers autres quecumqes, de quel estat ou condicion q'ils soient." Ibid.

81. Ibid., 376.

82. *SR*, 1:277.

ates, earls, and barons, were commanded that they "not take in hand quarrels other than their own, nor the same maintain by them nor by another, secretly or openly, for gift, promise, amity, favor, doubt, or fear, nor for any other cause." This was so that "every man may be free to sue for and defend his right in our courts and elsewhere, according to the law." The king claimed that he had personally commanded his son, the Black Prince, and several earls and magnates to uphold the ordinance.[83]

In another section of the same ordinance, the king commanded the lords to "void from their retinue, fees, and robes all such bearers and maintainers in the country without showing to them any aid, favor, or comfort in any manner." It had reached the royal ears that many maintainers were themselves "maintained and borne by lords, whereby they be more encouraged to offend." As a result of all this maintenance, it was said, "many people be disinherited, and some delayed and disturbed of their right, and some not guilty be convicted and condemned or otherwise oppressed." The king also promised to hold inquests in the shires against maintainers, who would be ordered to cease their practices or else face "grievous pains."[84]

Sometimes, however, it seemed that the clamor against maintenance was overstated. In 1354 and 1355, the commons complained that "good people" were being accused of being "conspirators, confederators, and maintainers" before the justices of trailbaston by reason of their accusers' "malice and falsehood."[85] The last mention of maintenance made by parliament under Edward III came in the last year of the reign, 1377. Once again, accusations of maintenance had been made without adequate proof. At a previous parliament, Hugh Fastolf of Yarmouth in Norfolk had been impeached of "diverse extortions, misprisions, champerties, maintenances, and oppressions," apparently on account of the malice and hatred of his enemies.[86] A general inquest had been ordered in the counties of Norfolk and Suffolk in order to investigate the matter and had acquitted Fastolf of

83. Ibid., 304.

84. Ibid., 304–5.

85. "A nostre seignur le roi et son conseil prie la comune de son roialme, que come nostre dit seignur le roi fait envoier ses justices en pais, ascun fotz son baunk, et ascun foitz autres justices trailbaston et d'autres enquerres, et sur ceo diverses gentz de lour malice et fausyne propre font faire billes en defesance des bones gentz du pais ou les sessions serront, surmettantz par meismes les billes, qe les gentz avant ditz sont conspiratours, confederatours, et meintenours des touz autres mals." *RP*, 2:259, 266.

86. "Item les communes prierent as seignurs du parlement entendre, coment Hugh Fastolf de Grant Jernemuth estoit empeschéz par malice et hayne d'aucuns de ses veisines, ses malveulliantz . . . de diverses extortions, mesprisions, champerties, maintenance, et oppressions." Ibid., 375.

any wrongdoing. Consequently, the commons at the present assembly asked that Fastolf be publicly "restored to his good fame."[87]

At first glance, the evidence of the rolls of parliament and the statute rolls for Edward III's reign may seem an impressive indictment against the maintenance and bastard feudalism that traditionally have been held responsible for a breakdown in law and order in late medieval England. This was not by any means the last the king and his council was to hear from parliament about the evils of maintenance; if anything, the clamor was to get louder. Complaints and statutes against maintenance and the giving of liveries were made in 1377, 1379, 1381, 1389, 1397, 1399, 1401, 1403, 1406, 1411, 1427, 1429, 1461, 1467–68, 1472–73, 1485, and 1495.[88] Nevertheless, most of the complaints about maintenance made under Edward III came at the beginning of the reign, which followed a particularly turbulent period of rule under his father. Moreover, according to the later petitions, many accusations of maintenance were unfounded and were themselves a manipulation of the law. Finally, one must consider this paradox: If maintenance was really so pervasive among the aristocracy, as some scholars contend, how is it that the most powerful maintainers, who would have sat in the House of Lords, and the recipients of such maintenance, the members of the gentry, who in all likelihood were themselves guilty of the practice and who controlled the House of Commons, have legislated against their own self interest?[89] The overmighty subject theory demands that the nobility as a whole, characterized by new bastard feudal ties, be entirely responsible for the perversion of the law and the encouragement of crime, yet this was the very class that clamored in parliament that something be done about these evils.

As early as 1945, the Oxford historian K. B. McFarlane challenged the traditional approach to maintenance and bastard feudalism on two grounds: first, that the money contracts between master and client—commonly known as indentures—which had replaced traditional feudal bonds by the later Middle Ages were not so disruptive of the social order as had been thought. An indenture was often entered into for life and once made, could not be so easily dissolved. Bastard feudalism therefore is not to be understood in the sense of an evil corruption of the old order, as Plummer claimed, but in the sense of being a variation on the theme of an enduring

87. "Em priantz humblement que desicome il y estoit mains vraiement accuséz au dit temps, en esclaundre et diffame de sa persone, q'il ent fust ore en cest parlement restoréz a sa bone fame." Ibid.

88. *RP*, 3:83, 100, 265–66, 339, 345, 404, 428, 444, 452, 478, 523, 601, 662; 4:329–30; 5:487, 633; 6:8, 287–88; *SR*, 2:3, 74–75, 93, 155, 240–41, 589.

89. M. C. Carpenter, "Law, Justice and Landowners in Late Medieval England," *Law and History Review* 1, no. 2 (1983), 226.

and necessary relationship between a lord and his man.

McFarlane's second point is that it is wrong to place the blame for the poor state of order in late medieval England entirely on the nobility. A large portion of the responsibility for good government must by shouldered by the king, who in medieval times was the ultimate source of authority. The steady complaints about maintenance in the rolls from the reign of Edward III on do not necessarily signify an increase in lawlessness among the aristocracy. What the complaints reflect, McFarlane suggests, is a greater awareness among contemporaries of these misdeeds and higher standards of good conduct.[90]

Modern scholarship has tended to confirm McFarlane's reinterpretation of bastard feudalism, if not go beyond it.[91] The bastard feudal ties based on indentures are no longer seen as an aberration of traditional feudalism, but as its logical successor. Indeed, far from weakening the master-client relationship, money contracts strengthened feudal bonds by helping to define the terms and length of service and the conditions under which those bonds could be broken. The origins of bastard feudalism have likewise been steadily pushed back in time until it is seen as nearly as old as feudalism itself. All this makes nonsense of the idea that bastard feudalism somehow corrupted "legitimate" feudal ties that had held the nobility together, and led to its destructive behavior during the fourteenth and fifteenth centuries. If the nobility misbehaved during the later Middle Ages, it had always done so.[92]

Aside from bastard feudalism, McFarlane's work inspired a renewed interest in magnate and gentry families and their affinities. Previously, historians of late medieval politics and society tended to emphasize the centralizing effects of crown policy emanating from Westminster, a view first championed in the nineteenth century by the constitutional historian Bishop William Stubbs.[93] The focus now, however, has shifted from the macrocosm to the microcosm, toward the perspective of local society

90. K. B. McFarlane, "Bastard Feudalism," *Bulletin of the Institute of Historical Research* 20 (1945), 161–80; reprinted in idem, *England in the Fifteenth Century*, 23–43.

91. A good overview of the scholarship up until 1981 is to be found in G. L. Harriss's introduction to McFarlane, *England in the Fifteenth Century*, ix–xxvii. For an overview of the scholarship since then, see M. A. Hicks, *Bastard Feudalism* (London, 1995), 1–42, 110–36.

92. For the major works on the subject, see B. D. Lyon, *From Fief to Indenture: The Transition from Feudal to Non-Feudal Contract in Western Europe* (Cambridge, Mass., 1957); J.M.W. Bean, *The Decline of English Feudalism, 1215–1540* (Manchester, 1968); idem, *From Lord to Patron*; S. L. Waugh, "Tenure to Contract: Lordship and Clientage in Thirteenth-Century England," *EHR*, 101 (1986), 816–39; Coss, "Bastard Feudalism Revised," 21–64; J. G. Bellamy, *Bastard Feudalism and the Law* (London, 1989); D. Crouch, "Debate: Bastard Feudalism Revised: Comment 1," *Past and Present*, no. 131 (1991), 165–77; D. A. Carpenter, "Debate: Bastard Feudalism Revised: Comment 2," *Past and Present*, no. 131 (1991), 177–89; P. R. Coss, "Reply," *Past and Present*, no. 131 (1991), 190–203; Hicks, *Bastard Feudalism*.

93. Stubbs, *The Constitutional History of England*.

in the shires. As a result, studies of individual magnates and gentry communities have blossomed in recent years, studies that have altered fundamentally the way historians view aristocratic violence and the extent of the nobility's responsibility for medieval crime.

In general, the new research on magnate and gentry relationships consists of biographies of great magnates and their affinities and of local studies of gentry society within a particular county or group of counties of England. These studies, naturally, tend to be sympathetic to the concerns and aspirations of the upper class; as a result, they do not view the nobility as the irresponsible authors of late medieval disorder and rebellion, as is fashionable among the traditional interpreters of bastard feudalism. On the contrary, great magnates often provided the only authority strong enough to maintain order in the shires; far from trying to undermine the crown, they depended on a strong monarchy to help maintain stability and act as final arbiter in disputes. The gentry, on the other hand, were not so beholden to their social superiors as has been thought. In many parts of the country they maintained a striking degree of independence and were therefore not so protected from criminal prosecution as the critics of maintenance believe. Often members of the gentry community were able to police themselves.[94]

Indeed, it has been argued that magnates had a disincentive to maintain criminals among their retinues. Simon Walker, in his study of the duchy of Lancaster under John of Gaunt, Edward III's third son, from 1376 until 1399, contends that if the duke tolerated too much corruption among his officials, his tenants and the local gentry would begin to look elsewhere for justice. In a sense, then, Gaunt was just as much a victim of his retainers' depredations, both in terms of lost revenue and lost connections, as were the actual plaintiffs. A delicate balance therefore had to be maintained by a great magnate such as the duke between showing good lordship to his followers and acting as lawgiver to the shire.[95] It was a position the duke took publicly at the parliament of 1384. Gaunt, in response to complaints by the Commons about maintenance, asserted that

---

94. A sampling of magnate studies includes M. C. Carpenter, *Locality and Polity: A Study of Warwickshire Landed Society, 1401–1499* (Cambridge, 1992); idem, "The Beauchamp Affinity: A Study of Bastard Feudalism at Work," *EHR* 95 (1980), 514–32; Walker, *Lancastrian Affinity*; Goodman, *John of Gaunt*. For the gentry, see Saul, *Knights and Esquires*; idem, *Scenes from Provincial Life: Knightly Families in Sussex, 1280–1400* (Oxford, 1986); M. J. Bennett, *Community, Class and Careerism: Cheshire and Lancashire Society in the Age of Sir Gawain and the Green Knight* (Cambridge, 1983); S. M. Wright, *The Derbyshire Gentry in the Fifteenth Century* (Derbyshire Record Society, 8, 1983); Payling, *Political Society*.

95. Walker, *Lancastrian Affinity*, 181, 248; idem, "Lordship and Lawlessness in the Palatinate of Lancaster, 1370–1400," *Journal of British Studies* 28, no. 4 (1989), 331–32, 335–36, 348.

magnates were perfectly capable of regulating their retinues and that he would set the example.[96] In at least one instance, the gentry may have modified their behavior in order to conform to the duke's standards.[97]

Even those magnates who conform to the pattern of the overmighty subject need to be understood in context. From 1400 until 1433, the Courtenays, earls of Devon, were unable to provide political leadership in the county as one earl after another proved inadequate. As a result, when Thomas Courtenay succeeded to the earldom in 1433, he found a changed political landscape, one consisting of a number of powerful patrons besides himself who could rely on active support from the crown. Earl Thomas tried to reestablish his authority by force, as when his men collided with those of his chief rival, William, Lord Bonville, in 1455. But Courtenay, and most of his colleagues in Devonshire, hesitated to start a civil war so characteristic of the War of the Roses. Instead, the earl exhausted all avenues of peace before embarking on his bloody course. Indeed, it was the fact that a great magnate had been excluded from his rightful position of power that led to violence in the county.[98]

Perhaps the very model of overweening magnate power is George Plantagenet, duke of Clarence. In 1477 he forced a jury to convict his servant, Ankarette Twynho, whom he suspected of poisoning his wife.[99] Nevertheless, there was another side to Clarence, one that showed himself as a discriminating and fair arbitrator, who endeavored to settle feuds and preserve peace.[100]

The role of magnates and gentry in arbitration has been another means by which historians have attacked the traditional assumptions about a violent medieval English nobility. Previously, scholars assumed that violence inevitably resulted when medieval litigants became frustrated with the slow progress of their suits before the bench. Their impatience expressed itself in resorts to "self-help" of a forceful nature, since the law apparently could not help them resolve their grievances.[101] In recent years, however, greater emphasis has been placed on peaceful alternatives to the law that medieval men found to their conflicts.

96. *The Westminster Chronicle, 1381–1394*, ed. L. C. Hector and B. F. Harvey (Oxford, 1982), 82–83.

97. Goodman, *John of Gaunt*, 334. For other examples, see Hicks, *Bastard Feudalism*, 126–28.

98. M. Cherry, "The Courtenay Earls of Devon: The Formation and Disintegration of a Late Medieval Aristocratic Affinity," *Southern History* 1 (1979), 71–97; idem, "The Struggle for Power in Mid-Fifteenth Century Devonshire," in R. A Griffiths, ed., *Patronage, the Crown and the Provinces in Later Medieval England* (Gloucester, 1981), 123–44.

99. Bellamy, *Crime and Public Order*, 24.

100. M. A. Hicks, "Restraint, Mediation and Private Justice: George, Duke of Clarence as 'Good Lord,'" *Journal of Legal History* 4, no. 2 (1983), 69.

101. Bellamy, *Crime and Public Order*, 25; Hanawalt, "Fur-Collar Crime," 11–12.

Arbitration was an informal procedure that lay outside the jurisdiction of the English common law but had its origins as early as the twelfth century in the canon law administered by the Church. The two parties who submitted their suit to arbitration agreed to abide by the award of a third party, often pledging a sum of money as a guarantee of future good faith. The arbitrator could be a single person or a panel of judges, chosen usually by the consent of both parties, who often attempted to decide a case in a way that would be agreeable to both sides. Arbitration was popular because it was quick and thus avoided the expense of long, drawn-out litigation and, even if it did punish one of the disputants, usually tried to mollify the loser by offering something in the way of compensation. Unfortunately, because of the informal and voluntary nature of the exercise, the settlement by arbitration was not legally binding and could easily break down, although many litigants used arbitration in conjunction with legal procedures.[102]

That arbitration was a genuine force in medieval English society has been shown by the legal historian, Edward Powell. Powell presents a radically different view of arbitration: as a permanent feature of the medieval English legal landscape rather than a temporary aberration of it, one with a long and continuous history alongside the institutional development of the common law. Many litigants used arbitration as part of an overall strategy that included a formal suit in court and, on occasion, violence. But arbitration presented a number of advantages, including speed, flexibility, and reduced expense, which often made it a favored alternative over the other two.[103] Some of the great lords and their councils who acted as arbitrators in late medieval England include Richard, duke of York, Richard Beauchamp, earl of Warwick, Humphrey, duke of Buckingham, Humphrey, duke of Gloucester, and George, duke of Clarence.[104]

To sum up, then, the most recent historiography on magnate and gentry behavior in England during the later Middle Ages has focused attention on their legitimate concerns and responsibilities within the context

---

102. E. Powell, "Arbitration and the Law in England in the Late Middle Ages," *TRHS*, 5th series, 33 (1983), 53–57; idem, "Settlement of Disputes by Arbitration in Fifteenth-Century England," *Law and History Review* 2, no. 1 (1984), 33–37.

103. Powell, "Arbitration and the Law," 49–53, 66–7; idem, "Settlement of Disputes," 21–26, 39–41.

104. J. T. Rosenthal, "Feuds and Private Peace-Making: A Fifteenth-Century Example," *Nottingham Medieval Studies* 14 (1970), 84–90; C. Rawcliffe, "The Great Lord as Peacekeeper: Arbitration by English Noblemen and their Councils in the Later Middle Ages," in J. A. Guy and H. G. Beale, eds., *Law and Social Change in British History: Papers Presented to the Bristol Legal History Conference* (London, 1984), 34–54; Hicks, "Restraint, Mediation and Private Justice," 56–71.

of their local communities and emphasized their role as peacekeepers in arbitration. On the whole, the late medieval English nobility seem to have been a conservative and peaceful lot, even during the upheavals of the fifteenth century. When violence did break out, it was usually a last resort employed when all other options had failed.[105] Far from consistently trying to undermine the law, the nobility of late medieval England engaged in a complex dialogue with the crown concerning the maintenance of order; justice, to a large degree, depended on local cooperation, although it is clear that people still looked to the king as the ultimate guarantor of peace. Indeed, much of the initiative for improving order in the shires during the reign of Edward III came from the Commons in parliament; nevertheless, it could be argued that it was Edward's failure to enforce the new legislation that kept for fourteenth-century England its violent reputation.[106]

Therefore, those relatively few noblemen who did commit crimes, such as the notorious "robber barons," Sir John Moleyns of Stoke Poges in Buckinghamshire and Sir Thomas Bradeston of Gloucestershire, or the gentry outlaw gangs such as the Folvilles of Leicestershire and the Coterels from the Midlands, seem to have been the exception rather than the rule. Nonetheless, these exceptions could make an impression that far exceeded their numbers. Moleyns, for example, terrorized the tenants of Buckinghamshire unimpeded between 1330 and 1340. Prior to that, in 1326, he had murdered his wife's uncle and nephew in order to gain the manor of Stoke Poges itself.[107] Bradeston, another favorite of King Edward III, was said to be "like a little saint" at the king's court, but "in his own country, like a raging lion."[108] The Folvilles and Coterels combined forces in 1332 to kidnap a puisne justice of the king's bench, Sir Richard Willoughby, and ransom him for the enormous sum of 1300 marks, or £866.[109]

105. P. C. Maddern, "Violence, Crime and Public Disorder in East Anglia, 1422–1442" (D.Phil. diss., Oxford, 1984), 299–300; S. J. Payling, "Inheritance and Local Politics in the Later Middle Ages: The Case of Ralph, Lord Cromwell, and the Heriz Inheritance," *Nottingham Medieval Studies* 30 (1986), 94–95; A. Smith, "Litigation and Politics: Sir John Fastolf's Defence of his English Property," in T. Pollard, ed., *Property and Politics: Essays in Later Medieval English History* (Gloucester, 1984), 73; E. Powell, *Kingship, Law and Society: Criminal Justice in the Reign of Henry V* (Oxford, 1989), 97.

106. See pages 191–201.

107. N. Fryde, "A Medieval Robber Baron: Sir John Molyns of Stoke Poges, Buckinghamshire," in R. F. Hunnisett and J. B. Post , eds., *Medieval Legal Records Edited in Memory of C.A.F. Meekings* (London, 1978), 202–5.

108. Saul, *Knights and Esquires*, 77.

109. Stones, "The Folvilles," 119–22; Bellamy, "The Coterel Gang," 707–11.

Corruption of the Law

But if unruly magnates and gentry were not the leading, or at least the only, cause of medieval English crime, who or what else was? A clue is provided by the complaints in parliament about maintenance. At the heart of these complaints was the charge that certain men were subverting the law in order to protect their followers, who could then commit crimes and get away with them. In fact, petitions and statutes in parliament addressing corruption of the law, whether of its officers—judges, sheriffs, gaolers, and coroners—or through the issuance of too many pardons, were more numerous during the reign of Edward III than those concerning maintenance.

An especially popular target of the Commons' petitions were corrupt sheriffs. At the parliament held in the first year of Edward's reign, 1327, the Commons complained that "false sheriffs," "false guardians of the gaols," and coroners conspired to use evidence supplied by approvers, suspect criminals who had turned king's evidence, in order to indict, imprison, and fine innocent people.[110] In 1334, a year that also saw complaint against "false jurors," the Commons asked that sheriffs be appointed for one year only, a request that was to be repeated in 1343, 1346, 1354, 1355, 1368, 1371, 1372, and 1376.[111] In 1343 it asked that anyone accused of "confederacy or conspiracy" not be appointed sheriff or any other of the king's officers.[112] Likewise, in 1354, the Commons demanded that "the sheriffs be good men and loyal, having good renown."[113]

The crown responded to these complaints by ordering an inquiry throughout England into the abuses committed by sheriffs, gaolers, coroners, and other royal officers: In 1327 the investigation was to be conducted by the justices of the central courts, of assize, and of gaol delivery and in 1330 by those of oyer and terminer.[114] Also in 1330, a statute was enacted that made it an offense for sheriffs and gaolers to demand fees before accepting suspect criminals into their gaols.[115] In 1340 another stat-

---

110. "Et pur ceo qe leaus gentz sount sovent grevetz, et malement enprisonéz, a grant anientissement de lour estatz par . . . d'apellours qe par les faux viscountes, et faux gardeins des gaoles, sount fait a force, et par outrageous distresses . . . de coronours." *RP*, 2:9.

111. Ibid., 142, 161, 261, 265, 296, 308, 313, 334–35, 376.

112. "Item pri la commune, que nul de ceux qi sont atteintz de confederacie ou conspiracie n'eit mes office de nostre seignur le roi, ne des roignes, ne des autres grantz de la terre, ne des visconts, ne des eschetours." Ibid., 142.

113. "Item prie la dite commune . . . que les viscontes soient bones gentz et loialx, eiantz bon renoun." Ibid., 261.

114. Ibid., 12, 60.

115. *SR*, 1:264.

ute confirmed the right of sheriffs to have custody of the town gaols, but threatened them with "judgement of life and of member" if any of their prisoners were compelled to turn approver.[116] Statutes also were passed against corrupt jurors: In 1327 the crown granted that a writ of attaint could be sued to recover damages incurred by the false accusation of jurors in cases brought on a writ of trespass.[117] In 1331 the writ of attaint was granted in all suits of trespass above 40s. and in 1354, in all such cases.[118] Also in 1331, it was enacted that jurors convicted of taking bribes could not sit on any jury and would be subject to imprisonment and a fine.[119]

The highest judicial officers, the justices, were not exempt from criticism. In 1346 a special Ordinance for the Justices was drawn up in order to address, according to the preamble, "divers complaints" made to the king about bribery, or maintenance, of the bench. All judges were required to swear an oath to the king, in which they loftily declared that they would "do equal law and execution of right, to all his subjects, rich and poor, without having regard to any person."[120] They promised not to accept gifts or bribes or take retainers of fees or robes from any man, nor give advice in cases prosecuted by the crown. Furthermore, they would endeavor to arrest those who sought to intimidate the court by force. Any justice who betrayed his oath would be "at the king's will, of body, lands, and goods."[121]

Edward III's justices seem to have been in dire need of reformation; perhaps at no other time was the bench so unpopular as during his reign, judging from the attacks and indignities it suffered. The kidnapping and ransom of Sir Richard Willoughby by the Folville and Coterel gangs in 1332 already has been mentioned. At his trial in 1340, it was alleged that Willoughby had "sold the laws as if they had been oxen or cattle" during his term as chief justice of the king's bench.[122] Justices were verbally abused in the streets, in the courts, and even in their homes.[123] In one instance, this had fatal results, as when in 1359 Justice Thomas Seton was stabbed in the belly at his home in Fleet Street, London.[124] But probably the most outrageous insult came in 1344, when shortly after the king's bench had left Ipswich, Suffolk, one of its officers, John de Holtby, was killed and his murderers feted by the townsmen, who gave them "presents such as food

116. Ibid., 284.
117. Ibid., 253.
118. Ibid., 267, 346.
119. Ibid., 267.
120. Ibid., 303–5.
121. Ibid., 305–6.
122. J. R. Maddicott, *Law and Lordship: Royal Justices as Retainers in Thirteenth- and Fourteenth-Century England* (Past and Present Supplement no. 4, Oxford, 1978), 43.
123. *Select Cases*, 3:cxxxvi; 5:121–23; 6:xxvi–xxvii, 29–30.
124. *CPR*, 1358–61, 280.

and drink and gold and silver and sang so many songs of rejoicing in their honour there that it was as if God had come down from heaven."[125] In mock imitation of the king's justice, the culprits sat on the steps of the town hall and summoned the chief justice, Sir William Shareshull, to appear on penalty of £100 and another justice, Sir William de Notton, to appear on penalty of £40. When asked why they did not arrest any of the murderers or their accomplices, the bailiffs of the town replied that the murderers' supporters were so many that it was outside their power, especially since they were old and feeble men.[126]

Finally, the Commons in parliament petitioned that pardons not be granted to convicted felons, a request it made in 1334, 1339, and 1346.[127] The Commons felt that pardons too lightly granted encouraged offenders, but the crown used them to recruit soldiers for its wars, since a criminal could often obtain a pardon in return for military service. Nevertheless, the crown forswore granting pardons in statutes passed in 1328, 1330, 1336, and 1340.[128]

How the crown enforced this legislation, and others concerning justice, and whether such measures were effective are issues that are discussed in Chapter 8.[129] For the moment, however, it has been shown that corruption of the law and of its officers was a substantial concern of members of Edward III's parliament and figured large in its legislative agenda. But those members represented a minority of the population at large, namely the upper echelons of society, the great lords and the gentry. Was legal corruption simply an elitist concern or did it have wider resonance?

Popular Complaints in Literature

More so than the issue of maintenance, the subject of bought justice found a popular outlet outside the petitions in parliament. In particular, complaint about corruption of the law was expressed in three forms: the so-called "poems of social protest"; the writings of clerical moralists such as John Bromyard, William Langland, and John Gower; and the famous outlaw ballads. Each of these will be discussed in turn.

Poems or songs giving voice to popular grievances in medieval England survive from the thirteenth to the fifteenth centuries and were writ-

125. *Select Cases*, 6:37.
126. Ibid., 37–38.
127. *RP*, 2:104, 161, 376.
128. *SR*, 1:257, 264, 275, 286.
129. See pages 193–98.

ten in Latin, Anglo-Norman French, and Old English. The earliest date from the reign of Edward I toward the end of the thirteenth century and the beginning of the fourteenth. Except for the *Song Against the Retinues of the Great*, they mainly address oppressions under the king's laws or under his taxes. The *Song on the Venality of the Judges*, dated to the early fourteenth century and composed in Latin, is a long diatribe against the entire judicial system, accusing not only judges but also sheriffs and court clerks. The message of the poem is simple: If one has money or gifts, one's case is heard speedily, but if one is poor, his case is heard last or not at all. Sometimes even hospitality toward the traveling justices is not enough; jewels must be distributed to their followers and robes to their wives.[130] A more subtle, allegorical approach is taken by *A Song of the Times*, also attributed to Edward I's reign, in which the lion, as king, judges the fox and wolf, both well-known criminals but who are acquitted through presents of birds and sheep. However, the ass, whose only crime is to eat grass but who has committed the unpardonable sin of bringing no gifts, promptly is sentenced to death and executed.[131]

Moving into the later fourteenth and fifteenth centuries, with the advent of the written English word, the *London Lickpenny* tells the story of a poor country bumpkin who journeys to the big city and receives nothing but an education in the ways of the world:

> tyll at the kynges bench I was come.
> before the Iudge I kneled anon,
> and prayd hym for gods sake to take heede.
> but, for lack of mony, I myght not speede.[132]

Another poem, *Truth is Unpopular*, also written in English, lists "men of lawe" among those who refuse to give an audience to the allegorical figure of Truth.[133]

The biting, satirical tone of these poems is reflected in another genre, the writings of clerical moralists such as the Dominican preacher John Bromyard, whose *Summa Predicantium* is attributed to the middle of the fourteenth century.[134] Bromyard, writing in Latin, attacks the retinues of the great, whom he compares to hounds, falcons, and locusts in their

130. *The Political Songs of England*, ed. T. Wright (Camden Society, 1839), 224–30.
131. Ibid., 197–201.
132. *Historical Poems of the Fourteenth and Fifteenth Centuries*, ed. R. H. Robbins (New York, 1959), 131.
133. Ibid., 146.
134. J. R. Maddicott, "Poems of Social Protest in Early Fourteenth-Century England," in W. M. Ormrod, ed., *England in the Fourteenth Century: Proceedings of the 1985 Harlaxton Symposium* (Woodbridge, Suffolk, 1986), 134.

greedy desire to prey on the poor.[135] But what lies behind such evil maintenance, argues Bromyard, is the fact that lords can protect their followers through bribery of the bench. Like the *Song on the Venality of the Judges,* Bromyard sees the whole judicial system as corrupt: Justices, juries, and lawyers all value money more than the truth. This produces a dangerous inequity, for the poor see one justice applied to themselves and another applied to the rich: "The poor man, indeed, if he steal the rich man's goods, is hung. The rich man is not punished at all for seizing the goods of the poor, even when he is worthy of the gallows."[136] The only true justice, according to Bromyard, occurs in heaven, where the victims will be able to turn the tables on their oppressors: "And with boldness will they be able to put their plaint before God and seek justice, speaking with Christ the judge, and reciting each in turn the injury from which they specially suffered."[137] God is the only incorruptible judge, before whom no riches will avail.

Another outraged clerical moralist, William Langland, wrote what is considered to be one of the masterpieces of later medieval English literature, *Piers Plowman.* A long allegorical poem in twenty-two chapters, *Piers Plowman* survives in three versions, known as the A, B, and C texts (all by the same author), written between 1360 and 1387.[138] It is a wide-ranging denunciation of the abuses of the age, and in Passus II, III, and IV, Langland's target is Mede, which for him symbolizes greed, or the desire for worldly goods, a vice that gives rise to a whole host of other abuses.[139] One of these can be considered to be maintenance, since Mede with all her wealth surrounds herself with a large and unruly retinue. But the striking aspect of Mede's retaining in Langland's poem is how many of her rapacious followers are connected with the law. In Passus II, when Mede is preparing herself for her marriage to False, she attracts "sysours" or assize jurors, summoners, sheriffs, beadles, and bailiffs. Her closest councilors are "simonye" and "cyvile," symbolizing canon and civil law. She rides to her marriage on a sheriff, while False rides a "sisoure."[140]

When Mede arrives in London to appear before the king and be betrothed to Conscience in Passus III, she has opportunity to distribute even greater largesse and to more influential people. Justices appear in her chamber, to whom Mede distributes:

---

135. G. R. Owst, *Literature and Pulpit in Medieval England* (Cambridge, 1933), 325.
136. Ibid., 303.
137. Ibid., 300.
138. William Langland, *Piers Plowman: An Edition of the C-Text,* ed. D. Pearsall (Berkeley and Los Angeles, 1979), 9.
139. Ibid., 55, note to line 19. See also J. A. Yunck, *The Lineage of Lady Meed* (Notre Dame, 1963), 5–11, 284–306, and A. P. Baldwin, *The Theme of Government in Piers Plowman* (Cambridge, 1981), 24–38.
140. William Langland, *Piers Plowman,* B-text, Passus II, lines 51–63, 161–64.

> Coupes of clene golde and coppis of silver,
> Rynges with rubies and ricchesses manye,
> The leste man of here meyne a motoun of golde.[141]

They assure her they will smooth her way to a wedding with Conscience, but when she is presented at court, Conscience refuses her. Among his objections to the match is Mede's corrupting influence on the law, pervading almost the entire hierarchy of the judiciary, from judges and sheriffs on down to gaolers and jurors. The result is that False goes free while Truth and Faith are punished.[142] Nevertheless, the corruption is not entirely Mede's fault, for it is well known that the wheels of justice are oiled by money:

> Lawe is so lordeliche and loth to make ende,
> Withoute presentz or pens she pleseth wel fewe.[143]

Embodying nearly all the complaints of moral satire are the poems of John Gower. His *Vox Clamantis*, a long Latin poem in seven books composed between 1378 and 1381,[144] is similar to *Piers Plowman* in that it is a dream vision of the poet who attacks the failure of each estate to live up to its social responsibilities. In book 7, Gower rails against the judiciary and its officers. In particular he despises lawyers, who are motivated only by their all-consuming desire for money. In chapter 1, he compares them to whores, who will sell their services to anyone for gold; in chapter 2, to hawks and wolves who devour innocent doves and lambs; in chapter 3, to a basilisk who poisons the air with its breath or to a fox who uses trickery to seize its prey.[145] Gower believes that the law can be good and just, but it is twisted and turned upside down by its ministers:

> Lawyers are clouds which darken the skies so that no one can see the light of the sun. For they obfuscate the clear justice of the law, yet their abominable darkness claims to be daylight. Splendor loses its radiance among these men; truth tells lies, fraud denies that honesty exists.[146]

Corruption of the law starts with lawyers, Gower explains in chapter 4, because they work their way up the judicial hierarchy, finally becom-

---

141. Ibid., lines 22–24.
142. Ibid., Passus III, lines 13–19, 133–40, 154–56.
143. Ibid., lines 160–61.
144. John Gower, *The Major Latin Works*, trans. E. W. Stockton (Seattle, Wash.,1962), 11–12.
145. Ibid., 221–24.
146. Ibid., 225.

ing the most powerful members of the bench, the judges. Hence, law is kept a prisoner to greed and can only be unlocked with a "golden key." Gower delivers a warning to justices in chapter 5, that they in turn will be judged by God. Once in heaven they will tremble with fear, for there true justice reigns and people are judged on their merits, not their goods. The other members of the court who habitually take bribes, sheriffs, bailiffs, and jurors, likewise are castigated by Gower in chapter 6. Here the poet gives voice to the climax of his indignation, bewailing the injustices done to the common people and comparing their oppressions to Christ's betrayal by Judas. Like the traitor of God, those "who sell justice to the wicked" will share his place in hell.[147]

The epitome of antijudicial literature, the popular outlaw ballads, have a long pedigree, finding antecedents in songs celebrating Hereward the Wake, the last Saxon to resist the first Norman king, William the Conqueror, in the fens of Ely during the latter half of the eleventh century.[148] The basic plot of these ballads as they evolved in the later Middle Ages is simple and well known: A member of the medieval aristocracy, usually from the lower orders of knight or yeoman, is deprived of his rightful inheritance or suffers some other injustice and seeks refuge in the forest where he cannot be hunted down. He is an outlaw, a legal term that means that he has been summoned before the court and refused to appear, so that he is declared literally "outside" the king's law and must forfeit his possessions and, if caught, his life. His enemy is the sheriff or another corrupt representative of the legal system who must be overturned before justice can prevail. As an expression of discontent with the law and its officers, there is no more powerful or entertaining complaint than the outlaw ballads.

The hostility toward the common law that is the ballads' trademark first appeared in songs dating from the 1300s, almost a century and a half after Henry II had established the jury system in the Assize of Clarendon in 1166. Another legal innovation, the commissions of trailbaston instituted by Edward I in 1305, were the target of the *Outlaw's Song of Trailbaston*, an Anglo-Norman French poem composed shortly after the commissions had gone into effect.[149] Originally intended to investigate assaults with a heavy club, known as the "baston," the commissions could nevertheless be used against a man whose only crime was "to punish my boy with a cuff or two," as the anonymous author complains.[150] Instead of going to prison, the author announces that he will seek refuge in the

---

147. Ibid., 225–30.
148. M. H. Keen, *The Outlaws of Medieval Legend*, rev. edition (London, 1977), 9–38.
149. *Anglo-Norman Political Songs*, ed. I.S.T. Aspin (Oxford, 1953), 67.
150. Ibid., 73.

"forest of Belregard" where "there is no deceit there nor any bad law."[151] He declares himself a loyal servant of the king, but of the "wicked jurors" who convicted him:

> I will teach them the game of Trailbaston, and I will break their back and rump, their arms and their legs, it would be right; I will cut out their tongue and their mouth into the bargain.[152]

Probably the most violent of the outlaw ballads is *The Tale of Gamelyn*, written in English around the middle of the fourteenth century.[153] Gamelyn, the youngest son of a knight, is disinherited by his elder brother and proves his prowess throughout the poem with plenty of breaking and cracking of limbs. When he comes out of the woods at the head of an outlaw band to seek revenge on his brother, now sheriff, at the next sitting of the court, he does so with an orgy of violence that overturns the whole, corrupt system. Without a word, Gamelyn approaches the justice sitting on his bench, cleaves "his cheeke-boon" and then throws "him over the barre and his arm to-brak."[154] Gamelyn next sits in his place and condemns the justice, his brother, the sheriff, and all twelve jurors to be hung "by the nekke and nought by the purs."[155] The sentence is speedily carried out despite the brother's pleas for mercy, for the punishment is just. Right justice triumphs completely when Gamelyn is made chief justice and all his fellow outlaws pardoned by the king and given offices.[156]

Of course, the most popular and most famous of the outlaw ballads is the *Gest of Robyn Hode*. First written down in English during the latter half of the fifteenth century, the Robin Hood ballads nevertheless are thought to have circulated in spoken form during the reign of Edward III, perhaps as early as the 1330s.[157] The story of the outlaw Robin Hood who hides out in Sherwood Forest with his band of "merry men" and struggles against the evil sheriff of Nottingham is too well known to be recounted here.[158] What is more interesting is the historiographical debate surrounding the ballads, such as whether there was a historical figure correspond-

151. Ibid.

152. Ibid., 74.

153. R. W. Kaeuper, "An Historian's Reading of *The Tale of Gamelyn*," *Medium Aevum* 52 (1983), 51.

154. Geoffrey Chaucer, *Complete Works*, ed. W. W. Skeat, 7 vols. (Oxford, 1894–97), 4:666, lines 850–52.

155. Ibid., 667, line 885.

156. Ibid., 666–67, lines 873–76, 891–94.

157. Keen, *Outlaws*, 135; J. R. Maddicott, "The Birth and Setting of the Ballads of Robin Hood," *EHR* 93 (1978), 198.

158. The original medieval Robin Hood ballads are printed in *Rymes of Robin Hood*, ed. R. B. Dobson and J. Taylor (London, 1976).

ing to the fictional hero, or the exact setting and date of origin of the narrative.[159] More relevant to our discussion is the hypothetical audience of the ballads. Who listened to the *Gest*, or to whom was it addressed?

That question has been the subject of much debate among Robin Hood scholars. In 1961 Maurice Keen put forward the thesis that the ballads were an "expression of peasant discontent," an argument he has since considerably revised.[160] Although the "stealing from the rich and giving to the poor" style of altruism lends itself to a proletarian interpretation, this is more a product of Hollywood's version of Robin Hood than the hero of the medieval ballads, who is more ruthless and violent. The ballads may very well have been disseminated through "the communal story telling of country people . . . at rustic festivals," as Keen originally argued.[161] But J. C. Holt contends that it is just as likely that they were also sung by professional minstrels to aristocratic and yeoman households, who had the money to patronize such entertainments.[162] Therefore, the audience of the Robin Hood ballads was not strictly confined to the poor and oppressed, but seems to have included all social classes.

The *Gest*, in fact, had almost universal appeal because its subject was one nearly everyone could identify with: corruption of the law and of its ministers. By one estimate, more than fifteen thousand people litigated before the court of common pleas during the 1330s, which implies that a wide range of folk, not just the first estate, experienced justice either as plaintiffs, defendants, or spectators.[163] Moreover, contrary to their portrayal in petitions against maintenance, aristocratic criminals are idolized in the outlaw ballads, which probably reflects to some extent the audience's sympathies. In 1331 the chronicler Henry Knighton wrote approvingly of the outlaw Richard Folville that he was "a fierce, daring, and impudent man."[164] Even William Langland, in his depiction of an ideal state in Passus XXI in *Piers Plowman*, would punish "false men with Foleviles lawes."[165]

A similar argument can be extended to the poems of social protest and the writings of the clerical moralists. While these works seem to express grievances on behalf of the peasantry, they were, in fact, written by, and

---

159. Maddicott, "Ballads of Robin Hood," 276–99; Keen, *Outlaws*, 174–90; J. C. Holt, *Robin Hood* (London, 1982), 40–61; J. G. Bellamy, *Robin Hood: An Historical Enquiry* (London and Sydney, 1985), 1–42; R. B. Dobson and J. Taylor, "The Medieval Origins of the Robin Hood Legend: A Reassessment," *Journal of Northern History* 7 (1972), 1–30; idem, *Rymes of Robyn Hood: An Introduction to the English Outlaw* (Gloucester, 1989), 1–36.

160. Keen, *Outlaws*, xiii–xvi, 145–90.

161. Ibid., xiii.

162. Holt, *Robin Hood*, 110.

163. R. C. Palmer, *The Whilton Dispute, 1264–1380: A Social-Legal Study of Dispute Settlement in Medieval England* (Princeton, 1984), 8.

164. Knighton, *Chronicon*, 1:460.

165. Langland, *Piers Plowman*, C-text, Passus XXI, line 247.

for, the up-and-coming middle class of literate townsmen and gentry.[166] "I cry out what the voice of the people cries out," wrote John Gower in book 6, chapter 1 of *Vox Clamantis*.[167] However, he recognized that if things were to improve, he had to bring the people's grievances to the attention of those in power. "I therefore," Gower continued, "direct my writings in particular to those whom the sin of avarice leads astray, and not to the others."[168] Gower's intended audience were the lawyers, justices, and sheriffs whom he was trying to reform. Although it may seem incompatible, these champions of the poor were patronized even by the aristocracy. In 1393 Gower dedicated his *Vox Clamantis* to Henry Bolingbroke, earl of Derby, and Thomas Arundel, archbishop of York.[169] Another fiery moralist, John Wycliffe, was protected from the stake by John of Gaunt, duke of Lancaster, until the former's natural death in 1384.

If corruption of legal officers is a more popular source of complaint in late medieval England than maintenance or aristocratic crime, then this would indicate that the majority of men viewed the former as the underlying cause of their troubled times. Society seems to have been preoccupied with the failure of the legal system to deliver justice and punish criminals—a serious indictment of the king's peace. Yet, the burgeoning sizes of the plea rolls by the fourteenth century may indicate that people were pleading before the courts in ever increasing numbers. In large part this discrepancy is explained by the fact that even though the courts were perhaps ineffectual in providing justice, they still served a useful purpose to their litigants. Many suits before the bench were merely part of an overall strategy to persuade the opposing party to compromise, usually by extralegal means such as arbitration.[170]

Arbitration provided a degree of flexibility that no doubt allowed many people to live with the law. Others expressed their frustration by resorting to violent self-help. Still others had to remain discontented. One of these last was De Lisle. Shortly after his conviction in 1355 for the arson of Lady Wake's houses, he approached the king in person with a complaint that he could not get justice, a charge that Edward took very much to heart. In a fascinating exchange of words, Edward offered to mediate in the dispute. The bishop refused the offer, perhaps because he suspected that the king could not remain neutral in an affair that involved his own cousin.[171]

166. J. Coleman, *English Literature in History, 1350–1400: Medieval Readers and Writers* (London, 1981), 64.

167. Gower, *Latin Works*, 220.

168. Ibid.

169. Coleman, *English Literature*, 127.

170. Powell, "Arbitration and the Law," 62–67; idem, "Settlement of Disputes," 39–41.

Here, on a very personal and at the highest level, we have epitomized the common complaint of medieval Englishmen against twisted justice.

Equally significant is the reaction of De Lisle's colleagues to his predicament. Whatever the issue of the bishop's guilt in the Lady Wake affair, the steadfast refusal of his fellow magnates and even churchmen to support his cause suggests that they disapproved of crime in general and in particular when associated with one of their community. Respect for the king and his popularity also played its part in isolating De Lisle.[172] From below, the bishop's tenants, particularly in Huntingdonshire, came forward soon after his fall from the king's grace to denounce what they perceived as his oppressive lordship.[173] Both classes clearly expected better behavior of a magnate and a bishop.

171. See pages 129–30.
172. See pages 167–74, 182–85.
173. See pages 144–47.

4

The Dispute with
Richard Spynk

The medieval city of Norwich was extremely fortunate to have as one of its citizens a man called Richard Spynk, for it is doubtful if anyone in Norwich during the fourteenth century did more to fulfill his civic duty than this wealthy and prominent merchant. When a tax was levied in the mid-fourteenth century to raise 500 marks (just over £333), for example, Spynk paid the greatest personal share, £9 and 12 marks (a total of £17), indicating that he was the richest citizen in the city at that time.[1] In 1344–45, Spynk provided that the city's history be commemorated in the "Old Free Book," one of the most valuable sources of Norwich's history to survive the Middle Ages.[2]

But the merchant's greatest contribution to civic pride was the 1343 completion of the city walls. In that year, Spynk's outlays on behalf of its defense were recorded in an indenture between him and the city that was copied into the Old Free Book. Spynk paid for all those who could not contribute 5s. toward the £200 murage to be raised for the building effort; paid for all those who could not afford 1s. for the king's tenth; paid approximately £20, representing the difference between expenses totaling 50 marks (just over £33), and £13 contributed by the city, to help build the wall between Coslany Gate and the River Wensum; and paid £100 of his own money to match the £100 that was all the city was able to raise from

1. NRO, Norwich City Records, 7(i): Assessment to Raise 500 Marks, 1350–51. An inscription on the outside of the roll erroneously states that it is "an assessment made to raise the sum of 100 marks." The pre-1835 sectional lists for Norwich City Records assign it a hypothetical date of 1350–51. However, the roll may date prior to 1343, since by the charter made in that year to commemorate Spynk's works upon the walls, the city exempted Spynk and his heirs from all future taxes.

2. *The Records of the City of Norwich*, ed. W. Hudson and J. C. Tingey, 2 vols. (Norwich, 1906–10), 1:xlii–iii, 261.

the murage. Moreover, Spynk personally took charge of the construction work since no one else was willing to do it. The work he supervised included the building of at least forty-five rods of wall; the strengthening of several towers and gates with portcullis machinery and a covering of timber, board, and lead; the provision of the towers and gates with engines of war such as *espringalds* (a type of catapult), *grauntz arblastes* (large crossbows), and *gogiouns* (projectiles); and the defense of the city's port by "two great chains of good Spanish iron" wound by a windlass across the River Wensum so that "no ship nor barge nor boat might come in or depart without leave."[3]

In gratitude the city agreed to exempt Spynk and his heirs from all future taxes and civic duties, and in addition, any merchant doing business with Spynk was to have free access to the city with his goods. These benefits were to extend to female heirs should Spynk die without male issue.[4] Although Spynk clearly profited from his generosity, his efforts and expenditure were considerable and betray some altruism. His activities on this occasion suggest that he was one of the first citizens of Norwich, both in terms of wealth and reputation.

Ironically, just three years after his completion of the city's defenses, it was Spynk himself who was to need defending. Less than a year after De Lisle had been enthroned in Ely Cathedral in November 1345, Spynk submitted his first complaints against the bishop in August 1346. If the merchant is to be believed, he was the victim of a violent and bloodthirsty campaign of physical intimidation masterminded by the newly created bishop of Ely. De Lisle's men were said to have stolen hundreds of pounds' worth of Spynk's sheep, cattle, and other goods. Spynk attempted to obtain redress through an extraordinary legal process known as a special commission of oyer and terminer, in which judges were assigned by the crown to investigate the matter. Before these commissions could go ahead, however, De Lisle's men, according to Spynk, resorted to strong-arm tactics to prevent him from pursuing his suit, tactics that allegedly included ambushes, death threats, bodily assaults, and posse-style manhunts throughout the county of Norfolk. The situation became so bad, Spynk said, that he was forced to live like a man besieged, not daring to venture out of the protection afforded by the city walls he had helped to build. As a result, he was not able to sell his merchandise or go about his ordinary business, losing much money in potential revenue. The feud dragged on

3. Ibid., 2:216–19; NRO, Old Free Book, fol. 4v; Domesday Book, fol. 33v. For a description of the Norwich walls, see H. L. Turner, *Town Defences in England and Wales: An Architectural and Documentary Study, A.D. 900–1500* (London, 1971), 129–38.

4. *Records of Norwich*, 1:220–22.

for seven years, at one point coming before the highest court in the land, the king's council in parliament, and finally was resolved in 1352 by a private out-of-court settlement.

It may seem improbable that an upright and law-abiding pillar of his community like Richard Spynk became involved in all this violent feuding with a bishop of Ely. For that matter, it is equally odd that De Lisle, so recently elevated to the wealthy and prestigious see of Ely, should come to be accused of leading a campaign of terror against a Norwich merchant. This chapter will attempt to determine if the bishop was guilty as charged, and if so, what induced him to attack the first citizen of Norwich. But beyond the personal issue of De Lisle's guilt or innocence, his legal feud with Spynk set an important precedent that was to have a profound impact on contemporary society. The judgment handed down in the Spynk case upheld *excepcio villenagii,* a legal procedure whereby lords in the Middle Ages could take exception to villeins impleading their masters in court. The debate between Spynk and De Lisle before the king's council in 1348 was therefore a test case for determining whether lords could still claim *excepcio villenagii* in the face of rising peasant challenges to such an objection. De Lisle and his attorneys were able to exploit this facet of the suit in order to help him win out over his rival.

Terror at Norwich and Dickleburgh

The legal, and sometimes not so legal, feud between De Lisle and Spynk first came to light through Spynk's purchase of special commissions of oyer and terminer, a unique category of medieval English legal documents dating back to the reign of Edward I. Few records of the actual sitting of the oyer and terminer courts survive—only an estimated 150 out of many thousands.[5] Usually our knowledge of the commissions comes from the original writ, issued out of chancery and enrolled on the dorse of the patent rolls, which authorized the court of oyer and terminer to be held. The information contained in the commission is very brief: It lists the justices who are to sit on the case, the plaintiff who brought the complaint, and the charge itself. As with other legal documents surviving from this time, the commissions of oyer and terminer present only the point of view of the plaintiff and must be treated accordingly.

The rise in popularity of oyer and terminer coincides with the decline and eventual abandonment of the eyre as a mechanism to investigate crime

---

5. Kaeuper, "Law and Order in Fourteenth-Century England," 755.

in the shires during the late thirteenth and early fourteenth centuries. By the middle of the fourteenth century, however, the total number of commissions issued began to decline: In 1346, the year Spynk purchased his first writ for oyer and terminer, just over 80 commissions were issued, compared to a peak of over 260 in 1327. The initial popularity of oyer and terminer owed much to the speed and success with which a plaintiff could prosecute his case compared to processes in other courts. Before 1360, plaintiffs often could select the justices who would sit on their commission, to be held at a time and place favorable to their cause. The commissions were set in motion by an informal petition, called a *querela*, submitted to the king's council in parliament, or by the purchase of the necessary letters patent for a fine, typically one mark, paid into the chancery. Usually the justices of oyer and terminer sat within months of the commission being issued and, since they often received a portion of the plaintiff's profit, handed down substantial awards. Most of the seekers of oyer and terminer commissions tended to be men of influence, the great lords and gentry who naturally engaged in much litigation over rival claims to land. But a sizable minority of plaintiffs—10 percent between 1358 and 1360—were merchants or townsmen such as Richard Spynk who were as adroit as anyone in manipulating the commissions to their advantage.[6]

Just as quickly as commissions of oyer and terminer began to be extensively used, complaints against them mounted. In 1285 the Second Statute of Westminster declared that henceforth commissions would be granted only in cases of "horrible" trespasses, a condition reaffirmed by the Second Statute of Northampton of 1328. The 1285 statute also stipulated that only justices of the king's bench, court of common pleas, or in eyre were to sit on the commissions.[7] A long petition submitted to the king in parliament in 1315 complained that commissions of oyer and terminer were granted too easily, and to the wrong people. Powerful lords were using them to compel helpless defendants to appear in hostile places where biased judges and jurors "from distant parts who know nothing of the trespass" convict them and award stiff fines.[8] Later in the century, the lords themselves would complain that they, too, were victims of the oyer and terminer process since their villeins were suing out writs against their masters in an attempt to prove their free status.[9] In 1327, a statute granted that a writ of attaint could be sued in oyer and terminer cases. This was in response to yet another complaint about the commissions and for the

6. Ibid., 740–58.
7. *SR*, 1:85, 258.
8. "Et si la partie defendant veigne al jour . . . [the plaintiff] serra procuré une jurre d'estraunge pays, qui riens soit du trespass." *RP*, 1:290.
9. *RP*, 2:180.

first time gave defendants a legal weapon with which to counteract purchase of an oyer and terminer writ.[10]

On 20 August 1346, the crown issued the first special commissions of oyer and terminer to investigate complaints against the bishop by Richard Spynk and his brother, William. Among the five men commissioned to investigate were Sir William Scot, chief justice of the king's bench, Sir William Basset, justice of the king's bench, and Sir William Shareshull, justice of the court of common pleas.[11] The two merchants said that at Marchford, Cambridgeshire, and at March, Norfolk, the bishop, his brother, John de Lisle, and others, including the bishop's nephew, William Michel, had several times laid ambushes for them and continued to do so day after day so that for "fear of death, mutilations of their members and capture and incarceration of their bodies they fled thence, wholly abandoning their dwelling places, and have not dared return." In addition, De Lisle's men were said to have stolen a total of 10 oxen, 15 cows, and 260 sheep belonging to the Spynks, worth £20 and 40 marks, or approximately £46, and carried away their goods valued at £400.[12]

In September 1346, more oyer and terminer commissions were issued in response to new complaints from the Spynks. This time each brother reported how Thomas and John de Lisle and more than twenty-five others, again including William Michel and also Osbern le Hawker, the bishop's keeper of his parks and warrens at Downham, Cambridgeshire,[13] "hostilely besieged him at Dickleburgh and Norwich and the suburb of that city, threatening his life and threatening him with mutilation of his members and capture and incarceration of his body, so that for fear of death he dared not go out [of those places] to pursue his trade by which he got food for himself and his household." On account of this siege, said the brothers, they had lost £700 in potential profit from merchandise they normally would have sold in market. What is more, according to the Spynks, De Lisle's gang had stolen goods worth £260 belonging to the merchants at Norwich and Dickleburgh, Norfolk, and at the latter place had assaulted their men and servants, wounding them so badly that they were not able to serve their masters "for a great time."[14]

By 6 December 1346 the crown, in response to new information, superseded all previous commissions issued on the Spynks' behalf with new ones, directed this time to Sir William Basset and four new justices of oyer

10. Ibid., 407; *SR*, 1:253.

11. For the appointments of these men, see *Select Cases*, 6:li, nn. 1, 4; lxvi, n. 7; lxvii, n. 4.

12. PRO, C 66/217, mm. 1d.–4d.; *CPR*, 1345–48, 186–88. The commissions were re-issued in September and October of the same year.

13. CUL, EDR, D 10/2/17–18.

14. PRO, C 66/217, m. 1d.; *CPR*, 1345–48, 188–89.

and terminer, including Sir William Thorp, the recently appointed chief justice of the king's bench.[15] The new commissions, although quite similar to those issued in August and September, made the important addition that the king had taken the Spynk brothers into his special protection and that De Lisle's gang had attacked them while they were so under this protection.[16] Meanwhile, the two parties were busily engaged in a war of suit and countersuit that benefited no one but their lawyers. The exasperatingly endless series of litigation even may have reached the ears of the king. On 29 August 1347 the crown, through the office of the privy seal, ordered the justices to review the record of the Spynk case and then call the parties before the bench and pronounce judgment "so that the king be not further solicited for lack of justice in the matter, as the king has learned that the said processes have been long delayed by pretext of divers of his writs and orders, obtained at the suit as well of Richard and William [Spynk] as of the bishop contrary to the law and custom of the realm."[17] But even this was not to satisfy the litigants, who were to carry their bitter dispute still further until finally, in 1348, both sides were given the opportunity to make their case before the highest tribunal in medieval England, the king's council in parliament.

Before the King's Council

The king's council in parliament was the highest court of appeal in England in the later Middle Ages and it was not available to just anyone. Prospective appellants first had to submit their written or oral petitions to the clerks of the chancery acting as receivers of petitions. Only those petitions deemed appropriate then were passed on to the council.[18] The petitions of both Thomas de Lisle and Richard Spynk are contained in a class of documents in the Public Record Office entitled "ancient petitions," a special collection created in 1892 but based on an earlier archival class called "parliamentary petitions" that originally was preserved in chronological order in the Tower of London.[19] Although there are no dating

15. Thorp was appointed chief justice on 16 November 1346. See *Select Cases*, 6:lii, n. 4.
16. PRO, C 66/218, m. 11d.; *CPR*, 1345–48, 237–38, 439–40; *CCR*, 1346–49, 169.
17. *CCR*, 1346–49, 381.
18. G. Edwards, *The Second Century of the English Parliament* (Oxford, 1979), 44–48; Powell, *Kingship, Law and Society*, 53.
19. PRO, SC 8: 45/2212, 162/8059, 342/16148; *Index of Ancient Petitions of the Chancery and the Exchequer Preserved in the Public Record Office*, rev. edition (PRO Lists and Indexes no. 1, New York, 1966), 2–4.

clauses in the documents themselves, the petitions of De Lisle and Spynk were entered by the eighteenth-century editors of *Rotuli Parliamentorum* as having been presented at the parliament held at Westminster from 14 January until 12 February 1348.[20] The editors numbered the petitions but worked from a transcript of the documents, now lost, made in the previous century by Sir Matthew Hale instead of from the original chronological bundles.[21] It may be impossible to check the accuracy of the dating in *Rotuli Parliamentorum* now that the petitions have been taken permanently out of context, but if the transcript by Hale remained faithful to the chronological series, then the date currently assigned to the documents should be correct.[22] The petitions are valuable evidence for the legal historian because, like the minutes of a modern court case, they contain the arguments both for the prosecution and for the defense, and thus allow us to make a more objective judgment as to whether a defendant charged more than six hundred years ago was guilty or innocent.

De Lisle presented the case for his defense in two separate petitions. The longer one, numbered seventy-one in the parliament rolls, claimed that the Spynk brothers were the bishop's villeins, born on his Doddington manor in Cambridgeshire, and that therefore he, the bishop, could take exception of villeinage (*excepcio villenagii*) against them. In medieval English law, the villein, unlike a free man, had no legal rights and was not allowed to bring a lawsuit against his lord.[23] Although some historians confuse the terms, an exception was not the same as a writ.[24] Whereas a writ was a formal document issuing out of chancery and sealed with the great seal, requiring that justice be done to the aggrieved party, an exception was simply an objection raised against an opponent's plea, either verbally or written down in a bill. Defendants often raised exceptions in the hope of defeating their opponent's case. *Excepcio villenagii* was an objection on the ground that the other party was incapacitated by reason of his villein status or his tenure.[25]

---

20. *RP*, 2:164, 192–93; *CCR*, 1346–49, 495; *RDP*, 3:572–75. The date of 1347 assigned to the parliament by *RP* does not take into account the medieval system of dating from 25 March. The mistake is repeated by R. H. Hilton, *The Decline of Serfdom in Medieval England*, 2d edition (Cambridge, 1983), 29.

21. *Index of Ancient Petitions*, 2.

22. A surviving transcript of some of the petitions in their original chronological order was made by F. Palgrave in 1824–27, but they mostly predate De Lisle. See PRO, PRO 31/7/104–5, and the handlist of parliamentary and council proceedings (C 49) in the Round Room of the PRO.

23. P. Hyams, *King, Lords and Peasants in Medieval England: The Common Law of Villeinage in the Twelfth and Thirteenth Centuries* (Oxford, 1980), 50, 95–96.

24. Hilton, *Decline of Serfdom*, 29; Ormrod, *Reign of Edward III*, 147.

25. Hyams, *King, Lords and Peasants*, 50, n. 7, and see the Glossary of Legal Terms, page 208.

Here the raising of an exception of villeinage before the king's council in parliament marks a change of tactic by De Lisle's attorneys. Spynk mentioned in his own petition that for the past two years the bishop had sued "writs under the great seal and letters under the privy seal" in order to counter the plaintiff's oyer and terminer commissions, "notwithstanding any mandate of our lord king or ordinance made by his council."[26] The former may refer to the writ of attaint granted by the statute of 1327 as a remedy against oppressive commissions of oyer and terminer, while the latter presumably refers to the crown's order of 29 August 1347 that had sought to bring the suit between the two parties to a conclusive end.[27] There is no mention of *excepcio villenagii* being raised by the bishop, which suggests that this was a new strategy adopted by the defendant, perhaps as recently as the parliamentary session.

The impression that *excepcio villenagii* was not De Lisle's usual defense is strengthened by the existence of another petition in the parliament rolls for early 1348 that likewise asserted the lord's right to take exception to a plaintiff's servile status. Numbered twenty-one by the editors of *Rotuli Parliamentorum*, the petition was not attributed to any one particular litigant but seems to have been drawn up collectively on behalf of all the lords in parliament.[28] The petition's main complaint was that serfs were impleading their lords "against right and good faith" in "foreign" counties, that is, places other than where the villeins had been born. The villeins were doing this, according to the lords, in order to have their free status recognized by the court, because in foreign counties the local people "cannot in any way have cognizance of their birth or of their blood," or in other words, they did not know that the plaintiffs were someone else's property.[29] In effect, the serfs were attempting to pass themselves off as free men with the same legal rights as free men.

---

26. "Et apres, a chescun session des justices a ceo assignéz, par suggestions noun veritables, a la seute del dit evesque, sont venuz briefs soutz le grant seal, et lettres soutz la targe, de surseer de les oiers et terminers avantditz . . . issint que pur la maintenance quele ad esté fait none resonablement countre la loy, le dit Richard ad esté destourbé de son recovrir par deux aunz, nouncontresteantz ascun mandement nostre seignur le roi ou ordeynance faite par son consail." PRO, SC 8/342/16148; *RP*, 2:193.

27. *SR*, 1:253; *CCR*, 1346–49, 381.

28. A similar petition, likewise undated, was sponsored by "all the prelates, lords, and peers of the realm and others having villeins in obedience" ("touz les prelatz, seignurs, et peres de roialme et autres qui ount vileyns des obeisans"). PRO, SC 8/134/6668.

29. "Qar altrement ensueroit grant meschief si la excepcion soit triée par gentz de forein countee, qe par tant les neifs serront enfranchiz par gentz qe ne purront en nule manere avoir cognissance de lour nestre ne de lour sank, en desheriteson des plousours seignurs q'ount neifs, quele herure q'ils soient ensi empledéz contre droit et bone foi." *RP*, 2:180.

The similarities in language and content which De Lisle's first petition bears to petition twenty-one are striking. De Lisle also complained that his "villeins," Richard and William Spynk, were suing him in a foreign county, Norfolk, in order to gain their liberty by having the court recognize their suit. They "have purchased against him and several others oyers and terminers in the county of Norfolk," De Lisle said of the Spynks, "maliciously feigning that he [the bishop] used to besiege them at Norwich and committed against them several other horrible trespasses . . . in order to enfranchise themselves by the people of the said county of Norfolk."[30] Both petitions asked the council to remedy the situation by ruling that, whenever the lord's exception be disputed by the plaintiff, who would assert that he was free and not servile, then the issue be decided by a jury from the county "where the villein was born, who have a true cognizance of his birth and or his blood."[31] In De Lisle's case, he requested that the inquiry into the Spynks' birth be held in Cambridgeshire, which he claimed was their native county. Finally, both petitions warned the council that if the defendants be convicted of anything their villeins accuse them of through their writs, then this would be "a very great mischief in law."[32]

Why did De Lisle not raise the objection of *excepcio villenagii* earlier? There may have been any one of a number of reasons, but if the lords' petition was heard before De Lisle's, as their numbering suggests, then there is the intriguing possibility that De Lisle adopted the *excepcio villenagii* strategy in the wake of his predecessors' arguments. The bishop may not have employed *excepcio villenagii* before submitting his petitions to parliament because in Norfolk, where the oyer and terminer commissions would have been held, Richard Spynk was well known as a free citizen of Norwich and De Lisle's exception would not have appeared credible. When his case came before the council, however, it was in the interest of De Lisle and his attorneys to identify with the interests and concerns of his peers.

30. "A nostre seignour le roi et a son conseil monstre le evesque d'Ely, que come Richard Spink, et William son frere, ses villeyns de sa eglise d'Ely, de son manoir de Dodington en le countee de Cantebr' [Cambridge], deinz quel manoir les ditz Richard et William et lour auncestres nesquirent, eyent purchacéz contre lui et autres divers oirs et terminers en le countee de Norff' [Norfolk], feignauntz maliciousement q'il les deveroit avoir en siege a Norwiz; et plusours autres horribles trespas a eux avoir fait, par cause de avoir les ditz oirs et terminers de les enfraunchier par gentz du dit countee de Norff' [Norfolk]." PRO, SC 8/8059; *RP,* 2:192.
31. De Lisle's petition: ". . . que la dite exception soit trié per gentz du dit counte de Cantebr' [Cambridge], ou les ditz villeins nasquirent, qui ount verrai cognissaunce de lour nestere et de lour sank." PRO, SC 8/8059; *RP,* 2:192. The Lords' petition: ". . . qe la dite excepcion si ele soit desdite, soit triée par gentz du countee en quel le neif nasquit, q'ont verraie cognissance de son nestre et de son sank." *RP,* 2:180.
32. De Lisle's petition: "Et estre ce le dit evesque serroit convitz de quanqe ses ditz villeyns lur surmettent en lors oirs et terminers, saunz avoir autre respouns, a ce que est trop grant meschief en ley." PRO, SC 8/8059; *RP,* 2:192. The Lords'

The council easily recognized that De Lisle and the lords shared common interests. Its responses to petitions twenty-one and seventy-one were exactly the same, word for word. Although the lords claimed that "many people of law are in various opinions" concerning the admissibility of their privilege,[33] the council was quite clear on this point. "It is agreed by the council in parliament," went the response, "that the exception of villeinage against the plaintiffs . . . be acceptable and allowed."[34] However, "if the said plaintiffs respond that they are free and of free estate . . . then, without going further in the said matter, the justices [who are hearing the case must] adjourn the parties before the king [king's bench] or before the common bench at the choice of the defendant."[35] The council made an important concession to the defendants by leaving the control of any further prosecution of the suit in their hands and by ruling that the inquest into the plaintiffs' birth should be taken by a jury from "the county where the said plaintiffs were born," rather than from the "foreign" county where the plaintiffs had brought their suit.[36]

Whereas his first petition was fairly certain of achieving its desired outcome, considering that it followed on the successful petition by the lords, De Lisle made a much more ambitious demand in his second appeal to the council (number seventy-two). In it, the bishop sought to deny the Spynks access to writs of oyer and terminer, leaving them with, as their only recourse for justice, the suing of a writ of trespass in the king's bench or the court of common pleas. De Lisle claimed that his innocence was well known by many "peers of the land, knights, and other good people."[37] If the "horrible trespasses" and especially the besieging alleged by the Spynks really had occurred, De Lisle argued, then these witnesses

---

petition: "Et, estre ceo, les seignurs serront convictz de quant que lour neifs les surmettont par briefs ou billes q'ils pursuent contre lour seignurs, sanz avoir autre respons a ceo; que est trop grant meschief en ley." *RP*, 2:180.

33. ". . . et plusours gentz de ley sont en divers oppinion." *RP*, 2:180.

34. "Il est assentu par le conseil en parlement, qe l'exception de neifte devers les pleinteifs, si ele soit par le defendaunt devant les justices purposé qe meismes les pleintifs sont ses niefs et néez en autre countee, soit resceu et allowé." PRO, SC 8/8059d.; *RP*, 2:180, 192.

35. "Et si les ditz pleintifs respoignent q'ils sont franks et de frank estat, et se offrent de ce averir, qe adonques, sanz aler plus ava[u]nt en la dite busoigne, ajournent les justices les [dites] parties devant le roi, ou en com[m]un bank a l'eleccion le defendant." Ibid.

36. ". . . et soit l'enqueste prise par gentz del visne du co[u]ntee ou les ditz pleintifs nasquirent." Ibid.

37. ". . . quelx horribles trespas, et nomement come de siege faire, ne purront si secrement estre faitz, que plusours des pieres de la terre, chevaliers, et autres bones gentz, deussent de ceo avoir cognissance s'ils eussent esté faitz." PRO, SC 8/2212; *RP*, 2:192.

certainly would have known about it. He therefore invited the council to seek out the good men's testimony, "and if through their information it be discovered that the said suit [brought by the Spynks against De Lisle] is false and malicious, then let the said oyers and terminers be completely revoked."[38]

The council denied De Lisle's request, pointing out that the law fully supported the Spynks' right to sue writs of oyer and terminer. The writs had been granted, the council said, "on account of the horribleness of the trespass" alleged by the Spynks. This is perhaps a reference to the second statute of 1328, which confirmed the stipulation made in the previous statute of 1285 that commissions of oyer and terminer would be granted only in cases of "horrible trespasses."[39] The commissions begun by the Spynks, ruled the council, were therefore to "remain in their force and not at all be rejected."[40]

Richard Spynk, in his own petition before the council (number seventy-three), seems to have followed a twofold strategy. One of his goals was to establish his right, as a free man, to plead against De Lisle and to counter the challenge to this right posed by *excepcio villenagii*. "Although the said bishop claims in his bills that the said Richard is his villein of his manor of Doddington," Spynk argued, "all the same Richard and his ancestors are and have been free and of free condition from time without memory, which fact is well known in the counties aforesaid [Norfolk and Cambridge]."[41] The "bills" Spynk mentioned could either refer to bills of exception sued by De Lisle or to the bishop's previous two petitions before the council. If parliament was the first court to witness the defendant pursuing *excepcio villenagii*, the bills of exception and the bishop's petitions would be virtually one and the same. This also would confirm that, in accordance with their numbering, De Lisle's petitions were heard before the plaintiff's. Spynk asked that "he not be deprived of the law accorded and granted by our lord the king and his council," notwithstanding De Lisle's "untrue suggestions" that he was the bishop's serf.[42]

---

38. "Et si par information de eux soit trové la dite sieute feinte et maliciouse, que adonques les ditz oiers et terminers soient de tout repellés." Ibid.

39. *SR*, 1:85, 258.

40. "Et sembloit adonques a la court et a consail que pur l'orribletee du trespas les ditz briefs d'oier et terminer furent grantables, par quoi il semble ore au conseil que meismes les briefs deivent demorir en lour force, et nemye estre repelléz." PRO, SC 8/2212d.; *RP*, 2:192.

41. "Et comment que le dit evesque surmet en ses billes, que le dit Richard soit son villayn de son manoir de Dodington, mesmes celuy Richard et ces auncestres sont et ount esté franks et de fraunche condition du temps dont memoire ne court, quele chose est bien notorie as counteez susditz." PRO, SC 8/342/16148; *RP*, 2:193.

42. "Par quoi prie le dit Richard, q'il ne soit destourbé de la ley accordé et granté par nostre seignour le roy et son consail par tiels suggestions noun veritables." Ibid.

Just as De Lisle tried to persuade the council to let the question of Spynk's birth be decided by a jury from Cambridgeshire rather than from the county of Norfolk, where the merchant had influence, so Spynk countered with the claim that a jury from Cambridgeshire would be unfairly weighted in the bishop's favor: "For all the people of value from the county of Cambridge are the tenants of the said bishop or otherwise [are beholden] to his fees and robes on account of this quarrel."[43] De Lisle's maintenance was so pervasive, according to Spynk, that he had been loath at first to complain about the bishop's transgressions against him, even though the bishop had stolen goods worth a total of 1,000 marks, or approximately £667. Finally, Spynk enlisted the aid of a legal principle of his own: *favor libertatis,* the notion that since the law was in the habit of favoring liberty, its justices ought to err on the side of keeping a man free than in a state of servitude.[44] As Spynk himself put it, "The law is more favourable for the freedom of a man's body than to put him back into bondage."[45] It seems that this was the first time that *favor libertatis* was invoked in court, and if so, this would add significance to the case.[46]

The rest of Spynk's long, rambling petition was devoted to his other goal, that of convincing the council of the "horribleness" of the trespass committed against him and the urgency of completing the oyer and terminer processes begun two years ago. In passages reminiscent of the charges made in the oyer and terminer commissions, Spynk described how De Lisle had commissioned Osbern le Hawker and "a great number of malefactors, armed men, and archers" in the bishop's pay "to spy out through all the neighbourhood of Norfolk in order to arrest and seize the body of the said Richard alive or dead, in whatever place he could be found," notwithstanding that Spynk had been taken into the king's protection.[47] To carry out their sinister task, De Lisle's men, according to Spynk, had held "improper assemblies" in the neighborhood around Norwich, and for this reason, Spynk said, he "did not dare go out of the city [of Norwich] with his merchandise, but kept himself inside in order

43. ". . . qar touz les gentz del value de countee de Cantebr' [Cambridge] sont tenantz del dit evesque, ou autrement a ces fees et robes, par cause de ceste querele." Ibid.

44. Hyams, *King, Lords and Peasants,* 206; Hilton, *Decline of Serfdom,* 26–27.

45. "Et si est la ley plus favourable a la fraunchise del corps d'ome que lui mettre en servage." PRO, SC 8/342/16148; *RP,* 2:193.

46. Hyams, *King, Lords and Peasants,* 201–19.

47. "Et nouncontresteant la dite protection le dit evesque manda sa comission a Osbern le Haukere, et a grant nombre des maffaisours, gentz arméez, et archiers a ses custages, de espier par tut le pays de Norff' [Norfolk] d'arestier et prendre le corps du dit Richard vif ou mort, quel part q'il poait estre trovéz." PRO, SC 8/342/16148; *RP,* 2:193.

to escape death, like a man besieged, as a result of which he suffered damages of £1,000 and more."[48]

Indeed, De Lisle's menace was so great, complained Spynk, that he neither dared venture into Cambridgeshire, comprising the bishop's diocese, in order to pursue his affairs, nor did he even dare come to Thetford, Norfolk, where he was to plead his case before the king's justices. Even now De Lisle, through his thugs and bullies, "threatens the said Richard as regards his life and as regards his members wherever he can be found," and "makes to chase the said Richard from one day to another throughout the various places in the said county of Norfolk . . . in order to capture him or put him to death. For this reason," Spynk continued, "he does not dare show himself nor pursue" his case except through his friends.[49] Spynk concluded his petition by asking the council to "mandate to your justices that they go forward in the quarrel in accordance with law and reason, notwithstanding any writs [of attaint?] . . . purchased or to be purchased by the said bishop in order to contradict [the plaintiff's writs of oyer and terminer] with another suggestion."[50]

The Council's Verdict

The final ruling on the dispute came in the council's reply to Spynk's petition. The verdict was decidedly against the plaintiff, largely because he or his lawyers had let slip numerous inconsistencies that the justices were quick to point out. In the first place, the charges made in the petition differed from those advanced earlier in the writs of oyer and terminer. The plaintiff's description of his harassment, comprised in the first part of his petition, did not conform to the definition of a besieging, as stated

48. "Par quoi le dit Osberne et les autres par colour de la dite commission ount fait assemblez noun covenable, ou grant affray du poeple, en meintes places en pays entour Norwiz. Par quoi le dit Richard n'oseit la citee isser a ses marchaundises, mais se tynt dedeinz pur sa mort escheure come un home assiegéz, dont il est endamagé de M. livres et plus." Ibid.

49. "Et le dit Richard manace de vie et de membre ou q'il poet estre trovéez . . . que ore le dit evesque continuant sa malice fait getter le dit Richard de jour en autre, per diverses places en le dit countee de Norff' [Norfolk] par les maffaisours susditz de lui prendre ou mettre a la mort: Par qoi il ne se ose monstrer, ne lui meismes pursure par la ley ses dites bosoignes, mais les fait pursuire par ses amys." Ibid.

50. "Et que vous pleise de vostre grace maunder a voz justices, que eux aillent avant en la querele solonc lay et reson, nouncontresteant ascuns briefs . . . lettres purchacéz ou a purchacer par le dit evesque du contraire par ascun suggestioun." Ibid.

in the oyer and terminer writs, but was more properly defined as an ambush, and therefore this charge, said the council, was untrue. The plaintiff failed to mention in his petition that goods and livestock had been stolen at Norwich and Dickleburgh, as described in the oyer and terminer writs, and therefore this charge, too, said the council, was untrue. In addition, Spynk owed money to the crown for oyer and terminer writs served in Cambridgeshire, according to the council, and since "the king still is not paid [for the writs]," the council ruled that the sheriff of Cambridgeshire had no legal obligation "to maintain the oyers and terminers."[51]

Nor did this exhaust the faults found in Spynk's argument. The plaintiff's charge that De Lisle had obstructed, through the suing of counterwrits, the oyer and terminer commissions that were to arrange for the investigation of Spynk's complaints held true concerning the court's first session during Christmas week. The council conceded that the justices had not sat then in judgment on the Spynk case by reason of crown writs sued against such a sitting. But Spynk's petition proved false regarding the second session of the court held during Easter week, the council said, because at that time no writs to suspend the sitting had been sued. Rather, the justices had not sat then by mutual consent of both parties, who had drawn up a formal agreement on the matter witnessed by De Lisle and Spynk's proxy, John de Norwich.

The plaintiff's charge that the bishop was maintaining "people of value" in Cambridgeshire was "notoriously untrue," ruled the council, "for [there are in the] county more than 1000 said people of importance and of virtue who are not his tenants nor [are beholden] to his fees or robes. And this can be discovered through the good people of the aforesaid county [attending] this parliament."[52] The plaintiff's other accusation "that the bishop continues his malice, and even now makes to lie in wait for the said Richard in order to seize him, etc., can be well understood to be untrue," the council decided, because Spynk had been seen speaking with De Lisle "at his ease . . . in several places in the counties of Cambridge and Huntingdon and wherever the said Richard often comes."[53] This in-

---

51. ". . . et du mark pur les brefs en le counte de Cantebr' [Cambridge] le roi n'est unqore servy, car le viconte ne . . . en sa baillie quele fyn ne . . . de droit estre cause de meyntenir les oiers et terminers." PRO, SC 8/342/16148d.; RP, 2:193.

52. "Item, la ou il dit que touz les gentz de value del counte de Cantebr' [Cambridge] sont tenantz l'evesque, ou a ses fees et robes, ceo est notoirement nient veritable, car . . . counte plus que M. ditz gentz de value et de bien qui ne sont ses tenanz, ne a ses feez ne robes: Et ceo poet estre trové par les bones gentz de ycell counte . . . cest parlement." Ibid.

53. "Item, par la ou il dit, que l'evesque continue sa malice, et fait unqore gauter le dit Richard de luy prendre et cetera ceo poet bien estre entendu nient veritable; car le . . . l'evesque a Ely apres la Pasche, et illoeques luy em parla tout a l'eise, et climacha ovesque luy, voloit avoir pris il le p . . . fait, et auxint en plousours lieuz en

formation probably also came to the council's attention through third-party testimony, namely De Lisle's peers in parliament.

The end result of the council's deliberations was an entirely satisfactory one for De Lisle. The council ruled that since Spynk "does not deny his birth [at Doddington, Cambridgeshire] . . . the exception of villeinage . . . should be tried by the people of the said county [of Cambridge] where he was born." Moreover, it granted the bishop's request comprised in his second petition (number seventy-two), that the writs of oyer and terminer purchased by Spynk "be completely rejected" because, according to the council, they were "conceived out of a false malice and suggestion, as appears by his [the plaintiff's] own petition."[54]

Oddly enough, De Lisle never pressed his advantage against Spynk through the courts. It was not until four years later, after an absence abroad from 1348 until 1350,[55] that De Lisle chose to submit his suit to arbitration, a popular alternative in the Middle Ages to expensive and drawn-out litigation whereby both litigants agreed to abide by the decision of an unbiased (it was hoped) third party.[56] The arbitrator in this case was Robert de Ufford, earl of Suffolk. He had witnessed the king's charter, dated 9 August 1345, which, in recognition of the recent expenses to complete the city walls, granted Norwich exemption from the jurisdiction of the royal clerk of the market.[57] Since Spynk had been primarily responsible for the work celebrated by this charter, it is possible that the earl was persuaded to intervene in memory of the merchant's previous good deed. Moreover, the earl's kinsman, John de Ufford, had witnessed the agreement between De Lisle and Spynk to suspend the Easter session of oyer and terminer as mentioned by the king's council.[58]

The document setting out the conditions of the agreement that finally ended the dispute was witnessed by De Lisle on 21 May 1352. Although no mention was made of it in the agreement, Spynk probably had to pay a monetary concession to the bishop to ensure his future goodwill. Certainly the wording of the document conveys the impression that De Lisle had the upper hand: "At the request of and out of reverence for the

---

les countez de Cantebr' [Cambridge] et Huntingdon et aillours ou le dit Richard sovont foitz vient." Ibid. The original petition is damaged and unreadable in places.

54. "Par quoi, depuis que les oiers et terminers . . . conceuz de fauce malice et suggestion come piert par sa bille demesne, soient ils de tout repellés, et de ceo q'il ne dedit pas son nestre en que . . . exception de villenage, quele heure q'ele soit alleggé contre le dit Richard, soit trié par gentz du dit counte ou il nasquit." Ibid.

55. CUL, EDR, G/1/1, Reg. De Lisle, fols. 16v, 17r, 37r.

56. Powell, "Arbitration and the Law," 55–57; idem, *Kingship, Law and Society,* 98–100.

57. *Records of Norwich,* 1:26.

58. PRO, SC 8/342/16148d.; *RP,* 2:193.

honourable lord, my Lord Robert de Ufford, earl of Suffolk, and *by reason of the good behaviour and humility of the said Richard*," De Lisle agreed to give up "all manner of actions, claims, challenges, and demands which he ever has or could have [brought] against the aforesaid Richard and William [Spynk]" (italics mine).[59]

The Historian's Verdict

It is puzzling why Richard Spynk, after the expenditure of so much money and effort to bring his case before the council, should have wasted his opportunity by presenting such a slipshod argument. Perhaps the blame should be borne by his attorney, John de Norwich, although the merchant was certainly wealthy enough to hire competent legal advice. On the other hand, the long and costly suit may have drained Spynk's financial resources; he could not have matched those commanded by De Lisle. While not immune to financial difficulties himself, the bishop, as his biographer testifies, seems to have spared no expense to surround himself with lawyers.[60]

The success of De Lisle's defense lay in his identification with the in-terests of his peers in parliament. Although legal disputes between ten-ants and their masters go back to the beginning of the common law in the twelfth century,[61] petition twenty-one on behalf of the lords warned of a new threat to the beloved privilege of *excepcio villenagii*. De Lisle's suit gained in importance as the first test case for the lords' defense of this privilege. Much was at stake. If Spynk had been successful, his prece-dent would have started a stampede of legal actions against lords by their freedom-loving serfs, or at least that is probably how the nobility viewed the implications of a verdict for the plaintiff. In the decades after the Black Death of 1348–49 and leading up to the Peasants' Revolt of 1381, lords everywhere increasingly were determined to preserve the profits of their lordship and halt the emancipation of the villein.[62] This determination found expression in the Ordinance of Labourers of 1349,[63] the Statute of

59. BL, Add. MS 41612, fols. 114r–v, and see Appendix B, pages 239–40.

60. See *AS*, 1:655, and Appendix B, pages 228–29.

61. S.F.C. Milsom, *The Legal Framework of English Feudalism* (Cambridge, 1976), 8–35; Hyams, *King, Lords and Peasants*, 221–65.

62. R. H. Hilton, *Bond Men Made Free: Medieval Peasant Movements and the English Rising of 1381* (London, 1973), 153–57; idem, *The English Peasantry in the Later Middle Ages* (Oxford, 1975), 60–61; Bolton, *The Medieval English Economy*, 213–15; Dyer, "Rural Revolt of 1381," 23–24; Swanson, *Church and Society*, 201–4; Waugh, *England in the Reign of Edward III*, 109–13.

63. *SR*, 1:307–9.

Labourers of 1351,[64] and in a lesser-known statute of 1352, which gave lords the right to plead exception of villeinage against plaintiffs who had purchased a writ of *libertate probanda*. The common law had traditionally favored lords over villeins.[65] However, in the context of increasing peasant challenges to serfdom in the later Middle Ages,[66] lords became increasingly concerned about what they perceived as potential manipulations of the law that would be prejudicial to their ancient rights. *Libertate probanda* required plaintiffs to prove their free status in court but, in the meantime, granted them protection from their lords. In its petition to the council that gave rise to the statute, the commons complained that villeins were using the writ to delay actions against them by lords seeking to reclaim their serfs. The new statute provided that lords could seize the persons of their villeins even after the writ of *libertate probanda* had been sued.[67] Spynk's case also may have anticipated lords' complaints expressed after 1381, in which villeins were said to be escaping to towns in an attempt to win their liberty through the community's protection.[68]

Despite the council's verdict, it seems difficult to believe that Spynk would have troubled himself to prosecute his case without some genuine grievance. There is the possibility that Spynk was trying to change his legal status from that of unfree serf of Doddington to free citizen of Norwich through his suit against De Lisle. From the latter's point of view, then, the merchant's complaints of theft and harassment would be misrepresentations of the legitimate actions of a lord defending his legal rights. Although he did not use his privilege of *excepcio villenagii* until much later, the bishop, from the very outset of the case, seems to have taken the position that Spynk was his villein trying to pass himself off as a free man. The stealing of Spynk's goods and his harassment then could be excused as a perfectly lawful attempt to distrain and capture a fugitive bondman. Although the court appears to have decided that Spynk was indeed De Lisle's villein, there is no record of a Spynk living at Doddington in an inquisition made in 1251 listing all the tenants who had to pay rent or perform services for the bishop of Ely.[69] It is possible that De Lisle and his

64. Ibid., 311–13.

65. Hyams, *King, Lords and Peasants,* 29–31, 167–69.

66. R. H. Hilton, "Peasant Movements in England before 1381," in E. M. Carus-Wilson, ed., *Essays in Economic History,* 3 vols. (London, 1954–62), 2:78–85; M.J.O. Kennedy, "Resourceful Villeins: The Cellarer Family of Wawne in Holderness," *Yorkshire Archaeological Journal* 48 (1976), 107–17; Z. Razi, "The Struggles Between the Abbots of Halesowen and their Tenants in the Thirteenth and Fourteenth Centuries," in T. H. Aston, P. R. Coss, C. Dyer, and J. Thirsk, eds., *Social Relations and Ideas: Essays in Honour of R.H. Hilton* (Cambridge, 1983), 151–67.

67. *SR,* 1:323: c. 18; *RP,* 2:242; P. R. Hyams, "The Action of Naifty in the Early Common Law," *Law Quarterly Review* 90 (1974), 331, n. 31.

68. Hilton, *Decline of Serfdom,* 29.

69. CUL, EDR: G/3/27, Liber R, The "Old Coucher" Book, fols. 25v–30r.

lawyers had some more recent record that connected Spynk, already a well-established citizen of Norwich before De Lisle's elevation to the see of Ely, with the bishop's Doddington manor, a connection that then gave De Lisle the legal basis to distrain Spynk's possessions and seize his person. Without this connection, the bishop's entanglement with a merchant based far outside his diocese is hard to explain.

Nevertheless, on balance, the evidence points more toward De Lisle's attack on Spynk as a case of barely lawful extortion rather than law-abiding indignation. Suspiciously, this was not to be the only instance where De Lisle used alleged servile status to justify forcible confiscation of another man's person or goods. In Michaelmas term 1352 the bishop's bailiff, Henry de Burton, had to answer charges brought against him by Robert Mody of Doddington in the court of common pleas. Mody alleged that Burton had come to Hitcham, Suffolk, armed with swords and other weapons and carried off four of his horses, six oxen, and five cows, worth £10, and caused further damage to the value of £40. Burton said in his defense that Mody was the bishop's villein, "and that all the predecessors of the bishop from time without memory by right had been seized of the antecedents of Robert as his neif."[70] Burton also claimed that, on De Lisle's orders, he had taken Mody's animals in lieu of amercements owed to the bishop by the plaintiff.[71]

A similar defense had to found for still another of Burton's actions against an alleged villein. On 1 May 1354, the crown ordered the sheriff of Cambridge, John de Harwedon, to free Richard Bythwall, who had been arrested by Burton and still was being held in De Lisle's prison in spite of numerous royal writs to obtain his release. If the sheriff was unable to carry out the king's mandate, he was to report back before the king's bench in Trinity term of that year and explain the reason for his failure. On the appointed day, 16 June 1354, Harwedon reported to the bench that he could not release Bythwall because De Lisle's bailiff of the liberty of Ely, John de Essex, who had return of all royal writs served within the Isle, had refused to execute the writ on the grounds that Bythwall was the bishop's serf and had been captured legitimately at Sutton, Cambridgeshire.[72]

De Lisle never had any intention of dragging Spynk all the way back from Norwich to Doddington and forcing him to live once again as a villein on his manor.[73] This much is clear from the fact that, once the bishop had

70. "Et quod omnes predecessores ipsius episcopi a tempore quo non extat memoria de antecessoribus ipsius Roberti ut de eius nativis seisiti fuerunt ut de iure." PRO, KB 27/369, civil pleas, m. 66d.

71. Ibid.

72. PRO, KB 27/376, rex m. 13; KB 27/378, rex m. 22d.

73. Hilton, *Decline of Serfdom*, 53.

the upper hand in the dispute, that is, once he had gained the right to try his claim to Spynk in Cambridgeshire and the plaintiff's accusations had been discredited by the council, De Lisle never pursued his claim. Instead, Spynk paid De Lisle what was in effect a bribe to obtain his manumission, or release from servitude, which is what the 1352 agreement, disguised as arbitration, really was. It is even called *manumissio Ricardi Spynk* in the Ely Priory register.[74] The fact that Spynk was a wealthy and established citizen of Norwich makes his manumission appear more as an unsavory form of extortion than as an honest pursuit of a runaway villein. This form of blackmail was not unknown, as the case of Simon de Paris, a former sheriff and alderman of London who brought a suit in the king's bench in 1308 for wrongful imprisonment as a villein, makes clear.[75] But the practice was to become more widespread in the fifteenth century, when more nobles fell on financially hard times and turned to extortion of rich townsmen as an alternative source of income.[76]

At first, however, De Lisle tried to cash in on his claim to Spynk by simply seizing the rich merchant's valuables, probably justifying this seizure on the grounds that he was owed backdated amercements or villein dues, as was the case with Robert Mody of Hitcham. The confiscation of Spynk's goods was done in a simple but effective manner. After frightening the Spynk brothers away from their Marchford and March residences, De Lisle's men took what was left in the abandoned dwellings and enclosures. It was only after this action had resulted in the oyer and terminer commissions of August 1346 that we hear, through the commissions of September later that year, of the next escalation in the dispute. De Lisle's men now were besieging the Spynks at Norwich and actively trying, with apparent success, to restrict the merchants' movements. Later, in Richard Spynk's petition of 1348, we learn that this besieging was accompanied by chases and manhunts and was designed to stop Spynk from pleading before the justices at Thetford. If the charge is true then it would suggest that De Lisle felt he needed to resort to violence because his claim to Spynk as his villein was tenuous. Although a record may have existed that showed that Spynk or one of his ancestors had been a tenant on the bishop's Doddington manor, the record may also have showed that Spynk had been a free tenant, with all the rights of a free man, rather than an unfree serf.[77] It is interesting to note that despite all his complaints of

74. BL, Add. MS 41612, fol. 114r.

75. *Year Books of Edward II*, ed. F. W. Maitland, 2 vols. (SS, XVII, 1903), 1:11–12.

76. Hilton, *Decline of Serfdom*, 51–55; McFarlane, *Nobility of Later Medieval England*, 221.

77. The legal distinction between free and unfree tenants is explained in Hilton, *English Peasantry*, 125–26. For a detailed analysis of the complex variations among the bishop of Ely's tenants, see Miller, *Abbey and Bishopric*, 113–53.

being threatened and pursued, Spynk never once alleged that De Lisle's men had laid a hand on him or his brother, only on his servants. This conforms to the pattern of violence between medieval litigants: The threat to use that violence is far more common than the physical assault itself.[78]

There seems little doubt, therefore, that De Lisle's motivation in this case was the financial profit to be had from Spynk rather than any principle of tenurial lordship. There is considerable evidence that at the time of his attack on the Spynk brothers, De Lisle, in spite of his see's wealth, already was deeply in debt and desperately short of money. His biographer relates how, on ascending the episcopal throne, he proceeded to squander his resources on an ostentatious retinue.[79] Although the bishop, according to the biographer, later pruned his court in line with more prudent fiscal practices, this improvement may have been short-lived. Soon the Black Death was to arrive in 1349, causing an immediate drop in the bishop's manorial revenue, and the resulting depression, despite a later recovery, may have persuaded De Lisle to continue to extort money from whomever possible.[80]

There was, indeed, another witness to the financial hardships that the bishop faced at this time: De Lisle himself. On 11 May 1347 he wrote to Edward III explaining why he could not honor the king's request for a loan of wool from his bishops. De Lisle's excuse was "the incumbent burdens and various debts and unjust persecutions to which we are subjected, and also . . . the sterility and paucity of the harvest of our present first year, in which our whole faculty and substance consists." The upshot of all this, the bishop complained, was that "we are so exhausted of money and in debt to so many creditors that we cannot, without the greatest expense and difficulties, raise a loan for our own needs."[81] De Lisle offered to give the king outright six sacks of wool by way of compensation, yet the crown repeated its demand for a loan of gold or silver equivalent to the price of fourteen sacks of wool. The bishop's second reply,

78. See Chapter 3, note 105.
79. *AS*, 1:655, and see Appendix B, pages 228–29. The biographer's testimony supports Spynk's charge in his petition that De Lisle was maintaining men of influence in Cambridgeshire.
80. See pages 43–50.
81. "Sumus etiam, tam propter incumbencia onera et debita varia ac persecuciones iniustas quibus subiacemus hucusque, tam etiam propter sterilitatem et paucitatem annone presentis anni nostri primi in qua consistit tota nostra facultas et substancia, pecunia sic exhausti, et erga creditores plurimos obligati, quod pro necessitatibus propriis absque maximis dispendiis et difficultatibus non possumus mutuum invenire." CUL, EDR, G/ı/1, Reg. De Lisle, fol. 72v. Although the letter is not dated as to year, this can be inferred from Edward's original loan request. See *Registrum Johannis de Trillek, Episcopi Herefordensis, A.D. 1344–1361*, ed. J. H. Parry (CYS, vıı, 1912), 298–99.

dated 8 September 1347, again was to plead poverty, claiming that "we have been oppressed for a long time by debts owed elsewhere and are worn out by continuous persecutions from day to day, having neither wools of our own nor being able to find a loan of wool or money from anyone."[82] Although De Lisle would have had good reason to exaggerate his poverty to the king, his letters nonetheless add some weight to the biographer's testimony. Moreover, the "unjust" and "continuous persecutions" he mentioned may have been an oblique reference to his protracted lawsuit with Spynk.

Given the complex and imperfect nature of the evidence, we never will know whether De Lisle technically was guilty of the charges of theft, intimidation, and extortion outlined above. It was not unusual at this time for lords, feeling the pinch of the economic effects of the Black Death of 1348–49, to be particularly hard-headed and mercenary toward their tenants, squeezing every bit of profit out of them as they could get.[83] What makes De Lisle's exploitation of Spynk different is the blatant nature of the extortion: A rich and established citizen of Norwich is hard to pass off as a runaway villein of Doddington. De Lisle may have been exonerated by the council, but there remains the uneasy suspicion that he exploited a purely nominal villeinage claim to his utmost advantage. His successful defense of his actions on this occasion may have encouraged him to become more audacious, both in terms of the nature of the crimes and the social status of the victims. If this is so, then it was this audacity that was to bring about the bishop's downfall when he became entangled with the king's cousin, Lady Wake.

For Richard Spynk there was to be no justice. But perhaps the merchant derived some comfort from his former adversary's comeuppance. De Lisle was to spend the last five years of his life in exile at Avignon, vainly trying to win back his confiscated temporalities. Spynk was to outlive him by several years: The earliest date we have confirming his death is 30 July 1384. He left behind a widow, Cecily, and a son and heir, John, who, like his father, was a prominent citizen of Norwich but seems to have had no more trouble from the bishops of Ely.[84]

---

82. "Ceterum excellentissime domine, pro novo mutuo quatuordecim saccorum lane, quos in auro vel argento petivistis, nos cogit inopia sic cum cordis displicencia et amaritudine resondere quod oppressi a diu alieno ere et de die in diem continuis persecucionibus fatigati, nec habentes lanas de proprio nec potentes apud quemquam mutuum lane vel pecunie invenire . . ." CUL, EDR, G/1/1, Reg. De Lisle, fols. 75v–76r. Date of letter is inferred from Edward's original loan request. See *Registrum Johannis de Trillek*, 308–9.

83. See Dyer, "Rural Revolt of 1381," 30–32, and Bolton, *The Medieval English Economy*, 213, for examples.

84. NRO, Norwich City Records, 3/4(9), 3/4(12); Norwich Private Deeds: St. Peter Mancroft parish (1377–1655), no. 305; St. Vedast parish (fourteenth century), no. 37.

5

The Dispute with Lady Wake

The *cause célèbre* of De Lisle's career was his protracted lawsuit with the Lancastrian noblewoman, Blanche, Lady Wake. The affair, which was to eventually involve King Edward III and Pope Innocent VI, caused a stir among the chroniclers of the day. Henry Knighton, a canon of St. Mary's Abbey, Leicester, located within the duchy of Lancaster, portrayed De Lisle, not surprisingly, as the aggressor whose men had terrorized the Wake household and who justly had been condemned and punished by the king and his justices.[1] However, three other chroniclers, all clerics, sided with their fellow churchman. Thomas Walsingham, monk of St. Albans, and John de Reading, monk of Westminster, both described the bishop as "unjustly vexed" by Lady Wake, while Stephen Birchington, monk of Christ Church, Canterbury, likewise claimed that De Lisle had been "wickedly convicted" in the king's courts.[2] Whether the bishop was indeed guilty or innocent of the crimes imputed to him by his accuser is still open to debate.

De Lisle was rather unfortunate in his choice of adversary. Aside from the king himself, he could not have chosen an opponent more well connected among the contemporary nobility than Lady Wake. In her own right, she was the sister of Henry of Grosmont, duke of Lancaster, and therefore, like her brother, she was the cousin of King Edward III. Her grandfather, Edmund, earl of Lancaster, was the second surviving son of Henry III, and her father, Henry, Edward III's uncle, was a major participant in the young king's accession. Through two of her sisters, Mary and Eleanor, she was related respectively to Henry Lord Percy and Richard

---

1. Knighton, *Chronicon*, 2:103–4.
2. *AS*, 1:44–45; Walsingham, *Historia Anglicana*, 1:285–86; Reading, *Chronica*, 129–30.

FitzAlan, earl of Arundel.[3] Her brother was reckoned among Edward's best generals during the Hundred Years' War and was one of the founding members of the Order of the Garter.[4] According to one account of his life, he was "a perfect knight, . . . a wise counsellor, and was loved and trusted by Edward III beyond any other of his lords."[5] With connections like these, it is hardly surprising that King Edward took a personal interest in his cousin's dispute with the bishop.

It was perhaps the Black Death that made Lady Wake a wealthy and independent woman. Her husband, Thomas, Lord Wake of Liddell, died without issue in May 1349.[6] On 17 and 20 June in the same year, the crown granted her back her husband's domains without fee.[7] The widowed Lady Wake never seems to have remarried; no doubt her inheritance enabled her to live out the remaining thirty-one years of her life alone in considerable comfort.[8] That her household was indeed a large one is indicated by the entourage allowed to travel with her to Rome to attend the 1350 jubilee: She was to be accompanied by three squires, thirty men, and twenty-four horses.[9] It is possible that, like Chaucer's pilgrims, she found a traveling companion in De Lisle, her future enemy, who likewise heeded the pope's call to congregate in Christian fellowship.[10]

What started out as a private property dispute between servants of the respective antagonists was to escalate into a vengeful feud involving arson and murder. But for all the interest, both among contemporary and modern historians, that this famous dispute has generated,[11] its origin remains shrouded in mystery. One of the aims of this chapter is to explain it. Equally challenging is the attempt to arrive at a verdict on De Lisle's guilt or innocence independent of the bias of the medieval records. The indictments recorded against the bishop in the king's bench plea rolls generally reflect the viewpoint of the plaintiff and are expressed in formu-

---

3. *DNB*, 26:100–101; G. E. Cokayne, ed., *The Complete Peerage of England, Scotland, Ireland, Great Britain and the United Kingdom*, rev. V. Gibbs et al., new edition, 13 vols. (London, 1910–59), 1:243–44, 7:378, 10:463.

4. K. Fowler, *The King's Lieutenant: Henry of Grosmont, First Duke of Lancaster, 1310–1361* (London, 1969), 219–20; M. Prestwich, *The Three Edwards: War and State in England, 1272–1377* (London, 1980), 175; J. Vale, *Edward III and Chivalry: Chivalric Society and its Context, 1270–1350* (Woodbridge, Suffolk, 1982), 87–88.

5. *DNB*, 26:105. Fowler and Prestwich seem to concur with this assessment. See Fowler, *King's Lieutenant*, 218–19; Prestwich, *Three Edwards*, 189.

6. *DNB*, 58:444; *Complete Peerage* 12, part 2, 304; *The Victoria History of the Counties of England: Northamptonshire Families*, ed. O. Barron (London, 1906), 318.

7. *CPR*, 1348–50, 324–25.

8. She was dead by July 1380. See *Complete Peerage* 12, part 2, 304; *VCH Northamptonshire Families*, 318.

9. *Foedera*, 3, no. 1, 203.

10. CUL, EDR, G/1/1, Reg. De Lisle, fol. 21r.

11. See Introduction, note 6.

laic language, allowing little room for opposing argument. This is balanced somewhat by the Ely biographer's account of the feud, which is perhaps even more heavily biased, in the bishop's favor, but is more intimate and revealing than the legal briefs. In the aftermath of Lady Wake's successful prosecution, many other alleged victims came forward to complain against De Lisle. Their evidence, as well as that of others enrolled at various times in the rolls of king's bench, gaol delivery, and court of common pleas, also needs to be factored into any general assessment of the bishop's supposed criminal activity. Finally, Edward III's efforts to punish De Lisle for his perceived injustices against his cousin aroused no little controversy among his subjects. The king's hasty seizure of De Lisle's temporalities in 1355 met with resistance from his ministers and council, who required that the bishop be punished only after due process of law. It can be said that the incident posed the greatest crisis to Edward's home government since the king's bitter conflict with Archbishop John Stratford in 1340–41.[12]

A Case of Arson at Colne

It is not immediately clear why, on the night of 28 July 1354, just two years after the end of De Lisle's feud with Richard Spynk, some of the bishop's most trusted officials, including his brother John, who acted as chief steward of the episcopal estate, should have burned down property claimed by Lady Wake in Colne, Huntingdonshire. That indictment, the result of an inquest held before Sir John Dengayn, justice of the peace for Huntingdonshire, and Sir Henry Green, justice of the court of common pleas, on 30 October 1354, marked the opening salvo in the hostile legal battle that was to occupy the two parties for the next two years.[13] The motive for the alleged crime does not seem to have been material gain, since theft does not figure in the original indictment.[14] Rather, the inci-

12. W. M. Ormrod describes the disputed seizure of De Lisle's temporalities as "the one disruption in the king's government in a period characterized by harmony and cooperation." See W. M. Ormrod, "Edward III's Government of England, c. 1346–1356" (D.Phil. diss., Oxford, 1984), 259.

13. PRO, KB 27/379, rex m. 9; CPR, 1354–58, 128, and see Appendix B, pages 240–42.

14. Only De Lisle's letter of petition to the pope shortly before 6 October 1356 mentions "theft" (*furti*) in addition to arson. Robbery is not mentioned in the commissions of oyer and terminer or in any record of the indictment. See LPL, Reg. Islip, fol. 138v; LAO, Episcopal Reg. VIII (Reg. John Gynwell), fol. 93r, and see Appendix B, page 247. All references to Gynwell's register are taken from microfilm MS 8232 in the CUL.

dent probably was the product of revenge and willful destruction on the part of De Lisle's men. However, the feud did not originate between De Lisle and Lady Wake, since there is nothing surviving from the years leading up to 1354 that would have given the two reason to hate each other. Instead, the origin appears to lie in a local land dispute between two servants of the respective patrons. Eventually, De Lisle and Lady Wake were drawn into the dispute once it escalated and entered the courts, where both parties were obliged to show their good lordship by taking the side of their respective followers.

Prior to the feud, however, contact between the main protagonists was minimal. On 18 September 1346, De Lisle granted a license for private oratory to Thomas, Lord Wake, Blanche's husband, one of many such grants the bishop was to make during his episcopate.[15] On 12 July 1350 an oyer and terminer commission was issued by the crown to investigate complaints made by Lady Wake's brother, Henry of Grosmont, then earl of Lancaster, that John de Lisle and more than twenty other men had broken into and burned his houses in Lincolnshire and carried off his goods there.[16] However, no record exists of any resulting trial or inquest, and the matter seems to have been dropped. The wealthy and extensive Lancaster estate was a popular target of criminal depredations: The infamous Coterel gang, for instance, raided the earl's parks in three counties in 1329.[17]

The origin of hostilities between De Lisle and Lady Wake probably is embedded in an ancient and complicated dispute over property rights so typical of land feuds in the Middle Ages.[18] The manor of La Leghe in Colne, containing the houses that were to be destroyed by De Lisle's men, originally belonged to the bishops of Ely as part of their "soke" of Somersham. Throughout the thirteenth century, the property was held by the Argentein family in exchange for feudal service owed to the bishop. The Argenteins, in turn, rented the land out to the Wacheshams of Suffolk who owed allegiance to the Lancastrian party.[19] Thus, by the all too familiar process of subinfeudation, the manor's ownership could be contested by two different masters through their respective vassals.

By the mid-fourteenth century, La Leghe became the subject of several competing local claims. Sir Robert de Waschesham declared the manor his by right of succession from his great-grandfather, Giles de Wachesham. But a new claimant, William de Herleston, king's clerk and keeper of the

15. CUL, EDR, G/I/1, Reg. De Lisle, fol. 1v.
16. *CPR*, 1348–50, 592.
17. *CPR*, 1327–30, 432.
18. For recent studies of other late medieval land disputes, see J. G. Bellamy, *Bastard Feudalism and the Law* (London, 1989); Maddern, *Violence and Social Order*; and works cited in Chapter 3, note 94.
19. *VCH Hunts.*, 2:167–69.

royal writs, appeared on the scene. It is possible that Sir Robert pledged La Leghe to Herleston as collateral for a loan, but the exact relationship between the two men is unclear.[20] In Michaelmas term 1346, Sir Robert brought a suit in the court of common pleas against Herleston in order to reclaim the manor. Wachesham pleaded that La Leghe devolved on him through the original deed by Giles, his great-grandfather, to his grandparents, Gerard and Joan. Herleston contested the deed, but the outcome is unrecorded.[21] In 1347, however, Herleston was recorded in possession of the manor.[22]

In the meantime, Herleston, it seems, needed to fight off other claims. On 20 January 1342, he bought off the claim of Richard and Joan Rikedown, who surrendered their stake to "a messuage, 200 acres of land, and eight acres of meadow with appurtenances in Somersham, Colne, and Bluntisham [Huntingdonshire]" in exchange for the payment of eleven and one-half marks, or £7 13s. 4d., per year.[23] On 18 November 1343, Herleston came to terms with Henry de Broughton, chaplain, who quitclaimed the same parcel for an unspecified sum. An important stipulation, however, was that after Herleston's death the manor would revert to Lawrence de Herleston and Margaret Holm.[24] The last record of a legal transaction concerning the manor dates to 18 November 1347, when Henry de Broughton and Lady Wake's valet, William Holm, conveyed La Leghe to William de Herleston and to Holm's sister, Margaret.[25]

Nevertheless, this is not the last we hear of the Holms. It is apparent that Margaret Holm was busy acquiring property in the area. On 3 February 1347, she was granted "a messuage and seven acres of land with appurtenances in Somersham and Colne" by Simon and Amicia Dyke of Graveley, Hertfordshire, in return for 20 marks, or just over £13.[26] The Holm family was no stranger to quarrels prior to their entanglement with De Lisle. In Hilary term 1350, William Holm brought a suit in the court of common pleas against John Stubbard of Colne on a charge of forcible en-

20. Ibid., 169.
21. PRO, CP 40/348, m. 83d.
22. PRO, CP 25/1:94/26, m. 70 (old pagination: m. 71).
23. "Hec est finalis concordia facta in curia domini regis . . . inter Willelmum de Herleston' clericum querulum et Ricardum Rikedon' et Johannam uxorem eius deforciantes, de uno mesuagio, ducentis acris terre, et octo acris prati cum pertinentiis in Someresham, Colne, et Bluntesham." PRO, CP 25/1:94/26, no. 51.
24. PRO, CP 25/1:94/26, no. 52.
25. PRO, CP 25/1:94/26, m. 70 (old pagination: m. 71).
26. "Hec est finalis concordia facta in curia domini regis . . . inter Margaretam de Holm querulam et Simonem Dyke de Gravele et Amiciam uxorem eius deforciantes, de uno mesuagio et septem acris terre cum pertinenciis in Somersham et Colne." PRO, CP 25/1:94/26, m. 72 (old pagination: m. 73).

try and theft. Holm alleged that Stubbard had broken his close at Colne, killed his sow pig worth 10s., and carried away his goods to the value of £5.[27] Five years later, Holm was murdered for the part he had played in helping to convict De Lisle and his men for the Colne arson. On the day after the murder, Margaret Holm led an unruly mob against the bishop in protest of her brother's untimely death.[28]

The bitter antagonist of the Holms was De Lisle's chamberlain, Ralph Carles. He was keeper of the bishop's park, warren, and free chase at Somersham, the next village to Colne in Huntingdonshire.[29] In addition, the bishop had granted Carles for the term of his life "a messuage, and twenty-eight acres of arable land, and two and a half acres of meadow with appurtenances" in Colne.[30] These holdings may have impinged on lands held by the Holm family and led to hostilities between the two parties. It is also possible that Carles, and perhaps De Lisle, sought to revive the bishop of Ely's ancient claim to La Leghe itself. De Lisle seems to have been trying to acquire land in the area around this time: On 31 March 1347, John Mowyn brought a suit in the assize courts against the bishop and four other men whom he accused of "unjustly" disseising him "of common pasture in Somersham and Bluntisham which pertains to his freehold in Woodhurst [Huntingdonshire]."[31] Carles was one of those indicted for burning down the houses of La Leghe: According to one indictment, the deed was done with his "assent" in his role as parker of Somersham.[32] The chamberlain also was identified as Holm's murderer.[33]

The dispute over La Leghe, therefore, was almost exclusively between Carles and Holm, who called in their respective patrons only when the feud turned violent and necessitated legal counsel. De Lisle and Lady Wake even may have entered the fray unwillingly. It is extremely unlikely that the raid on La Leghe threatened Lady Wake personally or that

27. PRO, CP 40/360, m. 2.
28. See pages 130–32.
29. BL, Add. ms 41612, fol. 113v; PRO, KB 27/382, rex m. 17.
30. ". . . predictus Radulphus Careles . . . tenuit ad terminum vite sue ad voluntatem Thome episcopi Elien' [Ely] apud Colne iuxta Somersham in predicto comitatu Hunt' [Huntingdon] . . . unum mesuagium et xxviij. acras terre arabilis et duas acras prati de dimidietate cum pertinenciis simul cum custodia chace de Somersham." PRO, KB 27/382, rex m. 17.
31. "Assisia venit recognoscere si Thomas episcopus Elien' [Ely], Robertus Willard, Robertus de Hotost senior, et Johannes le Heggere iniuste et cetera disseisiverunt Johannem filium Willelmi Mowyn de Woldhirst de communa pas[tura] sue in Somersham et Blundesham, que pertinet ad liberum [liberam] tenuram suum [suam] in Woldhirst." PRO, JUST 1/1431, m. 36d.
32. "Thomas de Baa per assensum Radulphi Carles parcarii de Somersham cum auxilio aliorum ignotorum posuerunt ignem super domos domine de Wake apud Colne." PRO, KB 27/381, rex m. 24.
33. PRO, KB 27/384, rex m. 11d., and see Appendix B, pages 245–46.

Fig. 4. Great seal of Thomas de Lisle (left) and seal of Alan Walsingham.

she ever resided in the manor. The domains that she inherited from her husband lay primarily north of the river Trent in the counties of York, Cumbria, Lincoln, Leicester, and Northampton.[34] Nevertheless, both De Lisle and Lady Wake probably felt themselves obliged to support their retainers' causes and assume them as their own; this was expected as part of good lordship and was considered necessary in order to attract and maintain loyal followers. Maintenance is the term generally used to describe such a wielding of a lord's influence on behalf of his retainers in order to protect them from legal prosecution. Although traditionally maintenance was held responsible for much of the crime and corruption in late medieval England, more recent studies of magnate and gentry be-

34. *CPR*, 1281–90, 35.

havior have arrived at a different conclusion. The violence surrounding a lord's retinue usually was circumscribed by the respect in which he wished to be held in the local community. Habitual maintainers of criminals, such as De Lisle, probably were uncommon.[35]

It was not long after the arson had been committed at Colne in July 1354 that legal prosecution on behalf of Lady Wake began in the succeeding Michaelmas term. On 3 October 1354, the crown issued a special commission of oyer and terminer to investigate Lady Wake's complaint,[36] quickly followed by the inquest at Huntingdon on 30 October. The jury determined that four houses at Colne said to belong to Lady Wake had been burned down along with a stack of sedge and an unfortunate horse complete with its saddle and bridle. The total value of the damage was assessed at £200. Among those who were said to have participated in the crime were the bishop's brother John de Lisle, chief steward of the episcopal estate; William de Pecham, a friar preacher who acted as one of the bishop's vicars-general; Robert de Godington, parson of Newton, Cambridgeshire, and one of the bishop's auditors; Thomas Durant (or Darent), parson of Stretham, Cambridgeshire, and the bishop's steward; Henry de Shankton, parson of Hadstock, Cambridgeshire, and the bishop's auditor; Stephen de Brokesbourn, custodian of St. Lawrence's Chapel-by-Wormeley, Hertfordshire; Robert Hale of Earith, De Lisle's bailiff of Somersham; John Balhorn of Colne; Thomas de Baa, the bishop's constable of Wisbech Castle, Cambridgeshire; and Ralph Carles. Bishop De Lisle himself was charged with having ordered and consented to the arson and of having received the culprits at his nearby manor at Somersham.[37]

On 15 May 1355, the indicted men, except the bishop, appeared before Chief Justice William Shareshull and his fellow justices of king's bench, where they pleaded not guilty to the charges.[38] Their case never came to trial. For seven years, the trial was repeatedly adjourned from one term to the next because either the jury failed to appear in court (*pro defectu juratorum*), the sheriff failed to submit his original writ of *venire facias*

---

35. See pages 70–82.

36. PRO, C 66/243, m. 5d.; C 66/244, m. 13d.; *CPR*, 1354–58, 128. The damages were assessed at five houses, a horse worth £10, and stacks of hay and rushes valued at 100 marks, or £66 13s. 4d.

37. PRO, KB 27/379, rex m. 9, and see Appendix B, pages 240–42. Other copies of the indictment were recorded in Michaelmas term 1355 and Trinity term 1356. See PRO, KB 27/381, rex m. 24; KB 27/384, rex m. 11d. The former copy mentions that five houses were burned and a stack of rushes ("integre concremaverunt quinquedomos et unum tassum rosci"). The commission of oyer and terminer issued on 10 November 1354 also names Henry Ferour and Richard Carter as perpetrators, but their names do not appear in the indictment. See *CPR*, 1354–58, 162.

38. PRO, KB 27/379, rex m. 9, and see Appendix B, page 242.

(*vicecomes non misit brevem*), or the defendants themselves failed to appear (*ipsi non venierunt*).[39] During Easter and Trinity terms of 1355, the defendants were allowed to make bail and were released into the custody of four knights: Sir John de Colville of Cambridgeshire, Sir Henry Waleys of Kent, Sir John Bardolph of Berkshire, and Sir Gerard de Braybrook.[40] However, it was while he was free on bail that Ralph Carles allegedly murdered William Holm in August 1355.[41] Thereafter, the crown's policy toward the other defendants changed. In the following Michaelmas term they were denied bail and consigned to prison in the custody of the marshal, while the court, in accordance with the wishes of the king and council, did not proceed with the trial despite the jury being present.[42] It is quite possible that John de Lisle and several other defendants were kept in prison until the bishop's death in July 1361 at Avignon.[43] Before he left England for the papal court in the autumn of 1356, De Lisle complained to the pope that his brother and other men had been languishing in the king's gaols for the past year and a half.[44] By 30 May 1362, four of the defendants, William de Pecham, Robert de Godington, Henry de Shankton, and John Balhorn, received royal pardons, which they presented before the bench in Hilary term 1363.[45] John de Lisle still was being sought by the court in Michaelmas term 1362 for failing to appear on the date fixed at his bail.[46] His fellow prisoner, Thomas Durant, was assigned a court

39. PRO, KB 27/380, rex m. 4d.; KB 27/382, rex m. 18; KB 27/383, rex m. 21; KB 27/384, rex m. 8d.; KB 27/385, rex m. 9d.; KB 27/386, rex m. 19d.; KB 27/387, rex m. 27d.; KB 27/388, rex m. 7d.; KB 27/389, rex m. 15d.; KB 27/390, rex m. 12d.; KB 27/391, rex m. 12d.; KB 27/392, rex m. 13d.; KB 27/393, rex m. 16; KB 27/394, rex m. 7d.; KB 27/395, rex m. 13d.; KB 27/396, rex m. 13; KB 27/397, rex m. 8; KB 27/398, rex m. 15d.; KB 27/399, rex m. 19; KB 27/401, rex m. 15; KB 27/402, rex m. 12d.; KB 27/403, rex m. 17; KB 27/404, rex m. 16d.; KB 27/405, rex m. 12; KB 27/406, rex m. 12d.; KB 27/408, rex m. 48.

40. PRO, KB 27/379, rex m. 9.; KB 27/380, rex m. 4d., and see Appendix B, 246.

41. *RP*, 2:267, and see Appendix B, page 244.

42. PRO, KB 27/381, rex m. 7.

43. In Hilary and Easter terms 1356, Easter term 1357, Easter term 1358, and Hilary term 1359, they were recorded as "committed to prison in the custody of the marshal [of England]" ("interim commituntur prisone in custodia marescalli"). See PRO, KB 27/382, rex m. 18; KB 27/383, rex m. 21; KB 27/387, rex m. 27d.; KB 27/391, rex m. 12d.; KB 27/394, rex m. 7d. John de Lisle's fellow inmates were William de Pecham, Robert de Godington, Henry de Shankton, and, until Easter term 1358, Thomas Durant. For the date of Thomas de Lisle's death, see *AS*, 1:662, and Appendix B, page 238.

44. LPL, Reg. Simon Islip, fol. 139r; LAO, Episcopal Reg. VIII (Reg. John Gynwell), fol. 93v, and see Appendix B, page 248.

45. *CPR*, 1361–64, 199–200, 215.

46. PRO, KB 27/408, rex m. 50d.

47. PRO, KB 27/403, rex m. 17.

date for Trinity term 1361, but no judgment was recorded against him.[47]

Aside from Carles, who went missing since his alleged murderous deed,[48] three other men indicted for the Colne arson managed to escape the long confinement imposed on their partners in crime. Robert Hale and Stephen de Brokesbourn presented king's pardons and were set free by the bench on 2 December 1355.[49] Such favors did not come without a price. On the same day that the crown issued its pardon, 28 November, Hale served on the sheriff's inquest into the lands held by the now outlawed Ralph Carles.[50] He also served on the inquests into the bishop's estate at Somersham after the crown had seized De Lisle's temporalities in October 1356.[51] In addition, the pardoned men may have served as witnesses for the prosecution against De Lisle for his role in Holm's murder or even have spied on the bishop's movements prior to his court appearance. Despite De Lisle's efforts at secrecy, the king learned that he was preparing to flee to Avignon to appeal his case to the pope, contrary to the Statute of *Praemunire* of 1353, and therefore on 23 October 1355, he ordered the bishop to attend the ensuing parliament.[52] Two weeks earlier, on 8 October, Edward had excused a third defendant, the bishop's constable, Thomas de Baa, from his scheduled court appearance because "the said Thomas may be engaged therein in our service."[53] Baa was allowed to make bail in Easter term 1356 and Easter term 1357 while his companions languished in the Marshalsea.[54] Moreover, he retained his constableship after the Ely temporalities had fallen into the king's hand in 1356. His reward was short-lived, however, for he surrendered his office back to the crown on 3 May 1358, at which time it was granted to the king's yeoman, John Herlyng.[55]

While the case against the bishop's men was allowed to languish, the case against De Lisle himself was pursued quickly and vigorously, presumably because the bishop was the only defendant rich enough to pay

48. Although Ralph Carles was recorded as committed to the Marshalsea in Easter term 1356, he did not appear in court for trial during the following Trinity term and consequently was outlawed (PRO, KB 27/383, rex m. 21; KB 27/384, rex m. 11d., and see Appendix B, page 246). He died on 20 June 1362. See Aston, *Thomas Arundel*, 260.

49. *CPR*, 1354–58, 313–14.

50. PRO, KB 27/382, rex m. 17.

51. PRO, E 143/9/2, mm. 17, 50.

52. *Foedera*, 3, no. 1, 314; *CCR*, 1354–60, 159.

53. ". . . et le dit Thomas soit ia entendant a nostre service en nostre present viage par quoi il ne poet estre devant vous a la dite quinzaine." PRO, KB 27/381, rex m. 7.

54. PRO, KB 27/383, rex m. 21; KB 27/387, rex m. 27d.

55. *CPR*, 1354–58, 462; 1358–61, 43.

the hefty damages claimed by the plaintiff. A second commission of oyer and terminer, which named De Lisle as one of the principal instigators of the arson, rather than a mere abettor, was issued on 10 November 1354 to Sir John Dengayn and Nicholas de Stukeley, justices of the peace for Huntingdonshire, and to Sir Henry Green, justice of the court of common pleas, and Robert Thorp, king's serjeant.[56] These four men accordingly presided at a trial held at Yaxley, Huntingdonshire, which is described by De Lisle's biographer but is unrecorded in the king's bench plea rolls. In the biographer's rather colorful account, the arson was committed by "certain sons of iniquity" rather than by De Lisle and his men, and the justices presiding at Yaxley pressured a reluctant jury to return a guilty verdict. When the jurors named De Lisle as only an accessory to the crime, the justices ordered them to go back and deliberate a second time in order to determine if the bishop was not really guilty as principal along with the others. When the jurors subsequently returned the desired verdict, the justices immediately sentenced De Lisle to pay £900 in compensation to Lady Wake, even though the damages claimed in the first inquest had only amounted to £200.[57]

De Lisle was not about to accept quietly such a punitive decision, however, and he made several attempts to overturn his conviction. The bishop's biographer, fuming that his hero had been "unjustly condemned," describes how De Lisle sued a writ of attaint on the grounds that the jurors at Yaxley had used false testimony to convict him.[58] In her own account, Lady Wake presented the appeal not as a gallant attempt to correct injustice but rather as a means whereby the bishop "could harass and trouble" the plaintiff "her whole life with little damage and cost" to himself.[59] In any case, the retrial had to be abandoned because the transcript from the previous trial at Yaxley could not be found. According to the biographer, foul play was afoot as the keepers of the transcript deliberately stonewalled attempts to recover it.[60]

De Lisle's next appeal came in Easter term 1355, when he sued a writ of error in another attempt to invalidate his conviction. He claimed that three mistakes had been made at the trial that had convicted him of arson against Lady Wake. The first was that the justices of oyer and terminer had mistranslated the Latin word *juxta* in a writ of trespass, so that the place where the crime was said to have occurred, at "Colne *juxta* Somersham" ("Colne beside Somersham"), was assumed to be "a place

56. *CPR*, 1354–58, 162.
57. *AS*, 1:655–56, and see Appendix B, pages 229–30. De Lisle's fine was recorded as £895 in the king's bench plea rolls. See PRO, KB 27/379, attorneys, m. 1.
58. *AS*, 1:656, and see Appendix B, page 230.
59. *RP*, 2:267, and see Appendix B, page 244.
60. *AS*, 1:656, and see Appendix B, page 230.

in Somersham." In other words, two separate towns in Huntingdonshire, Colne and Somersham, were assumed to be one and the same place. The second error alleged by the bishop was that the writ of *venire facias* (summons of the indicted man to appear in court) had failed to specify before whom of the justices De Lisle had to appear. A third error, according to De Lisle, was that the justices had not ruled on a penalty once he had been convicted of the arson.

Arguing on behalf of the original plaintiff (Lady Wake), Robert Thorp, king's serjeant, attempted to nullify the first objection by referring to the record of the Yaxley trial (which must have been the transcript supposedly "lost" in the previous suit on writ of attaint). The record proved, Thorp maintained, that the scene of the crime had been identified in English as "Colne beside Somersham," a fact that De Lisle allegedly had acknowledged at the trial. The place-name was then translated into Latin as *Colne juxta Somersham* in the writ of trespass and signified the same place as the English version. William de Witchingham, king's serjeant pleading for the defense, argued that a name in English did not carry always the same meaning as its counterpart in Latin. *Juxta* usually was interpreted temporally, Witchingham contended, in which case Colne would be understood to be another village outside of Somersham and not "in" Somersham. Yet the English version, "beside Somersham," was not to be taken as an adverbial surname of Colne, and therefore the two versions, in English and Latin, did not signify the same thing. Chief Justice William Shareshull ruled that, "Latin is a formal language to be put in writs, and English is the language of laymen. Therefore, since [a word in] Latin comprises the same signification as does the English [one], we hold them to be all one, and the record good."[61] The plaintiff also contended that since she originally had sued a writ of trespass, which sought only damages and not possession of freehold, any name of "a village or hamlet" would be sufficient in order that a jury be impaneled from the neighborhood, an interpretation the bench agreed with.[62]

The court then turned to the second objection. William Fyfield, king's serjeant pleading for the plaintiff, argued that once again the trial record proved the objection to be insupportable. The writ of *venire facias*, Fyfield asserted, had been entered as part of the original plea, which was recorded in Latin as "Pleas [held] before Henry Greenfield [Henry Green] and others." Since this had seemed sufficient to both parties at the time, there was no misunderstanding as to who would preside at the trial. Witchingham countered that the record was insufficient, since an oyer

61. *Yearbooks* 2–3, Easter term, 29 Edward III, 30–31, and see Appendix B, pages 242–43. Other, less complete versions of the same disputation are to be found in *Liber Assisarum et Placitorum Corone*, ed. J. Rastell (London, 1513), 29 Edward III, plea 33; *Select Cases*, 6:100–102.
    62. *Select Cases*, 6:101.

and terminer commission was directed to four men, all of whom ought to be named since two could sit one day and another two the next. Shareshull, however, dismissed the objection, declared the third of "no value," and the original judgment awarding £900 to Lady Wake was upheld.[63]

De Lisle by now was running out of appeals. If his biographer is to be believed, he decided on a desperate gamble to reverse his fortunes: an appeal to the king in person. He approached Edward III while his majesty was out hawking. De Lisle "humbly" asked the king to "command that a fulfillment of justice be done concerning the injuries inflicted on himself." Immediately Edward, as a precaution, called over Sir Richard la Vache, a household servant and a member of the Order of the Garter, so that he could later testify to the words exchanged by the two men. The king is then alleged to have said: "Lord bishop, the lawsuit that is contested between you and our beloved kinswoman, Lady Wake, is said to be extremely hateful to us and to our nobles and the people of our realm, out of which much injury to persons and many subversions and dangers could result in future. Therefore, we intend to take the aforesaid lawsuit into our hands so that neither your will nor hers may be done in all things, but by proceeding along the middle way, peace and harmony may be restored amongst you." But the bishop was by no means satisfied with this reply.

"Most excellent lord," he said, "let it be arranged, if it please your Serenity, that the aforementioned lawsuit between us be allowed to be decided in accordance with the law and justice of the realm."

"And who prevents you in our kingdom from having the law or justice?" Edward demanded.

"My lord," remonstrated De Lisle, "so it is that I am unable to have the law or justice in my lawsuit, being hindered, as I believe, by the royal power." Such an open accusation of obstruction could not go unanswered.

"Certainly you, Thomas de Lisle, speak falsely!" Edward angrily responded, "for you were never so hindered. But you will have the law, without the favor of the law!" De Lisle then had to withdraw from the place, reports the biographer, "with the indignation of the king [upon his head], having been comforted very little or not at all in his lawsuit."[64]

De Lisle's personal appeal to Edward thus ended in complete disaster, leaving the bishop in an infinitely worse position than before. If the story is true, it would help explain Edward's overeager desire to punish De Lisle at a later stage in the feud with Lady Wake.[65] The king's position as arbitrator of disputes among the high nobility was a carefully nurtured one that accorded well with the chivalric mold of his reign.[66] De Lisle, in

---

63. *Yearbooks* 2–3, Easter term, 29 Edward III, 31, and see Appendix B, page 243.
64. *AS*, 1:657, and see Appendix B, page 231.
65. See pages 134–37.
66. P. Johnson, *The Life and Times of Edward III* (London, 1973), 114–15; Ormrod, *Reign of Edward III*, 55–56.

his confrontation with the king, challenged this role, thereby inspiring in his sovereign a well of animosity toward himself that no subject would have envied. The incident also points up a curiously stubborn and undiplomatic streak in the bishop that was to reveal itself again and again, stifling any future chances of reconciliation between himself and the crown.[67]

Although the £900 judgment in Lady Wake's favor probably had been handed down before the end of 1354, De Lisle had managed to delay payment of the fine for at least the first six months of the new year. By 23 June 1355 Edward had determined to fulfill his promise to the bishop and intervene in the protracted suit against his cousin. On that date, the crown ordered Chief Justice Shareshull and his fellow justices of king's bench to grant Lady Wake a writ of *elegit*, which would allow her to collect the £900 fine awarded her against De Lisle. Apparently, a dispute had arisen over whether the writ of *elegit* could be granted against a bishop, since it had never been done so before. The crown cited, as its authority for granting the *elegit*, the Second Statute of Westminster of 1285, which authorized a plaintiff to sue such a writ in order to have execution of judgment against any defendant without exception.[68] In Trinity term 1355, Lady Wake came before the bench to collect her fine, but De Lisle's counsel made a last-ditch effort to persuade the justices that *elegit* did not apply to the bishop since there was no precedent for such an execution against a "peer of the realm and a prelate of Holy Church, who does not have [this status] in effect except during his lifetime." The bench replied that the Second Statute of Westminster was general and applied to peers as well as to others. If De Lisle was indeed only a lifetime peer, the court noted, then his lands would be forfeit. Robert Thorp, king's serjeant representing the plaintiff, then asked that De Lisle's temporalities be confiscated, since he was a prelate and his person could not be imprisoned like that of another man. Under this threat, De Lisle finally agreed to pay the fine, sent for his money, and handed it over there and then to Lady Wake.[69]

The Murder of William Holm

De Lisle's payment of the fine by no means ended his feud with his noble adversary. Instead, it was merely the prelude to a bloody escalation of hostilities between the two camps. Again, the primary actors in the vio-

---

67. See pages 134–35, 141–42, 243–44.
68. *CCR*, 1354–60, 137; *SR*, 1:82: sec. 18.
69. *Yearbooks*, 2–3, Trinity term, 29 Edward III, 42, and see Appendix B, pages 243–44.

lence were Ralph Carles and William Holm. On 28 August 1355, a little over a month after the end of the Trinity term in which De Lisle had surrendered his money to Lady Wake, Carles and another man, Walter Ripton of Little Whyte, allegedly murdered William Holm at the hour of high noon in "Gunnoklye" wood near Somersham. The murder supposedly was in revenge "for the suit which the aforesaid William Holm made on behalf of the king for the burning of the manors of Blanche, [Lady] de Wake."[70] It is possible that Carles carried out the vendetta on the orders of his master, but it is equally likely that the murder was yet another manifestation of a private feud between the two men, with Carles egged on by the reversal suffered by his patron. According to De Lisle's biographer, Carles (a Norman by birth) was inspired by the devil to kill Holm while they were engaged in a heated argument.[71]

Whatever the exact circumstances of the murder, the local people of Somersham seem to have been convinced that the bishop lay behind the deed. On the morning after the killing, De Lisle's entourage was set upon by an angry mob led by the dead man's sister, Margaret, as it left the bishop's Somersham manor on its way to London. Among the rabble that shouted curses and abuses at the bishop from all sides was Henry de Colne, one of the jurors who had indicted De Lisle and his men of arson at the first inquest held in October 1354 at Huntingdon.[72] It is likely, therefore, that the crowd that surrounded the detested bishop included political foes riding on the back of popular sentiment as well as people like Margaret Holm who perhaps had a genuine grievance against him. De Lisle's biographer, who provides a full account of the mob's attack, describes how the bishop bravely confronted the rabble's wrath, likening his conduct to that of the biblical King David as he was cursed by Shimei.[73] Margaret Holm, that "extremely malicious woman," reports the biographer, began screaming at the bishop: "A curse upon you, Thomas de Lisle, a curse, a curse upon you, most wicked murderer, a curse upon you! You have killed my brother William Holm! A curse upon you, a curse!" De Lisle turned and faced his accuser, saying: "You accuse me unjustly, woman. I am innocent of the blood of your brother. For I did not kill him, nor did I ever command that he be killed. But he was killed without my knowledge or consent. God only knows [who killed him]."[74]

Obviously, De Lisle's tormentors did not believe his protestations of innocence, for they proceeded to follow him all the way from Somersham

---

70. PRO, KB 27/384, rex m. 11d., and see Appendix B, pages 245–46.
71. *AS*, 1:657, and see Appendix B, page 232.
72. PRO, KB 27/379, rex m. 9, and see Appendix B, page 241.
73. 2 Samuel 16:5–14. The biographer erroneously quotes the second book of Kings. See *AS*, 1:658, and Appendix B, page 232.
74. *AS*, 1:657–58, and see Appendix B, page 232.

to St. Ives, Huntingdonshire, a distance of approximately five miles. When they arrived at the latter village, the mob, making a "horrible din," roused the whole community with its noise. The swelling crowd then blocked off the village bridge,[75] which De Lisle and his men could cross only by leaving behind their carriages containing all their provisions. The bishop and his entourage then escaped the mob by riding hard toward his manor at Little Gransden, Cambridgeshire, which they reached by midday.[76] De Lisle confirmed that this incident occurred in a petitionary letter he wrote to the pope sometime between 8 July and 6 October 1356. The bishop complained that at St. Ives he had been detained forcibly by the mob, who had taken advantage of their blockade of the bridge to assault his retinue, which included both horsemen and footmen. Some of his men, De Lisle said, had been dragged from their horses and thrown to the ground, whereupon the frenzied populace savagely had beat them and torn their clothes. In addition, all his baggage left behind at the bridge had been seized by his pursuers.[77]

This incident, so says the biographer, made De Lisle reflect on his future implication in the Holm murder. Anticipating that his temporalities could be seized, he wrote letters to the administrators of his estate, ordering them to sell quickly, but cautiously, all livestock and movable goods on the manors except for necessary supplies. He then entrusted the money to merchants for safekeeping until he needed it again, presumably when he was ready to flee England.[78] In spite of the precautions for secrecy, however, the king got wind of De Lisle's plans, possibly with the aid of spies recruited from among the bishop's men indicted for arson.[79] One month before the parliament to be held on 23 November 1355, the crown issued a special writ to De Lisle commanding his presence at the forthcoming assembly. Edward was concerned, he said, because he had learned that the bishop was "preparing to cross over the sea to foreign parts around the aforesaid day [of parliament]."[80] De Lisle was warned that if he failed

75. This would not have been difficult to do, if the original wooden structure was of similar dimensions to the surviving stone one built in the early fifteenth century. The present bridge of St. Ives measures only thirteen feet across. See C. H. Evelyn-White, "The Bridge and Bridge Chapel of St. Ives, Huntingdonshire," *The Transactions of the Cambridgeshire and Huntingdonshire Archaeological Society* 1 (1904), 81.

76. *AS*, 1:658, and see Appendix B, pages 232–33.

77. LPL, Reg. Islip, fols. 138v–139r; LAO, Episcopal Reg. VIII, fols. 91v, 93v, and see Appendix B, page 248.

78. *AS*, 1:658, and see Appendix B, page 233.

79. Edward also may have been alerted by the departure from England, reported in August and October 1355, of two friar preachers who probably were carrying messages from De Lisle to the pope in Avignon concerning the Lady Wake dispute. See page 126.

80. "Jamque intellexerimus quod vos, ad mandatum nostrum praedictum con-

to attend, his temporalities would be forfeit, a punishment Edward could have enforced using the recently enacted Statute of *Praemunire* of 1353. The statute forbade anyone from appealing to a foreign court judgments handed down in the king's courts or matters pertaining to them. Outlawry and forfeiture were to be the penalties should the appellor fail to respond within two months of being served a writ of *praemunire facias*.[81]

At the parliament that took place at Westminster from 23 until 30 November 1355, Lady Wake presented a petition to the king that most likely was read out to the assembly, to De Lisle's great embarrassment. The injured noblewoman presented a long list of grievances: First, the bishop and his men "have, against the peace and law of the land, burnt her houses," complained Lady Wake, after which "she recovered through the law [at the Yaxley trial] a great mischief pursued without favour." She thought that from then on she would have "peace and repose," but De Lisle continued to contest the suit through a writ of attaint, which caused great inconvenience to her and her neighbors, since they had to appear yet again in court. Then, while the perpetrators of the arson were let out on bail, the plaintiff's valet, William Holm, was "wickedly" murdered around the hour of high noon in Somersham wood. By her own account, Lady Wake's situation had deteriorated to such an extent that she and her circle were now living in a perpetual state of terror of their enemy. All she wanted, she said, was that "she and her men can live in peace, for they are greatly menaced from day to day." She asked the king to take the quarrel into his hand, so that her case would be tried *coram rege*, in the king's court, rather than in a local forum. "May it please your very honourable lord to do this," concluded her impassioned plea to Edward, "for the love of God, at the request of the said Blanche."[82]

The latter part of the appeal perhaps was more melodramatic than truthful. It already has been noted that Lady Wake's inheritance from her deceased husband lay well outside the county of Huntingdon, and therefore her interest in La Leghe was through her servant, William Holm, and her personal association with the property was minimal. Nevertheless, the strategy probably was successful in eliciting the sympathies and indignation of the members of parliament. Through blood relations alone, Lady Wake could expect the attentive interest in her plight of not only her cousin, Edward, who was doubtless present in person, but also of at least three important noblemen: Lancaster, Percy, and Arundel, the last two having married the plaintiff's sisters. Moreover, Edward, the self-

---

siderationem non habentes, ad transfretandum ad partes exteras, citra diem praedictum, vos paratis, quod in nostri ac mandati nostri praedicti contemptum cederet manifeste." *Foedera*, 3, no. 1, 314; *CCR*, 1354–60, 159.

81. *SR*, 1:329.

82. *RP*, 2:267, and see Appendix B, pages 244–45.

acknowledged model of chivalry, founder of the Order of the Garter, and arbitrator of noble behavior, could hardly fail to come to the rescue of a widowed lady in distress.

Technically, however, the king's interference in the dispute was illegal, for the Ordinance of Justices of 1346 forbade, as part of measures to limit corruption and combat maintenance, the king and his magnates from maintaining quarrels other than their own.[83] But even if Edward wished to remain impartial, the wellspring of support for Lady Wake among the lords assembled in parliament, created by this picture of a defenseless woman being hounded by the bishop of Ely, gave the king little choice but to intervene. Before parliament had convened, he had announced to De Lisle his intention of mediating in the dispute, as recounted by the bishop's biographer. Therefore, it must have come as no surprise to the assembly when Edward responded to the petition by saying out loud: "I take the quarrel into my hand."[84]

Probably soon after this announcement a second confrontation, even more dramatic than the first, allegedly took place between De Lisle and Edward at this very parliament. Again, our only source for the event is De Lisle's biography, but the account does fit in with other recorded incidents.[85] The king addressed the bishop directly before all the prelates and nobles gathered there.

"O Thomas de Lisle," said the king, "you have recently accused us, that in your lawsuit you were not able to have the law, being obstructed by our royal power." De Lisle flatly denied that he had ever uttered such words. Edward's ire was aroused.

"Most certainly you, Thomas de Lisle, lie openly!" the king cried. "For you have said such words!" He called over Sir Richard la Vache, the witness to their previous conversation, and the knight testified that De Lisle indeed had accused the king of obstruction, as Edward said. Simon Islip, the archbishop of Canterbury, and the other bishops present then came forward, hoping to calm the situation and placate the king's anger. They went up before Edward, got down on their knees, and sued for mercy on their colleague's behalf. They begged the king to forgive De Lisle his indiscretion and receive him back into the royal grace. De Lisle, however, did not help matters by remaining upright. According to the biographer, he was unsure what to do in the situation. Others standing by, who did not see the bishop incline even a little toward their sovereign, took De Lisle's posture for arrogance and were amazed. De Lisle was

83. *SR*, 1:304.
84. *RP*, 2:267, and see Appendix B, page 245.
85. See pages 136–37.

forced to withdraw once more before the king's anger. It was to be their last confrontation, for the bishop was never to see the king's face again.[86]

There is some confusion in the biographer's account about the next sequence of events. He places the Holm murder after his description of De Lisle's encounter with the king in parliament, whereas in actual fact the slaying occurred nearly three months prior to the autumn assembly.[87] Bertie Wilkinson interpreted the biographer's mistake as a deliberate manipulation to make De Lisle appear blameless in parliament.[88] The murder was, however, irrelevant to the confrontation, since what it really concerned was De Lisle's previous insult to the king's honor when he had accused Edward of partiality in his lawsuit. The Ely monk's account, in this instance, is hardly flattering to De Lisle, for by reporting the previous confrontation, the biographer proves that De Lisle did indeed perjure himself in parliament, as the king claimed. Therefore, if he really wished to exonerate De Lisle in the parliament, he would have omitted the first confrontation altogether. Instead of consciously manipulating his account, the biographer may have genuinely misunderstood the true sequence of events because the logic of continuity dictated to him otherwise. The incident in parliament follows naturally on the previous confrontation, for example, whereas the aftermath of the Holm murder, in which De Lisle had to appear before the king's bench and which also is recounted by the monk, did not occur until Trinity and Michaelmas terms of 1356, long after the assembly had adjourned.[89]

It is not certain when exactly the coroner's inquest into the Holm murder took place.[90] If, as the biographer claims, it was held shortly after the deed itself,[91] then Edward may have felt that this gave him enough justification to proceed with De Lisle's punishment without trial. The inquest, held before the coroner for Huntingdonshire, Robert de Waldeschef, at Somersham,[92] named Carles and Ripton as the principal felons but indicted De Lisle of consent to the murder. The jury also accused the bishop

86. *AS*, 1:657, and see Appendix B, pages 231–32.

87. *AS*, 1:657, and see Appendix B, page 232. According to the coroner's inquest, Holm was killed on 28 August 1355, while parliament met from 23 until 30 November 1355. See PRO, KB 27/384, rex m. 11d.; *RDP*, 4:603–8; *CCR*, 1354–60, 241–42, and Appendix B, pages 245–46.

88. B. Wilkinson, "A Letter of Edward III to his Chancellor and Treasurer," *EHR* 42 (1927), 249.

89. See page 138.

90. The transcript of the inquest, which was returned into the king's bench in Trinity term 1356, does not record the date. See PRO, KB 27/384, rex m. 11d., and Appendix B, pages 245–46.

91. *AS*, 1:658 and see Appendix B, page 233.

92. LPL, Reg. Islip, fol. 139r.

of receiving the felons at his Somersham manor after the deed had been done and of conducting them, in person with an armed escort, across county lines, where presumably they were safely out of reach of the local sheriff.[93]

As punishment for aiding and abetting this crime, the king attempted to seize De Lisle's temporalities almost immediately after parliament had ended on 30 November. He apparently had given orders to his ministers, John Thoresby, archbishop of York and royal chancellor, and William Edington, bishop of Winchester and royal treasurer, to carry out the seizure before he traveled up North to conduct a winter campaign against the Scots.[94] Thoresby and Edington, however, took advantage of the king's absence from Westminster to stall the proposed punishment of their colleague. Their insubordination probably was motivated less by an altruistic affinity for a fellow cleric as by a concern that such a hasty judgment could provide an ominous precedent for other arbitrary seizures of ecclesiastical estates, including their own. On 30 December 1355, Edward wrote an angry letter to Thoresby and Edington from Newcastle, demanding to know why the Ely temporalities still were not seized. He was dismayed at their inactivity, he said, "seeing that a wrong has been done to us so openly in our full parliament." Edward almost certainly was referring here to De Lisle's arrogant behavior toward him in the parliament a month earlier, thus confirming the biographer's account. As in the Stratford crisis of 1340–41, the king expressed his distrust of clerical ministers, who could not be relied on to carry out his orders. "If the matter had touched a great peer of the realm other than the bishop," Edward complained to Thoresby and Edington, "you would have made an altogether different execution."[95]

The one snag in the king's plans to seize De Lisle's temporalities before the end of 1355 was that it was illegal. Although an inquest already may have taken place that indicted the bishop of wrongdoing, a formal trial into De Lisle's guilt or innocence had yet to occur. This was the verdict of the king's council that met after December in order to resolve doubt about the king's actions raised by his rebellious ministers, Thoresby and Edington. The council consisted of the justices of both courts of king's bench and common pleas, the barons of the exchequer, and the king's serjeants. They bluntly advised Edward that "the temporalities of the bishop of Ely be not seized at present," because in a statute of parliament enacted in 1340, "it is expressly contained that our lord king will not act

93. PRO, KB 27/384, rex m. 11d., and see Appendix B, page 246.
94. On 23 December 1355, the king at Durham ordered his sheriffs to raise an army which was to meet him at Newcastle on 1 January 1356. See *Foedera*, 3, no. 1, 314.
95. Wilkinson, "A Letter of Edward III," 250–51.

to seize the temporalities of archbishops, bishops, abbots, priors, nor of anyone else without true and just cause in accordance with the law of the land." In order for the king to have "true and just cause" for seizing De Lisle's temporalities, the bishop first had to be convicted in a court of law. No such judgment yet had been rendered; indeed, De Lisle, according to the council, had "contradicted the charges which our lord the king accused him of in the said parliament." Here again we have another confirmation of the bishop's confrontation with the king in parliament as described by his biographer. The council concluded that the king's actions, as they now stood, were "expressly against the said statute [of 1340]."[96]

To Edward's credit, he had authorized the council's meeting in his letter to Thoresby and Edington in order to break the stalemate that had arisen between them. He evidently had learned from his mistakes of 1340–41, when he had tried to dismiss his then chancellor, John Stratford, archbishop of Canterbury, and try him for treason without consultation with the barons. On that occasion, his unilateral move had frightened and alienated the magnates into a concerted, although short-lived, opposition.[97] After 1341, however, Edward adopted a more mature political policy in which he encouraged the nobility's participation in his government through such incentives as his French campaigns, the granting of titles, and the Order of the Garter.[98] Nevertheless, the disturbing fact remains that Edward, by now an experienced and capable king, tried to flout the law, against the will of his own advisers, in order to satisfy a personal agenda in which his main motive seems to have been to defend the honor both of himself and of his cousin, Lady Wake, against De Lisle's impudent behavior. Since it is hard to believe that Edward did not know of the statute of 1340, it seems that he arbitrarily and conveniently ignored it. Moreover, his letter of December to Thoresby and Edington makes it clear that he already was convinced of De Lisle's guilt well before the trial of his case. For him, the seizure of the bishop's temporalities was simply a formality that inconveniently had to be delayed as a result of his ministers' objections. All he wanted to know, he told them, was how De Lisle's lands could be confiscated "without offense to the law."[99] Edward's complete disregard of legal procedure during what was supposedly the zenith of his kingship raises serious questions about his entire judicial and domestic policy, questions that are explored in a later chapter.[100]

96. H. G. Richardson and G. O. Sayles, *The English Parliament in the Middle Ages* (London, 1981), 32, n. 73; *SR*, 1:294, sec. 3.

97. On the Stratford crisis, see works listed in Chapter 1, note 30.

98. Prestwich, *Three Edwards*, 148–50; Vale, *Edward III and Chivalry*, 88–91; Ormrod, *Reign of Edward III*, 102–10; Waugh, *England in the Reign of Edward III*, 120–30.

99. Wilkinson, "A Letter of Edward III," 250–51.

100. See pages 187–201.

Although the council's decision proved a setback to Edward's drive to punish De Lisle, it did not stave off the day of the bishop's reckoning for long. The crown's prosecution of those deemed responsible for Holm's murder soon acquired an irresistible momentum. On the basis of the coroner's indictment, De Lisle and the other felons, Carles and Ripton, were summoned to appear before the king's bench on 8 July 1356. The latter two men, who were indicted for the actual murder, failed to appear in court on the assigned date and consequently were outlawed and their possessions declared forfeit.[101] An inquest into the lands and goods belonging to Carles and Ripton was made by the sheriff of Huntingdon, John de Harwedon, and returned into the king's bench in Hilary term 1356.[102]

De Lisle, however, duly appeared before the justices in person. According to his biographer, he arrived in the company of his ordinary, Simon Islip, archbishop of Canterbury, and of John Sheppey, bishop of Rochester. De Lisle denied the charges that he had consented to the murder or aided the culprits and claimed that he never had seen Carles after the felony had been committed. The biographer asserts that the bishop even had ordered Carles's arrest to his steward and custodian of the Isle of Ely, William Stansted. De Lisle then asked to be tried by his noble peers in parliament instead of by a jury of twelve commoners, but his request was denied.[103] According to the official record of the king's bench, on the other hand, De Lisle claimed benefit of clergy and refused to plead, instead asking that he be delivered to his ordinary, Islip, who was present in court. Ignoring this demand for immunity, the justices set a date of 6 October next when De Lisle was to appear again in court and be tried by a jury from Somersham. On the appointed day in Michaelmas term, the jury convicted De Lisle of receiving the murderers at Somersham in full knowledge that they had committed their crime, but acquitted him of consent. De Lisle then was handed over to his ordinary, but the king now had the legal basis with which to seize his temporalities.[104]

On 13 October 1356, orders to make an inquest into the bishop's estates were sent out to the sheriffs of Cambridgeshire, Huntingdonshire, Hertfordshire, Norfolk, Suffolk, and Essex: all the counties, in short, where the bishop had manors. The sheriffs were to return their inquests into the exchequer by the following 12 November.[105] Orders to seize the bishop's

---

101. PRO, KB 27/384, rex m. 11d., and see Appendix B, page 246.
102. PRO, KB 27/382, rex m. 17.
103. *AS*, 1:659, and see Appendix B, pages 233–34.
104. PRO, KB 27/384, rex m. 11d., and see Appendix B, pages 246–47.
105. PRO, E 143/9/2, mm. 1, 16, 18, 26, 30; E 143/13/1, m. 10/i; KB 27/384, rex m. 11d., and see Appendix B, pages 246–47.

temporalities came on 21 October 1356.[106] By 1 February 1357, Edward had leased out the Ely temporalities to a merchant, John de Wesenham, to hold yearly from 6 October. In return, Wesenham was to render 3,740 marks, or approximately £2493, per year into the king's wardrobe to be paid in four quarterly installments.[107]

At the sheriff's inquests held in Norfolk, the jurors reported that many goods and chattels were not to be found on the manors because around 1 August 1356, De Lisle had "sent letters to his ministers and custodians" of his estate, ordering them to sell as much property as they could before 6 October following, the date of his trial.[108] The jurors' timeframe for the liquidation conflicts with the biographer's testimony that De Lisle had ordered the sell-off shortly after Holm's murder and before the coroner's inquest.[109] Considering that De Lisle went to some trouble to keep his plans secret, the local people who sat on the Norfolk juries may not have known about these plans until much later, whereas the biographer had perhaps the benefit of inside information, which also seems to have been shared with the king. We know from Edward's prohibition to De Lisle of 23 October 1355 that the bishop was contemplating flight at least a year before his trial.[110]

On 16 February 1357, the king ordered a further investigation into the Ely temporalities to his clerk, Robert de Clown. Clown's task was to inquire into the goods and chattels that had gone missing from the Ely estate after 6 October 1356 and into the debts owed to the bishop. He discovered, through jurors' testimony, that De Lisle's ministers had continued to sell off property from the manors and hand over the proceeds to the bishop's receivers even after 21 October, when De Lisle's temporalities were supposed to have been in the hands of the crown. At Hartest manor in Suffolk, for example, Richard Pompy, reeve, had handed over £4 to

---

106. PRO, E 403, m. 382. The roll records a payment made to various messengers sent to deliver writs handed down in the court of common pleas to seize the Ely temporalities. Neither I nor Dr. Ormrod have been able to find the corresponding writs in the common plea rolls (CP 40). See Ormrod, "Edward III's Government," 258, n. 3.

107. CCR, 1354–60, 392; CFR, 7:28. Wesenham's rent later was reduced to 3000 marks, or £2000. See CFR, 7:172.

108. "Et dicunt ulterius predicti jurati quod plura bona neque catalla in predictis terris et tenementis de predicto episcopo ad presens non inveniuntur pro eo quod circa festum Sancti Petri Advincula proximum ante dictas octabas, dictus episcopus misit litteras suas custodibus terrarum et tenementorum suorum predictorum ad vendenda festinanter omnia bona sua et catalla que vendi poterunt quod venderentur ante festum Sancti Michaelis proximum sequentem sub pena que versus ipsum forisfacere poterunt." PRO, E 143/13/1, mm. 10/ii–x.

109. AS, 1:658, and see Appendix B, page 233.

110. Foedera, 3, no. 1, 314; CCR, 1354–60, 159.

John Dunsterre, the bishop's clerk, on 28 October. At Shipdham, Norfolk, the manor's reeve, Andrew Joman, had delivered £3 8s. to Dunsterre on 8 November. Another receiver, Richard de Middleton, was indicted and convicted by the crown for his role in alienating to the bishop what was now crown property, but he was pardoned his offenses on 1 June 1362.[111]

In all, £114 10s. 7d. had been raised by De Lisle's manorial officials from his estates after his conviction of complicity in Holm's murder. This total does not represent all of the goods estranged by De Lisle's agents, however. In many instances, the reeves had kept a portion of the money owed to the bishop or appropriated the goods for themselves. Inevitably, much of the reeves' activity had escaped the sheriffs' previous investigations. At Willingham, Cambridgeshire, Clown's inquest revealed that William Prick, reeve, had sold five quarters of wheat from the manor that had not been reported in the sheriff's survey. At Glemsford, Suffolk, the bishop's reeve, Robert Brice, had kept in a grange fourteen quarters of wheat that also had been overlooked by the sheriff.

Clown's commission from the crown may have been motivated by much more than the incompleteness of the sheriff's inquests. In Norfolk and Suffolk, Clown's inquests revealed that the sheriff of the two counties, Guy de Seintcler, not only had allowed De Lisle's ministers the freedom of the manors but also had participated in the liquidation himself through his deputies, Hugh Curzon, Gregory Hunt, and William Davy. At Northwold, Norfolk, for example, Curzon and the manor's bailiff, Walter Joldewyn, together had contrived to sell practically everything on the estate from horses, cows, hay, and grain to carts, plows and plowshares, hurdles, fish traps and nets, harnesses, sieves, a bronze pot, a watering trough, a pitchfork, a shovel, even the bucket and cord from a well. At the Norfolk manors of West Walton, Northwold, Terrington, and Walpole, Curzon and Hunt had used fodder from the manor to feed their horses and drive away oxen, presumably to work on the sheriff's land. The deputies eventually had returned the animals, but in a greatly deteriorated state. The sheriff's men also had interfered with the episcopal revenues. At East Dereham and Shipdham, Norfolk, Curzon had appropriated £1 2s. 4d. from leet courts held there by the sheriff's deputies.

Other instances speak of outright collusion between the sheriff's and the bishop's men. At Feltwell manor, Norfolk, Curzon had sold one quarter and five bushels of peas and a horse worth 8s. to John Inglond, the bishop's reeve. At Northwold, Walter Joldewyn had paid Curzon 3s. for transport of the bishop's plows. Nicholas Godard, reeve of Terrington manor, Norfolk, had bought four plows from Hunt and Curzon for 6s.

111. *CPR*, 1361–64, 204.

8d., and John Andrew, the manor's beadle, had given the sheriff's ministers 5s. out of the issues of a court held there. In Suffolk, Richard Pompy, reeve of Hartest, had paid 5s. of the bishop's money to William Davy when he had come to survey the manor there. And at Rettendon, Essex, the king's custodians of the manor had sold two cart-horses, an iron cart, seven steers, four oxen, and two old plows worth more than £5 to John de Hollewell, who in turn had paid £10 to Thomas Durant, De Lisle's steward.

Clown also had been charged by the crown to supervise defects in the palaces and other outlying buildings on the Ely episcopal estate. In the course of his investigation, Clown found evidence of a "scorched earth" policy pursued by De Lisle's ministers on some of the buildings. At Terrington, Clown's inquest reported that the bishop's officers had destroyed completely the hall and its adjoining chamber and that the cost of new buildings would be £30. The palace at Pulham, Norfolk, was missing its walls and doors and needed repairs to its roof, even though it was new. At Wilburton and Stretham, Cambridgeshire, De Lisle's agents had burned a cattleshed worth £10 and destroyed a sheepfold worth £3. At East Dereham, Norfolk, the timber from a dismantled sheepfold had been sold by the bishop's men and a new structure could only be rebuilt at a cost of over £6. Other manors were much dilapidated owing to, perhaps, neglect and depredations committed since the bishop's departure in 1356. At Shipdham, for example, the jurors of the inquest said that "there is not one house sufficient or whole in the entire manor."[112] Almost every single manor, it seems, belonging to the Ely temporalities needed some kind of repairs to its physical structures.[113] The damage arising from De Lisle's Pyrrhic departure was to continue to cripple the estate of his successors for at least the next two decades.[114]

Meanwhile, during the autumn of 1356 after his conviction on 6 October, De Lisle busied himself with his purgation, a process whereby convicted clerks appeared before their ordinary and attempted to clear their name so that they could be restored to their former status.[115] If De Lisle

---

112. "Et predicti jurati dicunt quod non est una domus sufficiens nec integra in toto manerio." PRO, E 143/9/2, m. 56.

113. PRO, E 143/9/2, mm. 34–75. Membranes are clearly labelled by manor. (Note, however, that Brandon, Suffolk, is misrecorded to be in Norfolk; Rattlesden, Suffolk, in Norfolk; and Pulham, Norfolk, in Suffolk.) There is evidence that De Lisle kept his manors in good repair during his episcopate. See CUL, EDR: D 7/1/6–10, *emende domorum* and *custume domorum*; D 8/1/19, *emende domorum*; D 8/2/1–12, *emende domorum* and *custume domorum*; D 10/2/17–20, *custume domorum necessariorum*.

114. Aston, *Thomas Arundel*, 264–66.

115. Good descriptions of the purgation process can be found in L. C. Gabel, *Benefit of Clergy in England in the Later Middle Ages* (Northampton, Mass., 1928–29), 94–104; Haines, *Administration of Worcester*, 181–86; R. H. Helmholz, "Crime, Compurgation and the Courts of the Medieval Church," *Law and History Review* 1 (1983), 1–26.

successfully had completed this procedure, he theoretically would have been entitled to resume possession of his temporalities. Simon Islip, archbishop of Canterbury, entrusted the proclamation of De Lisle's purgation to his kinsman and chancellor, William de Whittlesey, archdeacon of Huntingdon, on 17 October 1356. All those who wished to oppose the bishop's declaration of innocence were to appear in the church of Mayfield, Sussex, on the following 14 November. Whittlesey was to be De Lisle's spiritual judge on that day, with final admittance of purgation reserved to the archbishop himself.[116]

According to De Lisle's biographer, no opposers appeared at his canonical trial. De Lisle then approached Islip and asked for a firm date when he might complete the process and finally purge himself through his compurgators before the archbishop. Islip is said to have replied: "My most beloved brother, lord bishop, take my advice, I beg you, and God willing perchance it will go better for you. Go soon, as I advise, to our lord king, and reconcile yourself with him, since, as I hope, you will find him gracious towards you. And then you may return and by all means you will proceed freely to your purgation and without doubt be restored to your former status in all things." De Lisle remonstrated with Islip that he was bound by canon law to accept his purgation without any further conditions.

"Lord father," said De Lisle, "already everything has been carried out correctly which canonically had been required before you receive my purgation. Moreover, nothing else now remains, except that you choose to assign to me a day and place, as you are bound to do by [canon] law and which is incumbent upon your pastoral office, so that I canonically may be able to purge myself from the defamation laid upon me." However, Islip, who formerly had been the king's keeper of the privy seal, insisted on a reconciliation with Edward. To do otherwise would be to create another constitutional crisis in which he and his fellow prelates would be forced to choose between the crown and the Church.

"I will assign you a day and place when it is necessary," Islip said. "Nor do I intend to detract from your purgation in any way, although there is very little I can do of any great use, as your lawsuit only can be ended with the king's consent and by more mature counsel." De Lisle refused to accept these conditions and the two men parted. Soon afterward, De Lisle left England on 19 November 1356. He first made his way to Bruges in Belgium, where he rested before going on to arrive at the court of Pope Innocent VI at Avignon, where he was to spend the last five years of his life appealing the king's judgment in a vain attempt to win back his temporalities.[117]

---

116. LPL, Reg. Islip, fols. 125r, 128r.
117. AS, 1:659–60, and see Appendix B, pages 234–36.

6

The Bishop and His Unruly Retinue

By themselves, the Spynk and Lady Wake suits do not make a convincing dossier for a long career in criminal activity to be laid at the door of the bishop. De Lisle's actions against Richard Spynk can be represented as the legitimate distraint and pursuit of a fugitive bondman. The attack on Lady Wake originated in a private feud between servants of the disputing parties: Ralph Carles and William Holm. According to the bishop's biographer, there was a "long-standing enmity" between the two men,[1] and De Lisle remained steadfast in his denial of consent to Holm's murder. Moreover, unlike the feud with Spynk, De Lisle had little to gain by targeting such a well-connected noblewoman and indeed, as later events were to prove, risked harsh penalties. But this does not exhaust the evidence against De Lisle.

A motive for the bishop's disorderly conduct already has been suggested by the biographer's account of his financial troubles early in his episcopate, troubles that later may have been aggravated by the economic hardships brought on by the Black Death.[2] But to advance the case that the bishop doubled as a maintainer of criminals, it is necessary to establish two further points: first, that a pattern of crime over an extended period of time emerges out of the offenses of which De Lisle's men were accused; second, that De Lisle provided active support to these men who constituted a close-knit group occupying positions in the bishop's curia and who thus had the opportunity and the means to commit their crimes.

The most promising and potentially rewarding sources of information with which to address these issues are the records of the medieval courts, namely the plea rolls of the king's bench and of the court of common

---

1. *AS*, 1:657, and see Appendix B, page 232.
2. *AS*, 1:655, and see Appendix B, pages 228–29.

pleas and the gaol delivery rolls. The nature of these records has been described elsewhere;[3] what must be kept in mind is that they record primarily the point of view of the plaintiff and rarely give the defendant's side of the suit or even register a verdict on the case. Therefore, they must be approached with some caution and viewed in the context of other indictments. These are the records that form the foundation of this chapter. However, there are others that impinge on the question of De Lisle's criminality, most notably, the king's remembrancer extents and inquisitions from the office of the exchequer. These include two full surveys of the bishop's manors in seven counties, undertaken in the wake of Edward III's order to seize De Lisle's temporalities and the bishop's flight to Avignon in 1356. Together with the surviving manorial account rolls from Downham and Wisbech in Cambridgeshire, these provide much valuable information about the offices held by De Lisle's men and their length of service. Many of these officers of the bishop are among those frequently accused of carrying out the criminal raids described in this chapter. But most damaging to the bishop's reputation, neither were they disowned on that account by their patron, judging by their longevity of service.[4] It is a combination of all these factors that leads one to suspect that De Lisle indeed was a criminal gang leader in addition to being a bishop.

Nevertheless, for the majority of De Lisle's eleven-year tenure at Ely, he and his men succeeded in evading the law and its punishment. Like the careers of other unruly "robber barons,"[5] De Lisle's alleged criminal misdeeds only came to light when he fell out of favor with the crown. It was when his minions misguidedly attacked the property and person of someone with more powerful connections than he that they finally were brought to justice. Lady Wake's indictment of 30 October 1354,[6] when she brought a suit for arson, seems to have released the floodgates on a stream of grievances, some harbored for years, against the bishop and his men. A large number of these complaints were brought before two inquests taken at St. Ives and Woodston, Huntingdonshire, on 4 December 1354 and 12 January 1355 respectively.[7] Sir John Dengayn, justice of the peace for Huntingdonshire, presided, and among the jurors were Henry de Colne and William Holm, the two men who previously had helped convict De Lisle of arson. Although the new indictments never came to trial, the crown may have pursued them in order to put pressure on some of De Lisle's agents in order to convince them to cooperate with its ar-

3. See pages xxi–xxii.
4. See pages 50–58.
5. See the examples of Sir John Molyns and George, duke of Clarence, in Fryde, "A Medieval Robber Baron," 198–207; Bellamy, *Crime and Public Order*, 24–25.
6. PRO, KB 27/379, rex m. 9, and see Appendix B, pages 240–42.
7. PRO, KB 27/381, rex m. 24.

raignment of the bishop. Robert Hale, the bishop's bailiff, for example, obtained a pardon not only for his crime against Lady Wake but also for an assault on John Chaloner of Tydd St. Giles, Cambridgeshire, for which he had been indicted at St. Ives in December 1354.[8] Also suggestive is the fact that for three successive terms in 1355–56, Hale was bailed by the very jurors who had indicted him at St. Ives and Woodston.[9]

Abduction and Extortion

A total of sixteen separate indictments were recorded against the bishop and his men at the two Huntingdonshire inquests. Whereas most of the charges specify dates, places, and the names of perpetrators and victims involved in the crimes, a few are of a mysterious character that seem the result of local popular rumor. Among the latter is the complaint that on 25 December 1349, two friar preachers came to the bishop's manor at Somersham and presented him with a Christmas present of stolen precious objects worth £20. Instead of arresting the thieves, De Lisle, through his "evil custody," allowed them to get away.[10] Around 20 July 1349, Robert de Godington, De Lisle's bailiff, acting on the orders of John de Lisle and Thomas Durant, the bishop's stewards, allegedly rustled two hundred beasts at Somersham and within the year drove them outside the county of Huntingdon for the bishop's profit. No mention was made, however, of who formerly owned such a large and valuable herd. A third crime appears, on the face of it, to have had no other motive than gratuitous violence. It was said that on 25 August 1354, Robert Hale, the bishop's bailiff of Somersham, forcibly entered the house of John Sturdy at Earith, Huntingdonshire, and assaulted his servant, John Clynt. It may be that Hale, in his capacity as bailiff, was attempting to distrain something from the house, and Clynt sought to prevent the deed. If so, what Clynt got for his pains was a broken arm and some "ill-treatment" from his attacker. About a month later, on 29 September 1354, Hale was re-

8. PRO, KB 27/381, rex m. 24; *CPR*, 1354–58, 314.
9. PRO, KB 27/383, rex m. 5d.; KB 27/384, rex m. 2; KB 27/385, rex m. 3d. Hale's mainpernours were John Sturdy, Robert Woodhouse, John de Colne, Henry de Colne, William at Hall, Thomas de Earith, and John de Deen.
10. "Item circa festum Natalis Domini anno regni regis nunc vicesimo tercio, predictus episcopus apud Somersham contra pacem domini regis receptavit duos fratres ordinis predicatorum cum uno fardello iocalium furato ad valenciam xx. librarum, sciens ipsos esse fures et fardellum predictum esse furatum, et dictum fardellum devenit ad proficuum dicti episcopi. Et per malam custodiam dicti latrones, qui fuerunt in custodia dicti episcopi apud Somersham, evaserunt." PRO, KB 27/381, rex m. 24.

puted to have again assaulted Clynt at Earith, this time taking away Clynt's boat worth £3.

Nearly half of the complaints voiced at the inquests concern abduction with the intent of extortion; seven out of sixteen indictments are of this type. The standard form of the complaint is that De Lisle's men forcibly abducted the plaintiff and dragged him off to the bishop's prison where he was confined until he ransomed himself. On 8 December 1352, Robert Hale was said to have taken John Stobard at Colne, Huntingdonshire, and brought him to Somersham where he imprisoned him until Stobard paid half a mark, or 6s. 8d., to Hale and given two oxen worth 30s. to the bishop. Richard Mody, De Lisle's reeve at Somersham manor, allegedly captured Alice le Northern at Somersham on 4 December 1354 and imprisoned her until she paid the bishop half a mark, or 6s. 8d. About a month before De Lisle was due to be enthroned on 27 November 1345, Robert de Godington reputedly arrested Simon son of Hugh, a free man, and imprisoned him at Somersham until he paid £5.[11]

It is quite possible that most of these "abductions" and alleged thefts and assaults were simply attempts by De Lisle's manorial officials to compel tenants to pay fines or amercements incurred in the bishop's courts. As such, they would not have been out of place among similar efforts by lords all across the country at this time.[12] Like his attack on Richard Spynk, De Lisle indeed may have felt justified to use force against recalcitrant tenants. Particularly after the Black Death had struck in 1348–49, lords in general strove to maintain the profitability of their manors. Evidence from surviving manorial accounts indicates that from 1348 onward, profits from the bishop's manorial courts made up a greater percentage of his manorial income as a whole. At Downham manor in Cambridgeshire, for example, court profits in 1348–49 were more than twice the average registered for the previous five years, while at Wisbech Castle, Cambridgeshire, court profits in 1349–50 were higher by a third over the average (see Tables 3 and 7). Part of this profit may have been driven by more rigorous enforcement of court fines.

Nevertheless, there are indications that there was something more going on here besides mere harassment of tenants. In several cases, De Lisle's men may have been guilty of genuine, outright extortion. A number of plaintiffs alleging that they had been abducted and imprisoned by Robert Hale and Robert de Godington described themselves as "free men" rather than as the bishop's tenants.[13] It seems that a legal distinction was

---

11. Ibid.

12. Bolton, *The Medieval English Economy*, 213; Dyer, "Rural Revolt of 1381," 28–29.

13. For example, "Item dicunt quod circa festum Sanctorum Simonis et Jude anno decimo nono apud Somersham, predictus Robertus de Godyngton', tunc ballivus ipsius episcopi, per preceptum ipsius episcopi cepit contra pacem domini

being made between the two types of harassment, which needed to be punished accordingly. In the case of John Walles of Wornditch, Huntingdonshire, an indicted felon, it was specified that the victim was "neither the resident nor the tenant of the bishop."[14] Walles claimed that, on 22 May 1354, Robert Hale and John Motown had seized, with the bishop's assent and for the bishop's profit, twelve sheep, a mare, and three oxen, valued at £4 10s., belonging to him at Somersham. Another indicted felon, John Chaloner of Tydd St. Giles, Cambridgeshire, claimed that Hale had appropriated for himself at Earith stolen goods worth £1 on 10 May 1350.[15]

These cases argue the possibility that De Lisle was manipulating the law for his own, quite illegal, ends. As bishop of Ely, he was in a unique position to redefine legality. The bishop was entitled to the spoils of any criminals who resided on his lands as part of the so-called liberty of Ely, a series of legal privileges originally awarded to the abbey church by King Edgar in 970. By the later Middle Ages, these privileges had been extended to all the bishop's estates beyond the confines of the Isle of Ely. Not only did the liberty give De Lisle financial reward from the king's justice, it also accorded a great deal of autonomy to De Lisle's administration, which was allowed to operate with hardly any interference from representatives of the crown. All duties normally carried out by the sheriff, such as the arrest and imprisonment of criminals who were to appear in the king's courts, instead were carried out by the bishop's officials. Only within the Isle, however, did the bishop's courts supersede those of the central government.[16] In addition, De Lisle had to exercise his liberty within certain rules. He could not, for example, appropriate the property of felons such as John Walles or John Chaloner unless they first had been convicted in the king's courts. Clearly, the plaintiffs claimed that De Lisle had taken their goods while they merely had been indicted for their crimes. De Lisle was judged guilty of such hasty seizure when he appropriated the goods of his chamberlain, Ralph Carles, on 18 October 1355. Since Carles was not outlawed by the crown until 8 July 1356, the king's bench in the preceding Hilary term fined the bishop £21 14s. 10d. for his premature acquisition.[17]

---

regis Simonem filium Hugonis liberum hominem et ipsum imprisonavit et in prisona detinu[i]t quousque finem fecerat cum predicto episcopi de centum solidis." PRO, KB 27/381, rex m. 24.

14. ". . . et idem Johannes Walles nec residens nec tenens ipsius episcopi." Ibid.

15. Ibid.

16. For a history and description of the Ely liberty, see Miller, *Abbey and Bishopric*, 199–246, and an article by the same author in *VCH Cambs.*, 4:1–27. The liberty was confirmed by Edward III to De Lisle on 13 May 1348. See PRO, JUST 1/1431, m. 30/2.

17. PRO, KB 27/382, rex m. 17, and fines, m. 1; KB 27/384, rex m. 11d., and see Appendix B, page 246.

The form that this extortion and legal manipulation may have taken is suggested by a case heard against De Lisle and Robert de Godington before an inquest at Huntingdon on 6 November 1354. Abduction was once again charged, but it is clear that this had nothing to do with tenantry. The jury, which included William Holm and Henry de Colne, accused the defendants of having abducted and imprisoned Gregory at Hall, John Sturdy, and Adam Troke, free men, at Somersham on 2 October 1348 and detained them until they paid a total of £17 for their freedom. In the following Trinity term, on 7 June 1355, De Lisle's attorney, Stephen de Holborn, appeared before the king's bench at Westminster and endeavored to convince the court that his client's actions had been an attempt to uphold the law rather than break it. According to Holborn, the bishop's men had arrested a suspected thief, Thomas Milner, at Somersham and brought him before the coroner for Ely, Robert de Wilburton. Once before the coroner, Milner had turned approver and named Hall and the other plaintiffs as his fellow lawbreakers. The coroner then had issued a warrant for the arrest of the three men, which Godington, as the bishop's bailiff, dutifully had executed on 4 January 1348.[18]

Nevertheless, the bishop's liberty was insufficient grounds for innocence, according to the king's attorney, Simon de Kegworth. He argued that the coroner of Ely had no legal authority to order an arrest in another county, Huntingdonshire, and therefore De Lisle effectively had confessed to kidnapping the three men. Two king's serjeants, Robert Thorp and William Skipwith, made similar arguments on behalf of the plaintiffs. Skipwith contended that a coroner's jurisdiction extended only to the county where he was coroner (in this case, the Isle of Ely), and a bailiff was not authorized to make arrests except by mandate of the local sheriff. Thorp reminded the court that "although coroners may be called coroners of the liberties, each coroner is an officer of the king and each gaol belongs to the king and to no other."[19] Coroners should order arrests to no one but the sheriff, the king's officer, and if a suspect had to be arrested across county lines, only a justice of gaol delivery could authorize this. The court was prepared to hand down a guilty verdict against De Lisle, but William de Witchingham, king's serjeant pleading for the defense, seems to have lodged a successful appeal, and the final outcome remains in doubt.[20]

The arrest and extortion of fines from innocent victims on charges brought by approvers is a familiar pattern of medieval criminal behavior.

---

18. PRO, KB 27/379, rex m. 9d.
19. "Coment que coroners soient appellés coroners des franchises, chescun coroner est officer le roy et chescun goale est a le roy, et a nul autre de le terre." *Yearbooks* 2–3, Trinity term, 29 Edward III, 41–42.
20. Ibid., 42.

It was a well-known tactic among sheriffs and gaolers, which accounts for their unpopularity, both in the petitions submitted to parliament and the less formal means of complaint, the outlaw ballads such as the *Gest of Robyn Hode*.[21] Statutes were passed against the corrupt practices of sheriffs and their officers in 1327 and 1340, but seemingly to no avail.[22] Indictments from the king's bench plea rolls provide real-life examples of such complaints. On 6 November 1337, John de Nunwick Thorns, the gaoler of Ripon in the West Riding of Yorkshire, was said to have imprisoned Walter Sadelere of Penrith, Cumbria, and "tortured him with so many torments that his feet fell off because the same Walter did not want to make fine with him at his will."[23] In the following year, 1338, the sheriff of Cambridge, William Muschet, was convicted of extorting £1 from three men arrested on appeal while his gaoler, Thomas de Barrington, was accused of torturing prisoners in order to force them to become approvers.[24] In Hilary term 1352, Peter de Boxted, sheriff of Essex, paid a £20 fine on his own conviction that he had extorted a grand total of £351 from various people appealed by approvers.[25] Even coroners were not immune from accusations of extortion.[26]

Arson and Theft

Another well-documented and complex case involving possible manipulation by De Lisle of his legal privileges within his liberty of Ely centers around a "rescue." In legal terms, a rescue is an attempt to release a prisoner from lawful custody, and the writ sued to investigate such an offense had assumed a standard form by the fourteenth century.[27] The case,

---

21. See pages 83–84, 90–91, 196–97.

22. *SR*, 1:253, 384.

23. "Johannes filius Roberti de Nunwykthornes dum fuit custos gaole Ripon' die Jovis proximo ante festum Sancti Martini anno regni regis nunc Anglie undecimo apud Rypon' cepit Walterum Sadelere de Penreth' sine causa et ipsum ibidem imprisonavit colore officij sui et ipsum ibidem in prisona tantis penis cruciavit quod amisit pedes suos pro eo quod idem Walterum [Walterus] noluit finem facere cum eo ad voluntatem suam." PRO, KB 27/354, rex m. 68.

24. PRO, KB 27/314, rex m. 31. I am grateful to Dr. Jeus Röhrkasten for this reference.

25. PRO, KB 27/366, rex mm. 3–3d.

26. R. F. Hunnisett, "Sussex Coroners in the Middle Ages: Part III," *Sussex Archaeological Collections* 98 (1960), 50–51; idem, *The Medieval Coroner* (Cambridge, 1961), 72–73, 125–26.

27. *Early Registers of Writs*, ed. E. de Haas and G.D.G. Hall (SS, LXXXVII, 1970), 182.

interestingly enough, also involves arson and theft, a combination that suggests a favorite tactic employed by medieval thieves: to set fire to a house in order to "smoke out" the inhabitants, at which point the burglars would rush into the inferno to grab as much booty as they could before self-immolation.[28] Whether this was the actual technique employed by the bishop's men is uncertain, since the relevant indictments do not specify the purpose or order in which the arson and theft occurred.

The case first came before the king's bench in Michaelmas term 1352 at Norwich, where a Norfolk jury indicted the bishop of having ordered an attack on a "John son of Walter son of Stephen . . . against good faith and reason."[29] The jurors alleged that on the night of 10 or 13 October 1351, several men, including the bishop's bailiff, John Brownsley, forced their way into John's houses at Walpole, Norfolk, put the main house to the flame, and stole £10 worth of his goods, including silver and wooden bowls, a cloak, a saddle, and a sword. The hapless victim then was dragged off to Wisbech Castle, where he was imprisoned until he paid £20 over to the bishop. In a related indictment, the same men were said to have broken into the houses of John Daniel at Walsoken, Norfolk, on the night of 13 October 1351.[30]

Stephen de Holborn, De Lisle's attorney, appeared before the bench on 26 November 1352 to argue the defendant's case. Just as he was to try to dismiss the charge of abduction two years later, Holborn put forward an elaborate defense that portrayed De Lisle as an upholder of the law rather than its breaker. Yet again, the bishop's legal privileges enabled Holborn to cast the defendants as the agents of king's justice within the episcopal franchise. His client's only concern, argued the lawyer, had been to apprehend the wrongdoers, namely the plaintiffs, who in this instance had helped free from the bishop's custody a suspected criminal. Some time before, Holborn explained, the crown had issued a writ of judgment witnessed by John de Stonor, chief justice of the court of common pleas, which had authorized the arrest of John de Wilton who was to appear in court at

---

28. I am grateful to Dr. Jeus Röhrkasten for drawing my attention to this aspect of medieval crime through his work on approvers.

29. "Et quod ijdem Johannes de Bronesleye et alij venerunt vi et armis die Lune proximo post festum predictum eodem anno in Walpol in comitatu predicto et domos Johannis filii Walteri filii Stephani fregerunt et intraverunt et de qualibet parte capitale domus sue ignem ardentem posuerunt et ipsum Johannem per corpus suum ceperunt et ad castellum de Wysebech' ipsum duxerunt et ibidem ipsum detinuerunt per preceptum predicti episcopi quousque dictus Johannes finem fecerat prefato episcopo de viginti libris quas idem episcopus recepit ab eodem Johanne per extorsionem et contra bonam fidem et racionem." PRO, KB 27/369, rex m. 70.

30. PRO, KB 27/369, rex mm. 65, 70; KB 27/370, rex m. 19. Both dates of 10 and 13 October are given in the indictment for the crime against John son of Walter.

a certain date. Since Wilton had to be attached at Wisbech, Cambridgeshire, which lay within the bishop's liberty, the sheriff of Cambridge had returned the writ for execution to John de Brownsley, De Lisle's bailiff. With the aid of Robert de Godington, De Lisle's clerk, and Thomas Canville, porter of Wisbech Castle, Brownsley had arrested Wilton at Wisbech and was about to deliver him to the king's justices. Before he could do so, however, a mob of over twenty people, led by Wilton's mother and other relatives, allegedly had broken the attachment and freed the prisoner. Among the rescuers named by the defense were John son of Walter and Ralph and Robert Daniel, brothers of the plaintiff, John Daniel.

By 12 February 1350, Wilton had surrendered himself to the Marshalsea, and consequently the crown pardoned him of his outlawry for nonappearance before the justices.[31] Nonetheless, De Lisle had sued a writ of oyer and terminer, issued by the crown on 1 June 1350, to investigate the assault on his bailiff. Wilton's rescuers were presented not as ordinary citizens but as a confederation of "malefactors" out to disturb the peace. After they had freed Wilton, they allegedly besieged Wisbech Castle and daily threatened its constable, Thomas Lovet, with death and bodily injury so that he dared not stay there "without a great multitude of armed men" nor go out and perform his duties within the liberty.[32] An inquest held by the sheriff of Cambridge allegedly had found that Wilton and others were roaming armed around the shire "by day and night in order to impede the king's ministers."[33] Holborn repeated the sheriff's allegation as part of his defense, clearly intending to discredit the plaintiffs and show that they attacked not only the bishop's authority but also the crown's.

The sheriff's inquest had resulted in a commission of arrest of Wilton's rescuers, issued by the crown to Brownsley and others on 8 June 1350.[34] The commission, according to Holborn, justified Brownsley's visit to John Daniel's house, where his brothers had not been found, as well as the seizure and imprisonment of John son of Walter. In accordance with the commission of oyer and terminer issued on 1 June, John son of Walter had been brought before Justice Richard Willoughby at Cambridge later that same month. There the defendant had pleaded not guilty to a charge

31. *CPR*, 1348–50, 471–72.
32. *CPR*, 1348–50, 583.
33. ". . . super quo datum fuit domino rege intelligi de malefacto predicto, misit brevem suum vicecomiti Cant' [Cambridge] ad inquirendum de premissis, et premissa coram eodem vicecomite per inquisicionem reperta et in cancellaria retornata [fuerunt], et similiter compertum fuit quod predicti Johannes filius Reginaldi et plures alii in comitatu Cant' [Cambridge] infra libertatem et extra armati incederunt et vagabantur de die ac nocte ad ministros regis impediendos et cetera." PRO, KB 27/369, rex m. 70.
34. *CPR*, 1348–50, 584–85.

of trespass but had been found liable for damages of £40, half of which De Lisle already claimed to have received. Holborn thus accounted for the charge of abduction and extortion brought by John son of Walter, while the defendants denied that they had committed arson or "any other transgression by force and arms against the king's peace."[35] Indeed, according to the defense's account, the events in question had occurred more than a year prior to the dates in October 1351 contained in the indictment.

While De Lisle professed to have acted solely on the king's behalf, the king's attorney, Simon de Kegworth, asserted otherwise. The bishop and his men, he said, had perpetrated the arson, abduction, and theft of which they were accused and had done this for no other reason than to redress their own personal grievances. However, when the case finally came to trial in Easter term 1354, De Lisle and the other defendants, including John Brownsley, were acquitted.[36]

By no means was this an end to the litigation. Before De Lisle's acquittal could be handed down by the king's bench, one of the plaintiffs, John Daniel, had been able to have De Lisle's men convicted and fined £200 in a private suit brought before the court of common pleas at Norwich in Easter term 1353. Daniel's suit throws considerably more light on the assault alleged to have occurred at the plaintiff's home in Walsoken, Norfolk. On 13 June 1351 (not 13 October as in the indictment before king's bench), Brownsley, his brother Edmund, and other officers of the bishop were said to have approached Daniel's house armed with swords and other weapons "in a mode of war." The attackers broke Daniel's gates, doors, and windows, according to the indictment, and entered the house while Daniel lay in his bed in "great terror." Although Daniel's two brothers, the alleged rescuers of John de Wilton, were not to be found in the house, the invaders threatened Daniel that "they would run him through the middle of his body on the spot if he dared cried out there."[37] They

---

35. "Et predicti Johannes Clerk, Thomas Caunville, et Thomas Bacoun dicunt quod ipsi venerunt in auxilium predicti Johannis de Bronesle ballivi et cetera ad capiendos predictos Johannem filium Walteri et alios virtute commissionis predicte absque hoc quod ipsi ignem ardentem ex aliqua parte domus predicti Johannis filii Walteri posuerunt, seu aliqua transgressione vi et armis et contra pacem in premissis facienda et cetera, et hoc parati sunt verificare et cetera." PRO, KB 27/ 369, rex m. 70.

36. PRO, KB 27/369, rex m. 70; KB 27/370, rex m. 19.

37. "Johannes Danyel . . . querelatus [est] quod predicti Johannes de Brunneslee et alij simul et cetera, die Lune proximo post festum Sancti Barnabe Apostoli anno regni Anglie domini regis nunc vicesimo quinto, vi et armis, scilicet gladijs et cetera, domos ipsius Johannis Danyell' apud Walsoken' modo guerrino obsiderunt. Et portas, ostia, et fenestras ipsius Johannis Daniel fregerunt et vi armata intraverunt et in ipsum Johannem Daniel in lecto suo magnum terrorem fecerunt et ipsum manifeste minabantur quod si ipse ausus fuisset inde monendi quod ipsum statim per medium corpus suum percuterent." PRO, KB 27/371, civil pleas, m. 41d.

then proceeded to ransack the place, carrying off various personal effects, including bows, arrows, and linen and woolen clothes, worth £40, and causing other damages to the value of £200.

Brownsley's attorney, the ubiquitous Stephen de Holborn, repeated his argument that his client was only doing his job in accordance with the commission of arrest issued by the crown on 8 June the previous year. Brownsley had come to the house, according to the defense, on the information of "trustworthy witnesses" who had claimed that Daniel's brothers were staying there.[38] Moreover, Brownsley said that his suspicions had been aroused further when Daniel had shut his gates and doors on his approach. Daniel denied that he ever had given refuge to his brothers and countered that Brownsley had not shown any warrant for their arrest. The jury found in Daniel's favor, convicting Brownsley and the others except for Thomas le Parker, and awarded £200 damages to the plaintiff.[39]

Almost immediately, De Lisle retaliated against Daniel by bringing his own suit in the court of common pleas in the following Trinity term for the recovery of a £500 debt. De Lisle claimed that five years ago, on 26 August 1348, Daniel had acknowledged that he owed the bishop the money in a deed that Daniel asserted in his defense "is not his work."[40] In Michaelmas term 1353, Brownsley and his fellow defendants secured a retrial of Daniel's conviction on a writ of attaint; the final verdict, however, does not seem to have been recorded.[41] Although De Lisle was awarded his debt against Daniel, the bishop acquitted the debtor of his sum on 22 November 1354. Nevertheless, the unfortunate Daniel still had to pay a £2 fine to the crown for his denial of the incriminating deed.[42]

Other Crimes

Other indictments of criminal activity are uncovered by tracing the names of individual members of De Lisle's curia through the legal records. As expected, the familiar charges of abduction and extortion figure large

38. ". . . quia eidem Johanni de Brunnesle datum fuit intel[l]igi per testimonium fidedignorum quod predicti malefactores apud Walsokne in domo predicti Johannis Danyel fuerunt continue com[m]orantes." Ibid.

39. Ibid.

40. "Et dicit quod predictus episcopus ipsum de predicto debito virtute scripti predicti onerare non debet quia dicit quod predictum scriptum non est factum suum." PRO, CP 40/374, m. 169.

41. PRO, KB 27/373, civil pleas, m. 29d.

42. PRO, CP 40/374, m. 169; *CPR*, 1354–58, 129.

among such accusations. Although most of these indictments do not mention the bishop himself, they nevertheless shed light on the nature of his lordship. The fact that De Lisle employed many of the defendants over a long period of time suggests that his association with such "criminal types" was not accidental.[43] Unlike other lords who were more circumspect with their patronage, the bishop seems to have surrounded himself with unsavory characters and defended them when necessary.

One of the earliest accusations against De Lisle's followers fingered the bishop's own brother, John, and his nephew, William Michel. On 6 December 1346, a commission of oyer and terminer was issued by the crown "on frequent complaints by men of the counties of Norfolk and Cambridge" against John de Lisle, called here "John de Lisle of the county of Kent," as well as against William Michel and William de Cliff, who participated in the raids on the Spynks. The complainants charged that the three men would "ride armed in those counties, imprisoning men until they make fines and ransoms with them at their will, and perpetrating other trespasses, oppressions, extortions and grievances."[44] Another case of abduction involved the bishop's constable of Wisbech Castle, Thomas de Baa, along with its porter, Thomas Canville, and the castle reeve, Thomas Bacon. On 31 May 1352, they allegedly captured Nicholas de St. Botho at Walsoken, Norfolk, and detained him for eight days until he handed over seven marks, or nearly £5, to his abductors. Baa was acquitted by a jury from Norfolk on 5 November 1352, but in the same term he paid a £2 fine on his own conviction.[45]

Not even Cambridge dons, it seems, were immune from crime. In Michaelmas term 1355, Robert de Whitby, the bishop's clerk and a fellow of Peterhouse, was accused of abducting Nicholas de Werk at Puckeridge, Hertfordshire, and imprisoning him at Ware in the same county until he paid Whitby a £20 ransom.[46] Conversely, priests could be the victims of such extortion. At a gaol delivery session held at Ely, William de Stansted, De Lisle's steward, was fined for extorting a total of £13 10s. from various men of "good fame" (bone fame), including the vicars of Sutton, Cambridgeshire, and of St. Ives, Huntingdonshire. Stansted had imprisoned his victims on the basis of indictments brought by William Milneward, a thief who had turned approver before the coroner of Ely, Robert de Wilburton, on 8 February 1356.[47] In Trinity term 1356, John de Chippesby, parson of Elm, Cambridgeshire, brought a civil suit against

43. See pages 50–58.
44. *CPR*, 1345–48, 238.
45. PRO, KB 27/369, rex mm. 40d., 65, and fines, m. 7d.
46. PRO, CP 40/383, mm. 94d., 324d.
47. PRO, JUST 3, 8/4, mm. 1, 3. No date is given for Stansted's delivery.

Richard Michel, De Lisle's nephew, and Thomas Bacon, alleging that the two had stolen his grain stored at Elm over a one-and-a-half-month period from 17 August until 29 September 1355. The total damages claimed to have been sustained by the plaintiff amounted to £1000.[48]

On occasion the violence attributed to De Lisle's men escalated to assault, resulting even in death. Ralph Carles, the bishop's chamberlain, by no means was the only member of his curia alleged to have blood on his hands. However, English law did not recognize the distinction between premeditated murder and simple manslaughter until the sixteenth century, and therefore it is difficult to assess the exact nature of these crimes. Throughout most of the fourteenth century, culpable homicide, of whatever type, commonly was designated in the legal records as *felonice interficit* (or occasionally *occidit*), terms that referred to the killing of one man by another without admitting of further specificity. Even the rare term *murdravit* did not denote murder in the modern sense of killing "with malice aforethought."[49] When we do have a motive, such as in the feud between Carles and Holm, the act of killing nevertheless may have been accidental or have mitigating circumstances. According to the bishop's biographer, Carles killed Holm hotheadedly, in the heat of an argument, and thus the crime seems to have been unplanned.[50] Without more information, the record of an indictment for murder in the Middle Ages cannot be taken to mean that the deed was done deliberately.

Despite their ambiguity, the cases of violent assault and murder against various of the bishop's officers are worth noting. In 1356, William de Stretford, De Lisle's bailiff of Hadstock manor, Essex, and Thomas de Chilton, keeper of the bishop's parks and warrens at Downham, Cambridgeshire, were named as part of a gang of more than forty men who allegedly assaulted John de Grey, murdered one of his servants, and chased him to his house at Balsham, Cambridgeshire, in order to kill him.[51] In Michaelmas term of the same year, Thomas Bacon was accused in the court of common pleas of having assaulted, wounded, and ill-treated Adam Honyter at Wisbech.[52] The same term also saw Robert at Berne sue Bishop De Lisle and three other men for allegedly assaulting him at Hatfield, Hertfordshire, and stealing his goods and chattels worth £5.[53] At a gaol delivery in Norwich Castle on 28 July 1357, Thomas Wyliot,

---

48. PRO, KB 27/384, civil pleas, m. 42d.
49. J. M. Kaye, "The Early History of Murder and Manslaughter: Part I," *Law Quarterly Review* 83 (1967), 365–95.
50. *AS,* 1:657, and see Appendix B, page 232.
51. *CPR,* 1354–58, 453; PRO, CP 40/388, m. 247.
52. PRO, CP 40/388, m. 202d.
53. PRO, CP 40/388, m. 16d.

described as one of De Lisle's servants, was indicted on the charge that he and some others had killed John Wyffyn on 17 July 1354 at Shipdham, Norfolk.[54]

It may be that the mass of indictments just recounted against De Lisle and his followers represents nothing more than the complaints of disgruntled tenants who took the opportunity of the bishop's sudden fall from grace to object to his heavy-handed lordship. His support and association with his unpopular officials then may be understandable in the light of his obligations as a "good lord." However, two points argue against such an interpretation. One is that the indictments themselves, drawn from different parts of the country and at different times, give a remarkably similar pattern of criminal activity, namely extortion by means of abduction and imprisonment or theft accompanied by arson. Not all the accusers were the bishop's tenants; some allege legal manipulation of the bishop's liberty of Ely. These are clearly cases of outright crime and not simply an overeager defense of seigniorial rights.

It must be remembered, though, that hardly any of the indictments are conclusive. The objectivity of the record cannot be taken for granted. Witnesses, jurors, and justices all may have had their own prejudices against the defendant. William Holm, who before his murder had served several times on juries of presentment against De Lisle and his men, was also Lady Wake's valet. Two other jurors, John Sturdy and John Emmeson, were allowed to bring indictments even though they themselves had been alleged victims of De Lisle's oppressions, a situation said to be not uncommon in medieval legal procedure.[55] In Michaelmas term 1350, De Lisle brought a civil suit on a plea of trespass against Robert de Woodhouse of Somersham, who later was to serve on the jury that indicted De Lisle and his men of arson at the inquest held at Huntingdon on 30 October 1354.[56] The Huntingdonshire justice of the peace who was to preside at the trial at Yaxley, Nicholas de Stukeley, was around the same time embroiled in a civil suit over land in Huntingdonshire and Cambridgeshire with Thomas Canville, the bishop's porter of Wisbech Castle.[57] Sir Simon Drayton, one of the many men cited and excommunicated in Avignon for his role in the bishop's dispute with Lady Wake,[58] may have been a discontented tenant of the bishop. He was recorded in the bishop's manorial accounts as paying annually £2 13s. 4d. to De Lisle for 160 acres of land held in

---

54. PRO, JUST 3, 215/2, part 2, mm. 147, 155d.–156; JUST 3, 216/1, m. 120.

55. Powell, *Kingship, Law and Society*, 69. The service of Holm, Sturdy, and Emmeson on presenting juries against De Lisle is recorded in PRO, KB 27/379, rex m. 9d.; KB 27/381, rex m. 24; LPL, Reg. Islip, fol. 138v; LAO, Reg. VIII, fol. 93v, and see Appendix B, pages 247–48.

56. PRO, KB 27/361, civil pleas, m. 66d.; KB 27/379, rex m. 9, and see Appendix B, page 241.

57. PRO, CP 40/380, m. 99d.

58. See page 166 and note 17.

Wisbech Barton, Cambridgeshire.[59] He may have been the same Sir Simon Drayton retained by Crowland Abbey and indicted for murder.[60]

Comparisons with other magnates and their affinities indicate that lords generally tried to avoid the unpopularity demonstrated to De Lisle at St. Ives and toward his bailiff, John Brownsley, at Wisbech.[61] Such disfavor among neighbors and tenants could curtail disastrously the lord's income and influence. There was a limit, therefore, to how much disorderly conduct even a "good lord" could tolerate among his retinue.[62] These considerations may not have applied to a bishop hard up for money and free of dynastic ambitions for any heirs.[63] Those magnates who ignored such considerations, such as Sir John Moleyns of Buckinghamshire during the fourteenth century and George, duke of Clarence, during the fifteenth, usually found their misdeeds catch up with them when they eventually fell out of favor with the crown.[64]

The issue of good lordship leads to the second point, that of De Lisle's culpability in all these activities. It seems unlikely that the bishop would have countenanced criminal behavior among his officers unless he approved and supported their actions. It is striking how many of the men around him, including those who must have been intimate with his person, such as his brother, John, and his nephews, William and Richard Michel, were indicted at some point for disorderly conduct. Indeed, some of De Lisle's followers had acquired a criminal reputation even before they entered his service. John Poucher, the bishop's itinerant bailiff in county Suffolk, allegedly imprisoned and extorted £1 10s. from five men at East Dereham, Suffolk, in 1343.[65] John Botoner, a London priest, was perhaps introduced into the bishop's curia in 1345 because in that year he had to seek absolution from De Lisle for striking a colleague from the diocese of Ely.[66] By 1350, Botoner was dispensed from residence at his benefice in Wisbech in order to attend the bishop.[67] Also in 1345, Richard de Middleton, De Lisle's receiver, sought a dispensation from the pope because previously he had been involved in a deadly brawl while "in the service of a certain lord."[68]

---

59. CUL, EDR, D 8/1/12–19, *firme terrarum*; D 8/2/1–12, *firme terrarum*.
60. Jones, "The Church and 'Bastard Feudalism,'" 146; *CPR*, 1338–40, 242–43.
61. See pages 131–32, 150–51.
62. See pages 79–80.
63. See pages 13–16, 130.
64. Fryde, "A Medieval Robber Baron," 198–207; Bellamy, *Crime and Public Order*, 24–25.
65. KB 27/342, rex m. 24d.
66. CUL, EDR, G/1/1, Reg. De Lisle, fols. 1v, 61r–v.
67. Ibid., fol. 65r.
68. *CPP*, 102.

Although the bishop may have pleaded ignorance in his defense when charged with complicity in the murder of William Holm,[69] the fact that many members of his gang enjoyed long and continuous service with him argues against such a plea. Indicted criminals figured especially large among his manorial officials.[70] Two of the men, for example, who helped burn down the houses of Lady Wake, Robert de Godington and Henry de Shankton, were in De Lisle's employ since 1347.[71] Their employment continued despite the embarrassment and expense of defending such men, and, unless the bishop connived in their activities, went far beyond the dictates of "good lordship." To take the example of Ralph Carles, the bishop's chamberlain and parker of Somersham, the fine De Lisle incurred as a result of his servant's raid on Lady Wake's houses greatly outweighed any possible value of his loyalty: The £900 awarded to Lady Wake represented nearly half of the bishop's yearly income.[72] Yet, even after that loss, Carles was attached sufficiently to De Lisle to implicate him in Holm's murder. In many of the indictments, De Lisle was said to have ordered the crimes or at least to have known about them and given his consent. It is unlikely, however, that he ever personally participated in his men's raids. The practical business of organizing and leading such forays seems to have been left to his brother John, who had more experience in temporal matters as his brother's chief steward. Indeed, employment in manorial offices, inevitably giving an intimate knowledge of local people and terrain, seems to have been almost a prerequisite for membership in De Lisle's criminal gang.[73]

69. *AS*, 1:659, and see Appendix B, page 234.
70. See pages 50–58.
71. CUL, EDR, D 10/2/18, 21–22 Edward III, dorse, *avena* and *braseum*.
72. See pages 124–30.
73. See pages 50–58.

PART THREE

De Lisle as "Victim"

7

The Bishop Appeals His Case to Avignon

Rather than submit to the king's judgment in his suit with Lady Wake, De Lisle, toward the end of 1356, fled to the papal court at Avignon, where he lodged a vigorous appeal before the pope's auditors. Naturally, Edward III was not pleased. De Lisle had left England in secret without the king's permission, and his appeal flagrantly violated the recently enacted Statute of *Praemunire* of 1353. At the bishop's instance, the king's justices were cited to appear in Avignon and later excommunicated, to the consternation of many at home. On the other hand, De Lisle hardly could expect his would-be savior, Pope Innocent VI, to welcome him with open arms. The pope was attempting to arrange a much-needed truce in the Hundred Years' War between England and France, and the bishop's arrival could not have come at a worse time. Thus, De Lisle was rather like a political orphan whom neither side wanted and who only got in the way of greater events. From the isolated fens of Ely he had stumbled on the world stage where he was creating difficulties all around. A. B. Emden characterizes De Lisle's appeal as a "great embarrassment" to Anglo-papal relations, while J.R.L. Highfield concludes that "it was only with the death of the unreconciled Lisle at Avignon in 1361" that those relations "became friendly again."[1]

However unwilling, the pope was forced to support a fellow prelate against the crown's infringement on Church sovereignty. Nevertheless, Innocent and De Lisle were fighting a losing battle against a king whose power and popularity within his kingdom were at their height. The bishop had the misfortune to time his exile in Avignon

1. Highfield, "Relations Between the Church and the English Crown," 146; Emden, *Biographical Register of Cambridge*, 370.

Fig. 5. Papal palace at Avignon.

with some of Edward's greatest successes during the Hundred Years' War. In 1356, the king's son, Edward the Black Prince, defeated the French at Poitiers and captured the French king, John II. The fruits of this victory were finally realized in 1360, when, by the treaty of Brétigny, Edward reclaimed the Angevin inheritance of Aquitaine and extracted the enormous ransom of nearly half a million pounds for King John's release. To obtain even these terms, Pope Innocent, anxious for peace, had to negotiate long and hard with an English delegation fresh from victory and ill-disposed to compromise. In addition, Edward's subjects were deeply suspicious of the Avignon papacy. Ever since the Babylonian Captivity when Clement V had moved the Holy See from Rome to southeastern France in 1309, Englishmen began to see the pope as the puppet of the French king. "Because the pope always favored the French," wrote the chronicler Henry Knighton in 1357, and on account of the recent English victory at Poitiers, a familiar taunt was said to be written everywhere in Vienna and on other city walls all over Europe: "The pope has become French and Jesus has become English. Now it will be seen who is more favored, the pope or Jesus!"[2]

2. "Et quia papa semper favebat Francis, et eos fovebat in quantum potuit contra Anglos, et propter miraculum quod Deus tribuerat victoriam tam paucis viris contra tantam multitudinem Francorum, scriptum erat in pluribus locis in Vienna et in multis aliis locis: Ore est le pape devenu Franceys e Jesu devenu Engleys. Ore serra veou qe fra plus, ly pape ou Jesus." Knighton, *Chronicon*, 2:94.

Antipapal sentiment produced tangible results with the passage of clerical legislation in the early 1350s. The Statute of Provisors of 1351, which attempted to curtail the perceived avalanche of English benefices being granted by the pope to Frenchmen, was swiftly followed in 1353 by the Statute of *Praemunire*. The latter statute forbade appeals to a foreign authority of judgments handed down in the king's courts and was aimed specifically at anyone seeking to usurp the offices of native churchmen.[3] Ignored by the pope, the legislation was enforced selectively by Edward, who had approved it at the urging of a xenophobic commons. Edward still relied on the pope to reward his favorites with Church offices, but he quickly seized on *Praemunire* to quash any attempts to further De Lisle's cause in England. The result was that hardly any English prelate or cleric dared side with De Lisle and the pope on the question of Church sovereignty for fear of incurring the king's retribution. Indeed, the English clergy, as much as anyone else, was caught up in the tide of Edward's popularity and was instrumental in disseminating the crown's wartime propaganda.[4]

On nearly all counts, therefore, Edward was in a much stronger position than his rival, and De Lisle could little hope to regain his temporalities without the king's approval. Tragically, the bishop seems to have believed that the pope and his fellow prelates in England would unite on the principle of Church sovereignty to force the king's hand. However, this flew in the face of the reality of rising nationalism both in Church and state government during the later Middle Ages. Soon, De Lisle himself would be forced into the humiliating position of choosing between negotiating with his all-powerful sovereign or remaining in exile forever. But the fact that the bishop's appeal in Avignon achieved little in terms of restoring his former status does not mean that his years in exile were insignificant. Not only did De Lisle affect the politics of the Hundred Years' War at a crucial stage of negotiations, he forced his colleagues in England to take a stand on the age-old debate between Church sovereignty and royal supremacy. With but one exception, England's prelates sided with the crown. We need no better proof that Edward dominated the English clergy than his total success in stifling any support for De Lisle's cause within his kingdom. With his prelates and priests firmly behind him and his spectacular victories in France, Edward, in spite of the supposedly pro-French leanings of the Avignon papacy, could claim to dominate the international Church scene as well.

3. *SR*, 1:316–18, 329.
4. W. R. Jones, "The English Church and Royal Propaganda during the Hundred Years' War," *Journal of British Studies* 19 (1979), 18–30; Coleman, *English Literature*, 71–84; A. K. McHardy, "Liturgy and Propaganda in the Diocese of Lincoln during the Hundred Years' War," *Studies in Church History* 18 (1982), 215–27; Ormrod, *Reign of Edward III*, 132–34.

The Bishop's "Revenge"

Almost immediately after William Holm's murder on 28 August 1355, De Lisle, according to his biographer, had a foreboding that his days in England were numbered.[5] Not only did the bishop order his manors liquidated in preparation for flight, he seems to have maintained a private correspondence with the pope informing him of his growing predicament. De Lisle needed brave and trustworthy messengers who were willing to risk arrest and imprisonment by the king's officers. Edward no doubt anticipated his efforts to communicate with the papal authorities. Several times in 1355 and again in 1357 and 1358, he instructed the mayors and bailiffs of all the major ports to watch for subjects attempting to leave the country without royal license.[6] Nevertheless, at least two friar preachers ran the king's gauntlet on the bishop's behalf. On 10 August 1355, the crown issued a writ to arrest Thomas Hopeman, a friar preacher and De Lisle's penitentiary, for going abroad without the king's license. The following 12 October, another writ was issued, this time to apprehend William Jordan, also a friar preacher who had gone abroad without royal permission. Hopeman probably was carrying a message informing the pope that De Lisle had appealed his conviction for arson to no avail and finally had to pay the enormous £900 fine to Lady Wake. Jordan perhaps was entrusted with the latest news that the bishop had been indicted for complicity in Holm's murder.[7]

These leaks notwithstanding, Edward finally was closing the net around De Lisle with his arraignment before the king's bench on 8 July 1356.[8] Although he was to complain about it afterward, the bishop was fortunate to have his trial adjourned to the following Michaelmas term. This gave him time to draft still another letter to the pope that he completed sometime before his final sentencing on 6 October. In the letter or petition, which was to initiate the process of appeal before the papal auditors, De Lisle protested bitterly about his "persecution" at the hands of the king and his justices throughout the entire Lady Wake affair. His list of grievances was long: The bishop claimed that he had been indicted for his crimes by secret inquests to which he had not been summoned and at

---

5. *AS*, 1:657; PRO, KB 27/384, rex m. 11d., and see Appendix B, pages 233, 245–46.

6. *Foedera*, 3, no. 1, 295, 313, 353, 411.

7. *CPR*, 1354–58, 298. A connection between the two friar preachers and De Lisle's dispute with Lady Wake was first proposed by C.F.R. Palmer in "The Friar-Preachers, or Blackfriars, of Dunwich," *The Reliquary* 26 (1885–86), 210–11; and idem, "The Friar-Preachers, or Blackfriars, of Chelmsford," *The Reliquary*, new series, 3 (1889), 143.

8. PRO, KB 27/384, rex m. 11d., and see Appendix B, page 246.

which he had been accused by his enemies, "vile laymen and defamed and criminal persons," whom he named; that he had been convicted and fined for the burning of Lady Wake's houses with the help of "false witnesses corrupted by money," again giving their names; that he had been compelled to pay this fine "by force and fear" contrary to the statutes of England; that his brother and the other men indicted for arson had been imprisoned for a year and a half in spite of their clerical status; that, in the meantime, the goods on his episcopal estate had been occupied and laid waste by the king's ministers, who allegedly had assaulted his servants and familiars and expelled them from his manors; that, against canonical sanctions and the statutes of the realm, he had been arrested and detained in royal prison to await trial concerning Holm's murder; and that the judges sitting in judgment had adjourned his trial until Michaelmas term in order to have false witnesses present who would be "prepared to falsely convict him." Unless the pope came quickly to his aid, De Lisle tremulously declared, the coming Michaelmas term would see all his temporalities confiscated and his person banished from the kingdom. Anticipating his conviction, he asked Innocent to summon his stated enemies to appear before the papal auditors, since "otherwise he does not dare hope that a fulfillment of justice be attained."[9]

In tone, the bishop's petition to the pope is similar to that of Lady Wake to the king in parliament.[10] Both exaggerate their alleged sufferings in order to strengthen their cases. This is a common tactic among petitioners, who must cast themselves in the best possible light—as a victim of cruel injustice—if they wish to have the greatest possible chance of success. In De Lisle's case, many of his charges simply are inconsistent with more reliable records. The fact that the sheriffs turned a blind eye to liquidation of the estate even after 6 October casts considerable doubt on the bishop's claim that his manors and ministers were manhandled by the king's men prior to his trial.[11] It was not the case that the £900 fine paid to Lady Wake was extorted unlawfully. The crown quoted, correctly, the Second Statute of Westminster of 1285 as justification for granting the plaintiff her writ of *elegit*.[12] Equally puzzling is De Lisle's contention that his arrest and imprisonment to await trial was illegal. True, a statute on the books from 1341 specified that no peer of the realm be arrested, imprisoned, and brought to judgment without a trial by his peers or in contravention of Magna Carta. This was the very statute that Archbishop John Stratford wrested from Edward in the aftermath of the crisis of 1340–

9. LPL, Reg. Simon Islip, fols. 138v–139r; LAO, Reg. VIII, fols. 91r–v, 93r–94r, and see Appendix B, pages 247–49.

10. *RP*, 2:267, and see Appendix B, pages 244–45.

11. See pages 138–41.

12. See page 130.

41.[13] Within the year, however, the king felt confident enough to repeal the statute "on the advice of council."[14]

Once in Avignon, De Lisle set about turning the tables on his "tormentors." If a bishop could be dragged before a secular court and sentenced, then the king's justices could be summoned before an ecclesiastical tribunal in the papal palace so that, in De Lisle's words, "they receive their demerits."[15] The pope's chaplain and auditor, Aymeric Hugonis, cited an exhaustive array of people named in the bishop's petition as responsible for the reputed miscarriage of justice inflicted on him. They included Sir William Shareshull, the chief justice of the king's bench; Sir Robert Thorp, the chief justice of the court of common pleas; Sir William Thorp, former chief justice of the king's bench; Sir Thomas Seton, justice of the court of common pleas; Sir William de Notton, justice of the king's bench; Sir Henry Green, justice of the court of common pleas; John Knyvet, king's serjeant; Sir John Dengayn and Nicholas de Stukeley, justices of the peace for Huntingdonshire; Sir John de Stukeley, formerly coroner for Huntingdonshire; Robert de Waldeschef, coroner for Huntingdonshire; and John de Harwedon, sheriff of Cambridge and Huntingdon.[16] In addition, Hugonis cited the witnesses and jurors present at De Lisle's inquest at Huntingdon and at his trial at Yaxley in 1354 and several other men whom De Lisle described as "extremely hostile" (op[p]ido infesti) toward him but who otherwise have no obvious connection with his case.[17]

For these citations to have any effect, however, an attempt had to be made to publish them in England so that those cited could not plead ignorance.[18] According to indictments brought before the king's bench in Trinity term 1358, at least thirty-one masters, deans, beneficed priests, and

---

13. See works listed in Chapter 1, note 30.

14. *SR*, 1:295–97.

15. LPL, Reg. Islip, fol. 139r; LAO, Reg. VIII, fol. 94r, and see Appendix B, pages 240–42.

16. Green, Notton, and Robert Thorp were king's serjeants at the time of their alleged involvement in De Lisle's case. For their appointments, see *Select Cases*, 6:cvi.

17. The jurors were John de Deen, Ralph Chamberlain, Thomas de Earith, William at Hall, John de Colne, Henry Mateschall, John Emmesson, John Young, Nicholas Bray, Geoffrey Hildegar, William Botiller, John Lord, Richard White, Adam Manning, Andrew de Kelshall, John Huse, John Sturdy, Henry de Colne, and John Dengayn of Stilton. Witnesses included Sir Richard de Baiouse, Sir Thomas de Stukeley, Sir Robert de Baiouse, Sir John de Tilly, Richard Fuitz, esquire, Roger de Hurst, John Souche, William de Folkesworth, and Robert de Huntingdon. The following had no clear role in De Lisle's dispute with Lady Wake: Richard de Swineherd, canon of Lincoln, Henry de Walton, archdeacon of Richmond, Walter de Carlton, rector of Deeping, Lincolnshire, Sir Simon Drayton, Sir William de Siwardby, Sir Lucas de Burgo, Sir John Repynghale, Sir Thomas de Chaleres and his son, and Thomas Scot, esquire. See LPL, Reg. Islip, fols. 138v–139r; LAO, Reg. VIII, fols. 91r–94v, and Appendix B, pages 247–48.

18. *AS*, 1:661; LPL, Reg. Islip, fol. 139r; LAO, Reg. VIII, fol. 94r, and see Appendix B, pages 236, 249.

other clergymen in the counties of Cambridge, Huntingdon, and Northampton proclaimed the summons and the later sentences of excommunication. Among them were John Thursteyn, De Lisle's official and vicar-general, Henry de Kirkby, a friar preacher and one of De Lisle's penitentiaries, and two other members of the bishop's curia, Robert de Whitby, fellow of Peterhouse, Cambridge, and John Botoner, vicar of Wisbech.[19] De Lisle's biographer confirms that men affixed the bulls of citation to the doors of local parish churches "so that, traveling through those places, they were able to openly read and give attention to the names of those cited in the edicts."[20] According to another chronicler, Stephen de Birchington, De Lisle's agents even managed to nail the bulls to the doors of St. Paul's Cathedral in London.[21] In spite of such efforts, witnesses produced on the bishop's behalf in Avignon reported that the auditor's citation could not be read out in England, probably as the result of countermeasures taken by the king and his men. As a legal formality, the citation was nailed to the doors of Avignon church and of the papal palace.[22]

On 22 March 1357, Aymeric Hugonis wrote to several prelates and ecclesiastical officials in the southern province asking for transcripts of all legal processes held against De Lisle in relation to his dispute with Lady Wake. These were to include the inquest at Huntingdon and the trial at Yaxley in 1354 concerning the arson of Lady Wake's houses, the inquest into Holm's murder before the coroner, Robert de Waldeschef, at Somersham, and De Lisle's trial before Chief Justice Shareshull and the king's bench at Westminster in 1356. Among the dignitaries addressed were Simon Islip, archbishop of Canterbury; William Edington, bishop of Winchester and royal chancellor; Michael Northburgh, bishop of London; John Gynwell, bishop of Lincoln; Simon Langham, abbot of Westminster; and William de Whittlesey, archdeacon of Huntingdon. They were instructed to ask for the transcripts from the justices and coroner involved within six days of their receipt of Hugonis's letter. The justices, in turn, were to send the transcripts to the ecclesiastics within fifteen days of being warned, and the records were to arrive safely in Avignon within sixty days of being in the prelates' possession. Thus, the whole process was meant to be completed within roughly three months.[23]

With the king's officers on the lookout for any new arrivals from abroad, it is not certain how many of these letters reached their intended destination. On 10 October 1357, Edward ordered the mayor and sheriffs of London to arrest and imprison all those who were bringing "letters, processes,

19. PRO, KB 27/392, rex mm. 21–21d., 31–31d.
20. *AS*, 1:661, and see Appendix B, page 236.
21. *AS*, 1:44.
22. LAO, Reg. VIII, fols. 91v, 94r.
23. LPL, Reg. Islip, fols. 139r–v.

instruments, and other things prejudicial and hurtful to us . . . from foreign parts."[24] The offending messengers were to be kept without bail and the letters that they had been carrying were to be shown without delay to the king in person.[25] Nevertheless, on 28 November 1357, Robert de Whitby, calling himself De Lisle's clerk and proctor, appeared before the archbishop of Canterbury, Simon Islip, and handed over to him Hugonis's instructions.[26] The missive, which was transcribed into Islip's register, had taken more than six months to arrive in England from the time it had been issued in Avignon. Islip well may have been the only person to have received it.

Whitby's successful delivery put Islip in a difficult position. He owed the archbishopric to the king's patronage: For two years prior to his primacy, he had been keeper of the privy seal and had accompanied Edward on his Crécy campaign in 1346.[27] On the other hand, he risked papal censure if he refused outright to obey the pope's auditor. His solution was to attempt to obtain the transcripts within the stipulated time limit but to plead various excuses for why he ultimately was unable to do so. Among his obstacles, he told Hugonis in a letter dated 8 January 1358, was the difficulty in getting hold of the justices of the bench who "wander through various, separate, and distant parts of the kingdom as is their usual custom during the vacation between their fixed sessions."[28] Their itinerant habits notwithstanding, Islip had sent messengers to several justices asking for the transcripts. Sir John de Stukeley, who had sat on the first inquest in October 1354 at Huntingdon to investigate the arson committed against Lady Wake,[29] allegedly had died before the archbishop's letter reached him. Sir William Thorp, formerly chief justice of the king's bench, had declared before Islip "in good faith that he never was present as judge in any process held in this regard [to De Lisle's suit]."[30]

24. "Quia datum est nobis intelligi quod quamplures, nostri et regni nostri Angliae inimici, cum lit[t]eris, processibus, instrumentis, et aliis, nobis, magnatibus, proceribus, et toti regno praedicto valde praejudicialibus et dampnosis, a partibus exteris, infra regnum nostrum praedictum, venire . . ." *Foedera*, 3, no. 1, 380.

25. Ibid.

26. LPL, Reg. Islip, fol. 138v.

27. T. F. Tout, *Chapters in the Administrative History of Medieval England*, 6 vols. (Manchester, 1920–30), 5:24–26.

28. "Post quarum recepcionem litterarum et requisicionem per dictum magistrum Robertum clericum insimul nobis factam ad execucionem earum, ut subsequiter [subsequenter] processimus, eciam infra tempus nobis in eisdem litteris limitatum, quamquam nimis brevem nimisque artatum, attentis multitudine personarum movendarum varietatibus et distanciis domiciliorum suorum ac incertitudine locorum in quibus heedam [haedam] persone pro maiori parte per diversas, separatas, et distanciores regni partes iuxta morem suum solitum vacacione sessionum suarum fixarum, durante que tempore recepcionis predicte minebat pro tempore execucionis huiusmodi vagabant prout in appellacione quadam propter hoc et quedam alia gravamina sufficiencia in dictis litteris comprehensa . . ." LPL, Reg. Islip, fol. 139v.

29. PRO, KB 27/379, rex m. 9, and see Appendix B, page 241.

The most spectacular failure to solicit transcripts came when Islip's messenger approached Sir William de Notton, justice of the king's bench. Notton had the unfortunate envoy immediately arrested and imprisoned, a fate from which he still had not been delivered at the time of Islip's communication to Hugonis. Any other letters that the archbishop had written to justices and that had been found on the messenger's person had been confiscated by the crown, with Islip having no hope of recovering them. Not surprisingly, he could find no one else willing to carry his letters "on account of the very real fear of a similar punishment" to the one inflicted by Notton.[31] In any case, the transcripts had been for a long time literally "taken out of their hands," according to the judges, and "in accordance with habit and custom had been delivered, fully and completely, to a custodian of processes specially appointed for such a purpose." Even if the justices had the transcripts, Islip argued, "they could not in the least have delivered such processes to us" because it would mean violating their oath of loyalty to the king, "above whom a superior is not recognized," and consequently would be accounted as treason.[32] In short, no transcripts were forthcoming.

The papal camera was not satisfied with this answer. If justices could not deliver the transcripts, then their so-called custodian could. Without waiting for Islip's reply, the pope's auditor, Hugonis, seems to have summoned to appear at Avignon, in addition to the justices and other parties named above, the scribes, notary publics, and clerks employed in the king's chancery and exchequer who might be charged with the keeping of the court records.[33] One scribe thus cited was Thomas de Brembre, canon of

30. ". . . dictusque dominus Willelmus de Thorpe coram nobis postmodum bona fide asserint quod nunquam interfuit ut iudex in aliquo processu habito in hac parte." LPL, Reg. Islip, fol. 139v. In 1350 Thorp confessed to taking bribes and was removed from office. See *Select Cases*, 6:xxv–vi, liii; Maddicott, *Law and Lordship*, 48–50.

31. "Qua de causa et propter metum verisimilem consimilis pene, nullum extunc invenire potuimus qui onus deferendi litteras nostras huiusmodi in se voluit acceptare." LPL, Reg. Islip, fol. 139v.

32. Quin ymo [immo] nonnulli eorum se constanti animo excusabant, asserentes processus huiusmodi diu ante moniciones eis ut premittitur factas fuisse exiit manus et potestatem eorum ac custodi processuum huiusmodi ad hoc specialiter deputato, iuxta morem et ritum eorum plene et integre liberatos. Et dato quod in manibus ipsorum remansissent, eos tamen liberare nobis minime potuissent pro eo et ex eo quod processus huiusmodi iurisdiccionem regiam inmediate concernunt in qua non recognoscit su[pe]riorem ut dicunt, quodque iudices quicumque per dominum nostrum regem generaliter aut specialiter deputati processus coram eis habitos quam diu penes eos fuerint, tanquam porcionem thesauri regij fideliter servare et nulli, preter specialem regis licenciam, copiam seu transsumptum processuum huiusmodi liberare, virtute iuramenti in hac parte per eos prestiti, necnon et sub pena prodicionis seu lese [lesure] magestatis artissime obligantur." Ibid.

33. Ibid., fol. 139r.

Salisbury and king's clerk and secretary.[34] On the pretext of Brembre's citation, Edward III wrote several letters of protest to Innocent VI. The king complained that papal citations "in these days" were issued "at anyone's petition," whereas previously, they had been granted only "in the most troublesome cases against tyrants and rebels and enemies of the Roman Church." The summons issued at De Lisle's instance, declared Edward, contradicted his own laws, and the legal processes against the bishop were "duly held" by his justices. He asked the pope to refrain from citing anymore of his men since "henceforth he neither could nor ought show patience towards such things so prejudicial" to him and his kingdom.[35]

Innocent, who wrote back to the king on 31 May and 17 July 1357, remained inflexible and unmoved. His reply supports the contention, made by De Lisle's biographer, that the pope was upholding the bishop's cause as a defense of ecclesiastical liberty and in the wider interests of the Church.[36] Innocent accused the king's men of interfering with his citations: They prevented his summoners in England from visiting the places where those whom they were to cite lived. Furthermore, the king's justices, Innocent charged, had acted against De Lisle out of personal hatred and not in accordance with the duties of their office. As the vicar of Christ, the pope was obliged to "extend our right hand of comfort and consolation to prelates and their churches" who thus were being oppressed. Finally, Innocent urged Edward "to curb the license, temper the will, and restrain the noxious onslaught of your said familiars against prelates, clerics, and ecclesiastical persons," for whatever was inflicted on them "constitutes an injury inflicted upon the body of the universal Church." The pope observed the usual diplomatic courtesy of blaming the servants rather than the master. Nevertheless, he rebuked the king for what he saw as the tactlessness of the royal letters, suggesting that in future Edward keep a more watchful eye on what was being written by his scribes.[37] Even though the respective leaders may not have written or dictated diplomatic correspondence personally, they still were held responsible for its content.

Meanwhile, the papal court already had proceeded with the excommunication of those who had failed to appear in Avignon. On 19 April

34. On 27 July 1345, he was appointed chirographer of the court of common pleas (PRO, CP 40/344, m. 3).

35. R. Delachenal, *Histoire de Charles V*, 5 vols. (Paris, 1909–31), 2:387. This is a printed transcript of the pope's later letter dated 17 July 1357. The earlier one, dated 31 May, is a shorter version of the same letter. See ASV, Registra Vaticana 239, Innocent VI, fols. 85d.–86 (taken from a microfilm in the Seeley Historical Library, Cambridge). The letters are abstracted in *CPL*, 3:625, 627.

36. AS, 1:660, and see Appendix B, page 236.

37. Delachenal, *Histoire*, 2:387–90; ASV, Registra Vaticana 239, Innocent VI, fols. 86–87.

1357, Aymeric Hugonis fulminated sentences against all enemies whom De Lisle had named in his petition. If the auditor had allowed as much time for the justices to arrive as he did for the transcripts, the most likely date for his original citations would have been January 1357. On the following 4 July, the pope ordered that the excommunications be fulminated in England. However, more than eight months were to elapse before Gaucelin, abbot of Psalmody monastery in the diocese of Nîmes, France, was to dispatch on 20 March 1358 detailed instructions for the sentences to be carried out by English prelates.[38]

The long delay between Innocent's mandate and Gaucelin's execution undoubtedly was dictated by the realpolitik of the Hundred Years' War. Shortly after the English defeat of the French forces at the battle of Poitiers in September 1356, the papacy rushed in to make peace between the two sides. In the summer of 1357, Cardinals Perigord and Urgen arrived in London to negotiate the release of King John of France who had been captured by the Black Prince and was the "guest of honor" in the Tower. By 8 May 1358, Edward agreed to release his prisoner for the price of more than half a million pounds and the concession of French territory, including Aquitaine. This so-called First Treaty of London eventually broke down when the French failed to pay ransom money and Edward grew greedy for more concessions.[39] However, the English chronicler, Sir Thomas Gray, states that De Lisle's dispute with the king played a large role in the treaty's doomed outcome. According to Gray, the English parliament, when it met in February 1358, rejected the treaty because it distrusted a mediator who just had excommunicated the king's justices in Avignon.[40] But if the bishop's appeal in any way sabotaged the pope's negotiations, it is likely that Edward wanted it that way. At some point in the peace process, he may have seized on the affront to his justices as a convenient excuse to terminate a treaty he had no intention of honoring. Innocent, for his part, delayed the fulmination of the justices' excommunication in England for fear of upsetting the delicate diplomacy of his cardinals. Either way, De Lisle was merely a pawn in the chess game of international politics.

Gaucelin's instructions for the cursing procedure were elaborate and specific. On every Sunday and feastday in churches throughout England, the clergy were to denounce the excommunicate in the English tongue, individually and by name, and in a "high voice." This was to take place

38. LAO, Reg. VIII, fols. 91r–v, 93r, 94v. The dating clause on Aymeric Hugonis's instrument (fol. 94v) gives the wrong year (1358 instead of 1357) but the correct indiction (tenth) and the correct pontifical year (fifth).

39. Delachenal, *Histoire*, 2:73–82; E. Perroy, *The Hundred Years War*, trans. W. B. Wells (London, 1951), 137–38; J. Le Patourel, "The Treaty of Brétigny, 1360," *TRHS*, 5th series, 10 (1960), 27–30; C. Allmand, *The Hundred Years War: England and France at War, c. 1300–c. 1450* (Cambridge, 1988), 18.

40. Sir Thomas Gray, *Scalacronica*, trans. H. Maxwell (Glasgow, 1907), 129–30.

during Mass "with the bells pealed, the candles lit and then extinguished and thrown into the ground and with the cross erected."[41] The excommunications also were to be announced during sermons, including those delivered at the Universities of Oxford and Cambridge. If those cursed persisted in their excommunication and refused to seek absolution for a month after their sentence, they were to be forbidden from celebrating Mass, taking communion, receiving ecclesiastical burial, or participating in any of the Church's other sacraments. In the meantime, two of De Lisle's enemies, Sir Simon de Drayton and the coroner for Huntingdonshire, Sir John de Stukeley, had died while under sentence of excommunication and had been given a church burial. Their corpses were to be dug up from their tombs and thrown out into unconsecrated ground so that "the punishment of one may terrify many and in future restrain others from such excesses and contempt of the keys of the Church."[42] The official of the court of Canterbury and the dean of the court of arches in London were not to interfere with the censures. If the English prelates refused to execute the sentences, they were threatened with interdict within eight days of their receipt of Gaucelin's mandate and thereafter with suspension from office after sixteen days and finally with excommunication of their own persons in twenty-four days.[43]

Despite these harsh-sounding strictures, De Lisle's colleagues in general did little to support his cause. Even before he had left England in 1356, De Lisle had complained to the pope that the archbishop of Canterbury, Simon Islip, and the bishops of Lincoln and London, respectively John Gynwell and Michael Northburgh, had expressly refused to act against his enemies as he had requested. His colleagues's apathy had allowed him to sustain losses totaling 10,000 marks, or approximately £6667, and he had characterized their behavior as "an injustice to the Church and ecclesiastical liberty, the scandal of the clergy, a pernicious example to the faithful of Christ, in manifest contempt of Holy Roman Church and

---

41. ". . . secundum formam in eisdem litteris apostolicis contentam rite et publice excommunicatos . . . singulis diebus dominicis et festivis in ecclesiis vestris et aliis quibuscumque ecclesiis cathedralibus, collegiatis, conventualibus, et parochialibus regni Anglie supradicti intra Missarum solempnia, pullatis campanis, candelis accensis et demum extinctis et in terram proiectis, ac cruce erecta . . . singulariter et nominatim, alta voce, clero et populo in wulgari [vulgari] denuncietis." LAO, Reg. VIII, fol. 92r.

42. ". . . precipimus et mandamus quatinus [quatenus] cadavera Simonis de Drayton' militis et Johannis de Stivecle predictorum publice et realiter exhumetis, seu faciatis modo simili per alio exhumari, et cadavera huiusmodi a locis sacrosanctis, in quibus nunc tumilata dicuntur, vel saltim ipsorum ossa proiciatis, vel per alios proici faciatis, ut sic, lege docente, pene [pena] unius multos terreat et ceteros ab excessubus [excessibus] huiusmodi et contemptu clavium Ecclesie retrahat in futurum." Ibid., fol. 92v.

43. Ibid., fols. 92v–93r.

of your holiness, a grave injury and hurt to this bishop and his church, and in contravention of their oaths by which they are necessarily bound to preserve and defend the rights and liberties of Holy Mother Church."[44]

De Lisle's testimony was vindicated when, on 21 July 1357, Pope Innocent was forced to suspend his excommunication of one of the bishop's adversaries, Henry de Walton, archdeacon of Richmond, because Islip, Gynwell, and Northburgh refused to carry out the sentence.[45] Six days later, on 27 July, Innocent wrote to Archbishop Islip, sending similar letters to William Edington, bishop of Winchester and royal chancellor, and to John Sheppey, bishop of Rochester and royal treasurer. His holiness was displeased for many reasons, he said. The "oppression of clergy and prelates" displeased him, as did "the trampling of [ecclesiastical] liberty." He was displeased that "perverse minds conspire to turn the pure heart of this King [Edward] from royal rectitude." But most of all, scolded the pope to Islip, "it displeases us that you and other prelates and ecclesiastical men keep a hurtful silence concerning this and, as if your tongue cleaves to your palate, that you, like dumb dogs, dare not bark against the doers of such things [against the bishop of Ely]."[46] He closed the letter by raising the example of that "glorious martyr," Saint Thomas Becket, who "did not fear the swords of the impious on behalf of the Church of God." Islip was exhorted to "show by word and prove by deed that you [are] a true primate in these matters, so that, by your dignity and merits, you may be acknowledged to be the successor of Martyr Thomas."[47] The following January, in his reply to Hugonis's request for transcripts of De Lisle's trial, the archbishop was to demonstrate how far he was in the Becket mold.

In spite of the cold feet that he had shown earlier, John Gynwell, the bishop of Lincoln, apparently was the only prelate willing to brave the

44. LPL, Reg. Islip, fol. 139r; LAO, Reg. VIII, fol. 93v, and see Appendix B, page 249.

45. *CPL*, 3:584.

46. "Quod ex pluribus causis ferimus ad modum displicenter. Displicet siquidem nobis clericorum et prelatorum eorundem oppressio; displicet ipsius conculcatio libertatis; displicet quod perverse mentes purum ipsius regis cor satagunt a rectitudine regia trahere in obliquum; displicet quod tu et alij prelati et viri ecclesiastici tenetis super hoc nocive [nocivum] silentium, et quasi adheserit lingua palatui, sicut canes muti latrare adversus actores operum talium non audetis." ASV, Registra Vaticana 239, Innocent VI, fol. 155. The letter is abstracted in *CPL*, 3:627.

47. ". . . fraternitatem tuam attente rogamus quatinus [quatenus], prudenter considerans quod gloriosus martir [martyr] et pontifex Thomas, cuius successor es, pro Dei Ecclesia impiorum gladios non expavit, et quod ad te ut pote[m] metropolitanum ipsius episcopi cause sue cum iustitia et patrocinium et deffentio [diffentio] specialitate quadam pertinet diligenter attendens, te verum in hijs pontificem verbo exhibeas et probes effectu, itaque eiusdem Martiris [Martyris] Thome successor dignitate et meritis agnoscaris." ASV, Registra Vaticana 239, Innocent VI, fol. 155d.

king's certain wrath for the sake of obeying the papal mandates of excommunication. It is likely that he was of two minds about the dispute: On the one hand, as a member of the Church he was obliged to help his colleague, De Lisle; on the other, he was a close friend of Lady Wake's brother, Henry of Grosmont, duke of Lancaster, and he owed his bishopric to Lancaster's patronage.[48] Nevertheless, receiving Gaucelin's instructions on 18 May 1358, Gynwell, on the following Monday, 21 May, ordered his archdeacons and their officials to arrange for the excommunications to be fulminated in all the regular and secular churches in their respective archdeaconries.[49] To Gynwell also fell the unpleasant task of exhuming Drayton and Stukeley, since they both had been buried within his diocese, respectively at Botolph Bridge and Stukeley, Huntingdonshire. He conveniently excused himself from the exhumations on the grounds that he had to celebrate holy orders four times on the coming Saturday and for other "reasonable and just causes."[50] Instead, the abbots of Ramsey, Peterborough, Crowland, and Sawtry were to do the honors. Nevertheless, Gynwell's letters betray some unease over this ultimate insult to the king's men. He ordered the abbots to report back to him within six days of completing their task and ended his letter by disclaiming that, "we do not intend in any way to derogate the rights of our lord king and of his realm of England."[51]

A petition to the pope from Stukeley's brother, Gilbert, eventually secured an honorable reburial for the dead coroner, granted by Innocent on 31 August 1359.[52] Also working in Stukeley's favor was Gynwell's report of 9 October 1358 in which he confirmed that Stukeley, on his deathbed, "had tearfully repented of his contumacy" against the bishop of Ely and had declared that if he had been healthy enough, he would have gone to Avignon in person to make amends.[53] No such redemption was available to Drayton's corpse, which, according to the chronicler Stephen de

48. Fowler, *King's Lieutenant*, 179–80.

49. LAO, Reg. VIII, fols. 94v–95r.

50. "Cum autem propter execucionem nostri pontificalis officij, tam circa celebracionem ordinum, quos hac instante die Sabbati Quatuor Temporum celebrare personaliter nos oportet, prout officaciter intendimus deo dante, quam eciam circa alia et propter alias causas racionabiles atque iustas, contenta in dictis litteris apostolicis instrumentis et processibus, exequi personaliter nequeamus." Ibid., fol. 95r.

51. ". . . per predicta tamen non intendimus iuribus domini nostri regis et regni Anglie in aliquo derogare." Ibid.

52. *CPL*, 3:607.

53. ". . . dictum Johannem lacrimabiliter de dicta contumacia penituisse et verba penitencie publice emisisse ac dixisse in articulo mortis sue se fore paratum Deo et Ecclesie ac parti dicit episcopi pro huiusmodi contumacia satisfacere quatenus vires suarum se extenderent facultatum, et protestabatur publice coram eis quod, si Deus dare sibi voluisset de illa infirmitate corporalemque et potenciam laborandi, sedem apostolicam pro absolucione sua a dicta sentencia impetranda et pena canonica inde recipienda." LAO, Reg. VIII, fols. 95v–96r.

Birchington, had been thrown irretrievably into a "vile bog."[54] Another contemporary chronicler, Henry Knighton, reported that in addition to Drayton, Gynwell had ordered the abbot of Peterborough to exhume Sir John de Engan (probably Dengayn), but that the dead man's son forcibly prevented the ceremony from taking place.[55] No mention of Dengayn, however, is made in Gynwell's letters.

The King's Response

Just as Gynwell probably feared, these violations of the sanctity of the tomb shocked and outraged many in the royal circle, not least the king himself, who now resolved that something had to be done about De Lisle's supporters in England.[56] Among the first to feel the effects of Edward's vengeance was, naturally, the bishop of Lincoln. On 29 June 1358,[57] barely a month after he had ordered the offending exhumations, Gynwell was celebrating Mass in the church of Buckden, Huntingdonshire, when several men suddenly burst in and interrupted the service. Among the intruders were four men who had testified against De Lisle in the king's court and been summoned and excommunicated for their pains: Sir Thomas de Stukeley, Sir John de Tilly, Sir Robert Baiouse, and Richard Fuitz, esquire. Armed with "long knives" and other weapons, they rushed up to the high altar and uttered many "opprobrious words" at the bishop.[58] Finally, Sir Robert Baiouse, after another lengthy speech of abuse, read out a letter patent from the crown that he afterward handed over to Gynwell and then departed with his companions.

---

54. "Et postea idem Dominus Simon in huiusmodi excommunicatione decedens, per episcopum Lincoln' auctoritate domini papae fuerat exhumatus; eiusque corpus in paludem viliorem projectum." *AS*, 1:44–45.

55. Knighton, *Chronicon*, 2:104.

56. *AS*, 1:661, and see Appendix B, page 237.

57. The other date given in the register, 20 June, that fell on a Wednesday in 1358, may have been a scribal error (see below, note 58).

58. "Memorandum quod die Veneris in festo Apostolorum Petri et Pauli, videlicet vicesima die mensis Junij, anno Domini millesimo trecentesimo quinquagesimo octavo, Domini Thomas de Stivecle, Johannes de Tilly, et Robertus Bayouse milites, Ricardus Fuitz et Thomas Scot domicelli et alii quamplures viri cum eis, cum longis cultellis et aliis armis, ad magnum altare ecclesie prebendalis et parochialis de Buckeden' Lincoln' diocesis, in quo Venerabilis Pater Dominus Johannes dei gracia Lincoln' episcopus, pontificalibus indutus, Magnam Missam de Apostolis Petro et Paulo usque ad offertorium Misse cantatum cepit solempniter celebrare, et post ablucionem manuum suarum, cum magno impetu accesserunt et verba opprobriosa eidem domino episcopo publice intulerunt." LAO, Reg. VIII, fols. 95r–v.

The letter, dated 16 June 1358 and addressed to all the clerics and lay-men in England, matched the papal correspondence in hyperbolic lan-guage. The crown reasserted its ancient right to try felonies in its courts and said that it must uphold the laws and customs of England "by virtue of the sacred oaths" that the king had taken on his coronation.[59] Those who took their suits to a "foreign court" or who "put into effect sentences of excommunication and other intolerable processes" were the crown's enemies striving "to subvert and annul the judgments and other things which are rightly handed down, carried out, and determined in our royal courts."[60] Subjects were enjoined to desist from such activities on pain of forfeiture of their goods and by virtue of their loyalty to the government. The letter ended with a dire warning equal to that appended to Gaucelin's order of exhumation: "Know that we will punish without dissimulation as our enemies and violators of our crown all those who perpetrate the aforesaid things . . . so that their punishment will strike terror into others who henceforth transgress against us and our laws and customs."[61] On 15 November 1358, Edward issued yet another warning in the form of a general prohibition addressed to his ecclesiastics. "You are to attempt nothing in this regard," Edward declared in the prohibition after briefly summarizing the dispute between De Lisle and Lady Wake, "which can result in an offence against our crown or royal dignity or an impediment to Blanche's suit or a hurt against our jurors or other faithful [subjects]." If anything was so attempted it would be revoked "without any delay."[62] Both letters were witnessed by the king himself at Westminster.

59. "Cum nos et progenitores nostri . . . habuimus cognicionem de quibuscumque placitis feloniarum, transgressionum, et aliorum laicalium contractuum quorumcumque coram justiciis nostris infra regnum nostrum terminandis et nos ac dicti progenitores nostri, virtute sacramentorum in corona communibus nostris prestitorum, omnes et singulos dicioni nostre regie subiectos in legibus et consuetudinibus ipsius regni nostri Anglie manutenere teneamur . . ." Ibid., fol. 95v.

60. ". . . intellexerimus quod quamplures ligei nostri et alii nostri et regni nostri Anglie inimici quamplura, que ad cognicionem nostram regiam spectant, terminanda contra ligeancie et fidelitatis sue debitum ad alienum iudicium deduxerunt, et varios processus nobis et toti regno nostro nimis preiudiciales prosecuti fuerunt et prosecuntur de die in diem et iudicia et alia, que in curiis nostris regiis rite reddita, acta sunt, et terminata, subvertere et adnullari facere moliuntur, et super hoc excommunicacionum sentencias et alios processus intollerabiles execucioni in ipso regno nostro demandarunt." Ibid.

61. ". . . scientes quod omnes illos qui premissa perpetrarunt, seu decetero perpetrare presumpserint, vel execuciones huiusmodi fecerunt, vel facere presumpserunt, tanquam inimicos nostros et corone nostre violatores absque dissimilacione [dissimulacione] puniemus, quod eorum punicio aliis cedet in terrorem, [qui] contra nos et ipsos leges et consuetudines decetero delinquendi." Ibid.

62. "Et quia non est iuri consonum quod quis super hijs, que in curiis nostris secundum legem et consuetudinem regni nostri Anglie rite fiunt, trahatur in placitum in curia Christianitatis seu aliqualiter pregravetur, vobis et cuilibet

Edward was as good as his word in these strictures. His prosecutions against anyone found siding with De Lisle must rank among the most vigorous enforcements of the Statute of *Praemunire* of 1353.[63] *Praemunire*, like the Statute of Provisors of 1351, is generally seen by historians of Anglo-papal relations as a diplomatic tool that Edward implemented only when it suited him to do so, as a means of putting pressure on the pope to accede to his demands.[64] Although the new legislation was the culmination of a long series of complaints from the English clergy and commons against papal interference in their patronage, it reaffirmed the crown's domination of the English Church and gave the king vast new powers of enforcement. *Praemunire* stated that all those who appealed crown judgments in a foreign court would have their possessions forfeit and their persons imprisoned or outlawed unless they answered within two months for their contempt in the king's courts.[65] Edward used the statute to dissuade, by the example of those he punished, anyone in England who might have been tempted to heed the pope's call to assist De Lisle's appeal. The king's application of *Praemunire* thus went far beyond the original intention of its sponsors, which was to curtail papal patronage.

The most visible violator of *Praemunire*, John Gynwell, was summoned before the king's bench in Trinity and Michaelmas terms 1358.[66] Distrusting the courts, the bishop approached Edward III in person at Reading on 11 November in the same year and asked to be readmitted to the royal grace. With John Knyvet, king's serjeant, also present, Gynwell proposed that Edward appoint a special body consisting of men "learned in the law of Holy Church with others of the [king's] council," before whom Gynwell, on a day to be chosen by the king, would "come before them to show by what authority he did what he did." Edward's response was to take the bishop back into his favor but to deliberate further on the matter of an investigation into his conduct. In the end, the king seems to have been

---

vestrum districte prohibemus ne quicquam in hac parte quod in lesionem corone seu regie dignitatis nostre, aut prosecucionis ipsius Blanchie impedimentum, aut iuratorum, vel aliorum fidelium nostrorum predictorum dampnum cedere valeat, attemptetis, nec facere aliqualiter attemptari ex causa supradicta, et si quid minus rite per vos in hac parte attemptum fuerit, id sine dilacione aliqua revocari faciemus." PRO, KB 27/392, rex m. 18.

63. For other prosecutions under the statute, see E. B. Graves, "The Legal Significance of the Statute of Praemunire of 1353," in C. H. Taylor and J. L. La Monte, eds., *Haskins Anniversary Essays in Medieval History* (Boston, 1929), 74–79.

64. Highfield, "Relations Between the Church and the English Crown," 111, 147–48; Pantin, *English Church*, 82–87; P. Heath, *Church and Realm, 1272–1461: Conflict and Collaboration in an Age of Crises* (London, 1988), 130–33; Ormrod, *Reign of Edward III*, 126.

65. *SR*, 1:329.

66. PRO, KB 27/392, rex m. 32; KB 27/393, rex m. 1d.

satisfied by Gynwell's appropriate show of humility, and he let the matter drop.[67]

Others were not so fortunate. A judicial inquiry in the East Anglian shires resulted in the arrest and imprisonment of both clerics and laymen who had remained loyal to De Lisle and had helped publish the papal bulls on his behalf.[68] The witnesses for the prosecution had good reason to want their capture. Sir John Tilly, Richard Fuitz, esquire, and Andrew de Kelshall all had been summoned and excommunicated at De Lisle's instance.[69] According to the bishop's biographer, the prisoners were either stubborn or smart: "Some men . . . afflicted by various injuries, were punished with a twofold penalty of a bodily and monetary kind," while others, "taking the advice of their friends, threw themselves on the king's mercy and took a more lenient path."[70] Two men who chose the latter course were John Botoner, vicar of Wisbech, Cambridgeshire, and Robert Michel, De Lisle's nephew and rector of Tydd St. Giles, Cambridgeshire. Imprisoned in the Tower of London, they petitioned for and got release on bail on 22 November 1359 with the proviso that in future they not solicit, certify, receive, or publish "any letters, bulls or instruments prejudicial to the king, his crown and dignity."[71] By 30 May 1362, Edward officially pardoned Botoner, Michel, and Robert de Whitby, another violator of *Praemunire*.[72]

Other offenders were not treated so leniently. John Thursteyn, De Lisle's official and vicar-general, was outlawed and had his goods at Chichester, Sussex, seized into the king's hand by 28 January 1359.[73] The bishop's messenger, Thomas de Senanton, was arrested and thrown into the Tower after he had delivered papal bulls to John Sheppey, bishop of Rochester and royal treasurer. His companion in confinement was Thomas de Chilton, formerly keeper of the bishop's parks at Downham, Cambridgeshire, who had assisted Senanton in his mission. The two pris-

67. *CCR*, 1354–60, 534; Putnam, *Sir William Shareshull*, 142.

68. *AS*, 1:661, and see Appendix B, page 237.

69. PRO, KB 27/392, rex mm. 21–21d., 31–31d.; LAO, Reg. VIII, fols. 94r–v.

70. *AS*, 1:661, and see Appendix B, page 237.

71. *Select Cases*, 6:125–26.

72. *CPR*, 1361–64, 199–200, 215. Acting as De Lisle's messenger was not Whitby's only violation of *Praemunire*. In Hilary term 1361, Whitby was prosecuted by the crown for ousting Robert de Westbury, royal clerk, from the church of Barking, Suffolk. Whitby justified Westbury's ejection "by pretext of other collations or provisions [made] to himself in foreign parts" ("pretextu collacionum seu provis[i]onum aliquarum sibi in partibus exteris"). The provision no doubt was made at De Lisle's instance in Avignon; however, the patronage of the church along with the bishop's manor at Barking was seized by the crown in the wake of De Lisle's conviction in 1356. See PRO, KB 27/402, rex m. 23.

73. PRO, KB 27/394, rex m. 13; KB 27/397, rex m. 26d.; KB 27/398, rex m. 11d.

oners allegedly were starved before their trial and finally sentenced to perpetual imprisonment at Newgate, where they died "in great misery."[74] By other accounts, however, their agony was short-lived: They were sentenced summarily to death and hanged.[75]

It was becoming increasingly clear to Innocent and De Lisle that the papal bulls of citation and excommunication were being promulgated to no effect. No one now dared bring the bulls into England for fear of sharing the fate of Senanton and Chilton.[76] In addition, De Lisle's dispute was complicating the delicate diplomacy of peace, which continued until the conclusion of the Treaty of Brétigny in 1360. These new political realities were reflected in the latest round of correspondence between the pope and Edward concerning the bishop. Without waiting for a reply to his previous communication, Innocent wrote to the king on 25 January 1359. He began by complaining to Edward about the harsh treatment inflicted on De Lisle's agents. It soon becomes evident from the rest of the letter, however, that the pope had shifted dramatically his policy since the first year of De Lisle's exile from one of confrontation to reconciliation.[77]

In his letters of 31 May and 17 July 1357, Innocent had told Edward that he was directly responsible for his ministers' behavior. "For concerning these things, so that we may speak paternally to you," he had written to the king, "your ignorance does not excuse you, and should dissimulation perchance exist, then you are implicated in it, even if you rightly should put the blame on another." Dissimulation implied tacit consent, and doers and consenters were punished equally in the Lord's judgment.[78]

By 1 August 1358, Innocent had abandoned his strident, hectoring tone. Edward was no longer to blame for the injustices committed against De Lisle and his men, for the king was being "provoked" to do these things by "fabricated rumours" whispered into his ear by his advisers.[79] In fact,

---

74. *AS*, 1:45, 661; Corpus Christi College Library, Cambridge, MS 287, 135, and see Appendix B, page 237.

75. Walsingham, *Historia Anglicana*, 1:286; Reading, *Chronica*, 130.

76. *AS*, 1:661, and see Appendix B, page 237.

77. ASV, Registra Vaticana 240, Innocent VI, fols. 16d.–17 (taken from a microfilm in the Seeley Historical Library, Cambridge), and see Appendix B, pages 249–50. The letter is abstracted in *CPL*, 3:628.

78. Delachenal, *Histoire*, 2:389; ASV, Registra Vaticana 239, Innocent VI, fol. 86d.; *CPL*, 3:625, 627.

79. "Intelleximus, carissime fili, quod nonnulli tui subditi, quorum etiam aliqui in regiis officiis se excercent, illatis per eos, Venerabili Fratri Nostro Thomae episcopo Eliensi, ejusque ecclesiae, clericis, et servitoribus, jacturis et injuriis non contenti, sed adversus eum celsitudinem regiam provocare pro viribus satagentes, eidem episcopo penes eandem celsitudinem, quod de ipsa apud sedem apostolicam conquestus extiterit, confictis relatibus imponere studuerunt." *Foedera*, 3, no. 1, 403.

the bishop harbored no ill will toward his former sovereign and perse-cutor, according to the pope. "We wish your serenity to know," he had written, "that the bishop has not laid before us ever a complaint about your highness, nor has he asserted that his injuries and damages came about with your knowledge or by your mandate."[80] By the following January, Innocent went even further and asserted, somewhat disingenu-ously, that De Lisle still was the king's loyal friend and servant. In lan-guage reminiscent of that used by Clement VI in 1345 to persuade Ed-ward to accept De Lisle as bishop of Ely,[81] Innocent declared that his guest was "by all means your devoted and faithful subject and a zealot for your royal exaltation, ardently desiring to be on the look-out for your service and honor." Innocent ended the letter urging a settlement to the dispute. He implied that he would stop citing and excommuni-cating the king's justices and that he would convince De Lisle to com-promise. "Henceforth it may not be necessary for the parties to be sum-moned before us for judgement," he assured Edward, as "we hope that thus your royal benevolence will apply a remedy of swift provision, and the same bishop will acquiesce to our admonitions from God, so that, with your clemency taking the place of justice, the matter of such quarrels will be laid to rest and [the bishop] restored completely to your grace."[82]

The way finally was open for a rapprochement between the two sides. But just as he was on the verge of concluding an agreement that would have ended his long exile, De Lisle suddenly died on 23 June 1361.[83] It is quite possible that he was one of the many victims of the second outbreak of plague that is known to have ravaged Avignon as well as England.[84] He was laid to rest in the Dominican convent of St. Praxède at Montfavet in the outskirts of Avignon (see Fig. 6).[85] His tomb, if he had one, is unlikely to have survived the ruination of the church after it was abandoned in 1398.[86]

80. "Ne igitur hujusmodi pravorum conficta suggestio veritati praevaleat, et supplantet iniquitas innocentem, serenitatem tuam scire volumus quod idem episcopus nullam unquam de celsitudine tua apud nos querelam proposuit, nec praemissas injurias et jacturas de tua conscientia vel mandato asseruit processisse." Ibid.
81. See page 10.
82. ASV, Registra Vaticana 240, Innocent VI, fols. 17–17d., and see Appendix B, page 250.
83. AS, 1:662, and see Appendix B, page 238.
84. Mollat, Popes, 51.
85. AS, 1:662, and see Appendix B, page 238.
86. Précis de l'Histoire d'Avignon au Point de Vue Religieux, 2 vols. (Avignon, 1852), 1:186–87; L. H. Labande, Le Palais des Papes et les Monuments d'Avignon au Quatorzième Siècle, 2 vols. (Marseille, 1925), 2:158; J. Girard, Evocation du Vieil Avignon (Paris, 1958), 245–46.

Fig. 6. Ruined tower of Dominican Priory of St. Praxède, Montfavet.

On 10 July 1361, Pope Innocent lifted the sentences of excommunication that still lay on De Lisle's enemies.[87]

Edward's Checkmate

By almost any measure, Edward was the victor in the test of wills with his recalcitrant and stubborn opponent, the bishop of Ely. He all but blocked the pope's bulls from entering and being publicized in his kingdom. His bishops and archbishops, on the whole, turned a deaf ear to a call for help from one of their own number. And he forced his adversary to recognize his authority and even cultivate his goodwill. This was more than a personal struggle between two men. It affirmed the general trend throughout the later Middle Ages in which the supremacy of the state advanced at the expense of the sovereignty of the Church. That Edward was one of a growing number of monarchs who defied the waning power of ecclesiastical censure should occasion no surprise. But perhaps more than any medieval English monarch before or since, Edward III achieved unrivaled domination over his clerical subjects. The national Anglican Church first headed by Henry VIII by the Act of Supremacy of 1534 had its origin in Edward's medieval England.

Clearly, J.R.L. Highfield was right to point out in the 1950s that Edward had "tamed" the English episcopate.[88] But we in fact can go beyond Highfield's thesis to say that Edward dictated the agenda of the papacy itself in a way that few medieval English monarchs could. Although the Avignon popes were perceived to orbit in the French sphere of influence, the French kings who opposed Edward (Philip V and John II), were too weak and ineffective leaders to challenge the English hegemony. Ironically, Edward overawed the pope in the same way that the French king, Philip IV, of his grandfather's generation had done: through a combination of military terror abroad and political control and propaganda at home. The Black Prince's chevauchée through the south of France in 1356 caused panic among the French cardinals, who were ready to make terms at any price with the invaders about to knock on their gates. Meanwhile, the passage of the Statutes of Provisors and *Praemunire* in the early 1350s,

---

87. *Foedera*, 3, no. 2, 623. The sentences were suspended until 1 November, to be finally annulled when a new bishop of Ely was chosen. Sir William de Notton, justice of the king's bench, was absolved posthumously on 8 February 1364. See *Register of William Edington*, 2:57–58.

88. Highfield, "English Hierarchy," 136–38; Heath, *Church and Realm*, 138–39; Ormrod, *Reign of Edward III*, 122–23; Waugh, *England in the Reign of Edward III*, 148–51.

the dissemination of wartime benedictions by the clergy, and the failure of prelates to respond to De Lisle's appeal must have convinced Innocent VI that the English Church and commons were solidly behind their king. The myth of Church sovereignty in England now was debunked completely. Lacking any effective bargaining power, the papacy was forced to negotiate peace on Edward's terms, with the result highly favorable to the English. It is true that the French concessions in the Treaty of Brétigny of 1360 were slightly less than those proposed in the Second Treaty of London of 1359. Edward himself, however, had upped the stakes in 1359 and then failed to back them up with a military victory at Rheims later that year. The destiny of France, and of the supposedly pro-French papacy, was largely in his hands.

Edward's influence over the English Church therefore played an important part in his relations with Avignon. But how did the king convince his clerical countrymen that their interest lay more with the crown than with their pontiff? Edward used a heavy hand. At every opportunity he intervened in clerical disputes and seized the temporalities of recalcitrant churchmen. In addition to punishing De Lisle as a result of his suit with Lady Wake in 1356, Edward seized the lands of the bishop of Norwich, William Bateman, in his quarrel with the monks of Bury St. Edmunds in 1347; he confiscated the property of the bishop of Exeter, John Grandisson, in 1349; and he seized the temporalities of the bishop of Chichester, William Lynn, in 1365.[89] Edward's greatest coup came on 10 July 1372, when he ordered the temporalities of all the bishops of the Southern province be taken into his hand for nonpayment of a clerical subsidy. The move brought swift results; less than a month later, on 4 August, the king felt sufficiently satisfied to restore the confiscated estates.[90] It was an impressive display of royal supremacy that would have been unthinkable in the early part of the reign.

Edward's personal popularity and prestige, which owed much to his victories abroad, also contributed to his conquest of the Church at home. But his role was only half of the equation. The crown's control of the ecclesiastical hierarchy would not have been possible without a new breed of prelates who generally acceded to the king's wishes. Ironically, the popes, particularly Clement VI, appointed at Edward's request many of the so-called curialist bishops even as they increased their own powers of provision. This is not to say that the king's choices for the episcopal bench were completely devoid of independent thought or action. John

89. *CPR*, 1345–48, 251, 535; *CPR*, 1348–50, 427; *CPR*, 1364–67, 159. Also see Thompson, "William Bateman," 118–21; *Select Cases*, 6:143–45; Graves, "Praemunire," 76–77.

90. PRO, E 159/148, third membrane from bottom, dorse (no foliation); *Foedera*, 3, no. 2, 958; *CPR*, 1370–74, 190.

Thoresby, archbishop of York and Edward's chancellor between 1349 and 1356, dared to delay the king's seizure of De Lisle's temporalities until it conformed with legal procedure. On 27 November 1356, a week after De Lisle had left England for Avignon, Thoresby resigned the chancellorship. His resignation is thought to have been in protest of De Lisle's punishment, which Thoresby may have taken as an infringement on ecclesiastical liberty. Immediately, however, his place was filled by another long-standing royal servant, William Edington, bishop of Winchester and the king's treasurer, and no serious disruption in the government seems to have occurred.[91]

By contrast, the most subservient prelate to the crown was perhaps Simon Islip, archbishop of Canterbury.[92] The keeper of the privy seal before becoming archbishop, he remained forever afterward staunchly loyal to his former employer, even when the laws and interests of the Church demanded otherwise. In what was to be an ominous precedent for De Lisle, Islip, in 1352, helped implement crown policy designed to make criminous clerks more accountable for their deeds. In exchange for confirmation of clerical immunity in the statute, *Pro Clero*, the archbishop, on 18 February 1352, issued a decree that made it harder for defamed clerics to prove their innocence and imposed harsher punishments on those convicted.[93] It was in the spirit of this legislation that Islip, against the dictates of canon law, insisted on De Lisle's reconciliation with Edward as a condition of his purgation. Unlike Gynwell's courageous obedience to the papal mandates, Islip dragged his feet when asked to provide transcripts and otherwise assist the processes instigated by his colleague's appeal. De Lisle's fortunes may have been quite different had Islip's predecessor, John Stratford, still occupied the archbishopric. Stratford successfully had confronted his sovereign when accused of treason in 1340–41 and even had cast himself, if somewhat ambitiously, in the role of the martyred champion of Church immunity, Saint Thomas Becket. The great difference in character between Stratford and Islip is an indication of the change that Edward had effected among his bishops since 1341.

While Islip may have been too cooperative with the crown, it could be argued that De Lisle was too arrogantly inflexible. On at least two occasions he had the opportunity to make his peace with Edward and thus avoid the long and costly exile in Avignon. His refusal to humble himself in the parliament of 1355 and to take his ordinary's advice in 1356 hints of

---

91. *Foedera*, 3, no. 1, 344; *CCR*, 1354–60, 332. The connection between Thoresby's resignation and De Lisle's case has been made by Ormrod, "Edward III's Government," 258; and Hughes, *Pastors and Visionaries*, 135.

92. For an apology of Islip, see M. McKisack, *The Fourteenth Century, 1307–1399* (Oxford, 1959), 296–97.

93. *SR*, 1:325, sec. 4; Gabel, *Benefit of Clergy*, 134–35 (under a false date of 1351).

a contentious and intractable personality.[94] By contrast, other prelates who had their temporalities taken away by the crown managed to get them back through a show of personal submission to the king's authority. With his honor satisfied, Edward showed himself to be a forgiving ruler. Bateman, Grandisson, and Lynn all restored themselves to the king's favor and in turn had their temporalities restored to them within two years of confiscation.[95] Even De Lisle's lone supporter, Gynwell, quickly apologized for obeying his pope rather than his king. The day when the English episcopal hierarchy would rally round the principle of Church sovereignty belonged to a previous generation: Archbishop Stratford was perhaps the last of their breed. In contrast, the bishop appears more of a martyr to his own personal misfortune. Particularly undignified and vindictive was his senseless destruction of his manors prior to his departure.[96] We may admire his dogged persistence in a foreign country against formidable odds. But his unyielding defiance was unnecessary, futile, and, in the end, pathetic.

94. See pages 134–35, 141–42.
95. CCR, 1346–49, 338; CPR, 1350–54, 188–89, 190; CPR, 1364–67, 420.
96. See page 141.

8

The Crown's Response to Crime

On the death of Edward III in 1377, his contemporaries were in no doubt as to how to remember his long, fifty-year reign. One English poem compares the realm to a ship and Edward to its rudder: While he lived he guided his ship safely through rough waters.[1] Another commemorative poem, written in Latin, claims that Edward outshone even the sun, stars, and moon and outdid his illustrious predecessors.[2] The chronicler Thomas Walsingham christens him "The Favoured One," while Froissart remarks that "his like had not been seen since the days of King Arthur."[3] *The Brut* describes the king as "of a passyng goodnesse, and ful gracious amonge all the worthymen of the world."[4]

Modern historians are far less sure how to interpret the reign. There is ample justification to celebrate Edward's military and chivalric exploits: He and his eldest son, the Black Prince, were the victors at Crécy and Poitiers, and he founded the Order of the Garter.[5] Nevertheless, there remains a certain uneasiness among scholars about this king, particularly with regard to his domestic policies. This uneasiness first was voiced more than a century ago by the constitutional historian Bishop William Stubbs. Although Stubbs acknowledged Edward's greatness as a warrior, he also described him as "ambitious, unscrupulous, selfish, extrava-

1. *Political Poems and Songs relating to English History*, ed. T. Wright, 2 vols. (RS, XIV, 1859–61), 1:216; *Historical Poems*, 103.
2. *Political Poems*, 1:219.
3. Walsingham, *Historia Anglicana*, 1:327; Jean Froissart, *Chronicles*, trans. G. Brereton (Harmondsworth, Middlesex, 1968), 195–96.
4. *The Brut, or The Chronicles of England*, ed. F.W.D. Brie, 2 vols. (Early English Text Society, 1906–8), 2:333.
5. For works on Edward's military and chivalric exploits, see Johnson, *Life and Times of Edward III*; Vale, *Edward III and Chivalry*; M. Packe, *King Edward III*, ed. L.C.B. Seaman (London, 1983).

gant, and ostentatious," whose "obligations as a king sat very lightly on him."[6] Stubbs's main criticism of Edward was that, in order to secure financial support for his campaigns, he granted away too many royal prerogatives to parliament, thus diluting the powers of the central government.[7] The criticism has some resonance, for it is echoed in more recent works. Edward's reign is seen as one in which parliament came into its own and assumed more powers of government, particularly in matters of taxation and legal reform.[8]

Despite Stubbs's legacy, successive historians have been successively kinder to Edward. His peaceful reign compares favorably to the turbulence under his father, Edward II, and his grandson, Richard II. He fully lived up to contemporary ideals of kingship, excelling in war and chivalry. Thus, historians cautiously have been resurrecting the reputation of Edward III.[9] Finally, the first major study of Edward's domestic government appeared in 1990, by W. M. Ormrod. Ormrod attempts to reverse Stubbs's judgment of Edward as a constitutionally weak king. He argues that, instead of relinquishing royal power, Edward continued to dictate legislation and selectively enforced whatever he granted in statute. In addition, Edward surrounded himself with a loyal group of barons and a coterie of capable ministers who together formed a close-knit political community to support the king's policies. Thus, Edward admirably succeeded, where his father had failed, in establishing harmony among the various elements of his kingdom.[10] Ormrod expresses the hope that, once Edward's domestic as well as military achievements are appreciated fully, he will be admitted to "the august and select band of great medieval rulers."[11]

One consideration, however, that has received much less attention from historians, even from Ormrod, when assessing the reign is Edward's judicial policy. It can be argued that this is so because Edward did not have one, but the absence of royal interest in justice is a serious criticism and needs to be established. Justice indeed can be made the test of a king's rule: His ability to maintain peace and order within his realm marks the success of his government and the respect in which it was held. While it

6. Stubbs, *Constitutional History of England*, 2:393.

7. Ibid., 393–96.

8. M. H. Keen, *England in the Later Middle Ages* (London, 1973), 163–65; R. W. Kaeuper, *War, Justice, and Public Order: England and France in the Later Middle Ages* (Oxford, 1988), 176–77, 290–91; R. Butt, *A History of Parliament: The Middle Ages* (London, 1989), 354.

9. McKisak, *Fourteenth Century*, 270–71; G. A. Holmes, *The Later Middle Ages, 1272–1485* (London, 1962), 117.

10. Ormrod, *Reign of Edward III*, 199–202. Ormrod's views are echoed in another recent work on Edward III; see Waugh, *England in the Reign of Edward III*, 233–36.

11. Ormrod, *Reign of Edward III*, 203.

is important to keep Bertie Wilkinson's maxim in mind, not to judge Edward by modern standards,[12] justice clearly was a standard by which medieval Englishmen judged their kings. An important legal treatise dated to the mid-thirteenth century, Henry de Bracton's *De Legibus et Consuetudinibus Anglie*, made it clear that the king was the source of English law.[13] In the coronation oath that Edward took on 10 March 1327, he promised to uphold the "laws and customs" granted to Englishmen in the past and to be granted in the future, and furthermore to cause "equal and right justice" to be done in all his judgments.[14] The rolls of the king's bench typically began with the phrase *Placita coram domino rege* ("Pleas [heard] in the presence of the lord king"). Although the king long since had ceased attending the court in person, the *coram rege* expressed the idea that the king was ultimately responsible for justice.

Justice figures large in medieval manuals for princely behavior from the twelfth through the fifteenth centuries. Among the ideals prescribed for a perfect prince is that he be just. By adhering to justice, a prince keeps his realm in peace, whereas an unjust prince is a tyrant and forfeits the obedience of his subjects. Since he is subject to God, even a prince must obey the laws, and he should take care to appoint capable and trustworthy judges. He must be merciful but not so lenient that his laws are disregarded.[15]

A particularly influential treatise on government, one that enjoyed wide popularity in late medieval England, judging by the number of surviving copies in English,[16] was the *De Regimine Principum* of Giles of Rome. Written around 1287 at the request of King Philip the Fair of France, the *De Regimine* devotes three chapters of the second part of Book I to justice. Giles, a pupil of the famous philosopher, Saint Thomas Aquinas, follows his teacher's approach to the subject. Justice, Aquinas declares in the *Summa Theologiae*, is the supreme moral virtue because it proceeds from the rational intellect and benefits the common good of society instead of just the individual.[17] Giles likewise calls justice the "perfect virtue," without which kingdoms cannot exist.[18] Kings and princes ought to be just for four reasons, Giles argues. In the first place, they must be just in order to preserve their royal dignity, for the king is the law, and any inequality

12. B. Wilkinson, *The Later Middle Ages in England, 1216–1485* (London, 1969), 155.

13. Henry de Bracton, *De Legibus et Consuetudinibus Anglie*, ed. G. E. Woodbine, 4 vols. (New Haven, 1915–42).

14. *CCR*, 1327–30, 100.

15. L. K. Born, "The Perfect Prince: A Study of Thirteenth- and Fourteenth-Century Ideals," *Speculum* 3 (1928), 470–504.

16. I am grateful to Charles Briggs for this information.

17. Saint Thomas Aquinas, *Summa Theologiae*, Part 2–2, Question 58, Article 12.

18. Aegidius Romanus, *De Regimine Principum* (Rome, 1556), fols. 45v–46r.

reflects poorly on him. Second, justice ought to be pursued in and of itself, because it is so clear and beautiful a virtue that it outshines the stars, whose beauty is merely corporal and not of the spiritual kind. Third, justice, as Aquinas points out, extends its benefits to others and is a perfect good; the prince who practices it therefore shows himself to be perfectly virtuous. Last, the evil arising out of injustice is so great, again because it affects others besides the prince, that he must make every effort to be just.[19]

Another widely read treatise for the education of princes was the *Secreta Secretorum,* allegedly written by Aristotle for his pupil, Alexander the Great. A copy of the *Secreta* was made for presentation to Edward III at his coronation in 1327.[20] In its section on justice, the *Secreta* exhorts the king to be just so that he may imitate not only God's power over men but all His attributes. Justice makes the world go round and is the highest form of reason. Through justice, "the earth is populated and kings are established, subjects become obedient and are domesticated, enemies are subdued by it and remote places draw near, souls are saved and freed from all vice, and thereby its kings [are freed] from all corruption."[21] The people of India are said to have valued justice more than prosperity or rain.[22] The Englishman, Thomas Hoccleve, devotes several hundred lines of his English poem, *The Regement of Princes,* to justice. Written in 1412 as advice for the prince, the future Henry V, *The Regement* defines justice as the giving to each man his due. Justice comprises all the virtues: It prevents the shedding of blood, punishes the guilty, defends possessions, and protects the oppressed. The king is bound by his coronation oath to maintain justice, and in doing so, he becomes godlike. His justice is appreciated by his subjects more than rain, for it abounds with goodness. There follows several examples of just kings in history.[23]

A common theme thus emerges from these manuals for a just prince: Justice is the highest virtue and the foundation for a kingdom. By being just, the king wins the approbation of God and of his subjects. He oppresses the wicked and rewards the virtuous. His justice benefits all, not just himself. These ideals were not considered abstract notions with no place in the practical business of government. They were taken to heart by Saint Louis IX of France, who was considered by his contemporaries to be the ideal medieval king. According to Louis's biographer, Jean de

19. Ibid., fols. 48r–50r.

20. BL, Add. MS 47680. Unfortunately, chapter 19, *De regis iusticia* ("Concerning a king's justice"), has been cut out between fols. 17 and 18.

21. *Opera Hactenus Inedita Rogeri Baconi,* ed. Robert Steele, 16 vols. (Oxford, 1909–40), 5:123, 224.

22. Ibid., 124, 224.

23. Thomas Hoccleve, *The Regement of Princes, A.D. 1411–12,* ed. F. J. Furnivall (Early English Text Society, 1897), 89–100.

Joinville, the saint took a personal interest in justice, as when he used to sit under an oak tree in Vincennes and personally settle the disputes of all who approached him. In a sermon preached by an anonymous friar, Louis received his best advice. Kingdoms had been lost, the friar said, whenever justice had been ignored by its rulers. "Therefore," the preacher warned, "let the king . . . take good care to see that he administers justice well and promptly to his people, so that our Lord may allow him to rule his kingdom in peace to the end of his days."[24]

But in the England of the mid-fourteenth century, how exactly was Edward III to be just? There indeed was much to do in this regard. The reign opened with rampant lawlessness and the representatives of king's justice openly and brazenly vilified. The Folville and Coterel gangs terrorized the English midlands during the early 1330s, and bands of thugs were said to be preying on common folk all over England.[25] The eyre had declined long ago as an itinerant court of inquiry and complaints against commissions of oyer and terminer were on the rise.[26] Thus, some other way had to be found to investigate crime in the shires. The king's foreign campaigns, while producing victories, also were said to be producing brigands who returned to England with the promise of full pardons for their past misdeeds.[27] Perhaps most disturbing of all, corruption pervaded the bench and the entire judicial system, breeding open contempt for the king's officers. Verbal and physical attacks on royal justices gave real voice to complaints against the king's law as expressed in the Robin Hood ballads and other literature.[28] These attacks were a serious assault on the dignity of the crown: They indicated that not only were people dissatisfied with the poor state of justice, they were willing to flout the king's authority and disregard his rule. Government under such circumstances soon would become impossible.

It has been argued, however, that by the fourteenth century, the kings of England faced an insurmountable challenge: to be successful in war and maintain peace at home. Medieval government could not do both, and in the competition for administrative resources, justice was inevitably the loser. The problems involved in keeping public order had outgrown the government's capacity to solve them. Some of these problems Edward III had inherited from the turbulent reign of his father and were not of his own making. Without a standing police force to arrest suspects

24. Jean de Joinville and Geoffrey de Villehardouin, *Chronicles of the Crusades,* trans. M.R.B. Shaw (Harmondsworth, Middlesex, 1963), 176–77.

25. Stones, "The Folvilles," 117–36; Bellamy, "The Coterel Gang," 698–717; *RP,* 2:64.

26. Kaeuper, "Law and Order in Fourteenth-Century England," 773–74.

27. N. D. Hurnard, *The King's Pardon for Homicide before A.D. 1307* (Oxford, 1969), 324–26.

28. See pages 83–93.

and bring them to trial and without a more professional attitude on the bench and a legal system that produced more convictions, crime was to be a continuing and inevitable sore in the medieval body politic. Effective measures to combat crime in England would have to wait until the Tudors.[29]

This is a remarkably defeatist approach to late medieval disorder. It ignores the successes that the Middle Ages, in fact, were able to produce. The reign of Edward III was sandwiched between that of two English kings who ably combined achievements in war with effective justice. Both Edward I (1272–1307) and Henry V (1413–22) are praised by contemporaries and modern historians alike for their judicial innovations at the same time that they conducted campaigns abroad. Edward I, the "English Justinian," addressed, with arguably some success, the rising tide of crime through such measures as the Statute of Winchester of 1285, commissions of trailbaston, and an increasing "professionalization" of the judiciary.[30] Henry V gained a reputation for impartiality in judicial proceedings, even among his enemies in France, and he responded to lawlessness with a combination of rigorous enforcement of statutes and local visitations of the king's bench and commissions of inquiry.[31] Was anything comparable accomplished by Edward III?

Modern scholarship tends to discount the medieval English king's ability to affect significantly the state of law and order in the shires. A "dialogue" existed between local communities and the crown, in which the king necessarily relied on local officers, such as sheriffs, coroners, and keepers and justices of the peace, in order to administer the law. Medieval statutes had not the immediacy of modern decrees; their enforcement depended, to a large degree, on cooperation from the king's subjects. Yet it is clear that, whatever the obstacles, contemporaries still looked to the king to uphold the law and protect them from abuses. Even the Robin Hood ballads have the king set things right in the end. The crown was considered the fountainhead of justice and the one ultimately responsible if order broke down. Some allowance should, of course, be made for the difficulties a medieval king faced. But, in the end, there is no escaping the king's accountability for justice.[32]

29. Kaeuper, *War, Justice, and Public Order*, 124–33, 170–83, 383–87.

30. Brand, *Making of the Common Law*, 135–68; M. Prestwich, *Edward I* (London, 1988), 267–97.

31. Powell, *Kingship, Law and Society*, 269–75; C. Allmand, *Henry V* (Berkeley and Los Angeles, 1992), 323–26.

32. The "local view," ascribing importance to the shires and their inhabitants in the administration of justice, can be found in the studies listed in Chapter 3, note 94. The opposite view, of course, is taken in studies of medieval kingship. See in particular Prestwich, *Edward I*, 296–97; Powell, *Kingship, Law, and Society*, 29–30; Ormrod, *Reign of Edward III*, 54; Allmand, *Henry V*, 324.

Numerous remedies, in fact, were tried by Edward III and his government in order to improve the state of public order and address complaints about judicial procedure. Many of these measures arose out of petitions or pressure brought to bear by the commons in parliament and subsequently enacted in statute. They included special commissions of trailbaston to root out dangerous criminals, extending the law of treason to include offenses against the king's peace, eliminating pardons for murderers who fought in the king's wars, an ordinance to stop bribery of the bench, harsher penalties for extortionate sheriffs, and greater powers given to local judicial officers, culminating with the transformation of keepers into justices of the peace. Why then did Edward not acquire a reputation as a particularly just king? Why did lawlessness, or complaints about lawlessness, not decline substantially by the end of his reign?[33] It will be argued that this is so because the crown did not enforce effectively its legislation against crime and judicial corruption, since too often this legislation conflicted with the king's military goals or his own personal agenda. Unfortunately, Edward was unable to balance these goals or give enough priority to justice.

Early in the reign, the crown faced an unprecedented assault on the dignity of its bench and the authority of its law when the Folville and Coterel gangs kidnapped and held for ransom a puisne justice of the king's bench, Sir Richard Willoughby, in 1332. The incident provoked the chief justice of the king's bench, Sir Geoffrey le Scrope, to give a speech in parliament later that year denouncing such "great companies" who were imprisoning and despoiling liegemen, churchmen, and justices "in contempt of the king and in affray of his peace and to the destruction of his people."[34] Shortly thereafter, around Easter 1332, a special commission of trailbaston was sent to the midlands to investigate Willoughby's kidnapping and bring the culprits to justice. The importance of the commission was signified by the presence of both Scrope and the chief justice of the court of common pleas, William de Herle. Nevertheless, even this powerful court achieved very little: Hardly any of the principals or accessories to the crime were brought to trial, much less convicted. Much of the blame for the failure of this commission is placed on the crown's infirmity of purpose. The coming war with Scotland soon diverted both the king's and Scrope's attention away from the drudgery of hearing indictments and rounding up suspects. There is no better indication of where the crown's priorities lay than the fact that the leader of the gang that kidnapped Willoughby, Eustace Folville, received a king's pardon in July 1333 for serving in the "Scottish war." He was to be ordered again abroad to Scotland in 1337 and to Flanders in 1338.[35]

33. Bellamy, *Crime and Public Order*, 6.
34. *RP*, 2:64. For the full passage, see Chapter 3, note 18.
35. Stones, "The Folvilles," 122–29.

The crown's policy of indiscriminately granting pardons to hardened criminals like Folville in return for military service was a continuing source of complaint to the commons. The policy may have started under Edward I, but blossomed under Edward III. By one reckoning, nearly 900 pardons were granted by the crown in 1339–40, all as a reward for army service in Flanders, while by another count, at least 850 pardons were granted in 1339–40 to returning soldiers, of whom more than three-quarters were said to be murderers.[36] This was after statutes had been enacted in 1328, 1330, 1336, and 1340 in which the crown had promised to abandon the practice.[37] It has been argued that by granting pardons as an inducement to serve in his wars, Edward persuaded habitual criminals such as the Folvilles to trade in their life of crime for that of a professional soldier. Surprisingly, the crown even drafted such "reformed" felons as local peace officers.[38] However, pardons granted too freely were said to be encouraging men to commit crimes in anticipation of clemency and thus were contributing to disorder.[39] Moreover, it is naive to suggest that men like Eustace Folville would not revert to their former ways once they had finished their military campaigns. A widespread fear behind much of the commons' petitions against pardons was that returning soldiers would continue their depredations at home.[40] The later careers of men like Eustace Folville does not give much confidence that they were wrong.[41]

At the same time that the crown was pardoning notorious criminals, it was pursuing the contradictory policy of extending the law of treason to include even minor felonies such as highway robbery. Treason provided the government with a powerful tool against crime. The penalties were extremely harsh: In addition to forfeiture of property, men convicted of treason were hung, drawn, and quartered. It also allowed the crown to arrest on mere suspicion and to prosecute cases more vigorously.[42] But by 1352, the crown surrendered its expanded interpretation of treason in the statute for that year.[43] Edward's concession on this occasion, assuaging the commons' fear of government intervention in exchange for a grant of taxation, has been criticized for abandoning too quickly an effective instrument of justice.[44]

36. Hughes, *Study of Social and Constitutional Tendencies*, 218–19; *The English Government at Work, 1327–1336*, ed. J. F. Willard, W. A. Morris, J. R. Strayer, and W. H. Dunham Jr., 3 vols. (Cambridge, Mass., 1940–50), 1:119; H. J. Hewitt, *The Organization of War under Edward III, 1338–62* (Manchester, 1966), 30.

37. *SR*, 1:257–58, 264, 275, 286.

38. Bellamy, "The Coterel Gang," 712–13.

39. Hurnard, *King's Pardon*, 326; J. Barnie, *War in Medieval English Society: Social Values in the Hundred Years War, 1337–99* (Ithaca, N.Y., 1974), 40.

40. *RP*, 2:104, 161, 376.

41. Stones, "The Folvilles," 129–30.

42. Bellamy, *Law of Treason*, 59–101.

43. *SR*, 1:319–20.

44. Prestwich, *Three Edwards*, 233.

The examples discussed so far are drawn from the early years of Edward's reign when it is admitted that he showed little interest in justice.[45] An important test of his commitment to law enforcement during the more mature, middle years of his rule came in 1350. Previously, the Ordinance of Justices, enacted in 1346, had pledged all royal judges to take an oath forswearing the taking of bribes except meat and drink of small value and the giving of advice in any case prosecuted by the crown. As compensation for their loss of favors, the justices were to receive increased fees. However, if any judge violated his oath, his life and property were to be at the king's pleasure.[46] The initiative for the ordinance seems to have come from the commons. Although a petition did not call specifically for the measure, public opinion as expressed in parliament had been building for several years prior to 1346 against the corruption of the bench. At the same time, the king was preparing to embark on the Crécy campaign, which he did in the summer of 1346. The ordinance was probably a sop to such disgruntled opinion in preparation for the king's departure.[47]

Justices had been accustomed to taking oaths similar to the one administered in 1346 for almost a century earlier.[48] However, it was not until the reign of Edward I that such oaths were enforced. All together, the "English Justinian" convicted two justices of the king's bench, four of the court of common pleas, and four of the eyre, extracting fines totaling more than £18,000.[49] The chief justice of the court of common pleas, Sir Thomas Weyland, who was convicted of being an accessory to murder, was exiled from the realm and forfeited all his possessions.[50] These penalties are thought to have inspired more professional conduct among Edward I's judiciary.[51]

It is claimed that similar effects would have attended Edward III's enforcement of the ordinance of 1346. Once and for all, the crown had the opportunity to sever the ties between judges and their patrons and curtail the corruption of the bench. Of course, much depended for the ordinance's success on the goodwill and cooperation both of magnates as potential maintainers and of the justices themselves. But the crown inevitably played a major role in setting the example for impartial justice.[52] Unfortunately, this example was not forthcoming.

The first and greatest test of the crown's willingness to uphold the or-

---

45. Bellamy, *Law of Treason*, 77; Ormrod, *Reign of Edward III*, 54.
46. *SR*, 1:303–6.
47. Maddicott, *Law and Lordship*, 42–44.
48. Brand, *Making of the Common Law*, 149–52.
49. Ibid., 152–54.
50. Ibid., 103–12.
51. Ibid., 155–56.
52. Ibid., 41–42.

dinance came in the autumn of 1350. No less a man than Sir William Thorp, the chief justice of the king's bench, was accused of taking bribes while sitting at Lincoln. Thorp was reputed to be a notoriously corrupt judge, even for a bench whose venality made it so unpopular that it was subject to physical assaults.[53] He had been required to take his oath to obey the ordinance before the king in person in 1346.[54] A public confession of his crime condemned Thorp to a sentence of death and confiscation of all his possessions. Yet on the same day as his conviction, 19 November 1350, Edward pardoned Thorp his life and less than a year later, on 10 March 1351, he was restored to his lands and goods. By May 1352, he once again was acting in a judicial capacity, as a baron of the exchequer and justice of oyer and terminer. Edward apparently viewed Thorp's violation of his oath "as a personal breach of faith for which Thorp ought to be answerable to him alone."[55] This explains the chief justice's swift arraignment before a powerful commission of earls, which included the king's household steward and chamberlain. Yet just as quickly the king's resolve abated, and the example that Thorp's punishment was to provide became instead a demonstration that the king's law could be broken at will, a lesson that was sure to trickle down the judicial hierarchy. Not surprisingly, the ordinance of 1346 "was ignored almost from the start."[56]

The capricious and arbitrary nature of Edward's lawgiving likewise was demonstrated by the downfall in 1340–41 of another of the king's intimates, Sir John Molyns. Molyns's crimes for the previous decade, which included murder and extortion, were not brought to light until Edward's personal whims turned against him. He fell victim to the royal wrath that followed in the wake of the king's hasty return home in 1340 from his failed campaign in Flanders. Though his violent deeds were revealed fully in the ensuing judicial inquiry in the shires, it was more probably Molyns's theft of royal treasure and wool that caused a personal affront to Edward and resulted in his outlawry. Even so, Molyns subsequently was pardoned in 1345 and restored to his former status. His second fall from grace came in 1357 after he again had provoked the king's displeasure, this time for embezzlement of royal funds as steward of the queen's household.[57] The king's performance in this instance has drawn adverse comment from more than one legal historian.[58]

Compromises of judicial principles also were made when the crown was called on to curb the extortions of sheriffs and gaolers. The unpopu-

---

53. See pages 84–85.
54. *Foedera*, 3, no. 1, 208–10.
55. Maddicott, *Law and Lordship*, 50.
56. Ibid., 48.
57. Fryde, "A Medieval Robber Baron," 201–7.
58. Ibid., 207; Carpenter, "Law, Justice and Landowners," 235.

larity of these officers, who were known to coerce unlawful fines from their prisoners as a condition of release, is testified to by the Robin Hood ballads that cast the sheriff of Nottingham as the villain.[59] Statutes enacted in 1327 and 1340 set severe penalties for offenders. The latter statute warned sheriffs that they would have "judgement of life and member" if their abuses continued.[60] Nevertheless, leniency and corruption remained the norm, as the example of Peter de Boxted, the sheriff of Essex, makes clear. Boxted seems to have been a particularly unpopular sheriff: On 1 March 1350 some men came to Chelmsford, Essex, assaulted the sheriff's clerks and chased Boxted himself "into a certain chamber adjacent to the hall where the pleas of the crown were held, and there they made him remain by threats and the fear of death until he had made fine with them for four casks of wine." The assailants did this, according to a subsequent inquest, because Boxted had attempted to collect 25s. owed to the crown from their lord, Sir Thomas de Mandeville.[61] Nevertheless, Boxted seems to have extracted unlawful revenues as well: In 1352 he paid a £20 fine as penalty for extortions totaling £351.[62] Such penalties may have brought money into the crown's coffers to help fight the king's wars, but they cannot have seriously dissuaded men like Boxted, who still were able to profit enormously from their extortion.

Finally, in an effort to improve order in the shires, the crown gave greater powers to local officers of the peace. The commons in parliament long had clamored for such powers, and at the same time the central courts, except for the occasional session in a particular county, ceased traveling on circuits through the countryside. The best example of this localization of justice was the transformation of the keepers of the peace into justices of the peace by 1361. Keepers were established in the first year of Edward's reign in the second statute of 1327. They briefly were charged to keep and maintain the peace in each county and to be "good men and lawful."[63] In 1361 another statute upgraded keepers to justices. Four or five justices were to be appointed in each shire, with at least one of them being a lord and the others "the most worthy in the county . . . learned in the law." The justices were to have the power to arrest, imprison, and sentence suspects, just like any other of the king's justices. They also could be named on commissions of oyer and terminer, which had come in for a lot of criticism for imposing "foreign" justice on the counties.[64] Hence-

59. See pages 83–84, 90–91, 148–49.
60. *SR*, 1:253, 384.
61. *Select Cases*, 6:76–77.
62. PRO, KB 27/366, rex mm. 3–3d.
63. *SR*, 1:257.
64. See pages 98–99.

forth, justices of oyer and terminer were to be named by the court, not by the plaintiff, general commissions were to cease, and fines levied for trespass were to be reasonable.[65]

There has been much debate among scholars as to whether the accelerated decentralization of justice during Edward's reign was a good thing. One school of thought argues that the gentry were the natural representatives of the law in the shires, were generally loyal and trustworthy men, and that the crown had no choice but to share its peacekeeping duties with its subjects. Already the crown, lacking a modern, salaried police force, was forced to rely on local men to enforce its law as gaolers, sheriffs, and coroners. The addition of justices of the peace to this list heralded a new spirit of cooperation between the crown and gentry.[66] On the other hand, there are others who contend that the transformation of keepers into justices amounted to a renunciation by the central government of its legal obligations and administrative powers. The picture of local men valiantly upholding the law in the king's name is counterbalanced by the fact that justices of the peace were just as much, if not more, susceptible to corruption as their counterparts on the royal bench. Because justices of the peace were local appointments, powerful magnates easily could control their membership. It is only natural that patrons should seek men loyal to them rather than to the interests of the crown.[67]

In general, the crown under Edward III surrendered the initiative in justice to the commons and the shires. A pattern clearly emerges: Judicial reforms were proposed by parliament but foundered quickly on Edward's inability or unwillingness to enforce them. They succumbed to the higher priorities of the king's wars or the king's rather quixotic sense of honor. The inconsistent and intensely personal way in which Edward interpreted his role as lawgiver provided a poor example to the judicial hierarchy and society at large. What was needed was an impartial approach to justice, the kind that Shakespeare attributed to Henry V, who punished his old friend Bardolph, "for he hath stol'n a pax, and hanged must a' be."[68]

These criticisms are encapsulated in Edward's adjudication of De Lisle's dispute with Lady Wake. According to the bishop's biographer, the law was manipulated in De Lisle's disfavor during his appeal of his conviction for the arson attack on Lady Wake's houses. This perceived injustice

65. *SR*, 1:364–65. The standard historical account is B. H. Putnam, "The Transformation of the Keepers of the Peace into the Justices of the Peace, 1327–1380," *TRHS*, 4th series, 12 (1929), 19–48.

66. Ormrod, *Reign of Edward III*, 160.

67. Stones, "The Folvilles," 132–33; Bellamy, *Crime and Public Order*, 119–20; Hanawalt, *Crime and Conflict*, 45–50.

68. William Shakespeare, *King Henry V*, act 3, scene 6, line 42.

may have persuaded De Lisle to reject Edward's offer of mediation and to accuse the king to his face of favoritism in his suit. Clearly, De Lisle did not consider Edward III to be an impartial judge.[69]

The king's subsequent behavior rather confirms De Lisle's view. He attempted to confiscate the bishop's temporalities as punishment for his role in the murder of William Holm without the inconvenience of due process of law. Quite properly, he was rebuked by his ministers, Thoresby and Edington, and by his council.[70] Such an arbitrary seizure would have set an ominous precedent in the eyes of other landowners who displeased the king. Moreover, the king's defense of his cousin, although a chivalrous gesture, violated the ordinance of 1346, which, as part of measures to combat maintenance, pledged the king and all his magnates not to take in hand quarrels except their own.[71]

The whole episode of the king's intervention in De Lisle's suit with Lady Wake, coming as it did at the height of the reign, inspires little confidence that he took a more active interest in justice after 1340.[72] Even if he did so, it is perhaps to be lamented. His handling of the Lady Wake case indicates that his knowledge of the law remained limited and that he relied on advisers to set legal policy. Edward saw himself as an arbitrator par excellence of disputes arising among members of his nobility, a role that accorded well with the chivalric mold of his kingship.[73] However, the role of supreme arbitrator demanded a certain objectivity and circumspection in decision making, qualities that Edward lacked. Rather, his approach to the punishment of high-ranking lawbreakers was a highly personalized and remarkably unsophisticated one, based more on the degree to which they had offended the king's sense of honor than that they had offended the rule of law.

If we are to assign Edward to the pantheon of great medieval kings, surely it is right to ask whether he made any enduring contributions to English society that would qualify him for greatness. His successful pursuit of the two aims that took precedence over judicial principle, political harmony among the barons and war with France and Scotland, barely survived his lifetime. This was not a coincidence, for the much-praised partnership that Edward forged with his nobility was based on a militaristic and chivalric camaraderie with a relatively select band of men. By 1370, many of Edward's most reliable and trusted political allies, such as

69. *AS*, 1:656–57, and see Appendix B, page 231.
70. See pages 136–37.
71. *SR*, 1:304.
72. Ormrod, *Reign of Edward III*, 55.
73. Johnson, *Life and Times of Edward III*, 114–15. For Edward's chivalric program, see Vale, *Edward III and Chivalry*.

his longtime friends and advisers Henry of Grosmont, duke of Lancaster, and William Edington, bishop of Winchester, were dead, and predictably the coalition Edward had built on personal relationships fell apart dramatically in the Good Parliament of 1376. With the deposition of Richard II in 1399, we seem to come full circle to the tyranny and baronial revolts that ushered in the reign of Edward II's son. A slow war of attrition conducted by the French in the 1360s and 1370s frittered away the gains of spectacular English victories in the previous decades, and the heavy taxation used to finance the war eventually took its toll. A total of £1,120,900 was collected in twenty-eight separate levies from the laity alone during the reign, culminating in the first of the hated poll taxes that directly led to the Peasants' Revolt of 1381.[74] Indeed, it can be argued that the memory of Edward's successes and the warrior spirit enshrined in the Order of the Garter helped perpetuate a war even when it had become unpopular and burdensome.[75]

There are perhaps other accomplishments of the reign. It can be said that Edward laid the foundations for a national Church independent of a foreign and increasingly decadent pope. Although Gregory XI moved the see back to Rome before his death in 1378, the subsequent schism and the challenge from the Conciliar Movement in the next century was to sap the papacy of its moral authority and force from which it was not to recover for quite some time. But having freed itself from the corrupting influence of a declining institution, the English Church, one can argue, simply exchanged one master for another, and one more able to bend the Church to his will. Whether a cowed clergy answerable to the king was better than one answerable to the pope is debatable. Deprived of its independent voice, the English Church was unable to provide any moral leadership or censure during the political upheavals of the fifteenth century. W. M. Ormrod has traced some important reforms that William Edington, royal treasurer during the 1340s and 1350s, effected in the king's finances. Revenue from De Lisle's confiscated temporalities, for example, were paid into the wardrobe rather than the chamber so that the sums could be recorded by the exchequer.[76] Yet while Edington's reforms may have eased slightly the burden of taxation, it is difficult to see of what more immediate benefit they were to Edward's subjects.

Arguably, it was in the area of justice that reform was most needed and the most enduring contributions to be made. Edward I and Henry V demonstrated that legal reputations could be acquired at home at the same time that opposition was faced abroad. The ability to balance and give

74. Ormrod, *Reign of Edward III*, 204.

75. Barnie, *War in Medieval English Society*, 38–41, 117–38; Coleman, *English Literature*, 84–92.

76. Ormrod, "Edward III's Government," 257–60.

due consideration to both concerns—judicial and military—is the defining difference between a great king and a merely good one. Despite all the recent attempts to rehabilitate Edward III, therefore, the fundamental disquiet among historians about him probably will remain. The king's record on justice suggests that he was too enamored of the trappings of tournaments, chivalry, and warfare and too impatient with the mundane but essential day-to-day details of domestic government to be celebrated unreservedly. Lured by the popular, albeit transitory, conquests abroad, he neglected to maintain good order at home. Because fundamental grievances in the judicial system were not addressed (and Edward certainly had the opportunity and the means to address them), crime as a whole probably increased during the reign, creating a situation ripe for rebellion. Perhaps Edward wished to be king of France more than king of England. Certainly he could not be both. It can be argued that his abilities were barely up to the task of one.

Conclusion

This book has tried to prove that Thomas de Lisle, bishop of Ely from 1345 to 1361, was also the leader of a criminal gang that operated in East Anglia. The crimes of which De Lisle and his men were indicted fall into certain patterns: abduction and extortion on false charges brought by approvers, extortion of free citizens claimed to be villeins, arson and theft of houses, excessive distraint and fines levied on tenants, and finally, murder. These are all crimes familiar to anyone who has studied the activities of corrupt sheriffs, oppressive lords and robber barons, and the gentry outlaw gangs. The victims came from various social groups, ranging from free and unfree tenants, free men, merchants, and aristocrats. Perhaps most damning of all to the efforts of De Lisle's medieval biographer to exonerate the bishop of any wrongdoing is the latter's steadfast support of a core group of unsavory followers. The men who show up again and again in the indictments were long-serving retainers, most of them the bishop's manorial officials, who often occupied high positions and were on intimate terms with De Lisle himself. They included the chief steward, the bishop's brother John de Lisle; the bishop's chamberlain, Ralph Carles; his auditors, Henry Shankton and Robert de Godington; and his nephew, William Michel. De Lisle's failure to disown any of these men even after their activities had cost him much in expensive litigation, fines, and political favor, strongly suggests that he approved of their crimes.

The implications of De Lisle's career are many and profound. One of the most important conclusions to be drawn concerns the attitude of contemporary magnates toward crime. The general unwillingness of De Lisle's colleagues to come to his defense in the course of the Lady Wake affair indicates that they disapproved of one of their number becoming tainted with disorderly conduct. Good behavior seems to have been expected and was the norm. The traditional interpreters of maintenance and bastard feudalism who lay the blame for late medieval disorder at the door of overmighty subjects appear to have overstated their case. Recent studies of magnate and gentry affinities emphasize the beneficial rather than the detrimental effects of such associations.[1] Powerful lords

1. See pages 72–82.

often used their influence to prevent disorder by acting as arbitrators among rival factions in the shire. If a lord failed to act responsibly and did maintain many criminals, he stood to lose both influence and the profits of his lordship as tenants and others looked elsewhere for justice.

De Lisle therefore was not a typical example of the fourteenth-century English magnate. This is borne out amply by the way in which he rose to become bishop. He came from relatively humble origins, had little prior experience in manorial or household management on a grand scale, and had achieved his high position as bishop of Ely not through the usual channels of royal patronage or gradual ecclesiastical preferment, but through the favors of an extravagant pope. His inexperience, and perhaps the example of the decadent Pope Clement VI, led to overspending and reckless ostentation in his early years as bishop.[2] The need to balance the books may have encouraged him to look for alternative sources of income and precipitated his subsequent career in crime. The fact that he was lord only for life and had no heirs obviated the usual concerns for propriety and reputation that most noble families had to consider.

But if De Lisle indeed was guilty of at least some crime, the way in which Edward III sought to punish the bishop for his offenses against the royal cousin, Lady Wake, give some cause for alarm. The king, acknowledged to be the fountain of justice and upholder of the law in his realm, attempted to flout the law by seizing the bishop's temporalities in disregard of the statute of 1340.[3] It is a poor example of the king's solicitude for justice, one backed up by many other instances. The liberal granting of pardons to hardened criminals in exchange for military service, the failure to enforce the Ordinance of Justices of 1346 when presented with the corruption of Chief Justice William Thorp, the lenient fines handed down to criminal sheriffs, and the surrendering of judicial powers to the shires all speak of an agenda on which law and order was not high. Popular victories in battle may have been won abroad, but at a tremendous cost at home.

Finally, there is the enigma of De Lisle as a criminal bishop. The juxtaposition of religious and extremely secular characteristics in one man perhaps did not appear so contradictory to men of the Middle Ages. De Lisle's criminal involvement had little noticeable effect on the performance of his episcopal duties. Those duties were prescribed by tradition and an entrenched clerical bureaucracy. It was rather De Lisle's religious status that had important implications for his disorderly conduct. For a leader of a criminal gang, there were undoubted advantages to being a bishop. The most obvious one was benefit of clergy, which De Lisle claimed before the king's bench in October 1356 when he was convicted of complic-

2. *AS*, 1:655, and see Appendix B, pages 228–29.
3. See pages 136–37.

ity in the murder of William Holm. If his metropolitan, the archbishop of Canterbury, Simon Islip, had followed proper canonical procedure and accepted his purgation, De Lisle would have been restored to his temporalities against the king's wishes.[4] The benefit, of course, also extended to De Lisle's criminous clerks, although there is no indication that any of them used it when they were up before the king's bench in Easter term 1355 on a charge of committing arson against Lady Wake, since their case never came to trial.[5] However, the bishop's hunter, Thomas Brond, successfully claimed benefit of clergy when he was convicted of stealing thirty-six ells of woolen cloth worth £1 16s. at the gaol delivery session held at Cambridge on 15 or 22 July 1353.[6] Islip and Edward seem to have recognized the potential abuses of benefit of clergy and sought to correct them in the statute *Pro Clero* and Islip's proclamation for criminous clerks, both issued in 1352.[7] The chief justice of the king's bench, Sir William Shareshull, also probably took a hostile view of the clerical privilege.[8]

The jurisdictional immunities enjoyed by the bishop of Ely in his liberty provided De Lisle and his men with a defense for several trespasses of which they were accused in 1352–54. The attack on John Daniel in 1351, for example, was justified by a commission issued by the crown on 8 June 1350 to arrest the rescuers of John de Wilton, who had been apprehended by the bishop's ministers in lieu of the sheriff.[9] Most important of all, perhaps, was De Lisle's ability to appeal his case to the papal auditors at Avignon even after his temporalities had been seized, thereby prolonging a dispute that normally would have ended with the convicted man's punishment. Moreover, the auditors' excommunication of the king's justices caused sufficient distress in England to force Edward to take this appeal seriously. Precisely because he was a bishop, De Lisle proved to be a much more resourceful and elusive adversary of king's justice than any lay criminal in the Middle Ages could ever be.

Something of De Lisle's unique personality manages to whisper its way down through the centuries in the medieval records. According to even a favorable biographer, the bishop could be extravagant, stubborn, and proud. Endowed with an exasperatingly intractable and unyielding nature, he refused absolutely all attempts at reconciliation with a quick tempered but forgiving king. Yet the same author also bears witness to a charismatic and attractive side to De Lisle's character. He was a success-

---

4. *AS*, 1:659–60, and see Appendix B, pages 234–36.

5. PRO, KB 27/379, rex m. 9, and see Appendix B, pages 240–42.

6. PRO, JUST 3/136, m. 12d.; JUST 3/139, m. 11; JUST 3/215/2, pt. 2, m. 102.

7. *SR*, 1:325, sec. 4; Gabel, *Benefit of Clergy*, 134–35 (under a false date of 1351).

8. Putnam, *Sir William Shareshull*, 142.

9. See pages 149–53.

ful preacher, who "disseminated the word of God to the people who joined him fervent in spirit," and his messengers were willing to brave hardship and death to bring papal bulls back to England on his behalf.[10] We probably will never know the precise circumstances that led De Lisle to patronize criminal behavior. The elusive complexity of this man perhaps was evident also to his contemporaries. As one fifteenth-century commentator wrote in the margin of his biography: "This Thomas was the worst bishop. Concerning his death there are various opinions."[11] The latter comment proves no less true today.

10. *AS*, 1:655, 657, 659–61, and see Appendix B, pages 228–29, 231–32, 235–37.
11. "Fuit iste Thomas pessimus episcopus. De eius morte sunt varii [variae] opin[i]ones." LPL, MS 448, fol. 70r.

Glossary of Legal Terms

This glossary is not all-inclusive, but provides definitions for legal terms as used in their historical context.

amercement. A monetary penalty or fine, imposed by the court on a defendant convicted of trespass. The defendant was literally "at the mercy" of the crown.

arbitration. An informal procedure in which two parties agreed to abide by the decision of an arbitrator, judge, or panel of judges elected for this purpose. The arbitrator's judgment was not binding on the litigants under the common law.

arches, court of. An ecclesiastical court for the Southern province that met in the church of St. Mary-le-Bow in Cheapside, London. Presided over by the dean of the arches, it heard appeals from diocesan courts.

assize. A judicial body first established by Henry II in the Assize of Clarendon in 1166. Originally, a jury of twelve from each hundred and four men from each town would meet to bring indictments of criminal conduct against suspects, who then would be tried by the ordeal. Later, by the thirteenth century, the jury decided the guilt or innocence of the accused. Also, the name given to a possessory assize, such as the Assize of Novel Disseisin, assigned to settle disputes over possession of land.

attaint, writ of. A procedure whereby a defendant could obtain redress from a false accusation or conviction by a jury, first granted by statute in 1327.

auditor of causes. A member of the "sacred palace of causes" in the papal curia, who heard appeals brought by churchmen from their national courts.

benefit of clergy. Exemption accorded to churchmen from the jurisdiction of secular courts, usually on proof of literacy. The defendant then was handed over to his ordinary to be tried in an ecclesiastical court, but not before a verdict had been rendered by a jury.

Canterbury, court of. The ecclesiastical court of the archbishop of Canterbury, presided over by his official.

champerty. A variation of maintenance in which a third party agreed to prosecute a suit, provided that he shared the profits with the original plaintiff or defendant.

Chancery, court of. An administrative arm of the medieval English government that issued writs and commissions of oyer and terminer, received petitions to the king's council, and issued other kinds of judicial writs.

citation. A summons to appear before the auditors of the "sacred palace of causes" in the papal curia.

common pleas, court of. One of the central courts of Westminster that decided civil cases, usually concerning recovery of debt and property disputes.

coroner. A local officer of the crown who investigated unnatural or suspicious deaths.

distraint. The act of seizing the property of a defendant in lieu of payment of court fines.

elegit, **writ of.** Issued to a plaintiff in order to allow execution of a legal judgment, first granted by the Second Statute of Westminster of 1285. It authorized the sheriff to seize the defendant's property equivalent to the fine.

entry, *sine assensu capituli,* **writ of.** Issued to allow recovery of possession or damages from an unlawful entry into the plaintiff's property or dwelling, in this case "without the assent of the [monastic] chapter."

error, writ of. Issued to a court on appeal of a judgment handed down as a result of some "error" claimed to have been committed during the original trial.

excepcio villenagii. An informal objection raised against a plaintiff, claiming that he was of villein status and therefore could not plead in court.

Exchequer, court of. An administrative arm of the medieval English government that traditionally received all royal revenues and therefore recorded inquisitions into the property to be confiscated from a convicted defendant.

excommunication. A legal process under the jurisdiction of the court Christian, whereby the defendant, in a public ceremony, was excluded from "communion" with the Church. In the lesser version, the defendant was forbidden to receive the sacraments, whereas in the greater version, he was excluded from all contact with the faithful.

exigent, writ of. Issued during the early phase in the process of outlawry, in which the sheriff "demanded" that the defendant appear in court.

Eyre, court of. A body of itinerant royal judges who heard cases in the shires, established by Henry I during the twelfth century.

favor libertatis. A legal principle invoked to establish the free status of a litigant, whereby the weight of tradition "favored liberty."

felony. A category of medieval crime of a particularly serious nature, such as homicide, rape, theft, and arson, which merited the death penalty.

gaol delivery, court of. A judicial body presided over by an itinerant justice who "delivered" the town's gaol and tried the cases of all defendants contained therein.

halimote, court of. A judicial body dating from Anglo-Saxon times that consisted of the lord's court, or the manorial court, to decide tenant disputes. It was presided over by the steward.

hundred, court of. A local court that was larger than a halimote, since it was held for all the inhabitants of a hundred.

justice of the peace. A local judge appointed by the crown, formerly a keeper of the peace but given the status of justice by statute in 1361.

King's bench, court of. One of the central courts of Westminster that heard predominantly criminal cases involving trespass and felony.

King's council in parliament. The highest court in medieval England, which heard cases on petition delivered to chancery.

King's serjeant. A legal officer of the crown who pleaded cases before the king's bench on behalf of plaintiffs or defendants. The office was typically a stepping stone to that of justice.

leet, court of. A judicial body that met once a year within a hundred, lordship, or manor and that was presided over by the steward.

libertate probanda, **writ of.** Issued in order to provide protection from the seizure of serfs attempting "to prove their liberty" in the king's court, granted by statute in 1352.

liberty. Also known as franchise, a right granted to an individual or institution that exempted his territory from the jurisdiction of the royal court and its officers.

mainpernor. One who bails, or acts as surety for, a defendant.

maintenance. The act of sustaining a suitor at law by a party who has no legal interest in the case.

manumission. The act of releasing a villein from servitude.

Marshalsea. The prison belonging to the king's bench at Westminster, under the custody of the marshal.

nisi prius, **writ of.** Issued to a sheriff, authorizing him to produce a jury before one of the central courts in Westminster "unless before" that time an itinerant justice appeared in the shire.

outlawry. A judicial process whereby the defendant was declared "outside the king's law" for nonappearance in court, resulting in the confiscation of his property and, if apprehended, his life.

oyer and terminer, commission. A judicial procedure authorizing the sitting of a court presided over by specially appointed justices to "hear and determine" specified offenses in the shires. The commission could be either general or special to a particular offense, and was initiated by a writ purchased by the plaintiff.

petition. A written or oral bill presented to clerks of the chancery, and if received, stating the litigant's case before the king's council in parliament.

Praemunire, **Statute of.** Enacted in 1353 to forbid appeals of judgments handed down in the king's courts to an outside judicial body, on penalty of outlawry.

praemunire facias, **writ of.** Issued to a sheriff, authorizing him "to cause to warn" the defendant to appear in court to answer a charge of violating *Praemunire,* on penalty of outlawry.

Pro Clero, **Statute of.** Enacted in 1352, designed to end abuses of purgation. It imposed harsher conditions for acquittal and stiffer penalties for conviction.

prohibition, *de laico feodo,* **writ of.** Issued at the suit of a plaintiff in order to prevent his case being removed from the king's court to an ecclesiastical one. Such writs date from the reign of Henry II in the twelfth century.

Provisors, Statute of. Enacted in 1351 to prevent foreigners being "provided" to English ecclesiastical offices.

purgation. A legal process whereby a churchman accused of a crime proved his innocence before an ecclesiastical court by producing so many oath-helpers, or compurgators, who testified that they believed the defendant spoke the truth when he protested his innocence.

querela. An informal petition submitted to the king's council in parliament that set in motion a special commission of oyer and terminer.

rescue. The act of releasing a prisoner from the lawful custody of a sheriff or other officer authorized to apprehend a suspect.

sheriff. An officer of the crown who was authorized to arrest suspects, procure jurors, and hold his own local courts known as tourns.

soke. The territory within which the owner had the right to dispense justice.

trespass. A category of medieval crime, less serious than felony, that included assault, conspiracy, and extortion and for which a monetary penalty or fine was imposed.

venire facias, **writ of.** Issued to a sheriff, authorizing him "to cause to come" into court either the defendant or the jury.

waste, writ of. Issued against a defendant who had committed "waste," or destruction, of the plaintiff's property. Usually the defendant was the plaintiff's tenant who had legal possession of, but not full title to, the estate.

writ. A written order, usually issued to a sheriff, authorizing him to perform a specified act pertaining to the court.

Appendix A

Itinerary of Thomas de Lisle, 1345–61

(For the location of most place names, see Fig. 2)

1345	15 July	Avignon. Created bishop of Ely by Pope Clement VI. *CPL*, 3:19, 198.
	24 July	Avignon. Consecrated by Gaucelin, cardinal-bishop of Albano. *CPL*, 3:188.
	12–15 September	London. CUL, EDR, G/ɪ/1, Reg. De Lisle, fols. 1r, 2r, 54r, 85r.
	7 October	London. Ibid., fol. 1r.
	14 October	Lesnes, Kent. Ibid.
	23 October	London. Ibid., fols. 5r–v.
	3 November	Lesnes, Kent. Ibid., fol. 54v.
	5 November	Lesnes, Kent. Ibid., fol. 1r.
	8 November	Hatfield. Ibid., fol. 2v.
	11–12 November	Hatfield. Ibid., fols. 1r–v.
	18 November	Hatfield. Ordination to first tonsure. Ibid., fols. 1v, 84r.
	19 November	Hatfield. Ibid., fol. 1v.
	24 November	Balsham. Ibid., fol. 2r.
	25–26 November	Fen Ditton. Ibid., fols. 1v–2r, 85r.
	27 November	Ely Cathedral. Enthronement. *AS*, 1:655, and see Appendix B, page 228.
	28 November	Ely. CUL, EDR, G/ɪ/1, Reg. De Lisle, fol. 85r.
	29 November	Fen Ditton. Ibid., fol. 1v. Somersham. Ibid., fol. 87v.
	1 December	Somersham. Ibid., fols. 2r, 87v.
	4 December	Somersham. Ibid., fols. 5r, 16v.
	6–7 December	Somersham. Ibid., fols. 1v, 3v.
	11 December	Doddington. Ibid., fols. 1v, 7r.
	18 December	Downham. Ibid., fol. 85r.
	21 December	Somersham. Ibid., fol. 4r.

	23 December	Somersham. Ibid., fol. 7r.
	26–27 December	Somersham. Ibid., fols. 7r, 85r.
	30 December	Somersham. Ibid., fol. 5r.
1346	2 January	Somersham. Ibid., fol. 7r.
	9 January	Somersham. Ibid.
	17 January	Leicester. Attended provincial council. Ibid., fol. 56v.
	29 January	Fen Ditton. Ibid., fols. 4r, 59r, 87v.
	4 February	Great Bardfield, Essex. Ibid., fol. 4r.
	9 February	London. Ibid., fol. 4r.
	18 February	Hatfield. Ibid.
	1 March	Somersham. Ibid., fol. 57v.
	4 March	Somersham. Ibid., fol. 67v.
	9 March	Somersham. Ibid., fol. 4v.
	11 March	Somersham. Ibid., fol. 5r.
	14–15 March	Somersham. Ibid., fols. 5r, 57r.
	29 March	Cambridge. Ibid., fol. 4v.
	1 April	Ely Cathedral. Ordination. Ibid., fols. 85r, 91r.
	2 April	Downham. Ordination to first tonsure. Ibid., fol. 84r.
	3–4 April	Ely Cathedral Priory. Visitation. Ibid., fol. 5r. Downham. Ibid., fols. 5v, 59r, 61v, 67v, 87v.
	5 April	Ely Cathedral Priory. Visitation. Ibid., fol. 5r. Downham.[1]
	10 April	Downham. Ibid., fol. 5v.
	14 April	Ely. Ibid., fol. 89r.
	19–20 April	Downham. Ibid., fols. 16v, 62r, 85r.
	26 April	Downham. Ibid., fol. 62r.
	29 April	Downham. Ibid., fol. 85r.
	1 May	Downham. Ibid., fol. 60r.
	2 May	Cambridge. Ibid., fol. 69v.
	4 May	Fen Ditton. Ibid., fol. 7r.
	6 May	Cambridge. Ibid., fol. 69v.
	15 May	Ickleton Priory. Visitation. Ibid., fol. 5v.
	16 May	Swaffham Bulbeck Priory. Visitation. Ibid., fol. 5v.
	17 May	Fen Ditton. Ibid., fol. 60r.
	18 May	Barnwell Priory. Visitation. Ibid., fol. 5v. Fen Ditton. Ibid., fols. 6r, 85r.

1. Dating clause at Downham gives year as 1345 but this would predate De Lisle's creation as bishop. The scribe probably forgot to update the year after 25 March.

19 May	St. Radegund's Priory, Cambridge. Visitation. Ibid., fol. 5v.
20 May	Fen Ditton. Consecrated high altar. Ibid., fol. 60v.
23 May	Stow cum Quy, Cambridgeshire. Consecrated high altar. Ibid., fol. 60v.
24 May	Trumpington, Cambridgeshire. Reconciled cemetery. Ibid., fol. 60v.
27 May	Swaffham Prior, Cambridgeshire. Consecrated high altar. Ibid., fol. 60v. Swaffham Bulbeck. Consecrated high altar. Ibid., fol. 60v. Swaffham Bulbeck Priory. Consecrated high altar. Ibid., fol. 60v. Fen Ditton. Ibid., fol. 6r.
3 June	Downham. Ibid., fol. 60v.
5 June	Downham. Ibid., fol. 85r.
7 June	Downham. Ibid., fols. 67v–68r.
13–14 June	Downham. Ibid., fols. 7r–v.
23 June	Doddington. Ibid, fol. 7r.
26 June	Somersham. Ibid., fol. 60v.
5 July	Somersham. Ibid., fols. 7v, 61v.
12 July	Somersham. Ibid., fol. 87v.
16 July	Ely Cathedral. Ibid., fol. 6v. Somersham. Ibid., fol. 6r.
17 July	Somersham. Ibid., fol. 70v.
20–22 July	Somersham. Ibid., fols. 6v, 16v, 59r, 61r.
2 August	Somersham. Ibid., fol. 6v.
5 August	Somersham. Ibid., fol. 6v.
9 August	Somersham. Ibid., fol. 69r.
19 August	Somersham. Ibid., fol. 7v.
23 August	Somersham. Ibid.
15 September	London. Ibid., fol. 85v.
18–19 September	London. Ibid., fols. 9r, 63r, 70r.
21 September	Holborn, London. Ibid., fol. 63r.
22 September	London. Ibid., fol. 69v.
2–4 October	Thorney Abbey. Visitation. Ibid., fols. 5v, 48r.
4 October	Thorney. Ordination to first tonsure. Ibid., fol. 84r.
12 October	Anglesey Priory. Visitation. Ibid., fol. 5v. Fen Ditton. Ibid., fol. 8r.
14 October	Little Hadham. Ibid., fols. 63r, 70r.
15 October	London. Ibid., fol. 85r.
16 October	London. Attended convocation at St. Paul's Cathedral. Ibid., fols. 62v–63r.

20 October	London. Ibid., fol. 8r.
24 October	Chatteris Abbey. Visitation. Ibid., fol. 5v.
25 October	London. Ibid., fol. 85v.
26 October	Balsham. Ibid., fol. 8v. Little Hadham. Ibid., fol. 8v.
2 November	Balsham. Ibid., fol. 9r.
22 November	Somersham. Ibid.
25 November	Fen Ditton. Ibid., fol. 9r.
18 December	Downham. Ibid., fol. 70r.
15–16 December	Downham. Ibid., fols. 7v, 85v.
23 December	Downham. Ordination in manor chapel. Ibid., fol. 94v.
26–27 December	Downham. Ibid., fols. 7v, 87v.
31 December	Brandonferry, Suffolk. Ibid., fol. 9r.
1347 5 January	Downham. Ibid., fol. 8r.
7 January	Downham. Ibid., fols. 7v, 9r, 71v.
10 January	Downham. Ibid., fol. 87v.
16 January	Cambridge. Convened meeting of the clergy of the diocese at church of St. Peter outside Trumpington Gates in order to reply to the king's request for an anticipation of the biennial tenth. Ibid., fol. 71v.
1 February	Downham. Ibid., fol. 9r.
4 February	Downham. Ibid., fol. 87v.
8 February	Downham. Ibid., fols. 9r, 87v. Ely. Ibid., fol. 85v.
12 February	Downham. Ibid., fol. 9r.
15–17 February	Downham. Ibid., fols. 9r–v, 72r.
23 February	Downham. Ibid., fol. 89r.
24 February	Downham. Ordination in manor chapel. Ibid., fol. 94v.
25 February	Downham. Ibid., fol. 9v.
28 February	Downham. Ibid., fol. 10v.
2 March	Downham. Ibid., fol. 71r.
17 March	Ely. Ordination in church of St. Mary. Ibid., fol. 94v.
18 March	Stretham. Ordination to first tonsure. Ibid., fol. 84r.
19 March	Downham. Ibid., fol. 71r.
26 March	Downham. Ibid., fol. 10r.
28 March	Downham. Ibid., fol. 9v. Cosgrove parish church, Northamptonshire. Ibid.
31 March	Downham. Ordination in manor chapel. Ibid., fol. 96r.

5 April	Downham. Ibid., fol. 71r.
7 April	Downham. Ibid., fol. 72v.
21–22 April	Somersham. Ibid., fol. 10r.
25 April	Somersham. Ibid., fol. 10v.
29 April	Somersham. Ibid., fol. 50r.
1 May	Somersham. Ibid., fols. 76v–77r, 85v.
11 May	? Somersham. Ibid., fol. 72v.[2]
17 May	Somersham. Ibid., fol. 85v.
18 May	Willingham parish church. Examined and confirmed election of William de Haddon as abbot of Thorney. Ibid., fols. 50r, 51r.
20 May	Somersham. Consecrated abbots-elect of Thorney and Sawtry in parish church. Ibid., fols. 50v–51r, 87v.
21-22 May	Somersham. Ibid., fols. 10r–v, 85v, 87v.
25 May	Somersham. Ibid., fol. 10v.
26 May	Willingham. Ordination in parish church. Ibid., fol. 96r.
30 May	Somersham. Ibid., fol. 10r.
5 June	Somersham. Ibid., fol. 16v.
18 June	Thorney Abbey. Visitation. Ibid., fol. 48r.
26 June	Somersham. Ibid., fol. 10v.
28 June	Somersham. Ibid., fol. 77r.
11 July	Somersham. Ibid., fol. 11r.
19–20 July	Somersham. Ibid., fol. 75v.
29 July	Somersham. Ibid., fol. 11r.
7 August	Somersham. Ibid., fol. 76r.
12 August	Somersham. Ibid., fol. 11v.
17 August	Somersham. Ibid., fol. 64r.
26 August	Somersham. Ibid., fols. 11r, 85v.
3 September	Somersham. Ibid., fol. 11v.
8 September	? Somersham. Ibid., fol. 75v.[3]
9–10 September	Somersham. Ibid., fols. 16v, 85v.
16 September	Somersham. Ibid., fol. 85v.
21 September	Somersham. Ibid., fol. 12r.

2. Dating clause does not give the year, which is inferred from the context of a similar request for a loan of wool from the king to the bishop of Hereford, dated 28 March 1347. See *Registrum Johannis de Trillek Episcopi Herefordensis*, ed. J. H. Parry (CYS, VIII, 1912), 298–99.

3. Dating clause for 8 September does not give the year, which is inferred from the context of a similar request for an additional loan of wool from the king to the bishop of Hereford, dated 20 August 1347. See CUL, EDR, G/1/1, Reg. De Lisle, fol. 75v, and *Registrum Johannis de Trillek*, 308–9.

	11 October	Little Gransden. Ibid., fol. 11v.
	16–17 October	Little Gransden. Ibid., fols. 11v–12r.
	21 October	Balsham. Ibid., fols. 11v–12r.
	26 October	Balsham. Ibid., fol. 14v.
	28 October	Balsham. Ordination to first tonsure. Ibid., fol. 84r.
	29 October	Balsham. Ibid., fol. 11v.
	1 November	Balsham. Ibid., fol. 11v.
	5 November	Balsham. Ibid., fol. 12r.
	9 November	Holborn, London. Ibid., fol. 12v.
	11–12 November	Holborn, London. Ibid., fol. 12v.
	15 November	Hatfield. Ibid., fol. 12v.
	11 December	Somersham. Ibid., fols. 12v, 85v.
	13 December	Somersham. Ibid., fol. 85v.
	17 December	Titchmarsh, Northamptonshire. Ibid., fol. 12v. Somersham. Ibid., fol. 85v.
	23 December	Somersham. Ibid., fol. 13r.
	28 December	Somersham. Ibid.
1348	2 January	Somersham. Ibid., fol. 16v.
	14 January	? Westminster. First day of session of parliament at which bishop presented petitions against Richard Spynk before the king's council. *RP*, 2:164, 192–93; *RDP*, 3:572–73.
	21 January	London. CUL, EDR, G/1/1, Reg. De Lisle, fol. 13r.
	25 January	Holborn, London. Ibid., fol. 85v.
	26 January	London. Ibid., fol. 13r.
	28 January	Westminster. Ibid., fol. 85v. London. Ibid., fol. 14r.
	30 January	Holborn, London. Ibid., fol. 13r.
	1–2 February	Holborn, London. Ibid., fols. 13r, 85v.
	4 February	? Holborn, London. Ibid., fol. 14r.[4]
	8 February	Holborn, London. Ibid., fol. 13r.
	10 February	Holborn, London. Ibid., fol. 13v.
	12 February	Holborn, London. Ibid., fol. 14r. ? Westminster. Session of parliament ended. *CPR*, 1346–49, 495.
	25 February	Hatfield. CUL, EDR, G/1/1, Reg. De Lisle, fol. 14r.

4. Mandate of induction of John de Hatiston, poor priest of Haddenham, Cambridgeshire, to vicarage of Chatteris written and dated by the bishop's official.

12 March	Swaffham, Cambridgeshire. Ordination to first tonsure. Ibid., fols. 14r, 84r. Great Shelford. Ibid., fol. 85v.
15 March	Somersham. Ibid., fol. 14r.
19 March	Downham. Ibid.
22 March	Downham. Ibid.
13 April	Hatfield. Ibid., fol. 14v.
19 April	Little Hadham. Ordination in manor chapel. Ibid., fol. 96r.
25 April	Little Hadham. Ibid., fol. 14v.
30 April	Balsham. Ibid.
1 May	Balsham. Ibid.
2 May	Littlebury, Essex. Ibid., fol. 15v.
9 May	Little Hadham. Ibid., fol. 14v.
18 May	Somersham. Ibid., fol. 15r.
22 May	Somersham. Ibid.
31 May	Somersham. Ibid.
1 June	Somersham. Ibid.
3 June	Cambridge. Ibid.
11 June	Somersham. Ibid.
13 June	Somersham. Ibid.
14 June	Over, Cambridgeshire. Ordination in parish church. Ibid., fol. 96r.
15–16 June	Somersham. Ibid., fols. 15r, 77r.
25–26 June	Somersham. Ibid., fols. 15r, 77v.
1 July	Somersham. Ibid., fol. 87v.
8 July	Somersham. Ibid., fols. 15r, 77v.
4 August	London. Ibid., fol. 15v.
15 August	Cambridge. Ibid.
17 August	Downham. Ibid.
20 August	Downham. Ibid.
26 August	Somersham. Ibid.
1 September	Somersham. Ibid.
5 September	Somersham. Ibid., fols. 15v–16r.
9 September	Somersham. Ibid., fol. 16r.
	? Canterbury Cathedral. Profession of obedience to Canterbury. *Canterbury Professions*, ed. M. Richter (CYS, LXVII, 1972–73), 103.
10 September	Somersham. CUL, EDR, G/1/1, Reg. De Lisle, fol. 16r.
12–14 September	Somersham. Ibid., fol. 16r–v.
15 September	Great Shelford. Ibid., fol. 88r.

	17 September	Somersham. Ibid., fol. 16r.
	20 September	Yeoveney, Middlesex. BL, Add. MS 41612, fols. 107v–108r.
	29 September	Somersham. CUL, EDR, G/I/1, Reg. De Lisle, fol. 16r.
	1 October	Yeoveney, Middlesex. Ibid., fol. 17r.
	5 November	Bredhurst, Kent. Ibid., fol. 77v.
	27 November	Cambridge. Ibid., fol. 16v.
	6 December	Cambridge. Ibid., fol. 16v.
1349	9 April	Rome. Ibid., fol. 21r.
1350	15 November	Downham. Ibid., fol. 65r.
	20 November	Downham. Ibid., fol. 37r.
	18 December	Ely Cathedral. Ordination. Ibid., fol. 96v.
	20 December	Downham. Ibid., fol. 37r.
	24 December	Downham. Ibid., fol. 17r.
1351	15 January	Fen Ditton. Ibid., fol. 37v.
	4 February	Downham. Ibid., fol. 38r.
	16 February	Holborn, London. Ibid., fol. 37v.
	20 February	Holborn, London. Ibid., fols. 37v-38r.
	24 February	Holborn, London. Ibid., fol. 37r.
	29 February	London. Ibid., fol. 37v.
	11–12 March	Little Hadham. Ibid., fols. 87v–88r.
	14 March	Little Hadham. Ibid., fols. 38r, 65r.
	2 April	Ely. Ordination in church of St. Mary. Ibid., fol. 97r.
	3 April	Downham. Ordination to first tonsure. Ibid., fol. 84r.
	4 April	Downham. Ibid., fol. 64v.
	12 April	Downham. Ibid., fol. 89r.
	20–21 April	Downham. Ibid., fols. 38r, 43r.
	24 April	Downham. Ibid., fol. 38r.
	26 April	Downham. Ibid., fol. 64v.
	5–6 May	Downham. Ibid., fols. 65r, 89r.
	23 May	Downham. Ibid., fol. 38r.
	31 May	Downham. Ibid., fol. 38v.
	6 June	Downham. Ibid.
	11 June	Downham. Ordination in parish church. Ibid., fols. 38v, 97v.
	12 June	Downham. Ibid., fol. 88r.
	28 June	Somersham. Ibid., fol. 38v.
	3 July	Somersham. Ibid.
	7 July	Somersham. Ibid., fols. 39v–40r.
	30 July	Somersham. Ibid., fol. 39r.

	1 August	Somersham. Ibid.
	5 August	Somersham. Ibid., fol. 79r.
	7–10 September	Somersham. Ibid., fols. 39r, 78v.
	14 September	Thorney. Ordination to first tonsure. Ibid., fol. 84r.
	19–20 September	Somersham. Ibid., fol. 39r.
	24 September	Somersham. Ibid., fol. 40v. Willingham. Ordination in parish church. Ibid., fols. 84r, 98r.
	29 September	Somersham. Ibid., fol. 41r.
	3 October	Somersham. Ibid., fol. 40v.
	14-15 October	Little Hadham. Ibid., fols. 41r, 79v.
	20 October	Hatfield. Ibid., fol. 41v.
	31 October	Hatfield. Ibid.
	2 November	Hatfield. Ibid.
	6 November	Hatfield. Ibid., fol. 42r.
	27–28 November	Hatfield. Ibid., fol. 41v.
	1 December	Hatfield. Ibid., fols. 41v, 89r.
	19–20 December	Hatfield. Ibid., fols. 41v–42r, 79v.
	28 December	Hatfield. BL, Add. MS 41612, fol. 113v.
	31 December	Hatfield. CUL, EDR, G/I/1, Reg. De Lisle, fol. 42r.
1352	1 January	Hatfield. Ibid., fol. 45v.
	25 January	Holborn, London. Ibid., fol. 42r.
	28 January	Holborn, London. Ibid.
	18 February	Hatfield. Ibid.
	25–26 February	Balsham. Ibid., fols. 42r, 80r, 89r.
	29 February	Balsham. Ibid., fol. 89r.[5]
	2 March	Balsham. Ibid., fol. 42r.
	11 March	Balsham. Ordination to first tonsure. Ibid., fol. 84v.
	15 March	Cambridge. Dedicated high altar of church of St. Mary the Less (formerly St. Peter outside Trumpington Gates). Ibid., fol. 65v.
	16 March	Cambridge. Dedicated high altar of church of St. John. Ibid., fol. 65v.
	17 March	Teversham, Cambridgeshire. Dedicated high altar of church of All Saints. Ibid. Balsham. Dedicated chapel and burial ground. Ibid.
	18 March	Fen Ditton. Ordination to first tonsure. Ibid., fol. 84v.

5. 1352 was a leap year. See C. R. Cheney, *Handbook of Dates for Students of English History* (London, 1978), 118–19.

19 March	Cambridge. Reconciled cemeteries of churches of St. Benedict and All Saints. Ibid., fol. 65v.
24 March	Swavesey. Ordination in parish church. Ibid., fols. 84v, 98r.
7 April	? Downham. Ordination to first tonsure. Ibid., fol. 84v.[6]
9 April	Downham. Ibid., fol. 42r.
11–12 April	Downham. Ibid., fols. 42r, 102r: parchment cover.
16–17 April	Downham. Ibid., fol. 102r: parchment cover.
22 April	Downham. Ibid.
27 April	Downham. Ibid., fol. 42v.
30 April	Downham. Ibid.
9 May	? Great Childerley, Cambridgeshire. Dedicated church and cemetery. Ibid., fol. 65v.[7]
21 May	Downham. BL, Add. MS 41612, fol. 114v.
25 May	Downham. CUL, EDR, G/I/1, Reg. De Lisle, fol. 43r.
2 June	Fen Ditton. Ordination in parish church. Ibid., fol. 98v.
3 June	? Ickleton Priory. Dedicated church and cemetery. Ibid., fol. 65v.[8]
7 July	Somersham. Ibid., fol. 43v.
19 July	Somersham. Ibid.
1 August	Somersham. PRO, CP 40/378, m. 46.
15 September	Somersham. CUL, EDR, G/I/1, Reg. De Lisle, fol. 43v.
22 September	Over, Cambridgeshire. Ordination in parish church. Ibid., fols. 84v, 98v.
27 September	Chatteris and Chatteris Abbey. Dedicated parish and conventual churches. Ibid., fol. 65v.
28 September	Papworth Everard, Cambridgeshire. Dedicated church and cemetery. Ibid.
29 September	Little Gransden. Consecrated high altar. Ibid.
30 September	Caxton, Cambridgeshire. Consecrated high altar. Ibid., fols. 43v, 65v.
2 October	Hungry Hill, Cambridgeshire. Dedicated church and cemetery. Ibid., fol. 65v.

6. Year was given as 1351, but this would be out of sequence with neighboring entries in the register. The scribe probably forgot to update the year after 25 March.

7. Same as note 6 above.

8. Same as note 6 above.

	4 October	Kingston, Cambridgeshire. Consecrated high altar. Ibid.
	6 October	Toft, Cambridgeshire. Dedicated church and cemetery. Ibid.
	7 October	Clopton, Cambridgeshire. Dedicated church and cemetery. Ordination to first tonsure. Ibid., fols. 65v, 84v.
	9 October	East Hatley, Cambridgeshire. Dedicated church and cemetery. Ibid., fol. 65v.
	10 October	Arrington, Cambridgeshire. Dedicated church and cemetery. Ibid.
	15 October	Balsham. Ibid., fol. 44r.
	18 October	Balsham. Ibid.
	28 October	Balsham. Ibid.
	31 October	Balsham. Ibid., fol. 89r.
	1 November	Balsham. Ibid., fols. 44r–v. Hatfield. BL, Add. MS 41612, fol. 113v.
	3 November	Cambridge. Dedicated church of St. Mary the Less. CUL, EDR, G/I/1, Reg. De Lisle, fol. 65v.
	4 November	Swaffham Bulbeck Priory. Dedicated church. Ibid., fols. 44r, 65v.
	10 November	Whittlesford, Cambridgeshire. Consecrated high altar. Ibid., fol. 65v.
	15 November	Haslingfield, Cambridgeshire. Dedicated church of All Saints. Ibid.
	17–18 November	Balsham. Ibid., fol. 44v.
	25 November	Balsham. Ibid.
	7 December	Somersham. Ibid.
	10–11 December	Somersham. Ibid.
	22 December	Downham. Ordination in parish church. Ibid., fol. 98v.
	23 December	Downham. Ibid., fol. 44v.
1353	2 February	Downham. Ordination of William Michel, bishop's nephew, to first tonsure. Ibid., fol. 84v.
	3 February	Downham. Ibid., fol. 45r.
	16 February	Ely. Ordination in church of St. Mary. Ibid., fol. 99r.
	1 March	Downham. Ibid., fol. 45r.
	9 March	Downham. Ordination in manor chapel. Ibid., fol. 99r.
	13–14 March	Downham. Ibid., fol. 45r.

	1 April	Downham. Ibid., fol. 45v.
	12–13 April	Downham. Ibid., fol. 45r.
	23 April	Downham. Ibid., fol. 46r.
	25 April	Downham. Ibid.
	29 April	Downham. Ibid.
	4 May	Downham. Ibid.
	12 May	Downham. Ibid.
	21 September	Swavesey, Cambridgeshire. Ordination in parish church. Ibid., fol. 99r.
	21 December	Downham. Ordination in parish church. Ibid., fol. 99v.
1354	8 March	Downham. Ordination in parish church. Ibid.
	7 June	Doddington. Ordination in manor chapel. Ibid.
	20 September	Doddington. Ordination in manor chapel. Ibid., fol. 100r.
	7 October	Downham. Ibid., fol. 46r.
	19 October	Downham. Ibid.
	28 October	Downham. Ibid.
	10–11 November	Balsham. Ibid., fols. 46r–v.
	2 December	Holborn, London. Ibid., fol. 46v.
	16 December	Little Gransden. Ibid.
	30 December	Wisbech. Ibid., fol. 46r.
1355	28 February	Wisbech. Ordination in parish church. Ibid., fols. 84v, 100r.
	20 March	Hatfield. Ibid., fol. 46r.
	28 March	Hatfield. Ibid., fol. 46v.
	2 April	Wisbech. Ordination in parish church. Ibid., fol. 100v.
	4 April	Wisbech. Ordination in parish church. Ibid.
	20 April	Totteridge, Hertfordshire. Ibid., fol. 46v.
	14–15 June	Hatfield. Ibid., fols. 46v, 73r.
	22 June	Hatfield. Ibid., fol. 46v.
	4 August	Doddington. Ibid., fol. 74r.
	29 August	Somersham, St. Ives, Little Gransden. Attacked by angry mob for role in the murder of William Holm. PRO, KB 27/384, rex m. 11d.; LPL, Reg. Islip, fols. 138v–139r; LAO, Episcopal Reg. VIII, fols. 91v, 93v; *AS*, 1:657–58, and see Appendix B, pages 232–33.
	31 August	Doddington. CUL, EDR, G/I/1, Reg. De Lisle, fol. 74r.
	7 September	Doddington. Ibid.

	19 September	Doddington. Ordination in parish church. Ibid., fols. 84v, 100v.
	7 October	Doddington. Ibid., fol. 74r.
	20 October	Hatfield. Ibid., fol. 74v.
	23 November	? Westminster. First day of session of parliament at which Lady Wake presented her petition against the bishop. King took suit into his hand. *RP,* 2:267; *Foedera,* 3, no. 1, 314; *CCR,* 1354–60, 159; *RDP,* 3:603–8.
	28 November	Holborn, London. CUL, EDR, G/I/1, Reg. De Lisle, fol. 74v.
	30 November	? Westminster. Session of parliament ended. *CCR,* 1354–60, 241–42.
1356	19 March	Elm, Cambridgeshire. Ordination in parish church. CUL, EDR, G/I/1, Reg. De Lisle, fol. 100v.
	9 April	Wisbech Castle. Ordination in chapel. Ibid., fol. 101r.
	16–20 May	London. Attended provincial council at St. Paul's Cathedral. LPL, Reg. Islip, fols. 117r–v.
	18 June	Doddington. Ordination in manor chapel. CUL, EDR, G/I/1, Reg. De Lisle, fol. 101r.
	8 July	Westminster. Appeared before the king's bench to answer indictment for complicity in the murder of William Holm. Trial adjourned until 6 October. PRO, KB 27/384, m. 11d., and see Appendix B, pages 245–46.
	24 September	Ely Cathedral. Ordination. CUL, EDR, G/I/1, Reg. De Lisle, fol. 101r.
	6 October	Westminster. Tried and convicted of complicity in the murder of William Holm. PRO, KB 27/384, m. 11d., and see Appendix B, pages 246–47.
	14 November	Mayfield, Sussex. Canonical trial in the parish church. LPL, Reg. Islip, fols. 125r, 128r; *AS,* 1:659–60, and see Appendix B, pages 234–35.
	19 November	Departure from England. *AS,* 1:660, and see Appendix B, page 236.
1361	23 June	Avignon. Death. Buried in the Dominican convent of St. Praxède, Montfavet-by-Avignon, France. *AS,* 1:662, and see Appendix B, page 238.

——————— Appendix B ———————

Transcripts of Important Documents

The following transcripts are taken from documents and rare printed records which are cited extensively in the text. They are given here in the order in which they appear in the various chapters of the book.

Chapter 1

Anonymous Medieval Biography of Bishop Thomas De Lisle, from *Monachi Eliensis Anonymi Continuatio Historiae Eliensis.* Source: *AS*, 1:652–62. Latin words in brackets are from Corpus Christi College Library, Cambridge, MS 287, 118–36.

Post mortem quoque dicti Symonis Episcopi frater Alanus Prior ecclesiae praedictae et fratres omnes et singuli eiusdem ecclesiae ingressi sunt capitulum suum Elyense die vi. mensis Julii anno Domini MCCCXLIV [1345] de die praefigendo procedendi ad electionem futuri pontificis tractaturi, habita super hoc licentia regia. Et diem crastinum, i.e. diem septimum eiusdem mensis Julii cum continuatione et prorogatione dierum subsequentium unanimiter praefixerunt, et de consensu expresso omnium statuerunt. Et subsequente dicto die vii. mensis Julii praedicti, post Missam de Spiritu Sancto in ecclesia cathedrali praedicta ipso die mane celebratam, praedictus Frater Alanus et caeteri monachi omnes et singuli in domo sua capitulari se congregaverunt, et ibidem inter se tractaverunt, per quam formam ad praedictum electionem maturius et cautius esset procedendum. Et statim tunc ibidem idem Frater Alanus prior et omnes fratres monachi singillatim et nominatim requisiti asseruerunt, et quilibet illorum singillatim requisitus asseruit expresse sibi placere compromissi. Et subsequenter praedictus Frater Alanus prior et caeteri monachi omnes inter se super compromissariis in ea parte eligendis tractantes, in septem monachis eiusdem capituli consenserunt, dantes eisdem septem plenam et liberam potestatem vice sua et vice totius capituli eligendi personam idoneam in episcopum et pastorem sibi et ecclesiae suae viduatae. Et statim dicti compromissarii de capitulo recesserunt, et in locum secretum seorsim se receperunt. Et invocata Sancti Sp[i]ritus gratia, primo de diversis personis praeficiendis inter se tractare coeperunt. Et tandem in Fratrem Alanum priorem Elyensem vota sua unanimiter direxerunt, et ipsum in episcopum suum Elyensem et pastorem infra tempus eis limitatum [concorditer] elegerunt. Et ipsam electionem primo coram fratribus in capitulo, deinde in ecclesia Cathedrali Elyensi coram clero et populo, palam et aperte publicaverunt. Sed ante dictae electionis confirmationem Dominus Papa Clemens VIII [Sextus] ex suae potestatis plenitudine Fratrem Thomam de Lylde de ordine praedicatorum in episcopum Elyensem praefecit, et sic electio de praedicto Alano facta, sicut electio sui praedecessoris Fratris Johannis de Crandene, frustrata erat similiter per papalem reservationem. Tempore vero patris nostri venerabilis Domini Thomae Elyensis episcopi [quoddam] contigit miraculum, huic exili opusculo merito annectendum.

Regnante Dei gratia Domino Edwardo III post conquestum, rege Anglorum victoriosissimo, anno Incarnationis Dominicae MCCCXLIX et regni eiusdem regis xxiii. ac pontificatus eiusdem patris nostri Reverendi Thomae Elyensis episcopi anno quinto, quidam armiger, natione Anglus, in rebus bellicis strenuus, et arma bellica ab adolescentia sua viriliter prosecutus, optimi viri filius Johannis de Hyntoun [ipse Hugo de Hinton], vocitatus cum fratre suo Domino Willelmo de Hyntoun milite in transmarinis partibus, et in regno Hispaniae in exercitu Christiano contra inimicos Crucis properavit ad bellum, qui cum caeteris Christianis contra Saracenos viriliter dimicavit. Contigit autem in illa die bellum vehementer urgeri. Et cum varius sit eventus bellorum; quod nunc hos nunc illos consumit gladius, multi utriusque exercitus corruerunt. Inter quos miles ille strenuus cecidit Willelmus de Hyntoun, et ipse Hugo in illo conflictu lancea dire confossus est in osse lumborum suorum; et ita firmiter et profunde dicta lancea intravit in osse, quod illam evellere pati non potuit prae dolore. Unde de humana ope desperans, ad divinum confugit adjutorium; B[eatam] Etheldredam crebrius et devote invocans ac suppliciter efflagitans, ut Deus meritis almae suae matris ipsum in illa arta necessitate sua consolaretur pietate. Et statim post manum misit ad lanceam, et illam ita leniter extraxit, ac si in carne solum fuisset infixa; sed ex nimio labore vulneris ac in illo conflictu oppressione laboris fatigatus, in lectum decidit graviter infirmatus. Qui super medicos et chirurgicos varios medicinam secundum artem suam sibi porrigentes, nullo illorum potuit curari medicamine; sed semper interim invocavit dilectam matronam [suam Beatam] Etheldredam, ut suis precibus sacrosanctis Dominum Deum exoraret, quod a dira aegritudine, quam patiebatur, ipsum clementer liberaret. Illi vero in oratione et devotione perseveranti apparuerunt [in] quadam nocte quatuor venerabiles matronae religiosae: quarum una, ut sibi visum fuerat, caeteris honore praecellens pannum sericum ad modum manutergii vario colore diversimode listatum gestabat in brachiis. Dixit ad illum: "Amice, qualiter est tecum?"

A[i]t ille: "Valde male."

Et [illa] confortans illum dixit: "Confide filij sanus eris in brevi."

Et accipiens pannum sericum, inclinavit se; et involvit lumbos eius hiante vulnere sauciatos.

Et sic ex illo tactu confortatus est, quod vix aliquem sentiebat dolorem; et sicut postea fatebatur, quod ipse nunquam in tota vita sua tam delectabile tamque suave corpori vel carni suae aliquoties sensit adhaesisse. Et erigens se, virago illa venerabilis ait ad illum: "Ubi est lancea illa, cum qua vulneratus fuisti?"

At ille respondit, dicens: "Nescio, domina mea reverenda."

At illa: "Quaere illam diligenter, et inventam affer ad me apud Ely."

Et continuo quatuor illae matronae venerabiles disparuerunt.

Et ipse paulatim convalescens, nichil aliud medicinae ulterius vulneri apposuit nisi tantum lanam et oleum, et tempore modico sanus factus est per merita, ut creditur, B[eatae] Etheldredae Virginis. Quinetiam dictam lanceam quaerere fecit diligenter per triduum, sed tandem inventa est in custodia cuiusdam militis praedicto Hugoni familiaris. Assumens namque caput lanceae praedictae, detulit illam secum in Angliam. Et cum venisset ad Elyensem Insulam, ipse cum fratre suo Radulpho de Hyntoun ad illam pervenit ecclesiam. Et ad feretrum B[eatae Virginis] Etheldredae illud obtulit cum summa devotione, ac super paxillum ferreum ibidem ad miraculi huius memoriam infixit.

Aliud quoque [preclarum] contigit miraculum anno Domini MCCCLV et regni Domini Edwardi III post conquestum illustris regis Angliae anno xxix. Vir quidam bonus et religiosus, Dominus Johannes [de] Lavenham, monachus ecclesiae S[ancti] Regis Edmundi, circa Passionem Domini in Quadragesima coepit infirmari, et morbo squinanciae in collo, guttare, et maxillis graviter intumescere, et vehementer vexari, ita quod manducare vel bibere seu etiam loqui non poterat. Unde nil aliud nisi mortem ipsius credebant aestimandum. Quapropter certi fratres de conventu deputati fuerant ad custodiendum, confortandum, et cum opus fuerat, consulendum fratrem infirmum, sicut moris est inter religiosos facere fratribus in extremis languentibus: ut diligenter observantes statum infirmi, proponendo sibi crebrius verba aedificatoria de Passione Christi, de misericordia Dei, et alia huiuscemodi consolatoria; ut sic expectarent aut fratris languidi meliorationem, aut ultimi spiritus exhalationem. Ipse vero interim toto ex corde jugiter et devote in mente sua, eo quod loqui non valebat, Deum deprecatus est, ut meritis S[anctae Virginis] Etheldredae dolorem, quem dire passus est, leniret, et si suae pietati complaceret, sanitati iterum [ipsum] restitueret. His itaque gestis, circa

Parasceven Domini aegrotus ille paululum coepit dormire. Visionem quandam habuit, quod fuit in una parva capella, quae infra illam ecclesiam erat statuta, et ibi quaedam venerabilis matrona, religionis habitu induta, sibi apparuit. Quae confortans eum, collum ipsius, guttur et maxillas, ubi dolorem sentiebat, circumquaque manibus suis leniter palpavit, et hoc facto, se egredi dissimulavit. Et paulo post reversa dixit ad illum: "Duos annulos habes aureos. Offer unum ex hi[i]s apud Ely ad me, quoniam illum habere volo de te."

Et hi[i]s dictis disparuit. Et statim evigilans, clare locutus est, vocans socios suos, quos secum habuit pro sua custodia deputatos. Qui audientes illum loquentem, admirati sunt valde, et magno repleti gaudio, sciscitabantur ab eo, quomodo tam subito loqueretur, qui multis retro diebus verba proferre non potuit. At ille exponens eis visionem quam vidit, et quod per merita S[anctae] Virginis Etheldredae cito sanus fieret, asseruit. Unde quidam eorum praetextu istius miraculi Sanctam Etheldredam apud Ely nudis pedibus peregrinando se visitaturos promittebant; alii vero alia vota emittebant, qui postmodum [venientes] vota sua devotissime persolvebant. Denique vir ille praefatus Dominus Johannes, cum sanus fuerat et validus corpore, iter apud Ely pedibus gradiens coepit arripere, et illum annulum aureum per S[anctam] Etheldredam requisitum secum deferre. Quo perveniens, dictum annulum saphiro nobili ornatum, habentem et minuta granula lapidum diversorum in circulo per girum, obtulit B[eatae] Etheldredae maxima mentis devotione, ubi feretrum ipsius virginis ostenditur populo venienti ad honorem et laudem Dei et huius miraculi ostensionem.

Restat iam scribendum de praedicto patre et pastore nostro Fratre Thoma de Lylde de ordine praedicatorum, Elyensi dudum episcopo. Ipse enim praefectus erat in episcopum Elyensem per Dominum Papam Clementem VIII [Sextum] anno Domini MCCCXLIV [1345] mense Julii circa festum S[ancti] Jacobi, et in curia Avinionensi consecratus. In ipsa autem consecratione vas quoddam vitreum vino plenum super altare erat positum, sicut moris est curiae episcopos consecrari. Et circa salutaris hostiae consecrationem sine tangentis manu in altari confractum est subito et divisum, ac vinum, quod erat in vase, super altare discurrit effusum. Et qui praesentes aderant, hoc videntes, maximum arbitrati sunt praesagium fuisse futurorum. Nam in episcopatu suo multa postmodum adversa erat passurus. Eodem autem anno Angliam est ingressus, et a domino rege susceptus. Ac traditis sibi suis temporalibus, in prima Dominica Adventus eiusdem anni erat apud Ely solempniter intronizatus. In primiciis namque suis splendidus valde fuit in mensa. Milites quoque et armigeros valentes patriae, ac juris utriusque peritos, in magna copia ad suas robas et ad suum consilium retinebat, ut in parliamento et aliis locis communibus militum et armigerorum ac aliorum servientium multitudine vallatus, inter caeteros regni proceres apparuit gloriosus. Videns denique tantam sibi familiam nimis onerosam et in modico proficientem, quibusdam de electis secum retentis, caeteros vero quodam discretionis sarculo de sua familia resecavit.

In omnibus fere causis, quas tunc temporis ventilabat, foeliciter sibi et prospere succedebat. Egregius namque praedicator extitit, et per varia loca suae dioceseos discurrens, velut fidelis dispensator et prudens, familiae Dominicae mensuram tritici distribuendo, verbum Dei in populo sibi commisso ferventi animo disseminavit. Sed inimicus homo furtim venit et latenter, et in electo tritico superseminavit zizania; et invidiae suae antiquae nodum dissolvens, nimis illum fecit exosum populo terrae. Praesertim ex eo, quod in sermonibus suis misericordiam maxime commendabat, quam quidem misericordiam in se delinquentibus, justitia quadam nimia quasi in se veritatem mutata, quam prohibet scriptura dicens: "Noli esse nimis justus," absque satisfactione condigna de facili non concedebat. Quamvis idem pater et pastor noster in seipso bonus erat; quibusdam tamen adulatoribus et sinistra narrantibus, qui sibi erant a secretis, aures patulas et nimis credulas exhibebat. Nam quorundam malignorum instinctu, non sui proprii animi motu, ut creditur, erga priorem et conventum multum se reddebat difficilem, in tantum quod ad opus ecclesiae argillam fodere et arenam, sicut in omnium episcoporum temporibus consueverant, ad magnum scandalum sibis nimis diu denegavit. Crebris interim precibus et variis petitionibus prior et conventus, nunc per epistolas, nunc per fratres capituli iteratis vicibus sibi missos, suae paternitati deprecati sunt, ut argillam, zabulum, et arenam ad fabricas ecclesiae habere poterant, ut solebant. Ipse vero absque suae specialis gratiae rogatu licentiam zabulum habendi et arenam, ut superius dictum est, concedere recusavit. Tunc tandem prior et conventus ad placandum ipsius animum epistolam sibi miserunt deprecatoriam, mentionem suae specialis gratiae facientem. Epistolam illam gratanter acceptans, et ne in consequentiam traheretur in posterum, integram et clausam conventui tradendam in capitulum postmodum reportavit. Et deinceps argillam fodiendi, zabulum simul et arenam ad opus ecclesiae priori et conventui, ut hactenus usi fuerant, liberam concessit facultatem.

Postmodum namque, quod maxime dolendum est, oritur contra ipsum lamentabile infortunium. Nam quidam iniquitatis filii, suae salutis immemores, quasdam domos Dominae de Wake in mesuagio suo de Colne in comitatu Huntyngdoniae noctanter combusserunt, et totum crimen maliciose super episcopum et quosdam de suis imposuerunt. Super quo brevia regia emanaverunt, certis domini regis justiciariis ad inquirendum de huiusmodi incendii actoribus et fautoribus directa. Qui apud Yakesle sedentes, milites et armigeros ac alios de patria valentes coram eis ibidem fecerunt convenire. Et capta inquisitione per xii. juratos de praedictis militibus et aliis, qui super sacramentum suum erant onerati, quod in huiusmodi negotio incendii fideliter ac diligenter inquirerent, et quos huiusmodi sceleris reos invenirent, dictis justiciariis notificarent. Ipsi vero seorsum paulisper recedentes, in dictis negotiis tractaturi, et cum in causa concordes essent, ut dixerant, quosdam nominati actores esse sceleris, et episcopum illis consentientem asserebant. Justiciarii autem dicta illorum non acceptantes, iniunxerunt eis iterum per sacramentum suum, quod inter se diligenter investigarent, si episcopus actor esset criminis cum caeteris criminosis, vel non. Et [qui] inter se modicum colloquentes, dixerunt tamen injuste episcopum cum caeteris reum esse. Et statim fuit episcopus finaliter condempnatus in nongentis libris argenti Dominae Wake pro dampnis suis plenarie persolvendis, quae quidem pecunia in brevi post eidem extitit persoluta.

Thomas autem episcopus, retinens in memoria illud sapientis: "Esto forti animo, cum sis dampnatus inique," fortis erat in adversis. Et inter aspera viriliter incedens, super injuria sibi allata [illata] remedium habere cupiens, brevia impetravit regia super convictione superjuratorum, qui in prima sessione apud Yakesle falsum contra ipsum tulissent testimonium. Et hoc per numerum duplicem juratorum paratus est juris ordine declarare. Et cognoscendi in hac causa recti regis justiciarii fuerant deputati. Citati sunt enim ad comparendum coram eis [apud] Huntyngdoniae certo die valentiores patriae, qui ad diem assignatum ibidem congregati, et ad veritatem in hac parte dicendam parati comparuerunt. Sedentes autem pro tribunali, justiciarii praedicti petierunt statim dictamentum sessionis apud Yakesle, processum eiusdem sessionis justiciariorum et juratorum nomina continens, sibi ostendi. Quibus responsum est, quod fuit in manibus quorundam virorum, de quibus erant ibidem duo praesentes. Accersiti erant illi duo, et super hoc requisiti. Responderunt, quod id minime obtinuerunt. Dixerunt autem quod miles quidam modicum ab Huntyngdon distans dictamentum illud habuit custodiendum. Nuncius quidem [quidam] continuo a justiciariis est ad militem missus, ipsum ex parte illorum suppliciter deprecans, quatenus [illud] dictamentum eis mitteret indilate, quoniam ibi [ipsi] sedebant tota die quasi ociosi et taedio nimis affecti dictamentum expectantes praenominatum, quod sine illo in causa procedere non potuerunt. Respondens autem miles dixit nuncio, quod pro certo in sua non erat custodia sed in custodia alterius illorum, qui prius eodem die apud Huntyngdon coram justiciariis erant vocati et de re praedicta requisiti. Regressus est qui missus fuerat, sedentibus adhuc justiciariis, renuncians eisdem quid a milite audierat. Jusserunt justiciarii viros praedictos iterum inquiri, qui saepius iteratis vicibus vocati et per totam curiam quaesiti, minime sunt inventi. Advesperascente iam die surgentes justiciarii infecto negotio recesserunt. Episcopus autem Thomas, nolens sic vecorditer ab incoeptis desistere, sed ut iniuriatores sui ad satisfactionem de illatis sibi injuriis reducerentur, viis et modis legitimis, quibus poterat, coepit viriliter attemptare. Et cum in prosecutione causae praedictae modicum se senserat profecisse, quoniam aemuli sui ex adverso conati sunt, et processum ipsius causae in quantum poterant impedire.

Videns itaque episcopus, quod ab aemulis suis praedictis fuisset sic illusus, ad praesentiam domini regis, ubi in lusum avium cum falconibus, comitantibus secum militibus quibusdam et armigeris, spaciabatur, accessit. Et suam regiam magnificentiam humiliter requisivit, quod de injuriis sibi illatis fieri juberet justitiae complementum. Rex autem, continuo advocans sibi quendam militem Dominum Richardum de la Vache, qui erat ibidem, ut verba, quae inter ipsum et episcopum dicenda forent, posset audire et postmodum testificare, rex enim ait ad episcopum: "Domine episcope, causa quae inter te et dilectam nostram consanguineam Dominam Wake vertitur, nobis et proceribus nostris ac populo regni nostri odiosa valde fore perhibetur. Item ex illa dampna plurima personarum subversiones et pericula multa evenire forsitan potuerunt in futurum. Quapropter causam praedictam accipere intendimus in manus nostras, et non ut tua voluntas in omnibus fiat neque sua, sed per viam mediam incedendo, quod pax inter vos volente Deo et concordia reformetur."

Episcopus autem dixit ad regem: "Excellentissime domine, jubeat si placet serenitas vestra, quod secundum legem regni [vestri] et justitiam discuti valeat inter nos causa praenominata."

Cui rex, ut fertur, milite prius vocato praesente, dixit: "Et quis te prohibet in regno nostro legem habere vel justitiam?"

At ille respondit, dicens: "Domine, sic est quod legem in causa mea habere non possum neque justitiam, potestate, ut credo, regia praepeditus."

Rex autem audito hoc verbo, contra episcopum commotus erat vehementer, et ait: "Certe tu, Thomas [Thoma] de Lylde, falsum dicis! Nunquam enim fuisti praepeditus, sed legem habebis, absque tamen favore legis!"

Episcopus vero cum regis indignatione a loco recessit, parum vel nichil in causa confortatus. Modico post tempore lapso, [dominus] rex in parliamento suo Londoniae coram praelatis regni et proceribus ibidem congregatis dixit episcopo Elyensi: "O Thoma de Lylde, tu nuper nobis imposuisti, quod in causa tua legem habere non potuisti, nostra potestate regia praepeditus." At ille negavit expresse coram rege et magnatibus, dicens se nunquam talia verba protulisse. Ad quem rex ira succensus magna dixit: "Certissime tu, Thoma de Lylde, mentiris aperta! Talia enim verba dixisti!" Et advocavit in testem illum militem, qui verba, quae inter regem et episcopum in praemissis locuta fuerant, audivit. Et regiis dictis testimonium perhibuit, dicens episcopum ipso praesente et audiente talia verba dixisse. Videntes autem dominus archiepiscopus et alii episcopi animum regis contra episcopum Elyensem nimium fuisse commotum, surrexerunt. Et coram rege genua flectentes, ipsius suppliciter efflagitabant clementiam, ut episcopum Elyensem in suam reciperet gratiam, et sibi misericorditer indulgendo et suam regiam remitteret offensam. Episcopus vero interim stetit erectus, et quasi cogitans quid diceret in hoc casu aut quid ageret, nec se aliquantulum inclinavit, de quo plures qui affuerant, mirati sunt. Rege autem in ira adversus episcopum concepta perseverante, recessit episcopus, faciem regis de caetero amplius non visurus.

Contigit namque post haec, ut episcopo iam nimis afflicto major adhuc addita est afflictio. Nam quidam eius cubicularius nomine Radulphus, genere Normannus, orta inter ipsum et quendam Dominae Wake familiarem, Willelmum de Holm, saeva discordia, incidit in eundem Willelmum, et hoste incitante antiquo interfecit illum. Quod cum audisset episcopus, ingemuit, et tactus dolore cordis intrinsecus ait: "Coartor undique. Nunc scio vere, quod absque dispendio magno et discrimine non possum evadere, quoniam, ut ita dicam, totum pondus praelii versum est in caput meum," quoniam gentes patriae vicinae totum huius homicidii causam et flagitium mendaciter et maliciose super eundem imposuerunt. Die vero sequenti, comitante secum sacrista Elyensi, Fratre Roberto de Suttoun, iter cum suis versus Londoniam arripuit. Et ab ingressu manerii sui de Somersham circundante illum inopinate turba malorum quousque pervenisset ad S[anctum] Ivonem, quaedam Margareta de Holm, soror ipsius interfecti, mulier quidem maliciosa valde, adjunctis secum [quibusdam] perversis hominibus, una cum Henrico Colne ipsi episcopo nimis infesto, clamoribus magnis et tumultibus prosecuta est, ad instar Semei filii Gemini de cognatione Saul, ut Regem ii. legitur. Qui ingressus contra Regem David fugientem filium suum Absolon, proiiciens lapides et lutum, maledicebat regi dicens: "Egredere vir Belial, egredere vir sanguinum! Ecce, premunt te mala quae fecisti!" Sic et illa clamans et clamore terribili vociferans, dixit: "Harron super te, Thoma de Lylde, harron, harron super te homicida pessime, harron super te! Tu enim interfecisti fratrem meum Willelmum de Holm! Harron super te, harron!"

Episcopus vero conversus ad mulierem, simplici voce et lugubri dixit: "Mulier, injuste me persequeris [et possime agis contra me]. Innocens [ego] sum a sanguine fratris tui. Non enim illum interfeci, nec unquam illum interficere iussi. Sed me invito et nesciente omnino interfectus fuit; novit Deus."

Et Henricus de Colne et alii scelerati viri et perversi, qui secum erant, similiter insultantes episcopo, convicia, opprobria, verba contumeliosa, et varia improperiorum genera horribili strepitu inferebant. Et sic illum prosecuti [persecuti] sunt, ante et retro, a dextris et a sinistris, usque ad S[anctum] Ivonem; per mediam villam clamantes duxerunt et vociferantes, quod tota villa per illorum strepitum commota est, in tantum quod episcopus cum suis, relictis cariagiis suis ibidem cum victualibus, pontem vix transire poterat, et sic manus illorum evadere, ac ad manerium suum de Grantesdene velociter equitando hora prandendi pervenit. Vidit autem episcopus tanta sibi taedia imminere atque dispendia futura, caute respiciens et timens, ne forte per maliciam hominum, quae magna tunc erat contra ipsum, temporalia sua posse, quamvis non demeruit, confiscari. Et sic modicum haberet, per quod in sua necessitate sibi poterit subvenire. Discreto et utili usus consilio, scripsit lit[t]eras ad omnes et singulos maneriorum suorum ministros, illis districte praecipiens, quod omnia bona sua mobilia, averia et catalla, supplementis maneriorum duntaxat exceptis, cautela tamen convenienti, celeri exponerent venditioni. Et pecuniam pro rebus suis venditis acceptam in manibus mercatorum deposuit custodiendam, ut cum hi[i]s opus haberet, suis iterum usibus resolvendam.

Sedente modicum post coronatore illius patriae, et de morte dicti iam interfecti per inquisitionem xii. hominum legalium de vicineto districtius quaerente, onerati sunt xii. homines praedicti ex parte regis per eundem coronatorem super sacramentum suum, ut de interfectoribus huius mortui, et omnibus aliis, qui eis in hac felonia praebuerunt consilium, auxilium, vel favorem, seu quenquam illorum post factam feloniam receptarunt, diligentem inter se tractatum haberent, et quid in praemissis per sacramentum suum invenirent, indilate sibi fideliter significarent. Qui quidem jurati super hac causa inter se tractantes, praenominatum Radulphum episcopi cubicularium principalem Willelmi de Holm fuisse interfectorem, et episcopum neci ipsius consentientem, ac quosdam alios sibi adhaerentes et auxiliantes asseruerunt; episcopum vero dictum Radulphum post feloniam factam receptasse similiter affirmaverunt. Quod utique falsum fuit, et ex mendaci suspicione omnino processit, quoniam episcopus in mortem ipsius nullo tempore consensit, nec ipse Radulphus in comitiva sua post homicidium accessit, nec ab illo usquam postmodum visus est. Sed statim ut de morte audivit, accersiri [iussit] Willelmum de Stanstede senescallum suum et totius suae Insulae Elyensis custodem, sibi firmiter iniungendo mandavit, quod secundum iura regni homicidam illum per totam ballivam suam diligentius inquireret, et si illum forte alicubi inveniret, tanquam regis felonem secundum legem in regno traditam illum per omnia judicaret.

Cum autem dicta per praefatos xii. juratos in inquisitione per coronatorem dudum capta, et ad inquirendum super morte praefati Willelmi de Holm onerata, coram justiciariis de banco domini regis fuissent devoluta, vocatus est Thomas de Lylde episcopus Elyensis ad comparendum coram dictis justiciariis, super sibis obiiciendis in causa praemissa responsurus. Qui ad diem assignatum sedentibus pro tribunali justiciariis supradictis comparuit, comitantibus secum et astantibus ad ipsum locum judicii dominis Cantuariensi archiepiscopo et episcopo

Roffensi. Cui statim obiectum erat per justiciarios praedictos, quod ipse
contra justitiam et pacem regni consentiens fuerat in mortem cuiusdam
Willelmi de Holm felonice interfecti, consilium praebens et auxilium, ac
ipsum interfectorem quendam Radulphum Carles post feloniam factam
scienter receptavit, et in sua comitiva retinuit. Episcopus autem dictus
[dictis] justiciariis respondit, dicens quod non ex voluntate sua nec sua
scientia sed ipso invito et ignorante dictus Willelmus de Holm occisus
fuit, [et] quod ipsum Radulphum post feloniam factam nunquam vidit,
nec ipsum receptavit. Et hoc per pares suos, cum ipse erat de paribus
regni unus, discuti et discerni se sponte supposuit. Justiciarii vero super
hoc convocaverunt patriam xii. juratorum, non de paribus terrae, ut
episcopus pro se allegavit et petiit, sed de plebeiis. Et illos xii. juratos
super sacramentum suum oneraverunt, ut inter se diligenter inquirerent,
an Thomas de Lylde episcopus Elyensis consentiens fuerat neci Willelmi
de Holm nuper interfecti, consilium impendens vel auxilium, aut ipsum
Radulphum post feloniam scienter receptaverit vel non. Jurati autem in
casu praedicto modicum inter se tractantes, dixerunt quod Thomas de
Lylde episcopus Elyensis in mortem Willelmi de Holm nunquam consensit,
praedictum tamen Radulphum post perpetratam feloniam receptavit
scienter. Justiciarii vero ipsum episcopum de receptatione felonis regis
contra pacem regni tanquam clericum per legem illorum convictum
judicarunt, et statim omnia temporalia sua tam episcopatus Elyensis, quam
alia tempore episcopatus sui per ipsum episcopum perquisita, in manu
domini regis judicialiter per eosdem sunt seisita et confiscata.

   Cum vidisset Episcopus Thomas temporalia sua confiscata, et se coram
non suis videlicet de receptatione felonis regis, ut praedicitur, diffamatum
esse, cum per eos super hoc convinci non poterat, eo quod sui judices non
erant, cupiens itaque juris ordinem ad sua restitui, accessit ad dominum
Cant[uariensem] archiepiscopum, rogans illum suppliciter cum omni
justicia requisita, ut super diffamatione praedicta suam canonicam
admitteret purgationem. Dominus autem Cant' [Canterbury], justis
episcopi petitionibus libenter ac favorabiliter annuens, virum venerabilem
et discretum Magistrum Willelmum de Wythelysey, archidiaconum
Huntyngdoniensem, judicem sibi in praemissis constituit et deputavit.
Qui quidem judex proclamare fecit certis in locis, quod si quis obiicere
vellet, sciret vel intenderet contra Thomam de Lylde episcopum Elyensem,
quare ad purgationem suam canonicam super diffamatione sibi imposita
admitti non debeat, veniat obiiciens ille quicunque fuerit apud Manfeld
Cant' [Canterbury] dioceseos, et paratus ibidem sit personaliter die certo
per judicem praedictum assignato in dicta proclamatione exequenda.
Venientes vero praedicti episcopus et archidiaconus, comitantibus cum
eis Fratre Roberto Suttoun sacrista Elyensi et alii viris valentibus apud
Manfeld in diem praefixum, in ecclesia parochiali eiusdem villae sederunt.

Et dominus archidiaconus, judex ad praemissa deputatus, per praeconem suum fecit proclamare, ut si quis ibidem praesens esset, qui contra Thomam de Lylde episcopum Elyensem obiicere vellet, quod in dictam sibi purgationem canonicam admitti non debet, veniat nunc coram judice ibi praesente et pro tribunali sedente in hac causa, et obiiciat si quid habeat in hac parte obiiciendum, et dicta sua admitterentur, ac per viam justitiae discuterentur. Et hoc idem saepius in die iteratis vicibus jussit proclamare. Nemine quidem per diem totum ad obiiciendum comparente, circa vesperum eiusdem diei facta fuit peremptoria proclamatio, quod si aliquis ibidem esset, qui adhuc obiicere vellet, quod tunc demum sine mora veniret, quod post illam horam in posterum via obiiciendi cuiquam ulterius non pateret. Sed nec tunc quoquam comparente, judex praedictus in causa praemissa sententiam tulit diffinitivam, excludens cuicunque obiiciendi de caetero facultatem.

Recesserunt autem inde tam episcopus quam archidiaconus, et caeteri qui cum illis erant, iter arripientes ad archiepiscopum, nunciaverunt eidem res gestas per ordinem: qualiter certis die et loco pro proclamatione ex[s]equenda assignatis personaliter affuerunt, et proclamationem praedictam saepius per idem iteratis vicibus rite et legitime praeconizare fecerunt, sed nullus interim comparuit ad contradicendum, quin ad purgationem Thomae de Lylde episcopi Elyensis de jure foret procedendum. Unde Episcopus Thomas dictum archiepiscopum suppliciter rogavit ac instantissime petiit, ut super diffamatione sibi obiecta suam admitteret purgationem, nec non diem et locum, ubi et quando cum suis compurgatoribus ad se purgandum in hac parte compareret, certitudinaliter assignaret. Cui dominus archiepiscopus ait: "Dilectissime mi frater domine episcope, adquiesce rogo consiliis meis, et tibi volente Deo melius forte propitietur. Vade prius, ut consulo, ad dominum nostrum regem, et reconciliare sibi, quoniam, ut spero, illum tibi invenies gratiosum. Et tunc redeas, et omnia purgationem tuam concernentia pro libito consequeris, et ad statum tuum pristinum in omnibus sine dubio restitueris."

Ad quem Episcopus Thomas: "Domine pater, iam enim rite peracta sunt omnia, quae ante purgationem meam recipienda canonice sunt requisita. Nunc autem nichil aliud restat, nisi quod vos, prout de jure tenemini, ac vestro incumbit officio pastorali, diem mihi et locum velitis assignare, ut de diffamatione mihi imposita possim canonice me purgare. Quapropter vestram, ut prius, venerabilem rogo paternitatem, quod meam in hoc casu potero purgare innocentiam, diem adhuc mihi assignetis."

Respondit archiepiscopus, dicens: "Diem tibit et locum, cum opportuerit, assignabo. Nec tibi nec tua purgationi in aliquo derogare intendo, licet aliquantulum differo pro utilitate maiori, ut causa tua cum regis assensu consilio maturiori poterit terminari." Illo autem consiliis procedentes, pro multiplicatis illorum offensis censuras utique multiplicabant, et illos cum suis communicantibus [comitantibus] excommunicabant. Unde quidam de excommunicatis praedictis carnis universae viam interim sunt ingressi, et ecclesiasticae traditi sepulturae. Sed virtute quorundam processuum in curia contra illos factorum, eorum cadavera in conditionis humanae horrorem de suis sepulc[h]ris sunt extracta, et de loco sacro longius proiecta. Hoc autem plures arbitrati sunt genus fuisse nimiae severitatis, quod sepulturam quietam esse humatis hominum corporibus non indulsit. Propter quod episcopus et sui maximam regis indignationem et regni procerum incurrebant. Quapropter commissio regia certis justiciariis fuit directa ad inquirendum, qui essent fautores episcopi Elyensis in publicatione et prosecutione lit[t]erarum apostolicarum, citationes, et censuras in certi regni personis continentium [concernencium], consilium sibi in hi[i]s vel favorem aut auxilium impendentes. Justiciariis siquidem super praemissis inquisitionem capientibus, quidam vero viri religiosi et saeculares, clerici et laici fuerant indictati. Ex quibus quidam capti erant et incarcerati, ac variis afflicti injuriis, poena duplici, corporali et pecuniaria, sunt multati. Quidam vero amicorum consiliis adquiescentes, se regis gratiae summiserunt, et via leniori transierunt.

Episcopus autem, non obstante regis indignatione aut amicorum suorum prosecutione, ab incoeptis suis non desistit, sed suae causae processum viis et modis legitimis cum censurarum additionibus, quasi actor indefessus, contra suos adversarios continuavit. Unde factum est, quod quidam Thomas de Senauntoun clericus, de curia veniens Romana, quasdam secum lit[t]eras detulit apostolicas, continentes censuras graves quibusdam personis Angliae infligendas, ac ad publicandum et prosequendum vim et effectum illarum certis regni episcopis directas. Captus est cum quodam Armigero Thoma de Chyltoun, adjuncto secum socio altero quo sibi in auxilium occurrebant. Adducti sunt Londoniam [et apud turiem London] incarcerati, fame ibidem et inedia nimi afflicti. Justiciariis regis erant postmodum praesentati, ac demum [deinde] apud Newgate missi, unde [ubi] in magna miseria spiritum ultimum exhalabant. Cum autem rumores de morte virorum istorum ad aures pervenissent episcopi, ipse, dolens nimis et tristis effectus, ad dominum papam accessit. Et de atrocitate tanta suis nunciis illata flebiliter conquestus est, et quod ad hortandum suos adversarios nullus ibidem audebat accedere metu mortis. Unde dominus papa edicta iussit scribi publica, quae in valvis palatii erant affixa, et omnes, quorum nomina in illis edictis fuerant conscripta, sanxivit personaliter fore citatos. Unde processus incoepti in curia contra citatos per edicta, ac si essent personaliter praesentes, de die in diem, de termino in terminum, sunt continuati, quousque citati praedicti excommunicationis et interdicti sententiis et aliis censuris gravibus finaliter archiepiscopi non adquiescente, recesserunt alterutrum ab invicem, se postea non visuri.

Intellexit Episcopus Thomas animum regis esse contra ipsum nimis exasperatum, ac plures et graves se habere adversarios, qui de ipso mala citius domino regi procurarent quam bona, et in sua causa culpam agnoscere, ubi culpa non erat, se reputans non teneri. Idcirco maliciis hominum cedere et, corporis proprii pericula merito formidanda, censuit [sensuit] potius declinare, et ad partes transmarinas clam securus transfretare. Recessit igitur ab Anglia pastor et pater noster praedictus xix. die mensis Novembris per diem Sabbati anno Domini MCCCLVI. Et mari transito, ad villam de Bruges pervenit, et paululum ibi moram traxit.

Deinde ad curiam Avinionensem proficiscitur, ac domino papae et cardinalibus de illatis sibi iniuriis multiplicibus conqueritur. Et exponens eisdem dilucide et aperte in pleno consistorio totius causae suae ordinem et processum, subiecit se in omnibus et causam suam praedictam diffinitioni domini papae et cardinalium, ut secundum Deum et aequitatem justam in causa sua pronunciarent sententiam. Qui, examinantes causam praedictam diligenter et deliberato, invenerunt in processu adversus episcopum facto plurima libertati universalis Ecclesiae maxime repugnantia. Ideo causam ipsam non solum ipsius episcopi personalem, verum etiam totius Ecclesiae Catholicae causam esse universalem, diffinitiva sententia determinabant. Ipse vero petiit continue a domino papa, omni justitia requisita, judices sibi dari in causa. Et dominus papa, petitionibus justis annuens cum favore, certos sibi judices ad cognoscendum in causa praedicta inter ipsum et suos adversarios deputavit, ut, per formam juris procedentes, complementum justitiae sine personarum acceptione [exceptione] facerent inter partes. Judices itaque praedicti multos post [per] edicta publica clericos et laicos, milites et armigeros diversos decreverunt fore vocandos et citandos, ut, ad instantiam Thomae de Lylde Elyensis episcopi, super sibi obiiciendis certo die juridico personaliter comparerent in curia responsuri. Illis autem ad diem praefixum non comparentibus, ad instantiam partis accersitis, judices praedicti sententiam excommunicationis in non venientes pro sua contumacia fulminabant, decernentes eosdem contra diem certum vocari, et ad comparendum ibidem personaliter coram dictis judicibus peremptorie citari. Et super hoc edicta citatoria in Angliam [Anglia] fuerant delata, et in variis ecclesiis parochialibus et aliis locis communibus lecta et publicata. In quibusdam vero ecclesiarum hostiis erant affixa, ut per illa loca transeuntes, citatorum nomina palam in eis legere possent et intueri, ita ut per eadem dicta citati de ignorantia non poterant legitime excusari.

Sed nec sic quidem comparebant, nec procuratores pro eis responsuros in curia constituebant. Propter quod judices praedicti in causa [sentencialiter] fuerunt innodati.

Interim vero tractatus pacis et concordiae inter episcopum et suos in hac parte adversarios per quosdam procuratores a domino rege Angliae et magnatibus in hac causa ad curiam transmissos habitus fuerat et longo tempore continuatus. Sed ante finalem et concordem tractatus huiusmodi expeditionem, Episcopus Thomas, cuius memoria cum benedictione inter electos Dei antistites connumeretur, diem vitae suae clausit extremum. Cum autem iste episcopus noster Thomas ecclesiae suae Eliensi annis fere xvi. [xvii.] praefuisset, ix. calend[as] Julii in festo Depositionis S[anctae] Virginis Etheldredae et Vigilia Nativitatis S[ancti] Johannis Baptistae in curia obiit Avinionensi, anno Dom[ini] MCCCLXI. In ecclesia S[ancti] Praxèdis iuxta Avinionem inter sorores ordinis fratrum praedicatorum solempniter est sepultus.

Ipse vero paulo ante suum recessum de Anglia quaedam vestimenta sub custodia sacristae sibi et suae Elyensi ecclesiae deposuit conservanda: duas videlicet capas ex panno de serico purpurei coloris vineis intexto rubeis, unam casulam, cum tribus tunicis, duabus stolis, tribus favonibus, et tribus albis, cum paraturis eiusdem sectae de panno serico purpureo supradicto. Deposuit etiam episcopus penes praedictum sacristam unum calicem argenteum et deauratum, cum ii. urceolis de argento, et unam situlam argenteam pro aqua benedicta, cum aspersorio, et duobus parvis campanis pro capella similiter de argento. Sed haec omnia vestimenta simul et vasa argentea, in manus domini regis per suos ministros quasi devoluta [dedita], sunt seisita fisco. Rex tamen ex clementia sua omnia praedicta vestimenta simul et vasa argentea in usus Elyensis ecclesiae perpetuo fore statuit remansura. Quae quidem ad perpetuam Thomae de Lylde Elyensis episcopi memoriam et Domini Regis Edwardi III post conquestum munificentiam in Elyensi ecclesia conservantur.

Chapter 2

Letter from Richard de Sheningdon, abbot of Ramsey, to King Edward III concerning the abbey's dispute with Thomas de Lisle, undated. Source: BL, Add. Charter 33657.

Pleaise a nostre tresexcellente et tresdote seignur le roi de vostre haute et graciouse seignurie savoir et entendre des grantz mals, grevances, et torts que Thomas evesque de Ely avant son aler hors de vostre roialme fist et compassa par diverses voies de faire as voz houmbles chapeleins et servantz l'abbe et covent de Rameseie, sachant et aparseyvant qils furent trop poveres et en tiels meschiefs et estat qils ne poient eux mesmes defendre ne rienz n'avoyent apoi dout vivere blee n'aultres choses forsque d'achaat come overtement est conuz en celes parties. Et cele rancour et malice touz iours pensant et continuant ore de novel ad tret et tarié et grevé trop chargeantement voz dites servantz et chapeleins en la court de Rome a perpetuel destruccion de vostre dite meson de Rameseie, as toutz iours s'il ne soit le ples tost socourée, eaidé, et conforté par vostre real et sovereigne seignurie.

Et nyent meyns voz dites recomandéz liges, servantz, et chapeleins sont tretz et tariéz de iour en aultre devant diverses justices et en diverses contees par cause des processes et suytes que le dit evesque pursuyt en la dite court de Rome vers plousours des voz dites justices et aultres voz liges. Gentz et surmettent a eux diverses articles et choses qils ne firent unqes et coment qils sont de ceste matiere innocens et sanz coupe, sanz regarde a ceo avoir ou a nulle aultre chose forsque tut a plesance de vostre noble, benigne, et graciouse seignurie. Voz dites chapeleins se ount mys haut et bas en vostre haute seignurie et grace, et par tant les dites justices dient et voillont recorder que voz dites simples chapeleyns sont coupables et ount trespassé a vostre real seignurie et mageste et les ount manacé, qils sont et seront pur ceo a grosses et grevouses fins et ransouns, de qoi nostre tresdote seignur vous pleaise de vostre grande et haute realte et graciouse seignurie et bounte par charite penser, comander, et ordeyner issint que tiels fins et raunsouns ne soient sur eux mys ne de eux levéz. Qar certes ne vous despleaise ils ne la poont porter s'ils ne soient nettement destrutz, et la dite meson desolat, et les moynes enchacés, et la service Dieu de tut lessé et cessé.

Chapter 4

Agreement between Richard and William Spynk and Thomas de Lisle, witnessed by the bishop at Downham on 21 May 1352. Source: BL, Add. MS 41612, fols. 114r–v.

Manumissio Ricardi Spynk
A touz et ceux qui cestes presentes lettres orront et verront, Aleyn, priour de Ely, et le covent de mesme le leu, salutz en Dieux. Sachetz que come nostre treshonurable piere en Dieu, Thomas, eveske de Ely, eu relessé et quitclamé a Richard Spynk, citezeyn de Norwyz, et William, soun frere, toutez maneres d'actiounes, cleymes, chalenges, et demandes par ses lettres patentes compernaunz le tenour quele en suyt:

Conue chose seit a totes gentz que come diversis debatz et desencions ount esté moevés par entre l'onurable piere en Dieux, Thomas, par la grace de Dieux eveske de Ely, d'une parte, et Richard Spynk, citezeyn de Norwyz, et William, soun frere, d'altre parte. Les choses d'une parte et d'altre finalment debatues, acordé est a la requeste et reverence l'onurable seignur, Monsieur Robert de Ufforde, counte de Suffolk, et pur le bon port et humilite le dit Richard, issint qe l'avaundit evesque ad relessé et, contentrement pur cestez lettres, quytclamé pur ly et soz successours, quanqe en ly est, a les susdys Richard et William et a lours heirs toutes maneres acciouns, cleymes, chalenges, et demaundes qeux vers les avaunditz Richard et William unqe avoit, ou aver poeit, de comencement de mounde taunque al iour de la confeccioun dy cestes. En tesmoygniance de quele chose, a ceste lettre de quytclamaunce le dit evesque adz mys soun seal. Doné a Dounham, manoir le dit evesque, le vintisme un iour de Maij, la an del regne le Roy Edward Tierce puys la conqueste vyntisme syme, e de soun reigne de Fraunce tresizime.

Nous avaundiz priour et covent avoumes auxint relessé et quitclamé a les suzdiz Richard et William a la requeste et reverence nostre treshonurable seignur, Monsieur Robert de Ufford, le counte de Suffolk, et avandits a lours heirs toutes maneres acciounes, cleymes, chalenges, et demaundes queux vers eux avoms, ou aver poems, del comencement de mounde taunque al iour de la confeccioun dy cestez, ratefiauns et confermaunz pur nos et noz successours a touz iours le dit reles et quitclamaunce pur nostre ditz piere evesque a les avantdiz Richard et William fetes. En tesmoigniaunce de qele chose, a cestes presentes lettres avomes mys le comun seal de capitre. Doné a Ely, le vintisme secounde iour de Maij, l'an del regne nostre seignur le Roy Edward Tierce puis la conqueste vyntisme syme, e de soun regne de Fraunce tresizime.

Chapter 5

Indictment of John de Lisle and others for the arson of Lady Wake's houses, and of Thomas de Lisle as accessory, before Sir John Dengayn at Huntingdon on 30 October 1354, and their appearance before the king's bench on 15 May 1355. Source: PRO, KB 27/379, rex m. 9.

Dominus rex mandavit justiciariis suis hic brevem suum clausum in hec verba:

Edwardus, Dei gracia rex Anglie et Francie et dominus Hibernie, dilectis et fidelibus suis Willelmo de Shareshull' et sociis suis justiciariis nostris ad placita coram nobis tenenda assignatis, salutem. Quoddam ind[i]c[t]amentum coram dilectos et fidelibus nostris Johanne Dengayne et socijs suis, custodibus pacis nostre et justiciariis nostris ad diversas felonias et transgressiones in comitatu Hunt' [Huntingdon] audiendas et terminandas assignatis, de quibusdam feloniis unde Johannes de Ile, frater Thome de Ile episcopi Elien' [Ely], et quidam alij indictati sunt et quod coram nobis in cancellaria nostra certis de causis venire fecimus, vobis mittimus sub pede sigilli nostri, mandantes quod, inspecto indictamento predicto, ulterius inde fieri faciatis quod de iure et secundum legem et consuetudinem regni nostri Anglie fore videritis faciendum. Teste me ipso apud Westm' [Westminster], xvij. die Februarii, anno regni nostri Anglie vicesimo nono, regni vero nostri Francie sextodecimo.

Breve prefato Johanni Dengayne inde directum sequitur in hec verba:

Edwardus, Dei gracia rex Anglie et Francie et dominus Hibernie, dilecto et fideli suo Johanni Dengayne, salutem. Volentes certis de causis coram nobis et consilio nostro propositis certiorari super quibusdam indictamentis factis coram vobis et sociis vestris, custodibus pacis nostre et justiciariis nostris ad diversas felonias et transgressiones in comitatu Hunt' [Huntingdon] audiendas et terminandas assignatis, de quibusdam felonijs unde Johannes de Isle, frater Thome episcopi Elien' [Ely], et quidam alij indictati sunt, ut dicitur, vobis mandamus quod indictamenta predicta, cum omnibus ea tangentibus, nobis in cancellariam nostram sub sigillo vestro distincte et aperte sine dilacione mittatis et hoc breve, ut ulterius inde facere valeamus quod de iure et secundum legem et consuetudinem regni nostri Anglie fore viderimus faciendum. Teste me ipso apud Hampstede Mareschal, xxvj. die Decembris, anno regni nostri Anglie vicesimo octavo, regni vero nostri Francie quintodecimo.

Indictamentum, de quo in brevibus predictis sit mencio, sequitur in hec verba:

Inquisicio capta apud Huntyngdon', die Jovis proximo ante festum Omnium Sanctorum, anno regni Regis Edwardi Tercij post conquestum vicesimo octavo, coram Johanne Dengayne et sociis suis, custodibus pacis ac justiciariis domini regis in dicto comitatu Hunt' [Huntingdon] assignatis ad diversas felonias et transgressiones audiendas et terminandas, et virtute littere dicti domini regis eisdem justiciariis specialiter directe, per sacramentum Johannis Sturdy, Henrici de Colne, Johannis Dengayne de Stilton', Johannis de Foderyngeye, Thome Mevyll', Walteri Wastel, Thome de Keterynge, Johannis Jolyf, Simonis Cok, Johannis filii Andrei de Stilton', Roberti del Wodehous, et Ricardi le Eir. Qui dicunt quod Johannes de Ile, frater Thome de Ile episcopi Elyens' [Ely], Frater Willelmus de Pecham (qui per cartam), Robertus de Codyngton' (qui per cartam), persona ecclesie de Newton' iuxta Wysbech', Thomas Durant, persona ecclesie de Stretham in Insula de Ely, Henricus de Schanketon' (qui per cartam), persona ecclesie de Haddestok, Stephanus de Brokesbourne, custos capelle Sancti Laurencii iuxta Wormeleye, Robertus Hale de Ereth', Johannes Balhorn' de Colne iuxta Somersham, Thomas de Baa, constabularius dicti episcopi de Wysebech', et Radulphus Carles, servientes predicti episcopi, die Lune proximo post festum Sancti Jacobi Apostoli, anno regni regis vicesimo octavo, noctanter, per assensum, procuracionem, et preceptum predicti Thome episcopi, clausum Blaunche Wake domine de Lydell' apud Colne iuxta Somersham felonice fregerunt, et quatuor domos, unam tassam de seggis, et unum equun [equum] cum cella et freno in eodem clauso, et unam cameram et portas subtus cameram dicte ipsius Blanche precij ducenti liberi [librarum] ibidem felonice combustos fuerunt et comburerunt, et quod predictus Thomas episcopus, sciens predictam combustionem per predictos servientes suos esse factam, dictos servientes apud Somersham postea receptavit, et cetera.

Per quod preceptum est vicecomiti quod venire faciat predictum episcopum, et eciam quod capiat predictos Johannem Ile et alios si, et cetera, et salvo, et cetera, ita quod habeat corpora eorum coram domino rege a die Sancte Trinitatis in xv. dies ubicumque, et cetera.

Per recordum de anno xxix.: Postea, scilicet in crastino Ascensionis Domini isto eodem termino, coram domino rege apud Westm' [Westminster] veniunt predicti Johannes de Ile, frater Thome de Ile, Frater Willelmus de Peccham, Robertus de Codyngton', Thomas Duraunt, Henricus de Shanketon', Stephanus de Brokesbourn', Robertus Halle, Johannes Balhorn', Thomas de Baa, et Radulphus Carles, veniunt per vicecomitem ducti, qui committuntur marescallo. Et statim per marescallum ducti veniunt. Et allocuti sunt separatim qualiter se velint de feloniis predictis acquietare. Dicunt separatim quod ipsi in nullo sunt inde culpabiles. Et de bono et malo ponunt se super patriam. Ideo veniat inde jurata coram domino rege in octabis Sancte Trinitatis ubicumque, et cetera, et qui, et cetera, ad recognoscere, et cetera. Et super hoc venierunt Johannes de Colville, chivaler de comitatu Cant' [Cambridge], Henricus de Waleys, chivaler de comitatu Kanc' [Kent], Johannes Bardulph', chivaler de comitatu Berk' [Berkshire], et Gerardus de Braybrok, chivaler, qui manuceperunt pro predictis Johanne Ile et alijs, habendi corpora eorum coram domino rege ad prefatum terminum, videlicet corpora pro corporibus, et cetera. Et ulterius de die in diem quousque, et cetera.

Thomas de Lisle appeals his conviction of the arson of Lady Wake's houses by suing a writ of error before the king's bench, Easter term 1355. Source: *Yearbooks*, 2–3, 29 Edward III, 30.

Un recorde et proces, qui fuit devant justices d'oier et terminer, fuit fait venir en bank le roy. Et le primer error qui fuit assigné, fuit que l'ou fuit supposé par le brief de trespas que le trespas se fist a Colle *juxta* Someresham [Colne *juxta* Somersham], Colle fuit un place en Someresham. Et ceo fuit challengé devant Green, un des justices, come le record prova. Et non obstant ilz fuerent mys oustre. Autre error, quant il avoit pleadé de rien coulpable, le *venire facias* issuit, et le record ne fist pz mencion devant quel des justices le brief fuit retournable. Le tiers error, quant l'evesque, qui ore sue, fuit atteint de le transgres, il ne fuit paz ajuge quel sereit pris, et issint error.

Thorp: Quant a le primer brief, vous troveres par record, que en countant le challenge quel vous ditz fuit allegé que cele fuit nomé et apellé en Angloys Colle beside Somershem' [Colne beside Somersham], quel chose fuit conu de vous, come le recorde prove. Purque depuis que le lieu est appellé per tiel nom en Angloys, et ceo plus de reason de changer le lieu en Latin en le brief que met le nom en Angloys, de la heure que c'est meme la signification: Car *juxta* en Latin est beside en Angloys; issint le brief fuyt bon.

Wich. [Witchingham]: Un surnome en Angloys, et autiel en Latin, n'est pz tout tempz d'un meme significacion: Car ceste parol *juxta* en Latin tout tempz est materiall, et suppose cele estre horz de Som' [Somersham]. Car ceo ne puit my estre en Someresham, que est supposé autre ville, ou autre lieu hors de Somersham. Et coment que ce soit nomé et appellé en Anglois beside S[omersham], ce n'est pz qu'un surnome adverbialiter, et non significative, pur qu'ils ne sont pas d'un meme entent.

Sch. [Shareshull]: Latin est un language formal de mettre en briefs, et Angloys est parlance de lays. Purque depuis que Latin comprent meme le significacion come fait le Angloys, nous le tenons tout un, et le recorde bon; (non obstant ce) quant a l'ascun error:

Fiff. [Fyffield]: Vous voyez bien comment le recorde est tiel a le comencement: *Placita coram Henrico Grenefield [Green] et aliis.* Et cele agardé que le *venire facias* duist issuer retornable a certein jour, fuit parcele de le plea. Donque quant tout le plea fuit tenu devant eux (come le recorde prove par le title), chescun parcele fuit, et par consent en certein devant quel le brief fuit retorné.

Wiche. [Witchingham]: Sir, il n'est pas ainsi de justices d'oier et terminer come de justices de l'un bauk [bank] ou de l'autre: Car tiels sont en certein, issint que le recorde ne fera pz mencion en tiel cas, come il covient que ce face cy. Car icy le commission est directé a iv., issint que si eux iv. ou iii. ou ii. puissent tenir le plea, issint que mesque le ii. qui ne furent al primer jour n'ussent pas esté la, a un auter jour les auters ii. puissit aver tenu le plea. Et de ce covient que le record fait mencion. Purque jeo di, qu'ils duissent aver fait mencion en lour recorde, devant quel de ceux le brief sera retornable. Et de ce qu'ils ne firent pz, il est error.

Sh[areshull]: Nous ne veirrons nul cause de revercer ce pas rien qu'est dit. Et quant a le terce point, c'est de nul valu. Purque tout fuit affirmé, et cetera.

Final execution of the judgment handed down on De Lisle's conviction of the arson of Lady Wake's houses, Trinity term 1355. The bishop contests Lady Wake's *elegit*, which is upheld, and he pays the £900 fine to the plaintiff. Source: *Yearbooks*, 2–3, 29 Edward III, 42.

La Dame de Wake (a que suit l'evesque d'Ely fuit atteint in brief de transgres a certein damages) pri l'*elegit*. Et touch fuit, que l'evesque est pere de la terre et prelate de Seint Eglise, qui n'avoit in effect forsque pur sa vie, et il ne sera pas reasonable de guarrantier verz luy le *elegit*. A que fuit dit que l'Estatue [of Westminster of 1285] fuit general, qui auxy avant lié pere de terre, come autre person: Car devers luy gist brief de wast et autrez briefs donnés par l'estatue, come devers autres. Et quant a l'autre point, ce n'est rien a purpose quil n'ad forsque a terme de vie: Car le baron qui n'ad pas forsque par counture, le terre sera liveré.

Th[orp]: Nous prioms pur le roy que ses temporalties soient seisis, depuis quil est atteinte de transgres incontre le peace, et il ne sera pas pris, come autre home, pur ce quil est prelate. Et pur le party prioms *elegit*. Et puis l'evesque manda toutz les deniers, et lez livera a le party in court. Et pria de fine faire, et le tendra, et cetera.

Lady Wake submits a petition to the king in parliament concerning the murder of her valet, William Holm, November 1355. The king responds by taking the quarrel into his hand. Source: *RP*, 2:267.

Et puis mist Dame Blaunche de Wake sa petition a nostre seignur le roi en mesme le parlement, en la fourme qui s'ensuyst:

A son tres doute seignur le roi requert humblement la sue lige Blaunche de Lidell', que desicome el n'ad nul recoverir apres nostre seignur que de lui en qi sa sovereigne affiancé est, que se pleint de l'evesque d'Ely et les soens, que encontre la pees et la lei de la terre ses mesons ont ars. De quele chose ele avoit recoverir par la lei a grant meschief pursuy sanz favour, et ele quidoit de celle heure en avant d'avoir en pees et repos pur lui et les soens. Et sur ceo la il pursui un atteint sur la petit dozeine, et en quele il estoit nounsuy en sa suyte demesne, a grant meschief et costages de la dite Blaunche, et autres bones gentz du pais, qui viendrent par brief et commandement nostre dit seignur le roi. Par quoi, monsieur, ele ad entendue, que l'avant dit evesque la poet ensi tarier et travailler a tote sa vie, a poi des damages et costages du dit evesque. De quele chose ele prie a nostre seignur le roi et a son tres bon conseil remedie, pur lui et pur autres qi purront escheir en ce cas.

Et puis, monsieur, furent ces mesmes gentz lesséz a mainprise, et les mainpernours estoient Seignur Gerard de Braybrok, Seignur Johan de Covill, Seignur Henry de Valoyns, et autres. Et en mesme le temps q'ils estoient en mainprise, ils tuerent William de Holme, malveisement en treson, entour la haute nounne, en boys de Somersham, vadlet la dite Blaunche. Par quoi ele requert humblement a nostre seignur le roi et a tut son bon conseil, q'ils voillent sur ceste chose ordiner qu'ele puisse vivre en pees et les soens, qar ils sont grantement manacéz de jour en autre.

Par quoi jeo requer a monsieur le roi, que s'il ne puisse deliverer bonement a cest foitz, q'il voille prendre entierment la querele en sa tres graciouse main, tant qu'il soit de leisir de trier, et qu'ele ne soit mye trié hors de sa presence. Ceo voillez tres honure seignur faire, pur l'amur de Dieu, a la requeste la dite Blaunche.

Quelle petition entendue, nostre seignur le roi ottrohi a la darreine clause de sa petition, et dist overtement, "Jeo prenk la querele en ma main."

Thomas de Lisle appears before the king's bench and pleads benefit of clergy in response to his indictment for complicity in the murder of William Holm, while the principals, Ralph Carles and Walter Ripton, are outlawed for nonappearance, 8 July 1356. On the following 6 October, the bishop is tried and convicted of the crime and handed over to his ordinary, Simon Islip, archbishop of Canterbury, while the court orders an inquest into his temporalities preparatory to seizure. Source: PRO, KB 27/384, rex m. 11d.

Jurati diversorum hundredorum comitatus predicti [of Huntingdon] alias coram Johanne Dengeyne et sociis suis, custodibus pacis et justiciariis ad diversas felonias et transgressiones in eodem comitatu audiendas et terminandas assignatis, presentaverunt quod Johannes de Ile, frater Thome de Ile episcopi Eliens' [Ely], Frater Willelmus de Pecham, Robertus de Codyngton', persona ecclesie de Newton' iuxta Wysbech', Thomas Durant, persona ecclesie de Stretham in Insula de Ely, Henricus de Schanketon', persona ecclesie de Haddestok, Stephanus de Brokesbourne, custos capelle Sancti Laurencii iuxta Wormeleye, Robertus Hale de Ereth', Johannes Balhorn' de Colne iuxta Somersham, Thomas de Baa, constabularius dicti episcopi de Wysebech', et Radulphus Carles, servientes predicti episcopi, die Lune proximo post festum Sancti Jacobi Apostoli, anno regni regis nunc Anglie vicesimo octavo, noctanter, per assensum, procuracionem, et preceptum predicti Thome episcopi, clausum Blaunche Wake domine de Lydell' apud Colne iuxta Somersham felonice fregerunt et quatuor domos, unam tassam de seggis, et unum equum cum cella et freno in eodem clauso, et unam cameram et portas subtus cameram dicte Blaunche, precij ducenti librarum, ibidem felonice combustos fuerunt et combuserunt. Et quod predictus Thomas episcopus, sciens predictam combustionem per predictos servientes suos esse factam, dictos servientes apud Somersham postea receptavit, et cetera.

Item coram vicecomite et coronatore eiusdem comitatus [of Huntingdon], virtute cuiusdam brevis domini regis sibi directi ad inquirendum de morte Willelmi Holme, et cetera, presentatum fuit quod, die Veneris proximo post festum Sancti Hugonis, anno regni regis nunc vicesimo nono, Radulphus Carelees et Walterus Ripton' dictus Littelwatte felonice interfecerunt Willelmum Holm apud Somersham in bosco iuxta Gunnoklye pro secta quam predictus Willelmus Holm fecit pro rege pro incendio manerij Blaunchie de Wake. Et dicunt quod Thomas episcopus Eliens' [Ely] fuit de assensu felonie predicte (ad istud articulum de morte jurati onerantur). Et eciam quod predictus Thomas episcopus Eliens' [Ely] predictos Radulphum et Walterum post feloniam factam in manerio suo de Somersham scienter receptavit, et ipsos felones, in propria persona cum hominibus suis armatis, salvos conduxit quousque limites comitatus Huntyngdon' pertransierunt. Que quidem indictamenta dominus rex coram eo certis de causis venire fecit [ad] terminanda, et cetera. Per quod preceptum fuit vicecomiti quod caperet predictum episcopum si, et cetera.

Et modo, scilicet a die Sancti Johannis Baptiste in xv. dies isto eodem termino, coram domino rege venit predictus episcopus hic in curiam in propria persona sua. Et quia predicti Johannes Balhorn', Radulphus Careles, et Walterus Ripton' de principalibus felonie indictati, et cetera, utlagati sunt, prout patet per returna brevium regis de isto eodem termino. Dictus episcopus, allocutus est qualiter de feloniis sibi impositis se velit acquietare, dicit quod ipse est membrum Sancte Ecclesie et episcopus unicus et frater domini sanctissimi pape, et cetera, et quod ipse absque ordinario suo, videlicet venerabile patre Domino Simone [Islip] archiepiscopo Cantuar' [Canterbury], tocius Anglie primate, coram laico iudice respondere non potest. Et super hoc idem archiepiscopus, presens hic in curia, petit quod dictus episcopus Eliens' [Ely] de feloniis predictis sibi impositis hic coram laico iudice non cogatur respondere, et cetera.

Et ut sciatur inde rei veritas per inquisicionem patrie, et cetera, preceptum est vicecomiti Hunt' [Huntingdon] quod venire faciat coram domino rege in octabas Sancti Michaelis ubicumque, et cetera, viginti et quatuor, et cetera, de viscinu [vicineto] de Somersham per quos, et cetera, et qui, et cetera. Idem dies datus est prefato episcopo, et cetera.

Ad quem diem coram domino rege venit predictus episcopus in propria persona sua, et similiter jurati veniunt, qui electi, triati, iurati, et onerati si idem episcopus de assensu predictorum Radulphi et Walteri et de receptamento eorundem sit culpabilis necne, dicunt super sacramentum suum quod idem episcopus de assensu predictorum Radulphi et Walteri in nullo est culpabilis, set dicunt quod idem episcopus, post feloniam illam de morte predicta factam, receptavit ipsos Radulphum et Walterum apud Somersham, sciens ipsos feloniam illam fecisse, prout superius presentatum est. Ideo inquiratur de bonis et catallis, terris et tenementis suis, et cetera. Et super hoc predictus archiepiscopus [of Canterbury, Simon Islip], presens hic in curia, petit ipsum episcopum tanquam membrum ecclesie sibi liberari, et cetera. Et ei liberatur salvo [ad] custodiendum prout decet, et cetera. Et memorandum quod brevia de inquirendo de bonis et catallis, terris et tenementis ipsius episcopi liberantur vicecomitibus London', Cant' [Cambridge], Hunt' [Huntingdon], Hertford', Essex', Norff' [Norfolk], et Suff' [Suffolk], retornabilia coram rege in crastino Sancti Martini ubicumque, et cetera.

Chapter 6

Thomas de Lisle writes a letter of petition to Pope Innocent VI, in which he appeals his imminent conviction of complicity in the murder of William Holm to the "sacred palace of the auditors of causes" ("sacri palacij causarum auditorum") at Avignon, undated. Source: LPL, Reg. Islip, fols. 138v–139r. Words in brackets are from LAO, Episcopal Reg. VIII, fols. 93r–v.

Exponitur sanctitati vestre pro parte devote creature vestre Domini Thome episcopi Elien' [Ely] quod Nicholas de Stivekle [Stivecle], Ricardus de Swinarton' [Swynarton'], canonicus Lincoln', Henricus de Walton', archidiaconus Richemundie, Walterus de Carleton', rector ecclesie de Depyngg' [Deping'] Lincoln' diocesis, Simon de Drayton, miles, Willelmus de Siwardbi [Siwardeby], Johannes de Stivekle [Stivecle], Lucas de Burgo, Johannes Repinghale [Repynghale], Johannes Knyvet, Thomas de Chaleres [Deschalers] et eius filius, milites, Thomas Scot', Robertus de Walteschef' [Waldeschef'], Johannes de Harwedon', et alij eorum complices et fautores eidem episcopo op[p]ido infesti, ipsum de et super criminibus effraccionis domorum et clausorum, incendij nocturni, furti, et receptacione occisorum, furium [furum] et latronum apud bonos et graves nequiter et maliciose diffamarunt [defamarunt]. Et ipsum et Johannem de Insula, fratrem suum clericum, Willelmum de Peccham, fratrem ordinis predicatorum socium suum, Robertum de Godington' [Godyngton'], rectorem ecclesie de Neuton', Thomam Darent, rectorem ecclesie de Stretham, Henricum de Schanketon', rectorem ecclesie de Hadestoke, Stephanum de Brokesbourne [Brokesburn'], custodem capelle Sancti Laurencij iuxta Vormele [Wormele], Robertum Hale de Hereth [Hereth'], Johannem Balhorn' de Colne, Thomam de Baa, constabularium de Wisebech', et Radulphum Carles, familiares et servitores suos, procurarunt et fecerunt coram Dominis Johanne Dengaine [Dengayne], Henrico Grene, Roberto de Torp' [Thorp'], militibus, per quasdam inquisiciones clamdestinas, ipsis ad eas non vocatis set absentibus et indefensis per quosdam emulos suos laicos viles et diffamatas [defamatas] personas et criminosas, videlicet Johannem de Deen [Den'], Radulphum Chamberlayn [Chaumbirlayn], Thomam de Ereth', Willelmum Hartehale [atte Halle], Johannem Colne, Henricum Mateshale [Mateschall'], Johannem Emmeson [Emmesson'], Johannem Moun [Youn], Nicholaum Bray, Galfridum Hildegare [Hildegar], Willelmum Boteller' [Boteler], Johannem Lord', Ricardum White, Adam

Mannyng' [Maning'], Andream Keleshull', Johannem Huse, Johannem Sturdy [Sturdi], Henricum de Colne, Johannem de Colne, Johannem Dengaine [Dengayne] de Stilton', et eorum et cuiuslibet eorum complices et fautores factas super criminibus premissis indictari et falso deferri.

Ac ipsum et familiares suos, equites, et pedites cum eo apud Sanctum Yvonem L[incoln' diocesis ar]estari et detineri et quosdam ex ipsis de equis suis ad terram prosterni, verberari, et vestibus suis lacerari, ac omnia hernesia sua capi et detineri. Et propter huiusmodi incendia falso sibi imposita in curia seculari in mille trecentis et quinquaginta marcis sterlingorum per falsos testes et pecunia corruptos et super hoc confessos, videlicet Ricardum de Baiouse, Thomam de Stivekle [Stivecle], Robertum de Baiouse, Johannem [de] Tilly, milites, Ricardum Fuitz, Rogerum de Hurst', Johannem Souche, Willelmum de Felkesworth' [Folkesworth'], Robertum de Huntingdon' [Huntyngdon'], falso condempnari ad solucionem earundem [eorundem] et contra statuta regni Anglie compelli minus iuste, necnon in iniuriam et contumeliam ipsius, Johannem de Insula fratrem suum, et Willelmum de Pecceham [Peccham], fratrem predicatorum socium suum, ac Robertum, Thomam, Henricum, et Stephanum et alios clericos et beneficiatos predictos, et in possessione clericatus notorie existentes, familiares, et servientes suos per quos statum suum et ecclesie sue predicte regere consuevit, ut ipse auxilio et remedio eorundem esset penitus destitutus, per annum et dimidium iam effluxos incarcerari, et in carcere detineri, ac bona sua ecclesiastica et infra solum ecclesiasticum constituta per ministros curie secularis occupari et ea per ipsos rapi et destrui et consumi, et servientes et familiares suos verberari et male tractari, et de servicio suo ammoveri et expelli, ac ipsum episcopum per breve regium capi et eum in carcere regio salvo custodiri, et ad certum terminum ad respondendum domino regi predicto super premissis criminibus coram Domino Willelmo de Schareshull', Willelmo de Torp [Thorp'], Willelmo de Notton', militibus, contra canonicas sanctiones et eciam statuta regni Anglie, ad quorum observanciam omnes maiores regni eiusdem per iuramenta sua sunt astricti, trahi, et presentari.

Et quia non habuerunt falsos testes, ibidem paratos ad ipsum de falso convincendum super premissis, terminum predictum usque ad octabas Sancti Michaelis proximas iam futuras per ipsos prorogari, et illum terminum sibi pro termino peremptorie assignari, ac sibi per breve regium ac eciam in pleno parl[i]amento, sub pena forisfaccionis et perdicionis omnium bonorum ecclesie sue mobilium et inmobilium et que forisfacere posset erga dominum regem, ne regnum Anglie quovis modo exeat et ad Romanam curiam se transferat prohiberi. In quo quidem termino idem episcopus verisimuliter [verisimiliter] timet quod nisi per sanctitatis vestre graciam eidem celerius succuratur, ad bonorum suorum omnium et ecclesie sue predicte mobilium et inmobilium confiscacionem, et eciam persone sue bannicionem [banicionem] de regno Anglie procedatur, aliaque varia et diversa gravamina, dispendia, dampna, iniurias, et contumelias [violencias] realia et personalia sibi et ecclesie sue ac suis intulerunt et irrogarunt, sive procurarunt et fecerunt inferri et irrogari.

Et licet ipse sepius et cum maxima instancia requisiverit venerabiles patres, dominos archiepiscopum Cant' [Canterbury] metropolitanum suum, ac Lincoln' et London' episcopos, in quorum provincia et diocesibus premissa facinora contra ipsum fuerunt et sunt perpetrata, quod contra prefatos malefactores et ecclesiastice libertatis violatores notorios procedere[n]t, prout dictaret ordo iuris, ipsi tamen seu aliquis eorundem contra ipsos malefactores seu eorum aliquem ex officio suo seu ad partis instanciam procedere vel aliquos processus contra ipsos facere non curarunt, set recusarunt expresse, propterque omnia et singula premissa, idem episcopus dampnificatus est in decem milibus marcis sterlingorum et ultra, in preiudicium Ecclesie et ecclesiastice libertatis, cleri scandalum, ac Christi fidelibus perniciosum exemplum, et Sancte Romane Ecclesie et sanctitatis vestre manifestum contemptum, et ipsius episcopi et ecclesie sue iniuriam et grave dispendium et iacturam, et contra eorum iuramenta per que ad Sancte Matris Ecclesie iura et libertates defendenda et servanda necessario sunt astricti.

Supplicat igitur idem episcopus quatinus causas, quas super premissis excessibus tam enormibus commissis presertim in episcopum et in personam eiusdem ac Elien' [Ely] et tocius universalis Ecclesie et eorum, omni occasione monere vult et intendit communiter vel divisim contra predictos superius nominatos et eorum complices et fautores, eciam coniunctim et divisim committere dignemini audiendas et decidendas cum emergentibus, dependentibus, et connexis alicui ex reverentis patribus dominis auditoribus cum potestate citandi predictos, ut coram eo compareant pro demeritis recepturis, et eciam per edictum in valvis ecclesie Avinion' [Avignon] et alibi, si et ubi eidem videbitur affigendum, ut per ipsum perinde sint artati, ac si ad eos et eorum quemlibet citacio pervenisset si eidem per informacionem constiterit de infamia predictorum, cum idem episcopus non audeat nec speret aliter consequi iusticie complementum, ut eciam ex narratis superius postest liquide deprehendi.

Letter from Pope Innocent VI to King Edward III, urging an end to the dispute between him and Bishop Thomas de Lisle, 25 January 1359. Source: ASV, Registra Vaticana 240, Innocent VI, fols. 16d.–17d. (from a microfilm in the Seeley Historical Library, Cambridge).

Carissimo in Christo filio Eduardo regi Anglie illustri, salutem, et cetera.
    Celsitudinis tue litteras pridie paterna benignitate recepimus, earumque

diligenter intellecta serie tenore presentium respondemus. Siquidem, carissime fili, per dilectum filium Adam de Hilton' secretarium tuum, nostre recommendationis litteras Gallico sermone confectas pro venerabile fratre nostro Thoma episcopo Elien' [Ely] et sua Elien' ecclesia tibi meminimus destinasse, excellentiam tuam rogantes attentius per easdem, quatinus [quatenus] prefatos episcopum et ecclesiam susciperes benignitate regia commendatos. Verum prout ad nostras aures insinuatio fidedigna perduxit antequam ad nos predicte tue littere pervenirent, quod non sine admiratione percepimus plurique officiales et ministri tui nonnulla gravamina et iniurias, perturbationes etiam plurimas, et jacturas eidem episcopo seu officialibus et familiaribus suis et sue Elien' [Ely] ecclesie intulerunt, et inferre continuo temerarijs ausibus non desistunt, in grandem divine maiestatis offensam, proprie salutis dispendium et lesionem non modicam ecclesiastice libertatis. Nos igitur, attendentes illud maxime ad tue magnitudinis titulum pertinere ut, pro reverentia Regis Regum, ecclesias et ecclesiasticas personas non solum ab opprimentibus in regno tuo defendas, sed illis etiam, tamque princeps Catholicus et a progenitorum tuorum laudabilibus semitis non declinans, honorificentia debita favorabiliter prosequaris, serenitatem tuam, quam talia equanimiter ferre non decet, rogandam propensius duximus et hortandam, in remissione tibi peccaminum suadentes, quatinus [quatenus] divine pietatis intuitu ac pro nostra et apostolice sedis reverentia, episcopum predictum, utique devotum et fidelem tuum ac exaltationis regie zelatorem et tuis invigilare obsequijs et honoribus ardentius cupientem, sub tue gratie protectione suscipiens, et indignationis cuiuscumque conceptum, sique forte adversus eundem tuo ingesserit animo lingua detrahentium susurronum, de innate tibi affluentia pietatis astergens, super bonis et iuribus suis et sue ecclesie prelibate ab officialibus regijs vel quibusvis alijs tibi subiectis predictas inferri molestias non permittas, sic in premissis magnificentie ac mansuetudinis tue presidium laudabiliter impensurum, ut apud eterni Regis filium, qui exhibita uni ex minimis suis beneficia sibi potius quam illis ascripsit, cumulo meritorum crescas ac proinde tibi humane laudis incrementa proveniant. Neque super hijs de cetero apud nos expediat partes advocari justitie, in qua, cum ex iniuncto nobis de super licet immeritis apostolatus officio, facti simus omnibus debitores, negare illam petentibus non possemus, licet speremus quod taliter in predictis regia benignitas remedium celeris provisionis apponet.

Idemque episcopus a Deo nostris monitis acquiescet quod, justitie locum tua preoc[c]upante clementia, huiusmodi querelarum materia sopietur, tueque erga illum gratie restituetur integritas, et eius erga te sincere fidelitatis obsequia uberius subsequentur. Super premissis autem predictus secretarius tuus, lator presentium, intentionis nostre seriem, prout a nobis accepit, magnitudini tue poterit vive vocis oraculo diligentius aperire. Datum Avinion' [Avignon] viij. kalendas Februarij, anno septimo.

Bibliography

Manuscript Sources

Corpus Christi College, Cambridge
    Archives: XXVII-9, XXVII-17, XXVII-20, XXVII-21
    Library: MS 287

Gonville and Caius College, Cambridge
    Archives: RM I.11, RM I.25
    Library: MS 253/497

King's College, Cambridge
    Library: MS 15, "A Common-Place Book"

Pembroke College, Cambridge
    Archives: Box A.2

Peterhouse, Cambridge
    Treasury: Register Vetus

University Library (CUL), Cambridge
    Ely Diocesan Records (EDR):
        D 7: Wisbech Castle Manorial Accounts
        D 8: Wisbech Barton Manorial Accounts
        D 10: Downham Manorial Accounts
        G/I/1: Registers of Simon Montacute and Thomas de Lisle, 1337–61
        G/3/27: Liber R, The "Old Coucher" Book
    Maps.bb.36.64.2: Map from H. Hondius and J. Janson, *A General Plott and Description of the Fennes, etc.* (Amsterdam, 1646)

Lincolnshire Archives Office (LAO), Lincoln
Episcopal Register VIII: Register of John Gynwell, 1347–62 (from microfilm MS 8232 in the CUL)

British Library, London
    Additional Charter 33657
    Additional MSS 5822, 33491, 41612, 47680
    Cotton MS Cleopatra E.II

Cotton MS Nero A.XVI
Cotton MS Titus A.I
Seal LV 35
Seal LV 36

Lambeth Palace Library, London
  MS 448: *Chronica et Memoranda Eliensia*
  Register of Simon Islip

Public Record Office, London
  C 66: Chancery Patent Rolls
  C 84: Ecclesiastical Petitions
  CP 25: Feet of Fines
  CP 40: Court of Common Pleas, Plea Rolls
  E 143: Exchequer, King's Remembrancer, Extents and Inquisitions
  E 159: Exchequer, King's Remembrancer, Memoranda Rolls
  E 199: Exchequer, King's Remembrancer, Sheriffs' Accounts
  E 403: Exchequer of Receipt, Issue Rolls
  JUST 1: Justices Itinerant, Assize Rolls
  JUST 3: Justices Itinerant, Gaol Delivery Rolls
  KB 27: Court of King's Bench, *Coram Rege* Rolls
  PRO 31/7: Record Commission Transcripts, Series 1
  SC 8: Ancient Petitions.

Norfolk Record Office, Norwich
  Domesday Book
  Norwich City Records
  Norwich Private Deeds
  Old Free Book

Archivio Segreto Vaticano, Rome
  Registra Vaticana: 139, Clement VI; 239, Innocent VI; 240, Innocent VI (from
    microfilms in the Seeley Historical Library, Cambridge)

Primary Sources

Anglia Sacra, ed. H. Wharton, 2 vols. (London, 1691).
Anglo-Norman Political Songs, ed. I.S.T. Aspin (Oxford, 1953).
Annales Monastici, ed. H. R. Luard, 5 vols. (RS, XXXVI, 1864–69).
Bracton, Henry de, *De Legibus et Consuetudinibus Anglie*, ed. G. E. Woodbine,
    4 vols. (New Haven, 1915–42).
The Brut, or The Chronicles of England, ed. F.W.D. Brie, 2 vols. (Early English
    Text Society, 1906–8).
*Calendar of the Close Rolls Preserved in the Public Record Office: Edward III, 1327–
    1377*, 14 vols. (London, 1896–1913).

Calendar of Entries in the Papal Registers Relating to Great Britain and Ireland: Papal Letters, 14 vols. (London, 1893–1960).

Calendar of Entries in the Papal Registers Relating to Great Britain and Ireland: Petitions to the Pope, 1342–1419, 1 vol. (London, 1896).

Calendar of the Fine Rolls Preserved in the Public Record Office, 22 vols. (London, 1911–62).

Calendar of the Patent Rolls Preserved in the Public Record Office: Edward III, 1327–1377, 16 vols. (London, 1891–1916).

Canterbury Professions, ed. M. Richter (CYS, LXVII, 1972–73).

Cartularium Monasterii de Rameseia, ed. W. H. Hart and P. A. Lyons, 3 vols. (RS, LXXIX, 1884–93).

Chaucer, Geoffrey, *Complete Works*, ed. W. W. Skeat, 7 vols. (Oxford, 1894–97).

Chronicon Abbatiae Rameseiensis, ed. W. D. Macray (RS, LXXXIII, 1886).

Chronicon Angliae, 1328–1388, ed. E. M. Thompson (RS, LXIV, 1874).

Clement VI (1342–52): Lettres Closes, Patentes et Curiales Intéressant les Pays Autres que la France, ed. E. Déprez and G. Mollat (Paris, 1960).

Early Registers of Writs, ed. E. de Haas and G.D.G. Hall (SS, LXXXVII, 1970).

Foedera, Conventiones, Litterae et Cujuscunque Generis Acta Publica, ed. T. Rymer et al., 3 vols. in 6 parts (London, 1816–30).

Fortescue, Sir John, *The Governance of England*, ed. C. Plummer (Oxford, 1885).

Froissart, Jean, *Chronicles*, trans. G. Brereton (Harmondsworth, Middlesex, 1968).

Gower, John, *The Major Latin Works*, trans. E. W. Stockton (Seattle, 1962).

Gray, Sir Thomas, *Scalacronica*, trans. H. Maxwell (Glasgow, 1907).

Guisborough, Walter de, *Chronicle*, ed. H. Rothwell (Camden Society, 3d series, LXXXIX, 1957).

Historical Poems of the Fourteenth and Fifteenth Centuries, ed. R. H. Robbins (New York, 1959).

Hoccleve, Thomas, *The Regement of Princes, A.D. 1411–12*, ed. F. J. Furnivall (Early English Text Society, 1897).

Joinville, Jean de, and Geoffrey de Villehardouin, *Chronicles of the Crusades*, trans. M.R.B. Shaw (Harmondsworth, Middlesex, 1963).

Knighton, Henry, *Chronicon*, ed. J. R. Lumby, 2 vols. (RS, XCII, 1889–95).

Langland, William, *Piers Plowman: An Edition of the C-Text*, ed. D. Pearsall (Berkeley and Los Angeles, 1979).

Liber Assisarum et Placitorum Corone, ed. J. Rastell (London, 1513).

Murimuth, Adam, *Continuatio Chronicarum Robertus de Avesbury, de Gestis Mirabilibus Regis Edwardi Tertii*, ed. E. M. Thompson (RS, XCIII, 1889).

"The 'Nativity' Roll of Arms, Temp. Edward I," ed. J. Greenstreet, *The Reliquary* 15 (1874–75), 228–30.

Opera Hactenus Inedita Rogeri Baconi, ed. Robert Steele, 16 vols. (Oxford, 1909–40).

Paris, Matthew, *Chronica Majora*, ed. H. R. Luard, 7 vols. (RS, LVII, 1872–83).

The Paston Letters, ed. J. G. Gairdner, 3 vols. (London, 1896).

Political Poems and Songs relating to English History, ed. T. Wright, 2 vols. (RS, XIV, 1859–61).

The Political Songs of England, ed. T. Wright (Camden Society, 1839).

Reading, John de, *Chronica Johannis de Reading et Anonymi Cantuariensis*, ed. J. Tait (Manchester, 1914).

The Records of the City of Norwich, ed. W. Hudson and J. C. Tingey, 2 vols. (Norwich, 1906–10).

The Register of John de Grandisson, Bishop of Exeter, A.D. 1327–1369, ed. F. C. Hingeston-Randolph, 3 vols. (London, 1894–99).

The Register of William Edington, Bishop of Winchester, 1346–1366, ed. S. F. Hockey, 2 vols. (Hampshire Record Series nos. 7–8, 1986–87).

The Registers of John de Sandale and Rigaud de Asserio, Bishops of Winchester, 1316–1323, ed. F. J. Baigent (London, 1897).

Registrum Johannis de Trillek, Episcopi Herefordensis, A.D. 1344–1361, ed. J. H. Parry (CYS, VIII, 1912).

Registrum Thome de Charlton, Episcopi Herefordensis, A.D. 1327–1344, ed. W. W. Capes (CYS, IX, 1913).

Reports from the Lords' Committees for All Matters Touching the Dignity of a Peer of the Realm, 4 vols. (London, 1826).

Rishanger, William, *Chronica et Annales, 1259–1307*, ed. H. T. Riley (RS, XXVIiI, 1865).

Romanus, Aegidius, *De Regimine Principum* (Rome, 1556).

Rotuli Parliamentorum, 6 vols. (London, 1783–1832).

Rymes of Robin Hood, ed. R. B. Dobson and J. Taylor (London, 1976).

Sacrist Rolls of Ely, ed. F. R. Chapman, 2 vols. (Cambridge, 1907).

Select Cases in the Court of King's Bench, ed. G. O. Sayles, 7 vols. (SS, LV, LVII, LVIII, LXXIV, LXXVI, LXXXII, LXXXVIII, 1936–71).

Statutes of the Realm, 11 vols. (London, 1810–28).

Taxatio Ecclesiastica Angliae et Walliae Auctoritate P. Nicholai IV, circa A.D. 1291 (London, 1802).

Valor Ecclesiasticus Temp. Henr. VIII Auctoritate Regia Institutus, 6 vols. (London, 1810–34).

Walsingham, Thomas, *Historia Anglicana*, ed. H. T. Riley, 2 vols. (RS, XXVIII, 1863–64).

The Westminster Chronicle, 1381–1394, ed. L. C. Hector and B. F. Harvey (Oxford, 1982).

Year Books of Edward II, ed. F. W. Maitland, 2 vols. (SS, XVII, 1903).

Yearbooks: Les Reports des Cases en Ley, ed. R. Brooke and A. Fitzherbert, black letter edition, 11 vols. (London, 1678–80).

Secondary Sources

Aberth, J. S., "The Black Death in the Diocese of Ely: The Evidence of the Bishop's Register," *Journal of Medieval History* 21, no. 3 (1995), 275–87.

———, "Crime and Justice under Edward III: The Case of Thomas de Lisle," *EHR* 107 (1992), 283–301.

———, "A Medieval Norwich Feud: The Bitter Dispute between Richard Spynk and Thomas de Lisle, Bishop of Ely," *Norfolk Archaeology* 82 (1992), 294–304.

———, "Thomas de Lisle, Bishop of Ely, 1345–61: Edward III's Turbulent Priest" (Ph.D. diss., Cambridge, 1992).

Adams, N., "The Writ of Prohibition to Court Christian," *Minnesota Law Review* 20 (1935–36), 272–93.

Allmand, C., *Henry V* (Berkeley and Los Angeles, 1992).

———, *The Hundred Years War: England and France at War, c. 1300–c. 1450* (Cambridge, 1988).

Aston, M., *Thomas Arundel: A Study of Church Life in the Reign of Richard II* (Oxford, 1967).

Aston, T. H., P. R. Coss, C. Dyer, and J. Thirsk, eds., *Social Relations and Ideas: Essays in Honour of R. H. Hilton* (Cambridge, 1983).

Baker, J. H., *An Introduction to English Legal History*, 3d edition, 2 vols. (London, 1990).

Baldwin, A. P., *The Theme of Government in Piers Plowman* (Cambridge and Woodbridge, Suffolk, 1981).

Bale, J., *Scriptorum Illustrium Maioris Brytanniae Catalogus*, 2 vols. in 1 (Basle, 1557–59).

Barnie, J., *War in Medieval English Society: Social Values in the Hundred Years War, 1337–99* (Ithaca, N.Y., 1974).

Barron, O., ed., *The Victoria History of the Counties of England: Northamptonshire Families* (London, 1906).

Bean, J.M.W., *The Decline of English Feudalism, 1215–1540* (Manchester, 1968).

———, *From Lord to Patron: Lordship in Late Medieval England* (Manchester, 1989).

Bedford, W.K.R., *The Blazon of Episcopacy* (Oxford, 1897).

Bellamy, J. G., *Bastard Feudalism and the Law* (London, 1989).

———, "The Coterel Gang: An Anatomy of a Band of Fourteenth-Century Criminals," *EHR* 79 (1964), 698–717.

———, *Crime and Public Order in England in the Later Middle Ages* (London, 1973).

———, *The Law of Treason in England in the Later Middle Ages* (Cambridge, 1970).

———, *Robin Hood: An Historical Enquiry* (London, 1985).

Bennett, M. J., *Community, Class and Careerism: Cheshire and Lancashire Society in the Age of Sir Gawain and the Green Knight* (Cambridge, 1983).

Bentham, J., *The History and Antiquities of the Conventual and Cathedral Church of Ely* (Cambridge, 1771).

Blatcher, M., "The Workings of the Court of King's Bench in the Fifteenth Century" (Ph.D. diss., London, 1936).

Bolton, J. L., *The Medieval English Economy, 1150–1500* (London, N.J., 1980).

Born, L. K., "The Perfect Prince: A Study of Thirteenth- and Fourteenth-Century Ideals," *Speculum* 3 (1928), 470–504.

Brand, P., *The Making of the Common Law* (London: Hambledon, 1992).

Brault, G. J., *Early Blazon, Heraldic Terminology in the Twelfth and Thirteenth Centuries with Special Reference to Arthurian Literature* (Oxford, 1972).

Buck, M., *Politics, Finance and the Church in the Reign of Edward II: Walter Stapeldon, Treasurer of England* (Cambridge, 1983).

Burke, B., *The General Armory of England, Scotland, Ireland and Wales* (London, 1884).

Burns, C., "Sources of British and Irish History in the Instrumenta Miscellanea of the Vatican Archives," *Archivum Historiae Pontificiae* 9 (1971), 7–141.

Butler, L. H., "Archbishop Melton, His Neighbours, and His Kinsmen, 1317–1340," *Journal of Ecclesiastical History* 2 (1951), 54–67.

———, "Robert Braybrooke, Bishop of London (1381–1404), and His Kinsmen," (D.Phil. diss., Oxford, 1952).

Butt, R., *A History of Parliament: The Middle Ages* (London, 1989).

Cam, H. M. and G. Barraclough, eds., *Crown, Community and Parliament* (Oxford, 1951).

Cantor, N. F., *The English: A History of Politics and Society to 1760* (New York, 1969).

Carpenter, D. A., "Debate: Bastard Feudalism Revised: Comment 2," *Past and Present*, no. 131 (1991), 177–89.

Carpenter, M. C., "The Beauchamp Affinity: A Study of Bastard Feudalism at Work," *EHR* 95 (1980), 515–32.

———, "The Fifteenth-Century English Gentry and their Estates," in M. Jones, ed., *Gentry and Lesser Nobility in Late Medieval Europe* (Gloucester, 1986), 36–60.

———, "Law, Justice and Landowners in Late Medieval England," *Law and History Review* 1, no. 2 (1983), 205–37.

———, *Locality and Polity: A Study of Warwickshire Landed Society, 1401–1499* (Cambridge, 1992).

Carus-Wilson, E. M., ed., *Essays in Economic History*, 3 vols. (London, 1954–62).

Cheney, C. R., ed., *Handbook of Dates for Students of English History* (London, 1978).

Cherry, M., "The Courtenay Earls of Devon: The Formation and Disintegration of a Late Medieval Aristocratic Affinity," *Southern History* 1 (1979), 71–97.

———, "The Struggle for Power in Mid-Fifteenth Century Devonshire," in R. A. Griffiths, ed., *Patronage, the Crown and the Provinces in Later Medieval England* (Gloucester, 1981), 123–44.

Cokayne, G. E., *The Complete Peerage of England, Scotland, Ireland, Great Britain and the United Kingdom*, rev. V. Gibbs et al., new edition, 13 vols. (London, 1910–59).

Coldstream, N., "Ely Cathedral: The Fourteenth-Century Work," in N. Coldstream and P. Draper, eds., *Medieval Art and Architecture at Ely Cathedral* (The British Archaeological Association Conference Transactions 2, 1979), 28–46.

———, and P. Draper, eds., *Medieval Art and Architecture at Ely Cathedral* (British Archaeological Association Conference Transactions 2, 1979).

Coleman, J., *English Literature in History, 1350–1400: Medieval Readers and Writers* (London, 1981).

Coss, P. R., "Bastard Feudalism Revised," *Past and Present*, no. 125 (1989), 27–64.

———, "Reply," *Past and Present*, no. 131 (1991), 190–203.

Crouch, D., "Debate: Bastard Feudalism Revised: Comment 1," *Past and Present*, no. 131 (1991), 165–77.

Crown, Community and Parliament, ed. H. M. Cam and G. Barraclough (Oxford, 1951).

Dahmus, J. H., *William Courtenay: Archbishop of Canterbury, 1381–1396* (University Park, Pa., 1966).

Davies, R. G., "Alexander Neville, Archbishop of York, 1374–1388," *Yorkshire Archaeological Journal* 47 (1975), 87–101.

Delachenal, R., *Histoire de Charles V*, 5 vols. (Paris, 1909–31).

Déprez, E., "La Conférence d'Avignon, 1344: L'Arbitrage Pontifical Entre la France et l'Angleterre," in A.G. Little and F.M. Powicke, eds., *Essays in Medieval History Presented to Thomas Frederick Tout* (Manchester, 1925), 301–20.

A Dictionary of British Surnames, ed. P. H. Reaney, and rev. R. M. Wilson, 2d edition (Sheffield, 1976).

Dictionary of National Biography, ed. L. Stephen and S. Lee, 63 vols. (London, 1885–1900).

A Dictionary of Surnames, ed. P. Hanks and F. Hodges (Oxford, 1988).

Dictionnaire de Droit Canonique, ed. R. Naz et al., 6 vols. (Paris, 1935–57).

Dobson, R. B., and J. Taylor, "The Medieval Origins of the Robin Hood Legend: A Reassessment," *Journal of Northern History* 7 (1972), 1–30.

——, *Rymes of Robyn Hood: An Introduction to the English Outlaw* (Gloucester, 1989).

Dyer, C., "The Social and Economic Background to the Rural Revolt of 1381," in R. H. Hilton and T. H. Aston, eds., *The English Rising of 1381* (Cambridge, 1984), 9–42.

Edwards, G., *The Second Century of the English Parliament* (Oxford, 1979).

Emden, A. B., *A Biographical Register of the University of Cambridge to 1500* (Cambridge, 1963).

England in the Fourteenth Century: Proceedings of the 1985 Harlaxton Symposium, ed. W. M. Ormrod (Woodbridge, Suffolk, 1986).

The English Government at Work, 1327–1336, ed. J. F. Willard, W. A. Morris, J. R. Strayer, and W. H. Dunham, Jr., 3 vols. (Cambridge, Mass., 1940–50).

The English Rising of 1381, ed. R. H. Hilton and T. H. Aston (Cambridge, 1984).

Essays in Economic History, ed. E. M. Carus-Wilson, 3 vols. (London, 1954–62).

Essays in Medieval History Presented to Thomas Frederick Tout, ed. A. G. Little and F. M. Powicke (Manchester, 1925).

Evelyn-White, C. H., "The Bridge and Bridge Chapel of St. Ives, Huntingdonshire," *Transactions of the Cambridgeshire and Huntingdonshire Archaeological Society* 1 (1904), 77–85.

Flahiff, G. B., "The Writ of Prohibition to Court Christian in the Thirteenth Century: Part I," *Mediaeval Studies* 6 (1944), 261–313.

Fowler, K., *The King's Lieutenant: Henry of Grosmont, First Duke of Lancaster, 1310–1361* (London, 1969).

Fryde, N., "A Medieval Robber Baron: Sir John Molyns of Stoke Poges, Buckinghamshire," in R. F. Hunnisett and J. B. Post, eds., *Medieval Legal Records Edited in Memory of C.A.F. Meekings* (London, 1978), 198–207.

Gabel, L. C., *Benefit of Clergy in England in the Later Middle Ages* (Northampton, Mass., 1928–29).

Gentry and Lesser Nobility in Late Medieval Europe, ed. M. Jones (Gloucester and New York, 1986).

Girard, J., *Evocation du Vieil Avignon* (Paris, 1958).

Given, J. B., *Society and Homicide in Thirteenth-Century England* (Stanford, 1977).

Given-Wilson, C., *The English Nobility in the Late Middle Ages: The Fourteenth-Century Political Community* (London, 1987).

Godwin, F., *A Catalogue of the Bishops of England* (London, 1601).

Goodman, A., *John of Gaunt: The Exercise of Princely Power in Fourteenth-Century Europe* (Harlow, Essex, 1992).

Graves, E. B., "The Legal Significance of the Statute of Praemunire of 1353," in C. H. Taylor and J. L. La Monte, eds., *Haskins Anniversary Essays in Medieval History* (Boston, 1929), 57–80.

Green, T. A., "The Jury and the English Law of Homicide, 1200–1600," *Michigan Law Review* 74 (1975–76), 414–99.

Griffiths, R. A., ed., *Patronage, the Crown and the Provinces in Later Medieval England* (Gloucester, 1981).

Guy, J. A., and H. G. Beale, eds., *Law and Social Change in British History: Papers Presented to the Bristol Legal History Conference* (London, 1984).

Haines, R. M., *The Administration of the Diocese of Worcester in the First Half of the Fourteenth Century* (London, 1965).

———, *Archbishop John Stratford: Political Revolutionary and Champion of the Liberties of the English Church* (Toronto, 1986).

———, *The Church and Politics in Fourteenth-Century England: The Career of Adam Orleton, 1275–1345* (Cambridge, 1978).

———, *Ecclesia Anglicana: Studies in the English Church of the Later Middle Ages* (Toronto, 1989).

Hamil, F. C., "The King's Approvers: A Chapter in the History of English Criminal Law," *Speculum* 11 (1936), 238–58.

Hanawalt, B. A., "Community Conflict and Social Control: Crime and Justice in the Ramsey Abbey Villages," *Mediaeval Studies* 39 (1977), 402–23.

———, *Crime and Conflict in English Communities, 1300–1348* (Cambridge, Mass., 1979).

———, "Fur-Collar Crime: The Pattern of Crime among the Fourteenth-Century English Nobility," *Journal of Social History* 8, no. 4 (1975), 1–17.

Handbook of Dates for Students of English History, ed. C. R. Cheney (London, 1978).

Handlist of Parliamentary and Council Proceedings (C 49) in the Round Room of the PRO.

Harding, A., *The Law Courts of Medieval England* (London, 1973).

Harvey, P.D.A., *Cuxham Manorial Records* (Oxford Record Society, 1976).

———, *Manorial Records* (Gloucester, 1984).

Haskins Anniversary Essays in Medieval History, ed. C. H. Taylor and J. L. La Monte (Boston, 1929).

Hastings, M. *The Court of Common Pleas in Fifteenth-Century England* (New York, 1947).

Hatcher, J., *Plague, Population and the English Economy, 1348–1530* (London, 1977).

Heath, P., *Church and Realm, 1272–1461: Conflict and Collaboration in an Age of Crises* (London, 1988).

Helmholz, R. H., *Canon Law and the Law of England* (London, 1987).

————, "Crime, Compurgation and the Courts of the Medieval Church," *Law and History Review* 1 (1983), 1–26.

————, "The Writ of Prohibition to Court Christian before 1500," *Mediaeval Studies* 43 (1981), 297–314, reprinted in idem, *Canon Law*, 59–76.

Hewitt, H. J., *The Organization of War under Edward III, 1338–62* (Manchester, 1966).

Hicks, M. A., *Bastard Feudalism* (London, 1995).

————, "Restraint, Mediation and Private Justice: George, Duke of Clarence as 'Good Lord,'" *Journal of Legal History* 4, no. 2 (1983), 56–71.

Highfield, J.R.L., "The English Hierarchy in the Reign of Edward III," *TRHS*, 5th series, 6 (1956), 115–38.

————, "The Relations Between the Church and the English Crown from the Death of Archbishop Stratford to the Opening of the Great Schism, 1349–1378" (D.Phil. diss., Oxford, 1951).

Hilton, R. H., *Bond Men Made Free: Medieval Peasant Movements and the English Rising of 1381* (London and New York, 1973).

————, *The Decline of Serfdom in Medieval England*, 2d edition (Cambridge, 1983).

————, *The English Peasantry in the Later Middle Ages* (Oxford, 1975).

————, *A Medieval Society: The West Midlands at the End of the Thirteenth Century* (London, 1966).

————, "Peasant Movements in England before 1381," in E. M. Carus-Wilson, ed., *Essays in Economic History*, 3 vols. (London, 1954–62), 2:73–90.

————, and T. H. Aston, eds., *The English Rising of 1381* (Cambridge, 1984).

Hinnebusch, W. A., *The Early English Friars Preachers* (Rome, 1951).

Holmes, G. A., *The Estates of the Higher Nobility in Fourteenth-Century England* (Cambridge, 1957).

————, *The Good Parliament* (Oxford, 1975).

————, *The Later Middle Ages, 1272–1485* (London, 1962).

Holt, J. C., *Robin Hood* (London, 1982).

Hughes, D., *A Study of Social and Constitutional Tendencies in the Early Years of Edward III* (London, 1915).

Hughes, J., *Pastors and Visionaries: Religion and Secular Life in Late Medieval Yorkshire* (Woodbridge, Suffolk, 1988).

Humphery-Smith, C. R., *General Armory Two: Alfred Morant's Additions and Corrections to Burke's General Armory* (London, 1973).

Hunnisett, R. F., *The Medieval Coroner* (Cambridge, 1961).

————, "Sussex Coroners in the Middle Ages: Part III," *Sussex Archaeological Collections* 98 (1960), 44–70.

————, and J. B. Post, eds., *Medieval Legal Records Edited in Memory of C. A. F. Meekings* (London, 1978).

Hurnard, N. D., *The King's Pardon for Homicide before A.D. 1307* (Oxford, 1969).

Hyams, P. R., "The Action of Naifty in the Early Common Law," *Law Quarterly Review* 90 (1974), 326–50.

————, *King, Lords and Peasants in Medieval England: The Common Law of Villeinage in the Twelfth and Thirteenth Centuries* (Oxford, 1980).

Index of Ancient Petitions of the Chancery and the Exchequer Preserved in the Public Record Office, rev. edition (PRO Lists and Indexes, no. 1., 1966).

Jessopp, A., *The Coming of the Friars and Other Historic Essays*, 5th edition (London, n.d.).

Johnson, P., *The Life and Times of Edward III* (London, 1973).

Jones, E. D., "The Church and 'Bastard Feudalism': The Case of Crowland Abbey from the 1320s to the 1350s," *Journal of Religious History* 10 (1978–79), 142–50.

Jones, M., ed., *Gentry and Lesser Nobility in Late Medieval Europe* (Gloucester, 1986).

Jones, W. R., "The English Church and Royal Propaganda during the Hundred Years War," *Journal of British Studies* 19 (1979), 18–30.

Judd, A., *The Life of Thomas Bekynton, Secretary to King Henry VI and Bishop of Bath and Wells, 1443–1465* (Chichester, 1961).

Kaeuper, R. W., "An Historian's Reading of *The Tale of Gamelyn*," *Medium Aevum* 52 (1983), 51–62.

———, "Law and Order in Fourteenth-Century England: The Evidence of Special Commissions of Oyer and Terminer," *Speculum* 54 (1979), 734–84.

———, *War, Justice, and Public Order: England and France in the Later Middle Ages* (Oxford, 1988).

Kaye, J. M., "The Early History of Murder and Manslaughter: Part I," *Law Quarterly Review* 83 (1967), 365–95, 569–601.

Keen, M. H., *England in the Later Middle Ages* (London, 1973).

———, *The Outlaws of Medieval Legend*, rev. edition (London, 1977).

Kennedy, M.J.O., "Resourceful Villeins: The Cellarer Family of Wawne in Holderness," *Yorkshire Archaeological Journal* 48 (1976), 107–17.

Knowles, M. D., *The Religious Orders in England*, 3 vols. (Cambridge, 1948–59).

———, and R. N. Hadcock, *Medieval Religious Houses: England and Wales*, 2d edition (London, 1971).

Labande, L. H., *Le Palais des Papes et les Monuments d'Avignon au Quatorzième Siècle*, 2 vols. (Marseille, 1925).

Lapsley, G. T., "Archbishop Stratford and the Parliamentary Crisis of 1341," *EHR* 30 (1915), 6–18, 193–215; reprinted in H. M. Cam and G. Barraclough, eds., *Crown, Community and Parliament* (Oxford, 1951), 231–72.

Law and Social Change in British History: Papers Presented to the Bristol Legal History Conference, ed. J. A. Guy and H. G. Beale (London, 1984).

Leach, A. F., "A Clerical Strike at Beverly Minster in the Fourteenth Century," *Archaeologia* 55 (1896), 1–20.

Le Neve, J., *Fasti Ecclesiae Anglicanae, 1300–1541*, rev. J. M. Horn, B. Jones, and H.P.F. King, 12 vols. (London, 1962–67).

Le Patourel, J., "The Treaty of Brétigny, 1360," *TRHS*, 5th series, 10 (1960), 19–39.

Little, A. G., and F. M. Powicke, eds., *Essays in Medieval History Presented to Thomas Frederick Tout* (Manchester, 1925).

Lunt, W. E., *Papal Revenues in the Middle Ages*, 2 vols. (New York, 1934).

Lyon, B. D., *From Fief to Indenture: The Transition from Feudal to Non-Feudal Contract in Western Europe* (Cambridge, Mass., 1957).

McFarlane, K. B., "Bastard Feudalism," *Bulletin of the Institute of Historical Research* 20 (1945), 161–80; reprinted in idem, *England in the Fifteenth Century*, 23–43.

———, *England in the Fifteenth Century* (London, 1981).

———, *The Nobility of Later Medieval England* (Oxford, 1973).

McHardy, A. K., "Liturgy and Propaganda in the Diocese of Lincoln during the Hundred Years War," *Studies in Church History* 18 (1982), 215–27.

McKisack, M., *The Fourteenth Century, 1307–1399* (Oxford, 1959).

Maddern, P. C., *Violence and Social Order: East Anglia, 1422–1442* (Oxford, 1992).

———, "Violence, Crime and Public Disorder in East Anglia, 1422–1442" (D.Phil. diss., Oxford, 1984).

Maddicott, J. R., "The Birth and Setting of the Ballads of Robin Hood," *EHR* 93 (1978), 276–99.

———, *Law and Lordship: Royal Justices as Retainers in Thirteenth- and Fourteenth-Century England* (Past and Present Supplement no. 4, Oxford, 1978).

———, "Poems of Social Protest in Early Fourteenth-Century England," in W. M. Ormrod, ed., *England in the Fourteenth Century: Proceedings of the 1985 Harlaxton Symposium* (Woodbridge, Suffolk, 1986), 130–44.

Medieval Art and Architecture at Ely Cathedral, ed. N. Coldstream and P. Draper (British Archaeological Association Conference Transactions, 2, 1979).

Medieval Legal Records, ed. R. F. Hunnisett and J. B. Post (London, 1978).

Mertes, K., *The English Noble Household, 1250–1600: Good Governance and Politic Rule* (Oxford, 1988).

Miller, E., *The Abbey and Bishopric of Ely* (Cambridge, 1951).

Milsom, S.F.C., *The Legal Framework of English Feudalism* (Cambridge, 1976).

Mollat, G., *The Popes at Avignon, 1305–1378*, trans. J. Love (London, 1963).

Moorman, J.R.H., *Church Life in England in the Thirteenth Century* (Cambridge, 1945).

Morant, A. W., ed., *Papworth's Ordinary of British Armorials* (London, 1874).

Morris, C., "The Plague in Britain," *Historical Journal* 14 (1971), 205–15.

Ormrod, W.M., "Edward III's Government of England, c. 1346–1356" (D.Phil. diss., Oxford, 1984).

———, *The Reign of Edward III: Crown and Political Society in England, 1327–1377* (New Haven, 1990).

———, ed., *England in the Fourteenth Century: Proceedings of the 1985 Harlaxton Symposium* (Woodbridge, Suffolk, 1986).

Owen, D. M., *Ely Records: A Handlist of the Records of the Bishop and Archdeacon of Ely* (Cambridge, 1971).

Owst, G. R., *Literature and Pulpit in Medieval England* (Cambridge, 1933).

Oxford English Dictionary, 2d edition (Oxford, 1989).

Packe, M., *King Edward III*, ed. L.C.B. Seaman (London, 1983).

Palmer, C.F.R., "The Friar-Preachers, or Blackfriars, of Chelmsford," *The Reliquary*, new series, 3 (1889), 141–44.

———, "The Friar-Preachers, or Blackfriars, of Dunwich," *The Reliquary* 26 (1885–86), 209–12.

———, "The Friar-Preachers, or Blackfriars, of Winchester," *The Reliquary*, new series, 3 (1889), 207–15.

Palmer, R. C., *The Whilton Dispute, 1264–1380: A Social-Legal Study of Dispute Settlement in Medieval England* (Princeton, 1984).

Pantin, W. A., *The English Church in the Fourteenth Century* (Cambridge, 1955)

Papworth's Ordinary of British Armorials, ed. A. W. Morant (London, 1874).

Patronage, the Crown and the Provinces in Later Medieval England, ed. R. A. Griffiths (Gloucester, 1981).

Payling, S. J., "Inheritance and Local Politics in the Later Middle Ages: The Case of Ralph, Lord Cromwell, and the Heriz Inheritance," *Nottingham Medieval Studies* 30 (1986), 67–96.

———, *Political Society in Lancastrian England: The Greater Gentry of Nottinghamshire* (Oxford, 1991).

Perroy, E., *The Hundred Years War,* trans. W. B. Wells (London, 1951).

Plucknett, T.F.T., *A Concise History of the Common Law* (London, 1922).

Pollard, T., ed., *Property and Politics: Essays in Later Medieval English History* (Gloucester, 1984).

Pollock, F., and Maitland, F. W., *The History of English Law,* 2 vols. (Cambridge, 1899–1923).

Post, J. B., "Criminals and the Law in the Reign of Richard II" (D.Phil. diss., Oxford, 1976).

Powell, E., "Arbitration and the Law in England in the Later Middle Ages," *TRHS,* 5th series, 33 (1983), 49–67.

———, *Kingship, Law and Society: Criminal Justice in the Reign of Henry V* (Oxford, 1989).

———, "Settlement of Disputes by Arbitration in Fifteenth-Century England," *Law and History Review* 2, no. 1 (1984), 21–43.

———, "Social Research and the Use of Medieval Criminal Records," *Michigan Law Review* 79 (1980–81), 967–78.

Précis de l'Histoire d'Avignon au Point de Vue Religieux, 2 vols. (Avignon, 1852).

Prestwich, M., *Edward I* (London, 1988).

———, *The Three Edwards: War and State in England, 1272–1377* (London, 1980).

Property and Politics: Essays in Later Medieval English History, ed. T. Pollard (Gloucester, 1984).

Putnam, B. H., *The Place in Legal History of Sir William Shareshull, Chief Justice of the King's Bench, 1350–1361: A Study of Judicial and Administrative Methods in the Reign of Edward III* (Cambridge, 1950).

———, "The Transformation of the Keepers of the Peace into the Justices of the Peace, 1327–1380," *TRHS,* 4th series, 12 (1929), 19–48.

Rawcliffe, C., "The Great Lord as Peacekeeper: Arbitration by English Noblemen and Their Councils in the Later Middle Ages," in J. A. Guy and H. G. Beale, eds., *Law and Social Change in British History: Papers Presented to the Bristol Legal History Conference* (London, 1984), 34–54.

Razi, Z., *Life, Marriage and Death in a Medieval Parish: Economy, Society and Demography in Halesowen, 1270–1400* (Cambridge, 1980).

———, "The Struggles Between the Abbots of Halesowen and their Tenants in the Thirteenth and Fourteenth Centuries," in T. H. Aston, P. R. Coss, C. Dyer, and J. Thirsk, eds., *Social Relations and Ideas: Essays in Honour of R. H. Hilton* (Cambridge, 1983), 151–67.

Richardson, H. G., and G. O. Sayles, *The English Parliament in the Middle Ages* (London, 1981).

Röhrkasten, J., "Some Problems of the Evidence of Fourteenth-Century Approvers," *Journal of Legal History* 5, no. 3 (1984), 14–22.

Rosenthal, J. T., "Feuds and Private Peace-Making: A Fifteenth-Century Example," *Nottingham Medieval Studies* 14 (1970), 84–90.

St. Etheldreda's and Ely Place: A Brief Account of the Church and its Surroundings (Leicester, n.d.).

Saul, N., *Knights and Esquires: The Gloucestershire Gentry in the Fourteenth Century* (Oxford, 1981).

———, *Scenes from Provincial Life: Knightly Families in Sussex, 1280–1400* (Oxford, 1986).

Sayles, G. O., *The Court of King's Bench in Law and History* (London, 1959).

Shrewsbury, J.F.D., *A History of Bubonic Plague in the British Isles* (Cambridge, 1970).

Smith, A., "Litigation and Politics: Sir John Fastolf's Defence of his English Property," in T. Pollard, ed., *Property and Politics: Essays in Later Medieval English History* (Gloucester, 1984), 59–75.

Social Relations and Ideas: Essays in Honour of R. H. Hilton, ed. T. H. Aston, P. R. Coss, C. Dyer, and J. Thirsk (Cambridge, 1983).

Stones, E.L.G., "The Folvilles of Ashby-Folville, Leicestershire, and their Associates in Crime, 1326–1347," *TRHS,* 5th series, 7 (1957), 117–36.

Storey, R. L., *The End of the House of Lancaster* (London, 1966).

———, *Thomas Langley and the Bishopric of Durham, 1406–1437* (London, 1961).

Stubbs, W., *The Constitutional History of England,* 3 vols. (Oxford, 1874–78).

Swanson, R. N., *Church and Society in Late Medieval England* (Oxford, 1989).

Taylor, C. H., and J. L. La Monte, eds., *Haskins Anniversary Essays in Medieval History* (Boston, 1929).

Thompson, A. H., *The English Clergy and their Organization in the Later Middle Ages* (Oxford, 1947).

———, "Registers of John Gynwell, Bishop of Lincoln, for the Years 1347–50," *Archaeological Journal* 68 (1911), 300–360.

———, "William Bateman, Bishop of Norwich, 1344–1355," *Norfolk Archaeology* 25 (1935), 102–37.

Tout, T. F., *Chapters in the Administrative History of Medieval England,* 6 vols. (Manchester, 1920–30).

Turner, H. L., *Town Defences in England and Wales: An Architectural and Documentary Study, A.D. 900–1500* (London, 1971).

Vale, J., *Edward III and Chivalry: Chivalric Society and its Context, 1270–1350* (Woodbridge, Suffolk, 1982).

Van Caenegem, R. C., *The Birth of the English Common Law,* 2d edition (Cambridge, 1988).

The Victoria History of the Counties of England: Cambridgeshire and the Isle of Ely, 9 vols. (London, 1938–89).

The Victoria History of the Counties of England: Hampshire and the Isle of Wight, 5 vols. (London, 1900–12).

The Victoria History of the Counties of England: Huntingdonshire, 3 vols. (London, 1926–36).

The Victoria History of the Counties of England: Northamptonshire Families, ed. O. Barron (London, 1906).

Walker, S. K., *The Lancastrian Affinity, 1361–1399* (Oxford, 1990).

————, "Lordship and Lawlessness in the Palatinate of Lancaster, 1370–1400," *Journal of British Studies* 28, no. 4 (1989), 325–48.

Waugh, S. L., *England in the Reign of Edward III* (Cambridge, 1991).

————, "Tenure to Contract: Lordship and Clientage in Thirteenth-Century England," *EHR* 101 (1986), 816–39.

Wilkinson, B., *The Later Middle Ages in England, 1216–1485* (London, 1969).

————, "A Letter of Edward III to his Chancellor and Treasurer," *EHR* 42 (1927), 248–51.

Willard, J. F., W. A. Morris, J. R. Strayer, and W. H. Dunham, Jr., eds., *The English Government at Work, 1327–1336*, 3 vols. (Cambridge, Mass., 1940–50).

Wood, D., *Clement VI: The Pontificate and Ideas of an Avignon Pope* (Cambridge, 1989).

Woodward, J., *A Treatise on Ecclesiastical Heraldry* (Edinburgh, 1894).

Wright, S. M., *The Derbyshire Gentry in the Fifteenth Century* (Derbyshire Record Society, 8, 1983).

Yunck, J. A., *The Lineage of Lady Meed* (Notre Dame, 1963).

Ziegler, P., *The Black Death* (Harmondsworth, Middlesex, 1969).

Zutshi, P.N.R., *Original Papal Letters in England, 1305–1415* (Vatican City, 1990).

————, and R. Ombres, "The Dominicans in Cambridge, 1238–1538," *Archivum Fratrum Praedicatorum* 60 (1990), 313–73.

Index